WOMEN PHOTOGRAPHERS AND FEMINIST AESTHETICS

Women Photographers and Feminist Aesthetics makes the case for a feminist aesthetics in photography by analysing key works of twenty-two women photographers, including cis- and trans-woman photographers.

Claire Raymond provides close readings of key photographs spanning the history of photography, from nineteenth-century Europe to twenty-first century Africa and Asia. She offers original interpretations of well-known photographers such as Diane Arbus, Sally Mann, and Carrie Mae Weems, analysing their work in relation to gender, class, and race. The book also pays close attention to the way in which indigenous North Americans have been represented through photography and the ways in which contemporary Native American women photographers respond to this history.

Developing the argument that through aesthetic force emerges the truly political, the book moves beyond polarization of the aesthetic and the cultural. Instead, photographic works are read for their subversive political and cultural force, as it emerges through the aesthetics of the image.

This book is ideal for students of Photography, Art History, Art and Visual Culture, and Gender.

Claire Raymond teaches Art History at the University of Virginia. She is the author of *Francesca Woodman's Dark Gaze: the Diazotypes and Other Late Works*; *Witnessing Sadism in Texts of the American South*; and *Francesca Woodman and the Kantian Sublime*. Her research focuses on aesthetics, poetics, and the intersections of cultural trauma and representation.

WOMEN PHOTOGRAPHERS AND FEMINIST AESTHETICS

Claire Raymond

Routledge
Taylor & Francis Group
LONDON AND NEW YORK

First published 2017
by Routledge
2 Park Square, Milton Park, Abingdon, Oxon OX14 4RN

and by Routledge
711 Third Avenue, New York, NY 10017

Routledge is an imprint of the Taylor & Francis Group, an informa business

British Library Cataloguing-in-Publication Data
A catalogue record for this book is available from the British Library

Library of Congress Cataloging-in-Publication Data
A catalog record for this book has been requested

ISBN: 978-1-138-64427-4 (hbk)
ISBN: 978-1-138-64428-1 (pbk)
ISBN: 978-1-315-62891-2 (ebk)

Typeset in Bembo
by Apex CoVantage, LLC

"It's harder being a woman, and I guess that's part of what I want to show. I relate well to men, but I feel a real link with women because I understand their plight."

Mary Ellen Mark

CONTENTS

FIGURES

ACKNOWLEDGMENTS

Students in the many semesters of "Women Photographers and Feminist Aesthetics," a course I taught from 2008 until 2015 at the University of Virginia, shaped this book. I owe a debt to every one of them: for being interested in feminist theory when it was not fashionable, for caring about photography created by women when much of it is not grouped in the standard canon, and for bringing their energy and intelligence to this class. I hesitate to list names for fear of seeming to be less grateful to the many worthy who are not named, but a few students stood out for the intensity and thoroughgoing commitment they brought to this class, and their thoughts and questions percolate throughout this book. Without Shantell Bingham, Riley Blanks, Elisabeth Hogeman, Kristen Inglese, Conley Lowrance, and Megan Reilly, it would not have been the same class or the same book. Also, a thousand thanks are due to Daniel Weiss, Lawrence Goedde, and Christine Stevens Stinson, for providing varied and heroic forms of support for this project. I am also grateful to the Office of the Vice Provost for the Arts at the University of Virginia for supporting this project. And my gratitude to Natalie Foster, whose idea for this book set it in motion.

INTRODUCTION

Women photographers and feminist aesthetics

Women Photographers and Feminist Aesthetics draws on feminist and aesthetic theory to interpret a selection of photographers whose work carries a feminist aesthetic. I begin the book with a brief discussion of feminist theory in the twenty-first century and then move into a discussion of what might constitute a feminist aesthetic. Each chapter describes and assesses the photographic oeuvres of two or three photographers, as the book moves roughly chronologically from the nineteenth to the twenty-first century. Hence, the reader can look at chapters individually or read the book all the way through, following the thread of a theory of feminist aesthetics. I allow some indeterminacy of the definition of the term *woman* to work through the book, as the meanings of gender and being are addressed differently by various photographs. The question of what is a photograph runs parallel to this question of how one might define the term *woman*, for it is precisely in photography's fluidity and protean capacity – for better and for worse – that its relationship to gender emerges.

My aim is not to place the photographers in this book above other women photographers. This book is about feminist aesthetics, and consequently it is concerned with photographic images that carry the ethics of the feminist movement through formal contour and symbolic figure. It is not a book that attempts to devise a canon of women photographers. Instead, it is anticanonical in concept. I aim to show ways that some photographs overturn sexist thinking and how such subversion is the turn of a feminist aesthetic.

Feminist aesthetics, risk, and peripheral vision

Feminism in the early twenty-first century is a strange beast; it is contradictory and in many ways disconsolate in the West and faces multiple challenges outside of the West. At the end of the twentieth century, poststructuralist feminism, taking its cue from Judith Butler's influential book *Gender Trouble*, popularized the idea that gender is entirely performative, an argument that seemed to some to sidestep issues of gender-based violence and entrenched patterns of economic oppression.[1] Drawing heavily from Joan Riviere's 1929 essay, "Womanliness as Masquerade," Butler's argument for gender's layered but entirely fabricated ontological status effectively blamed feminist theorists for creating the very damaged and oppressed category "woman" that they claimed to be trying to revise.[2] In the wake of the immense twentieth-century popularity of Butler's theory of gender as a copy without an original, twenty-first-century feminists – especially those coming of age in the second decade of the twenty-first century – search for a more expansive ontological status for the category 'women.' They do so not only for reasons of theory but also for the practical necessity of understanding (a) why rates of assault against people gendered feminine remain high and (b) why people gendered feminine do not have functionally equal access to various forms of cultural power, including equal wages.[3] Likewise, theorizing from perspectives to which Butler gives scant attention (other than to myopically define non-Western lives as "precarious"), non-Western feminists pose significant and important questions, thus complicating the meaning of a poststructuralist lockstep of gender as entirely performative.[4]

The distance seems almost insuperable between twentieth-century poststructuralist feminism and twenty-first-century feminists' urgent need to address issues such as violence against women, wage disparity, and the gendering of poverty. If gender is entirely performative, how might we deeply understand and effectively contend with issues of gender-based violence and oppression such as rape and poverty – issues that move beneath and tragically in advance of the subject's capacity to achieve, much less reconceptualize, a performative subjectivity? Even as Butler's late-twentieth-century poststructuralist approach seems ill suited for many twenty-first-century concerns, her legacy remains a dominant force in feminist thinking in the academy. In addition, poststructuralist feminism and the new feminism on U.S. campuses, which focuses on the issue of college rape, tend to ignore earlier feminist work regarding gender-, class-, and race-based oppressions; they often elide the racialized economics of sexist oppression in a conversation that has, for decades, privileged the concerns of the Western, white bourgeoisie.[5]

If twenty-first-century feminism is caught in a web of contradictory impulses, so much so that we now speak of feminisms rather than feminism, what does it mean to say that something, or someone, is feminist?[6] Race and gender theorist bell hooks argues that rather than ascribing the quality or claiming the status of *being* a "feminist," an activist should instead "advocate feminism."[7] Feminism, then, should be an active force rather than a static attribution.[8] Drawing on hooks's vision of the feminist movement as an active force rather than a static descriptor, can one say that not only a person but also, possibly, certain photographs could "advocate feminism"? If so, on what grounds?

Fixed as any given photograph is in capitalist networks of viewership, can it advocate against the powerful dominating the powerless? Can a photograph advocate against sexist oppression? Giorgio Agamben and Jacques Rancière suggest that the *aestheton* – the aesthetic force that an image may produce – is a political force, one of the few left in the twenty-first century. This century is a time when, they argue, many other forms of political resistance have been hollowed out.[9] The feminist movement is certainly a political entity, but how can a photograph that is not obviously politically pitched advocate feminism? I answer this question by studying photographs that women have created, photographs that, I will argue, advocate feminism. It is not that each of these photographers necessarily saw or sees herself as a feminist. Instead, the photographic work expresses a feminist aesthetic. A feminist aesthetic is not monolithic but protean, an active force rather than a fixed, gridded frame. Indeed, in developing this notion of feminist aesthetics as mutable and unpredictable, I draw from the origins of aesthetic theory. Here, I locate the crux of the aesthetic event as an occurrence of a kind of motion, a force with which the image, or thing seen, crosses to affect, and deeply alter, the one who sees. Roland Barthes argues that, in photography, the aesthetic carries the political.[10] And, as bell hooks rightly argues, feminism means to "call for an end to patriarchal domination."[11] This book looks closely at ways that certain photographs visually agitate to end patriarchal domination.

In referring to the photographers I chose for this book, I use the word *woman*. Butler's *Gender Trouble* and *Bodies that Matter*[12] reiteratively argues that there is no such creature as a woman and that the concept "woman" is an illusory category created by habits of language. And yet, Teresa de Lauretis provocatively asks whether the ontology of gender might be more complicated than Butler allows. In various articles, some of which are collected in *Figures of Resistance*, de Lauretis suggests that a woman is the product of a historical accretion of patterns of perception: she contends that culturally produced and consumed images-of-self settle around the body of a person born female.[13] For de Lauretis, the difference between a *cultural construct*, the term usually used to describe Butler's skeptical view of the artifice that makes a woman, and an *historical construct* is the emphasis that the second term places on ways that the subject is born into history. However much one may verbally or declamatively rewrite the script of one's gender or – to use Butler's phrase – *reinscribe* within the hierarchical parameters of gender, many other people will yet read one's gender according to an inherited lens.[14] Hence, historical accretion creates the gendered subject, who may then resist being so seen. However, the subject may yet be caught between the desire of the self to resist oppression and the force of historical, sexist ways of seeing (and acting) that shape the matrix of the subject's material conditions.

De Lauretis, influenced by the work of Monique Wittig, does not see an easy performative solution to sexist oppression. Instead, de Lauretis suggests a process of dismantling and building anew an entity who might yet be called a woman.[15] She argues that – because we still live in deeply patriarchal structures of power – we do not yet know how to define the term, and yet the concept of woman can have meaning that eludes oppressive or performative structures. Similarly, hooks defines *woman* as a subject position, arguing that those who experience and are shaped by specific forms of sexist oppression may be socially configured as women. And Monique Wittig argues that, because the concept of woman is defined by a relationship to culture and a relationship that involves some kind of domination, the word itself may be ultimately discarded. But for now, Wittig sees the word as a practical term for describing a large number of people who are socially placed as women. Even as Wittig provocatively argues that lesbians are not women because they do not perform the submissive role of sexual object for a male partner, her writings yet describe myriad ways that lesbians are treated and oppressed as women as well as being socially punished for being lesbian.[16]

The title of my book, *Women Photographers and Feminist Aesthetics*, does not eschew the word *women* because, as yet, the world order is not a gender-equal society that would render this term obsolete. In using it, I am not ignoring Butler's twentieth-century effort to estrange and reinscribe our interpretation of gender. Instead, I write in recognition of the limits of this project of reinscription, limits that arise because Butler's work is so heavily based in interpretation of language and indebted to masculinist hierarchies. De Lauretis, a film critic, interprets gender as a product not merely of speech but of watching, looking, seeing, and being seen. A visual identity defines gender for most people, whether or not that identity feels like a source of inner truth. People born biologically female are overwhelmingly often interpreted by others as women not because of words or consciously held beliefs but because of historical accretions of ways of seeing, ways of watching. I contend that a woman is not so named but so seen. Needless to say, my emphasis in this book about photographs is on the visual – if the way she is seen socially creates a woman, then one way to combat sexist oppressions is to create other images, another visual discourse that neither elides the pain of sexist oppression nor gives in to the domination of patriarchal scripts, not even by reinscribing them in that dominance.

One may extend Jacques Derrida's notion of logocentrism to reveal ways that images, like the written word, take a secondary place to the spoken word in our concept of how culture is produced.[17] Roland Barthes argues that the image – with its subterranean force that is neither idea nor nonidea, neither language nor non-communication – remains in a suspended state between systems of meaning.[18] My project in this book is to read images for their intermediary, oneiric (dreamlike) power. By that I mean to pay attention to how an image can alter political meaning not despite but because of its muteness. Jacques Rancière states that an image that rearranges the sensible is at once aesthetic and political: the power of such an image is to disrupt our usual, quotidian pattern of thought. In this way, by aesthetic force, photographs may push the viewer to resee – to rearrange – what he or she has once seen to be real, natural, or given: to resee cultural structures of power and domination.[19]

Feminist aesthetics is a political force, political in the sense that Rancière defines the term – that is, communal, of the community's heart. This force is not necessarily overtly legibly political – what Rancière would call metapolitical – but instead works on the level of the visual, not as a reinscription but as a rearranging of the sensible to be seen anew. Rancière's argument that an image can send a message from the real does not mean that we must translate the image to words, but on the contrary it contends that aesthetic force, the message from the real, only extends from the image-idea. So when I interpret photographs in this book as participating in a feminist aesthetic, I do not mean a reinscription of gender but a rearranging of the visible, a message from the real – that space wherein the false consciousness of domination is overturned. Photography's relationship to the real is, of course, complicated. By using the term *real*, I emphatically do not make a simplistic claim about photography's documentary truth. Instead, I use the term as continental critical theory develops it, as the place of urgency, what Maurice Blanchot calls "the depths."[20] The real is that space wherefrom what harms and heals a life emerges; it is the vulnerable, mortal, and possibly transformative curve of social space where it intersects materiality. As such, photography's connection to the real is through its uncannily disembodied signification of embodiment. Photographs do not straightforwardly show lived embodiment, but they do limn its ineluctable echoes.

The photograph's materiality (a complicated aspect of its status to be sure, as there are a wide range of photographic practices productive of a very wide range of material photographic images) in one sense lends itself uncannily to aesthetic theory: the photograph, if it can be defined at all, is image as such. Yes, each individual photograph is produced by some technology of photography – be it silver collodion, diapositive slide, or digital image on a screen generated by algorithmic code. Yet what photographs have in common is an origin as light's mark and, hence, a relative lack of physical texture (they are very nearly the flat plane image). They are not created by paint (although paint can be applied to a photograph); they are not sculpture (although early photography was frequently compared to sculpture); and they are not performance (though Barthes insightfully finds the aesthetic origin of the photograph as theater). Instead, a photograph is an image, and as an image it translates across the boundaries of its own creation and performance. As Walter Benjamin, in *The Work of Art in the Age of Its Technological Reproducibility*, makes clear, the photograph is made to be copied, circulated, and repeated anew.[21] In this sense, it is the always-copied materiality of the photograph that makes it a political object. That is why I study the photograph in this book on feminism.

The risks

Griselda Pollock, in *Differencing the Canon*, and other works, warns of the risk of creating a kind of ghetto by studying women artists as a group, whereas Rita Felski, firmly in the poststructuralist camp, argues that a feminist aesthetic cannot exist because "woman" as a unified subject cannot exist.[22] And yet a feminist movement need not imply the existence of a singular unified subject "woman"; meanings of *woman*, *man*, or, for that matter, *human* can be fragmentary, protean, and multiple.[23] As Pollock indicates by her use of the term *ghetto*, the category of woman is created by the sequestering of social power in the masculine domain. And yet this congealing of social power around masculinity does not imply the existence of a uniform woman. Feminist, then, does not imply a monolithic, unary subject but instead, as bell hooks argues, it implies an advocacy of overturning multiple and variable structures of sexist, racist, and classist oppressions. Felski's literary argument in *Beyond*

Feminist Aesthetics glosses visual arts but fails to contend with the very different ways that the visual and verbal function. Contrasting with Felski's work, my focus on the visual contends with the differential structures of meaning that characterize photographs. Unlike literature, a photograph emanates a "message without a code"; that is, it transmits meaning through form and, if powerful aesthetically, rearranges the sensible such that references shift in their meaning.[24] The literary bent of dominant poststructuralist feminism occludes the reality of the visual as a force that structures the subject in advance of her conceptualization of self. Hence, the work of feminist image-makers is a crucial aspect of the feminist movement. That said, Pollock's concern that writing about women artists in the aggregate carries the risk of creating a ghetto is important.

The ghetto of the feminine – or as Abigail Solomon-Godeau memorably termed it, the nightmare of the feminine – describes the risk of grouping works produced by people whom others interpret as women in the common usage of the term and who may (or may not) interpret or categorize themselves as women.[25] Developing from Pollock and Solomon-Godeau, I suggest that the most salient risk of creating this gender aggregate is the danger of implying that women photographers cannot enter the canon dominated by male photographers, that instead there must be a separate and implicitly lesser canon of women photographers. There is also the obvious risk that by grouping women photographers one may seem to imply a kind of essentialism. That is, such a grouping may seem to imply that people born with certain physical characteristics, such as wombs or feminine facial features, are genuinely and meaningfully similar to each other.

With regard to the risk of essentialism, in that the term *woman* is already emergent from historical accretions of ways of seeing, referring to people whom others (and often themselves) see as women accurately reflects historical conditions as they overlap with contemporaneity. Photographs produced by people whom others perceive as women are feminist images according to their formality, temporal embeddedness, and material force, rather than according to the life of the photographer. It is not the photographer's life that anchors the photographic image in feminism; it is the image that transmits feminist aesthetics through its form. Could a man, then, create feminist photography? Almost certainly not in that it is extremely unlikely that someone who does not appear to others to be a woman would be sufficiently well and deeply versed in receiving sexist oppression to create an image that overturns it.[26] Could a woman who was born a boy and transitioned create feminist work? Julia Serano's powerful testimony in *Whipping Girl* suggests that a transwoman could create feminist photographic work.[27] Transwoman Zackary Drucker's collaborative works *Relationship* and *Translady Fanzine* evince the feminist potential of transwoman photographers. Developing from de Lauretis's, Wittig's, and hooks's positional definitions of the term *woman*, I will suggest in this book that a woman is someone who has learned firsthand how sexist oppressions, by way of hailing her, perversely produce and restrict her subjectivity.

The risk of lowering the status of women photographers by grouping them for study is very real, but the task of dismantling a more masculinist canon can only happen by women photographers becoming better known – that is, by having their names and work better circulated and lucidly discussed. I do not, in this book, propose an alternate canon. I do not propose a canon at all. Instead, I bring together a small number of women photographers whose work advocates feminism, even though some of these photographers would most certainly not have thought themselves to be doing so and even though I could have included other photographers' work in this book. My goal is to focus meaningfully on the works, so I discuss a relatively small number of images produced by a relatively small number of photographers. My attention is on the images themselves. As such, my book takes its cue from Agamben's and Rancière's theories regarding aesthetics and ethics. In arguing for a feminist aesthetic, I emphatically do not argue for a gaze or a vision that emanates from the embodied female subject as such. Instead, I interpret forms of photographic images that advocate feminism.

This emphasis on aesthetics is itself against the grain of important strands of postmodern photography theory. Allan Sekula and John Tagg, developing from Pierre Bourdieu and Michel Foucault, have created important counterdiscourses to formalist aesthetics.[28] For me, these anti-aesthetic arguments paradoxically are useful in understanding how a photographer produces work of aesthetic power. The theories of Foucault and Karl Marx on the subject of power are essential to my readings of the photographic practices I study here. I do not, then, propose a Clement Greenberg–style grid or matrix by which one could decide which photographs are feminist and which are not. Instead, I follow Immanuel Kant's insistence on the dynamic interiority of the aesthetic event. Although one can ascribe a formal arc to the experience of the aesthetic, one cannot map in advance which work will generate this force.[29] Indeed, for Rancière, the newness – the reordering of the sensible – is the defining force of the aesthetic. So to suggest that one could give a map by which images would be read would be to purloin the very power of newness that is the mettle of the aestheton.[30] There is no formalist litmus test for feminist aesthetics or, to use Felski's word, no "normative" principle of feminist aesthetics, as I interpret it in this book. Instead, I draw from Kant's theorization of the dynamic structure of perception as the locus of the aesthetic. If the photographic image viewed carries aesthetic force, then the form of the visible alters the perceiver of the photograph and hence alters politics (in the strictest sense of the word, politics as the communal people, the *polis*).

In this book, I have chosen a small number of women photographers whose work, to draw on Roland Barthes's phrase, wounds me, striking home.[31] And yet, I have been not idiosyncratic but systematic in bearing forward the argument that if a photograph advocates feminism – if it alters or rearranges the sensible; if it changes what we know of the sensed world, our politics, our knowledge of community – then it carries a feminist aesthetic.[32] The photographers discussed here are different enough from each other, socially and historically, that the notion of one community containing them all is absurd. In the twenty-first century, however, photographic images do hold a community of watchers. We watch photographs – obsessively – on electronic devices, in magazines, museums, and even classrooms.

The photograph is the medium of our time; its digitized spectral force swallows all other forms of image-making. In this sense, these disparate photographers are part of a photographic community, one that many of them never intended to join, while others actively sought and continue to seek to refashion it. The community of this book, at its core, is not a community of women but a community of watchers.

Peripheral vision

I also want to emphasize that articulating a space for a feminist aesthetic leads to specific gains. As Allan Sekula rightly has argued, to trace a history of photography is to trace a history of power.[33] The person who wields the camera – and who does so in such a way as to be named the photographic author of the image – is very often in a position of relative cultural and economic power. This photo-power for Sekula means that the traffic in photographs traces power structures and reveals photography's colonizing force.[34] Indeed, photography has been used to catalog and thereby dominate vulnerable populations through the racist discourse of the nineteenth century and early twentieth century.[35] Likewise, John Tagg has persuasively argued that the conceit that documentary photography showing truth belies the way that ideology and power create, inform, and circulate the documentary photograph and shape the viewer's interpretation of the image.

How then might individual photographs agitate against the broad systems of domination (economic and gendered) that photography in general supports? A feminist aesthetic subverts social patterns of domination. And yet some of the photographers included in this study occupied positions of relative economic and social power over their subjects. Julia Margaret Cameron, for example, made use of her female servants – housemaids – to pose for her photographs. Sally Mann photographed her children in the nude well before they were old enough to comprehend the meaning of, much less meaningfully grant, consent. Other photographers in this study have a different relationship to power. Ana Mendieta created a photographic oeuvre documenting her own earthworks performances: in this process, she stages and records abjection through the outline left by an absent person (Mendieta herself), her work oscillating between the power of wielding the camera and the staged submission of performing its abject object. Matika Wilbur (Swinomish and Tulalip), in taking photographs of every federally recognized Native American tribe, works with tribes to gain permission to take portraits of Native Americans that bespeak anything but these photographic subjects' disempowerment.

Discerning photo-power, which will always have some economic valence, is more complicated than simply following the money. The weight of sexist oppression, although profoundly and infinitely varied, shapes for some women photographers the possibility – never the certainty – of a challenging and subversive way of looking, what Amelia Jones calls "seeing differently."[36] A photograph has to be interpreted detail by detail and image by image for the qualities that make the viewer see what has been photographed differently from how he or she would see the object or scene itself. How does this occur? The answers are never uniform for the photographs in this book. Hence, my interpretation of feminist aesthetics has no place for Felski's rejection of the possibility of feminist aesthetics on the assumption that aesthetics and gender must be normative. Taking my cue and developing from Jones's important work, I reject the simplistic desire to locate a normative aesthetic. Instead, my argument is that seeing differently, as expressed in a photograph, entails a radical reordering of the sensible, with the sensible here meaning the visible. This radical reordering responds to different situations depending on the culture and time from which the photographs emerge. The photographs themselves act as watchers; that is, the act of taking the photograph is an act that both perceives and creates the aesthetic. The photograph is both the perceived and the perceiver, an uncanny object in the sphere of the visual.

The photographer, then, shows what she sees and also shows what she refuses; the frame delineates an act of presentation and a boundary. The photographer opens the space of the gaze in the created frame of the image. Jones's theory of a different way of seeing, a refusal to disavow embodied history and its effects on subjectivity, then, describes my approach to the photographs I interpret in this book. Needless to say, the culture, time, and place from which a photographer works will make a difference in the differentness of her vision. Clementina Hawarden is not responding to the same forms of sexist oppression as Carrie Mae Weems. Separated by more than a century, by massive shifts in history, and not least by different experiences of the effects of European imperialism and colonization, they produced works that contain no common normative code. And yet, these photographers are both exemplars of seeing differently. Hawarden photographed her teenage daughters with a gaze that merges maternal melancholia and sisterly eroticism. She subversively reveals the violent constrictions of nineteenth-century British patriarchal aristocracy – never giving away the enigmatic game at the heart of her photographic resistance. Weems also invokes tropes of nineteenth-century oppression, depicting enslavement and *plaçage* as forms of haunting in her works *The Louisiana Project* and *Sea Islands Series*. Hawarden and Weems share a sharp gaze at the architecture structures of containment and oppression, and they share a willingness to risk opposition in the place of stillness. They create photographs whose meaning of resistance hinges dangerously close to – and in this proximity radically critiques – the beautiful architecture that constrains and oppresses the female subjects in their photographs. And yet to claim that Weems and Hawarden share a normative aesthetic would be deeply incorrect. What they share is radicality, a fundamental reenvisioning of the visible in their photographs.

As noted, I have chosen to discuss a small number of photographers whose work resists quotidian vision. In that regard, my book crosses boundaries that might not usually be crossed in an art history format. I jump from Britain of the Victorians to France of the surrealists and from late twentieth-century United States to early twenty-first-century Ethiopia, but not to argue significant threads of influence. Instead, my concern is with the aesthetic force of the images. In this sense, I take something close to an anti–art history approach: I am less interested in tying knots of influence between photographers and more concerned with working through a paradigm of feminist aesthetics, however non-normative. How does the photographic image trouble, stir, or change the visible? That is the thread of questioning that I pull through these photographs and photographers.

As Carol Armstrong argues in "Francesca Woodman: A Ghost in the House of the Woman Artist," there is scant lineage between women artists, more a fractured happenstance.[37] This fractured lineage is an effect of patriarchal domination and therefore, Armstrong implies, an effect that will die away as we move deeper into the twenty-first century. And yet, if one takes a wider view, the accomplishment of a postfeminist world is far from obvious at this time. Rosi Braidotti, following a concern with the "posthuman" condition of experience lived in the twenty-first century, interprets the lives of women who are not supported by white European or white U.S. bourgeois systems of privilege.[38] For Braidotti, the posthuman entails an understanding of the position of the radically disempowered labor systems that render us less and less human, immersed in tools of information (laptops, iPhones, tablets) that are physically built by human labor, often women's labor. If in my choice to jump between countries and eras to study disparate photographs I mirror the very fractured lineage that Armstrong lays at the feet of patriarchal oppressions, it is not to repeat this injustice but to unearth it. My interpretation of feminist aesthetics is not postfeminist.[39] Instead, I am very keenly aware of the position of the subaltern, the woman who is not supported by wealthy, Western, so-called postfeminist reinscriptions of gender.[40] It is for her – she who occupies the most numerous and least-attended-to subject position – that a feminist aesthetic will have meaning and value. If there is any validity to a feminist aesthetic, it lies in its capacity to overturn dominant ways of seeing, including those embedded in the academy.

When bell hooks makes the claim that feminist theory will never be written by the women who know the most about sexist oppression, she means that by definition the women who lack the social position from which to claim the authority to write theory are the very ones who most intimately and personally know what it means to be oppressed.[41] And yet a photograph is a different object from a person: as John Szarkowski points out, the camera, unlike any other implement of art, may have an accidental clarity to its production.[42] The camera sees a different nature than the eye, and also the camera has a different nature from the eye.[43] Its clarity of accident, or ability to show the contingent, can cut through wrappings of social structure and pretense. As I said, some of the women photographers in this book work from positions of relative social privilege. Few occupy or occupied social positions that would place them with the most oppressed of women. But some of them led or lead relatively risky and unscripted lives. Indeed, some of these photographers remained very much outside any academy during their lifetimes. Such positioning occurred for several reasons: (a) partly because photography was long considered a bastard art form on the boundary of science, commerce, and fine art; (b) partly for reasons of sexist oppression; and (c) partly for reasons to do with racism and class-based oppressions. With photographs, in rare but notable instances, women can shift social codes that resist more scripted (that is, verbal) pressures for change. The temporally fragmented nature of photography, its self-enclosed quality, hence, lends itself to instances of visual resistance to power structures.

The position of photography as a fine art has similarities to the position of the feminine socially. Photography was originally interpreted as a passive art form; William Henry Fox Talbot described photography as taking the imprint of nature, calling his calotype process "nature's pencil" by which "she" (meaning nature) draws herself.[44] Allan Sekula implicitly compares the social position and use of the photograph to those of women when he alludes with his title "The Traffic in Photographs" to Gayle Rubin's earlier essay "The Traffic in Women." Sekula argues that photographs do not have an identity of their own but are merely circulated passively to serve other – capitalist – interests, comparing the exchange or traffic in photographic images to Claude Lévi-Strauss's argument that societies are cemented through the ritualized exchange of women.[45] This exchange, an example of which would be the Western tradition of a father giving away his daughter to another man in the marriage ceremony, places women in a culturally passive position. If the oppression of women is socially scripted, the reenvisioning of social fabrics overturns that position; some photographs achieve this reenvisioning, this rearranging the visible, and overturn that which can take place wrenching the framework of patriarchal capitalism.

Possibly as a consequence of radical vision, several of the photographers in this book did not achieve widespread public recognition for their work while they were alive. This oversight placed them in a somewhat disempowered social position but also, paradoxically, permitted them to create subversive work. Coming from inherited wealth, surrealist photographer Claude Cahun (born Lucy Schwob) did not need to earn her living as a photographer. Indeed, the images for which she is justly famous today were kept private during her lifetime. She shared many of the images only with her lover, Marcelle Moore (born Suzanne Malherbe), and stored the collection for decades in nothing more glorious than drugstore photograph packets.[46] Although the relatively wealthy Cahun was not oppressed by material want (until she was imprisoned by the Nazis, toward the end of her life), the fact that her most original images remained outside public discourse until many years after her death places her in a position of relative cultural powerlessness. That is, she could not, during her lifetime, insist on the public role of artist. In contrast to surrealist photographer Man Ray, for example, Cahun experienced a quiet social disempowerment as her photographs did not receive the public acclaim accorded to Man Ray. Although she did publish her writing and tucked photo-collages into it, Cahun was not able to assume the empowering identity of a major artist because she was not considered to be one during her lifetime. So unknown was Cahun that decades after her death, art historians assumed she was a man.[47]

Not all photographers who create images that advocate feminism experience this outsider status, but they do so frequently enough that I will return several times to what it means to have a posthumous career and how such a status relates to the feminist aesthetic. The photography of reclusive Vivian Maier was entirely unknown during her lifetime, and maybe she preferred it that way.[48] Only when her work was discovered after her death was she effectively created as a publicly recognized photographer. Cahun, Clementina Hawarden, Lee Miller, and Francesca Woodman – along with Maier – share the dubious honor of having become much more famous and well regarded after death than during their lifetimes. These photographers did receive some scant recognition while they were alive, but their posthumous fame overwhelms the small prizes, publications, and fellowships they achieved while living. Even Diane Arbus and Ana Mendieta, artists recognized during their lifetimes, garnered after their deaths a kind of fame that far surpasses their reputations while they were alive.

Although the usual interpretation of a woman's posthumous career is that the romantic narrative of her death is itself the engine of her fame, I posit a different theory and suggest that the countercultural force of these photographers' work prevented wider contemporary fame. Death performed a kind of sacrificial expiation for the radicality of each photographer's work, allowing viewers to approach the dead woman's photographic oeuvre without fearing her living embodiment of her feminist way of seeing. Her death generated the lasting image of a passive woman, and it thus created culturally acceptable space for her fierce work. Clementina Hawarden's photography may not seem to warrant description as radical, but I hope to show that her avowal of womanly silence and invisibility indeed formed a protest. The poet Emily Dickinson wrote, "I'm 'Wife' . . . I've finished that!" and expresses the "soft eclipse" that settles on the respectable wife.[49] Hawarden photographs from within this eclipse, showing its contours.

Of course, a posthumous career is not necessarily correlated, with creating images that move through a feminist aesthetic. Photographers Sally Mann, Nan Goldin, and Cindy Sherman have garnered notable fame and recognition and are still active in the field. *Time* magazine cited Mann as America's best photographer in 2001, and both Goldin and Mann have reputations that cross over from the art world into popular media, with Nan Goldin mentioned in the television series *Six Feet Under* and Sally Mann's work copied in the film *Titanic*.[50] Regardless of what one thinks of her work, it cannot be denied that Cindy Sherman is one of the most well-known artists of her generation.[51] Her work *Untitled #96* is among the most expensive photographs ever sold at auction. I cite these facts not to suggest that selling one's art for a great deal of money or that being lauded in popular media is a marker of aesthetic power or a sign of worthy art, assuredly not. Instead, I simply want to make clear to the uninitiated that by no means are women photographers uniformly ignored and rejected during their lifetimes.

In choosing photographs that advocate feminism, then, I am not driven by the impulse to resurrect the careers of women who were ignored while alive. Instead, I look for the turn in the image, something Walter Benjamin spoke of as the "spark of contingency" that sometimes – rarely, but brilliantly – illuminates the photographic object.[52] Benjamin's argument that some photographs have this spark, like Rancière's theory that some works of art reorder the sensible, grounds the aesthetic in the confluence of the act of perception with the formality of the image.[53] For Benjamin and Rancière, then, the aestheton cannot be predicted – if it is the spark of contingency, it is not lit until it is lit – but its force is not felt in an entirely individual or idiosyncratic way; the aesthetic cannot be predicted but multiple observers will see it, even though each may obliquely or even directly connect it to their own perceptions. Political, then, is perceptual as it drives home in the viewer an altered awareness of the polis.

Rancière defines as metapolitical that art which tries very hard and very clearly to be political. For Rancière such overtly political art does not reach the interior power and depth of art that draws from the inherent fusion of ethics and aesthetics. This ethics–aesthetics fusion grounds my interpretation of feminist aesthetic. A photographer's personal avowal or disavowal of feminism has changed meaning over time as feminism has changed meaning in its cultural use over time. I argue that the image, not the artist, carries ethics and hence aesthetics. I would not suggest that the camera is a tool that creates without input from the photographer, and I consider biographical facts about a photographer relevant to understanding her oeuvre. However, I do think it is important to avoid trying to form a point-by-point map that connects the artist's biography with her art. In this book, I interpret biographies as gossip, as Irit Rogoff suggests, or, to use Michel Foucault's term, "subjugated knowledge."[54] The biography of the photographer stands as a kind of politics and as such can be brought to bear on interpretations of the political and historical matrix from which the work emerges. But I reject the practice of interpreting women's art as narrowly biographical. Biography is political and cultural, and I draw on the photographers' biographies in that light.

Photographs that advocate feminism, that carry forward a feminist aesthetic, work through perception: the event of vision that takes place in the viewer. The photograph itself is an uncanny purveyor of perception. As Barthes writes, "It is not it that we see," meaning that when we see a photograph we experience not the frame, not the iPhone screen, but instead we experience seeing the person, object, or scene photographed.[55] A photograph is an image *par excellence*, commonly experienced as image rather than object (even though a photograph is a multitude, a wide array of objects, variously purveyed by paper, metal, and computer screen). For this reason, Susan Sontag complained in *On Photography* that photographs do not convey knowledge but must be supplemented by language to articulate meaning.[56] And yet in the paradigmatic antinarrative quality of the photograph is also its chance for aesthetic force. The aesthetic experience shifts the faculties of the perceiver, and this experience is non-narrative; that is, the aesthetic experience (as understood in Kantian terms) moves outside of narrative time. Aesthetic force by no means emanates from all photographic images.

Most photographs are banal and, as John Tagg points out, many are even inhuman: they are images created by machines to be read by machines.[57] Yet, as Agamben suggests, one does not enter an image, an image enters the viewer; not only does one stare at a photograph, but the photograph also stares at the viewer.[58] He argues: "According to the principle by which it is only in the burning house that the fundamental architectural problem becomes visible for the first time, art, at the highest point of its destiny, makes visible the original project."[59] The photograph presents both the inception of vision and its arrival; unlike other art forms, the photograph does not remember but instead replaces memory hauntingly in its material evasion. Photography is a formal art, one that demands a reading at the intersection of aesthetics and ethics.[60]

Terrain and time

I have arranged this book roughly chronologically to provide an accessible frame. Time is time, even if photographic practices do alter our perception of it. I carry into my interpretation of each artist's work an awareness of how her particular placement before and after the advent of other photographies informs her body of photographic work. My first chapter covers the 1860s and 1870s photographic works of Clementina Hawarden and Julia Margaret Cameron, British photographers whose careers illuminate the struggle early women photographers underwent to be considered anything other than amateurs who were amusing themselves. Hawarden's work is especially important in this regard; having won a few amateur awards and the admiration of Lewis Carroll, she never established herself publicly as a serious artist. Instead, her reputation now rests on photographs that she took of her young daughters, silver colloid photographs that were kept in family albums and given, with tattered corners, to London's Victoria and Albert Museum in 1939. Finally, in the 1970s, more than 100 years after Hawarden's death, her photographs began attracting serious critical attention. Although she was recognized before her death for a very small number of photographs that she displayed publicly, this recognition was nothing akin to canonical representation as an artist. I read Cameron, better known than Hawarden as a photographer in her day, through her relationship to the circle of artists and scholars, including Alfred, Lord Tennyson, with whom she was closely connected socially. I illuminate the way that Cameron deployed a canny strategy of aligning herself with established male artists, such as G.F. Watts, to create a space for reception of her own work. I also interpret the economy of gender and class as reflected in Hawarden's and Cameron's works.

My second chapter interprets surrealist photographers Claude Cahun and Lee Miller through the rubric of the interwar period and the impact of the world wars on European culture. I parse the "insider–outsider" status that Whitney Chadwick ascribes to surrealist women artists by working through some biographical information about Cahun and Miller and presenting their work in contrast to that of male surrealists, such as Man Ray. The chapter looks at the surrealist discourse of gender – concepts of *femme enfant, amour fou*, and convulsive beauty. It also compares Cahun's autoportraits and Miller's pre-World War II works with the dictums of surrealism, querying Rosalind Krauss's contention that women were implicitly at the center of the surrealist movement – for their peers accepted neither Cahun nor Miller in their day as prominent and important photographers. Their fame is decidedly posthumous. I close this chapter by interpreting Miller's war photography in light of several recent articles that suggest it shows a "feminine" gaze, a "female" sublime, or a "female" genius.[61] I leverage Cahun's refusal of the terms of gender – her claim that she was neither man nor woman but a third sex – to question what it might mean to say that Cahun's photographs, or for that matter Miller's, show a feminine sublime.

As proponents of straight photography (Group f/64) and documentary photography and in the cohort of Ansel Adams and Walker Evans, Imogen Cunningham and Dorothea Lange represent a high-water mark of belief in photography's capacity to document the real, the so-called truth. This book's third chapter considers Cunningham's work in typology and formalism and compares it to Lange's work in documentary photography and social realism. I explore the power of the belief that by showing what is physically present, photography might also reveal larger truths, a kind of transmission from the unseen into the visible. In this regard, I consider the tension between photography as document and photography as art and query the ideology of photographic claims to "truth." The fame and centrality of Adams and Evans stands in contrast to the more subsidiary positions of Cunningham and Lange. I interpret, then, representative photographs of Cunningham and Lange as implicit responses to this culturally feminized position of being lesser known for equal work.

My fourth chapter focuses on Diane Arbus's now canonical photographic works, and it juxtaposes Arbus's oeuvre with that of newly discovered mid-century photographer Vivian Maier. I trace the distinction between street photography and documentary photography, using Arbus and Maier as foils while also pointing to some similarities in their approaches. The presence of women photographers on the street I interpret as a form of implicit power. I repudiate arguments around Diane Arbus's supposed cruelty to her photographic subjects, as described in Susan Sontag's infamous essay on Arbus, "America, Seen Through Photographs, Darkly."[62] My argument centers on the question of the gendering of ethics – the demand that a woman photographer be empathetic. Moving beyond this question, I also explore formal aspects of Arbus's portrait photographs and interpret Arbus's choreographed work in contrast to Maier's more fractionary approach. The unifying aspect of both artists' work is mid-twentieth-century urban America and the slant and strange light in which Arbus and Maier cast this world.

In the fifth chapter, I consider the work of Francesca Woodman and interpret her photography in relation to the nearly contemporaneous oeuvre of earthworks and performance artist Ana Mendieta. In that Mendieta extensively recorded her performances by taking photographs of them – photographs upon which Mendieta's posthumous fame largely rests – I interpret her as a photographer. Woodman's work, like Mendieta's, contends with tropes of disappearance even while the photographs function as marks against vanishing. Woodman is an artist whose career – that is, her public recognition – began after her death; Mendieta was certainly not unknown at the time of her death, but her fame after death far exceeds her reputation while alive. In interpreting them, I pay careful attention to uncanny intersections of reception history – the critical and cultural apparatuses of the photographer's reputation's ascent – and themes of disappearance, dereliction, resistance, and persistence manifested in the photographs themselves. That Mendieta worked in the medium of 35-millimeter slides, while Woodman at the end of her life experimented extensively with diazotype, indicates the two photographers' compelling interaction with materialized themes of transience and loss in the discourse of the photographic image.

I focus on the photographs of Nan Goldin and Nikki Lee in my sixth chapter, also interpreting the work of Catherine Opie and Zackary Drucker. Developing from Sarah Ruddy's claim that Goldin's genre is "affective documentary," I extend an understanding of Goldin's seminal and passionate photographs of the demimonde in relation to Nikki Lee's work, created roughly a decade later, ironizing the snapshot aesthetic.[63] Both Goldin and Lee work with a framed-box structure by which the viewer is invited into an intimate interior relationship with the photographs' subjects. However, Goldin's work professes immense sincerity and functions, so claims Goldin, as an expression of love for her subjects, whereas Lee takes the postmodern approach of posing as an intimate with subjects whom she has categorically known less than a month. Goldin pioneers the photographic oeuvre as diary, and so I argue that her works operate most strongly in the elegiac register. This chapter describes cultural shifts from the 1980s to the 1990s and changes in the landscape of feminist theory, in particular as they relate to gender theory and queer theory. In this chapter I contend with Catherine Opie's work – photographs that have focused on queer sexuality and the body. I approach Opie's handling of these themes, drawing from paradigms of queer textuality of the body. I close the chapter with a discussion of collaborative artist Zackary Drucker's exploration of transfemininity in *Translady Fanzine*.

The book's seventh chapter emphasizes the photography of Carrie Mae Weems, reading Sally Mann's family and landscape photography as a counterpoint to Weems's. I explore class and race as motivating factors in Mann's immense popularity and acclaim. This chapter discusses the class and race issues embedded in the reception of Mann's portrait photography and its enmeshment with the American culture of whiteness. I read Carrie Mae Weems's magisterial body of work through the lens of race relations in the United States, and I explore Weems's requisitioning and radical repositioning of documentary photography by interpreting what Abigail Solomon-Godeau calls the haunting aspects of Weems's late twentieth- and early twenty-first-century series. I discuss *Family Pictures and Stories*, *The Kitchen Table Series*, *The Hampton Project*, and *The Louisiana Project*, in their relationship to Blanchotian theory. I interpret Weems's deployment of the witness figure and the ghost as figurations of her feminist vision.

The eighth chapter examines works by Zoe Strauss, Mary Ellen Mark, and Rineke Dijkstra as a means of engaging questions about the postphotographic era, after the broad advent of digital photography. During this time, Mary Ellen Mark absolutely rejected digital photography; Rineke Dijkstra works in film but scans her negatives into digital form; and Zoe Strauss states that the debate over film versus digital photography is specious and recommends that we "explore the differences."[64] I emphasize Dijkstra's evocation of traditional portraiture, a position that addresses the postmodern issue of fabricated digital images. In interpreting Mary Ellen Mark's seminal 1980s work in *Streetwise*, I focus on the politics of representation, while querying the terms of the photographic representation of vulnerable populations.[65] I compare Mark's street photography to Strauss's photography of American poverty, which Strauss approaches as a war photographer approaches war. The violence of Strauss's images, together with her insistence on placing her work where it was taken, in the rundown urban neighborhoods from which she and her photographs emerge, mark a resistance to the fabricated visual realm, the simulacrum of the postmodern.

In the ninth chapter, I interpret the work of Aida Muluneh and Lalla Essaydi. I interpret Muluneh in relation to Ethiopian Orthodox iconicity, an ancient tradition of image-making, and I connect images from Ethiopian Orthodoxy with the radical imagery in her *The 99 Series*. Drawing from Mel Y. Chen's theory of animacy, I argue that this series presents visual boundaries between life and death. The images contend with Ethiopia's recent histories of war and with the way that colonial and postcolonial Africa becomes a figure for death, the continent against which the West poses its concept of life.[66] Muluneh's photographs argue for the animacy of Ethiopian tradition and vision in photographs that eloquently symbolize resilience and life. I interpret Essaydi's recent turn to photography – after a career as a mixed-media artist – as a potent response to the role of imagery in creating an oppressive and damaging concept of the woman of Middle Eastern origin as utterly vulnerable and accessible to the male gaze fused with the colonizer's look. Essaydi's photographs counter and refuse this narrative that marks the body of the woman of Middle Eastern descent as "unmournable," thereby creating in response a vivid tableau of women caught in the intersecting nexus of various forms of patriarchal domination.[67]

The tenth chapter concerns Native American photographer Matika Wilbur and Canadian First Nations photographer Rebecca Belmore. I interpret indigenous North American women's photography in light of the long history of the camera being used to dehumanize indigenous peoples on the North American continent. Belmore and Wilbur forcefully work against this history of dehumanization, creating a counterhistory that rebuts and radically reframes photographic images of indigenous North Americans. Belmore has long incorporated elements of photography into her performance art, but in the twenty-first century she has created some works that are entirely photographic and that emerge thematically from her performance work. This chapter interprets Belmore's film and photographic work in *The Named and the Unnamed* and *Vigil*, as well as related series of photographic images. The chapter connects Belmore's works elegizing murdered indigenous women who lived on the streets with her photography produced in the twenty-first century. Matika Wilbur's *Project 562* directly tackles the misrepresentation of Native Americans in photography. *Project 562* positions itself as a postmodern – blogged and tweeted – rejoinder to Gertrude Käsebier's romanticized and falsified early twentieth-century photographic images of Native Americans as a vanishing race. Photographically insisting on the presence of twenty-first-century Native Americans, Wilbur deploys the image realm of the Internet to circulate these counterimages, photographs of members of every federally recognized Native

American tribe. Her project continues to date. In emphasizing Native American photographers who interpret and make use of digital media, *Women Photographers and Feminist Aesthetics* emphasizes the feminist potential of photography. The chapter argues that the historical construct of gender shapes ways of seeing – articulated in the photographic works of some women photographers – that tell us about our world even as they seek to change it. I interpret the challenge and éclat of Native American women photographers as exemplary of feminist aesthetics: Belmore and Wilbur create photographs that are political in the most aesthetic terms. The photographs charge the viewer to see anew.

As exergue, placed as a postscript, I interpret the work of artist Dayanita Singh. Singh's photographs construct a language of imagery in sensitive photographs that she combines to create displays called "museums" in the gallery or larger museum space. Singh's photographic books and "museums" bounce off the documentary tradition, curving toward an elliptical and evocative narrative, questioning always the frame (in the gallery or museum space and also, by implication, the cultural space) in which the image is seen. Singh creates intimate and enigmatic, emotive and hauntingly private realms of images that she exhibits in constantly revolving and evolving connectivity. She evocatively poses questions about how visual relations come to manifest under the rubric of fate or chance. The lyricism of her work carries considerations of cultural dispossession that are anticolonial, not postcolonial.[68] In Singh's refusal of the colonizing gaze inheres the turn of the feminist aesthetic: to resist and overturn the gaze of the dominant, to take apart the vision of the ideology of domination.

Notes

1 See Rosi Braidotti, "Feminism by Any Other Name," *Differences: A Journal of Feminist Cultural Studies* 6, no. 2 (1994): 47. See also Judith Butler, *Gender Trouble* (London: Routledge, 1990). In the opening chapter, Butler argues, "The appearance of an abiding substance or gendered self, what the psychiatrist Robert Stoller refers to as a 'gender core,' is thus produced by the regulation of attributes along culturally established lines of coherence. . . . In this sense, *gender* is not a noun . . . the substantive effect of gender is performativity produced and compelled by the regulatory practices of gender coherence" (24). For Butler, the copying of the putative "heterosexual original" demonstrates that "the original is nothing more than a parody of the *idea* of the natural original" (31).

2 See Mary Jacobus, *The Poetics of Psychoanalysis* (Oxford, UK: Oxford University Press, 2005), 35–60.

3 See Michele C. Black, Kathleen C. Basile, Matthew J. Breiding, Sharon G. Smith, Mikel L. Walters, Melissa T. Merrick, Jieru Chen, and Mark R. Stevens, *The National Intimate Partner and Sexual Violence Survey* (Atlanta, GA: National Center for Injury Prevention and Control, Centers for Disease Control and Prevention, 2010), www.cdc.gov/ViolencePrevention/pdf/NISVS_Report2010-a.pdf. See also Melanie Heenan and Suellen Murray, *Study of Reported Rapes in Victoria 2000–2003: Summary Research Report* (Melbourne, Australia: Office of Women's Policy, Department for Victorian Communities, RMIT University, 2006), http://mams.rmit.edu.au/igzd08ddxtpwz.pdf; Christopher P. Krebs, Christine H. Lindquist, Tara D. Warner, Bonnie S. Fisher, and Sandra L. Martin, *The Campus Sexual Assault (CSA) Study: Final Report* (unpublished report prepared for the National Institute of Justice, Washington, DC, December 2007), www.ncjrs.gov/pdffiles1/nij/grants/221153.pdf; Jen Roesch, "Protecting the University, Failing Rape

Survivors," *Socialist Worker*, www.socialistworker.org/2014/10/02/protecting-university-failing. See also the website of End Rape on Campus, http://endrapeoncampus.org/our-team-1/; Estelle Freedman, *Redefining Rape* (Cambridge, MA: Harvard University Press, 2013); Anne Marie Slaughter, *Unfinished Business: Women, Men, Work, Family* (New York: Random House, 2015).

4 See Josephine Ahikire, "Vulnerabilities of Feminist Engagement and the Challenges of Developmentalism in the South: What Alternatives?" *IDS Bulletin: Reclaiming Feminism: Gender and Neoliberalism* 39, no. 6 (2008): 28–33; see also, Josephine Ahikire, "African Feminism in Context: Reflections on the Legitimation Battles, Victories, and Reversals" in *Feminist Africa* 19 (2014): 7–23; Amina Mama, "Gender Studies for Africa's Transformation," in *African Intellectuals: Rethinking Politics, Language, Gender and Development*, ed. Thandika Mkandawire (London: Zed Books, 2005): 94–116; Charmaine Pereira, "Locating Gender and Women's Studies in Nigeria: What Trajectories for the Future," in *Gender Activism and Studies in Africa, Gender Series Vol. 3* (Dakar: CODESRIA, 2004), 1–26; J. Everjoice Win, "Not Very Poor, Powerless or Pregnant: The African Women Forgotten by Development," in *Feminisms in Development: Contradictions, Contestations and Challenges*, ed. Andrea Cornwall, Elizabeth Harrison, and Ann Whitehead (London: Zed Books, 2006): 79–86.

5 bell hooks argues that feminist theory has contended with the "plight of a select group of college-educated, middle- and upper-class, married white women-housewives" and that such theory fails to "discuss who would be called in to take care of the children and maintain the home if more women . . . were freed from their house labor," that is, it fails to theorize the position of the economically oppressed. *Feminist Theory: From Margin to Center* (New York: Routledge, 2015), 1–2. There are, of course, other feminist voices. Sarah Deer, Gloria Anzaldua, Amelia Jones, Grace Chang, and Cherie Moraga represent differences from Butler's white bourgeois paradigm. See Grace Chang, *Disposable Domestics* (Boston, MA: South End Press, 2000); see also Cherie Moraga, *This Bridge Called My Back* (Boston, MA: Kitchen Table Press, 1981).

6 For further reading on where feminism has come from and where it is going in twenty-first-century art, see Alexandra Kokoli, *Feminism Reframed: Reflections on Art and Difference* (Newcastle-upon-Tyne, UK: Cambridge Scholars Publishing, 2008); see also Eleanor Heartney, Helaine Posner, Nancy Princenthal, and Sue Scott, *After the Revolution: Women Who Transformed Contemporary Art* (New York: Prestel, 2013).

7 hooks, *Feminist Theory*, 40.

8 According to hooks, advocating feminism entails not simply what one does in one's personal life but what one advocates for other women. See bell hooks, *Feminism Is for Everybody: Passionate Politics* (Cambridge, MA: South End Press, 2000), 1–6.

9 See Jacques Rancière, *The Politics of Aesthetics* (London: A. and C. Black, 2006); see also Giorgio Agamben, *The Man without Content* (Palo Alto, CA: Stanford University Press, 1999).

10 Roland Barthes, *Camera Lucida: Reflections on Photography*, trans. Richard Howard (New York: Hill and Wang, 1980), 34–8.

11 See bell hooks, "Moving Beyond Pain," bell hooks Institute Blog, May 9, 2016, www.bellhooksinstitute.com/blog/2016/5/9/moving-beyond-pain.

12 Judith Butler, *Bodies that Matter: On the Discursive Limits of "Sex"* (New York: Routledge, 1993).

13 See Teresa de Lauretis, *Figures of Resistance: Essays in Feminist Theory* (Champaign: University of Illinois Press, 2007), 72–84.

14 In *Bodies that Matter*, Butler argues that "the 'being' of gender is an *effect*, an object of a genealogical investigation that maps out the political parameters of its construction in the mode of ontology" (38). In effect, she claims that ontology itself is a specious category, but this is an untenable position and one that misinterprets the Foucauldian theory of truth-effect to which she is yet heavily indebted. To carry this argument, she must claim a mode rather than an existence for ontology globally.

15 See Teresa de Lauretis, *The Practice of Love* (Bloomington, IN: Indiana University Press, 1994).

16 See Monique Wittig, *The Straight Mind* (Boston, MA: Beacon Press, 1992).

17 Jacques Derrida argues, "The written signifier is always technical and representative. It has no constitutive meaning. This derivation is the very origin of the notion of the signifier, the notion of the sign always implies within itself the distinction between signifier and signified, even if, as Saussure argues, they are distinguished simply as the two faces of one and the same leaf. This notion remains therefore within the heritage of the logocentrism which is also phonocentrism." *Of Grammatology*, corrected edition (Baltimore, MD: Johns Hopkins University Press, 1998), 11. See also Jacques Derrida, *The Truth in Painting* (Chicago: University of Chicago Press, 1987), 173–4.

18 Roland Barthes states, "Since every photograph is contingent (and thereby outside of meaning), photography cannot signify (aim at a generality) except by assuming a mask." *Camera Lucida: Reflections on Photography* (New York: Macmillan, 1981), 34.

19 Rancière, *The Politics of Aesthetics*, 30, 71.

20 Maurice Blanchot, *L'Espace litteraire* (Paris: Editions Gallimard, 1955).

21 Walter Benjamin, *The Work of Art in the Age of Its Technological Reproducibility and Other Writings on Media*, eds. Michael Jennings, Bridig Doherty, and Thomas Levin (Cambridge, MA: Harvard at the Belknap Press, 2008).

22 See Griselda Pollock and Rozsika Parker, *Old Mistresses* (New York: I.B. Tauris, 2013); see also Griselda Pollock, *Differencing the Canon: Feminism and the Writing of Art's Histories* (London: Routledge, 1999). See also Rita Felski, *Beyond Feminist Aesthetics* (Cambridge, MA: Harvard University Press, 1989), 22.

23 Griselda Pollock, "Writing from the Heart," in *Writing Otherwise: Experiments in Cultural Criticism*, ed. Jackie Stacey and Janet Wolff (Manchester, UK: Manchester University Press, 2013), 29.

24 Suggests Roland Barthes, "Certainly the image is not the reality but at least it is its perfect *analogon* and it is exactly this analogical perfection which, to common sense, defines the photograph. Thus can be seen the special status of the photographic image: *it is a message without a code*." "The Photographic Message," in *A Barthes Reader*, ed. Susan Sontag (New York: Hill and Wang, 1983), 196. Jacques Rancière argues that "the point of view of the reconfigurations of the shared sensible order . . . is also the configuration of a proper place, a non-polemical distribution of the sensible universe where what one sees, what one says, and what one makes or does are rigorously adapted to one another." *Le Partage du sensible: Esthetique et politique* (Paris: La Fabrique, 2000), 40; see also Rancière, *The Politics of Aesthetics*, 36.

25 Abigail Solomon-Godeau, "Just Like a Woman," in *Catalogue, Wellesley College Exhibition of Francesca Woodman Photographs* (Wellesley, MA: Wellesley College, 1986).

26 For a fuller argument as to why it matters that a photographer be somehow sincerely of the community from which she creates her body of work, see Arthur C. Danto, "The Naked Truth," in *Aesthetics and Ethics: Essays at the Intersection*, ed. Jerrold Levinson (Cambridge, UK: Cambridge University Press, 2001), 257–82; see also Claire Raymond, "The Crucible of Witnessing: Carrie Mae Weems's 'From Here I Saw What Happened and I Cried,'" *Meridians* 13, no. 1 (2015): 26–52.

27 Julia Serano, *Whipping Girl* (New York: Perseus, 2007). I consider the entire oeuvre of the artist Greer Lankton a feminist manifesto. If Lankton were primarily a photographer, her work would be in this book. For more about her, see Giancarlo Ambrosino, ed., *David Wojnarowicz: A Definitive History of Five or Six Years on the Lower East Side* (Los Angeles, CA: Semiotext(e), 2006).

28 John Tagg, *Grounds of Dispute: Art History, Cultural Politics, and the Discursive Field* (Minneapolis, MN: University of Minnesota Press, 1992).

29 Immanuel Kant, *Critique of Judgment* (Jersey City, NJ: Start Publishing, 2013), 250.

30 Rancière contends, "In the aesthetic regime, artistic phenomena are identified by their adherence to a specific regime of the sensible, which is extricated from its ordinary connections and is inhabited by a heterogeneous power, the power of a form of thought that has become foreign to itself: a product identical with something not produced,

knowledge transformed into non-knowledge. . . . The locus for a form of thought that has become foreign to itself, is the invariable core in the identifications of art that have configured the aesthetic mode of thought." *The Politics of Aesthetics*, 22–3.

31 For Barthes, the aesthetic is private and cannot be predicted. See *Camera Lucida*, 27, 40.
32 hooks, *Feminism Is for Everybody*, 23.
33 See Allan Sekula, "The Traffic in Photographs," *Art Journal* 41, no. 1 (1981): 15, doi:10.2307/776511.
34 Geoffrey Batchen, *Burning with Desire* (Cambridge, MA: MIT Press, 1999), 69–78.
35 See Anne Maxwell, *Picture Imperfect: Photography and Eugenics, 1879–1940* (Eastbourne, UK: Sussex Academic Press, 2008); Allan Sekula, "The Body and the Archive," in *The Contest of Meaning*, ed. Richard Bolton (Cambridge, MA: MIT Press, 1992): 343–390.
36 Amelia Jones, *Seeing Differently: A History and Theory of Identification and the Visual Arts* (London: Routledge, 2013), 2, 10.
37 Carol Armstrong, "Francesca Woodman: A Ghost in the House of the Woman Artist," in *Women Artists at the Millennium*, ed. Carol M. Armstrong and M. Catherine de Zegher (Cambridge, MA: MIT Press, 2006): 347–370.
38 Rosi Braidotti, *The Posthuman* (Cambridge, UK: Polity Press, 2013).
39 See Amelia Jones, "Feminism, Incorporated: Reading 'Postfeminism' in an Anti-Feminist Age," in *Afterimage* (December 1992): 10–15.
40 Gayatri Chakravorty Spivak, "Can the Subaltern Speak?" *Die Philosophin* 14, no. 27 (2003): 42–58.
41 hooks, *Feminist Theory*, 1.
42 See John Szarkowski, *The Photographer's Eye* (New York: Museum of Modern Art, 1966).
43 Walter Benjamin, "Small History of Photography (1931)," in *On Photography*, trans. and ed. Esther Leslie (London: Reaktion, 2015): 79–84.
44 William Henry Fox Talbot, *The Pencil of Nature* (Alexandria, Egypt: Library of Alexandria, 1969).
45 Allan Sekula, "The Traffic in Photographs," and Gayle Rubin, "The Traffic in Women: Notes on the 'Political Economy' of Sex," both in *Toward an Anthropology of Women*, ed. Rayna R. Reiter (New York: Monthly Review Press, 1975), 157–210.
46 Gen Doy, *Claude Cahun: A Sensual Politics* (London: I.B. Tauris, 2006).
47 Ibid., 9.
48 John Maloof, *Vivian Maier: A Photographer Found* (New York: Harper Design, 2014).
49 Emily Dickinson, *The Complete Poems of Emily Dickinson* (Cambridge, MA: Belknap Press of Harvard University Press, 1998), 19.
50 In the sketchbook of movie character Jack Dawson, one saw sketches strikingly similar to Sally Mann's work. See Maude Schuyler Clay, "Sally Mann's Vision," *Oxford American*, May 12, 2015, www.oxfordamerican.org/item/581-sally-mann-s-vision.
51 Anna Kerchy, "The Woman 69 Times: Cindy Sherman's Untitled Film Stills," *HJEAS: Femininity and Subjectivity* 9, no. 1 (2003): 181–190.
52 Walter Benjamin, "Little History of Photography," in *Selected Writings, Volume 2: 1927–1934*, trans. Walter Livingstone and others, ed. Michael W. Jennings, Howard Eiland, and Gary Smith (Cambridge, MA: Harvard University Press, 1999), www.chaffeyphoto1.com/items/02_Benjamin_LittleHistory.pdf.
53 Rancière, *The Politics of Aesthetics*, 4.
54 Irit Rogoff, "Gossip as Testimony," in *The Feminism and Visual Culture Reader*, ed. Amelia Jones (London: Routledge, 2010), 268.
55 Barthes, *Camera Lucida*, 6.
56 Susan Sontag, *On Photography* (New York: Macmillan, 1977), 69.
57 John Tagg, *The Burden of Representation: Essays on Photographies and Histories* (Minneapolis, MN: University of Minnesota Press, 1988).
58 Agamben, *The Man without Content*, 108.
59 Ibid., 110.
60 Rancière, *The Politics of Aesthetics*.

61 Jui-Ch'i Liu, "Beholding the Female Sublime: Lee Miller's War Photography," *Signs: Journal of Women in Culture and Society* 40, no. 2 (Winter 2015): 308–19; Jean Gallagher, *The World Wars through the Female Gaze* (Carbondale, IL: Southern Illinois University Press, 1998).

62 Susan Sontag, "America, Seen through Photographs, Darkly," in *On Photography* (New York: Picador, 2001): 27–51.

63 Sarah Ruddy, "A Radiant Eye Yearns from Me," *Feminist Studies* 35, no. 2 (2009): 347–80.

64 Zoe Strauss, "To Take a Picture and to Be Taken by a Picture," *Zoe Strauss* (blog), http://zoestrauss.blogspot.com/2008/09/to-take-picture-and-to-be-taken-by.html.

65 I refer here to the book *Streetwise*, not the film. See Mary Ellen Mark and John Irving, *Streetwise* (New York: Aperture, 1992).

66 Mel Y. Chen, *Animacies: Biopolitics, Racial Mattering, and Queer Affect* (Durham, NC: Duke University Press, 2012).

67 The term and concept of the *unmournable person* is one I draw from Teju Cole. Please see Cole, "Unmournable Bodies," *The New Yorker*, January 9, 2015, www.newyorker.com/culture/cultural-comment/unmournable-bodies.

68 bell hooks, "Carrie Mae Weems: Diasporic Landscapes of Longing," in *Inside the Visible: An Elliptical Traverse of Art, in, of, and from, the Feminine*, Ed. Catherine de Zegher (Cambridge, MA: MIT Press, 1996): 173–179.

1

MYTHS OF ORIGIN

Julia Margaret Cameron and Clementina Hawarden

A silence attends Clementina, Viscountess Hawarden, or Lady Clementina Hawarden (1822–1865), as she is better known. She left no written record explaining her photographs and apparently left very little written record of her thoughts on any subject. Instead, the traces she left are the many exquisite and enigmatically staged photographs that she took of her eldest daughters, Isabella and Clementina, in London in the early 1860s.[1] The daughters preserved these photographs in albums, as wealthy Victorian families typically did, with the difference that Hawarden's family considered Hawarden an important photographer: they kept the photographs she created as family treasures, private, but of public import. They considered them art, rather than memorabilia. Her granddaughter brought the photographs to London's Victoria and Albert Museum in 1939. Mark Haworth-Booth, a curator of photographs at the Victoria and Albert from 1977–2004, recollects:

> Lady Clementina Tottenham had seen the exhibition [commemorating 100 years of photography] and wished to know why her grandmother, Lady Hawarden – an important pioneer – had not been included. "Unfortunately, your ladyship," my predecessor replied, "the museum possesses no photographs by Lady Hawarden." Lady Tottenham returned with 775 photographs, which she gave to the Museum. The war soon intervened and it was not until 1968 that the photographs were all fully mounted, numbered and listed.[2]

A sleep of more than 100 years, from 1864 until 1968, enfolded Hawarden's photographs. In this chapter, I investigate the terms of that sleep and awakening, interpreting Hawarden's photographs as images that lucidly articulate the gendered terms of her silence.

Photographer Julia Margaret Cameron (1815–1879), also an aristocratic Victorian British mother, refused to be mistaken for a woman creating a family album.

Even so, she created albums of her photographs to send to male artists, scientists, and photographers whom she admired and from whom she hoped to elicit mutual admiration. Cameron, unlike Hawarden, left clear and strong written statements regarding her photography. In particular, her *Annals of My Glass House* makes the case that photography as such, and Julia Margaret Cameron's photography in particular, could aspire to and would accomplish the status of great art.[3] Cameron compared her photographs not so much to works by other photographers but rather to paintings, thus claiming for herself a place among artists of genius. Indeed, genius and greatness were concepts that very much drew Cameron's attention. She sought the company of men whom she considered geniuses, from Alfred, Lord Tennyson, the poet, to G.F. Watts, the painter, to John Herschel, the scientist. She sought to photograph men whom she saw as paradigms – exemplars – of male genius. In turn, Cameron argued that her photographs of such men, as well as the many photographs she took of her housemaids, demonstrated her own artistic genius.[4] In this chapter, I investigate the terms of Cameron's relationship to male artists as a way to unpack the photographs she created.

The social code of the "great" artist who has "genius" is no more real than the social code of the good Victorian mother.[5] Hawarden and Cameron worked under the rubric of these social myths, and their photographs contend with them. To understand their photographic oeuvres, I begin by interpreting the photographers' place in a society that did not regard women as capable of intellectual or artistic accomplishments comparable to those of men. Importantly, this was also a culture that did not regard photography as a proper medium for fine art. I read Hawarden and Cameron in contrast to and in conjunction with each other not only because of their obvious proximity in time, nationality, and class – both were wealthy women photographers living and working primarily in England during the Victorian era – but also because both photographers anchored their photographic projects with the use of widely circulated Victorian cultural myths. Here I use the term *myth* in the way that Roland Barthes develops its understanding in *Mythologies*.[6] By invoking myth, I do not refer to the way that Cameron uses names from classical mythology to title her photographs, although I will also consider her tactics in that regard. Instead, I indicate the way that Cameron deploys the cultural myth of the artist as a transcendent genius to leverage her photographic project, keeping in mind that photography was not universally considered a fine art, much less an expression of genius, in the 1860s as she began her short career. In a similar fashion, Hawarden positioned herself as the mythical good mother: giving birth ten times, she produced a family of eight living children, the youngest of whom was scarcely more than a toddler when Hawarden, then in her early forties, died suddenly of pneumonia. When she began to practice photography, Hawarden clearly undertook the work seriously and intensely, producing an oeuvre of nearly 800 images in some seven years, from the late 1850s to 1864, the year of her death. Working with silver collodion wet plate, she created photographic work that is radically different from today's digital photography. To create any photographic images, much less images as brilliant as those she produced, Hawarden had to master the complex technique.

Mastery of that material process, of course, did not mean that she would produce images worth seeing, but as it happened, she did produce an oeuvre of subtly melancholic, enigmatically claustral photographs. Her daughters stored these photographs in an album, which meant that the edges of the prints got torn. Hawarden's photographs of her adolescent daughters, for which she is best known, were taken in her home at 5 Princes Garden in London.[7] Photographically, one may say that Hawarden never departed from the role of aristocratic mother; in her most powerful photographs, she never leaves her beautiful home and never turns her gaze from her children. And yet, what she does with that gaze is to produce photographs that visually subvert the ideal of the home-enclosed mother.

Myths

The artist positioning himself or herself according to widely accepted contemporary myths is a practice hardly exclusive to Julia Margaret Cameron and Lady Clementina Hawarden. But because these photographers were at the vanguard of women in photography – indeed, the 1860s and the 1870s were among the first decades of photography, an era during which the idea that photography was a fine art was by no means generally accepted – their use of cultural myth to place themselves as artists is of special interest. For the desire to photograph (as Geoffrey Batchen usefully sets the phrase in *Burning with Desire*) arises broadly in the early nineteenth century, an amalgam of cultural, scientific, and aesthetic practices.[8] Hawarden and Cameron burned with this desire to photograph, thereby devoting immense energy and time to creating photographic images, the fate of which could not have been entirely clear to them. Even as Cameron positioned herself through her written rhetoric as an artist of genius, there was scant precedent and scanter agreement regarding whether and how photography could occupy the realm of fine art.[9]

Not only as a woman but also as a photographer, Cameron's path to being recognized for artistic genius was not clearly delineated in the early 1860s, when she created a darkroom in what had been the family chicken coop.[10] Hawarden and Cameron created their photographs using wet plate collodion technology: they mixed the chemicals with which to coat the plates to create their negatives, and they developed their own direct silver prints (meaning that their prints were the same size as their negatives).[11] As noted, Hawarden's photographs, as they have come down to us, are often torn at the edges, markers of their long sojourn in family albums. Critic Carol Mavor argues persuasively that this history is part of the images, part of their meaning.[12] Cameron's photographs were better preserved in that she became de facto artist-in-residence at the Victoria and Albert Museum, which began purchasing her photographs only a couple of years after she began taking them.

Cameron's claim to genius was an effective echoing of the terms used in her immediate social circle to describe men upon whom the Victorian role of sage, or man of genius, was inscribed. Cameron asked the well-known poets, painters, and scientists in her social circle to accept that her photographs of them captured the image of their genius. But in this claim, she also implied that the power of the images stemmed from *her* genius. Cameron leverages the idea of a generative force that is specially reserved for art, for the image, and for the artist who creates the image, thus pulling this term *genius* toward herself when she absolves her photographs of the need for technical perfection. Instead, her goal is the work of massing shadow and form and vivifying symbol. Time has proven Cameron right, as she is now regarded as a preeminent portrait photographer of the Victorian era.

If Cameron is best understood as a photographer who consciously and cannily positioned herself as a publicly recognized artist – however controversial the artistic reputation of her medium and her work in her day – Hawarden, having left no written record of her approach to photography, seems to retreat into a secret, enigmatic room. But that secret room is the very room where Hawarden spent hours, days, and years photographing her daughters. My suggestion is that Hawarden is less mysterious and rather more a photographer who, like Cameron, positioned herself by using cultural myth and widely held cultural beliefs. She created a persona as a decorous aristocratic mother who remained in the home and devoted herself to her children, using photographs to subvert this role. The photographs that Hawarden created in and of this private room quietly overturn the terms of entrapment that the images poignantly convey. The feminist resistance to stifling domesticity that is palpable in Cameron's claiming of her own genius might seem to be missing in Hawarden's ultratraditional life, but I suggest that Hawarden, like Cameron, availed herself of the most accessible myth to frame her artistic practice. Hawarden, like Cameron, used myth to launch, frame, and sustain the creation of a photographic oeuvre, forging a space in which to create art despite a relative lack of public esteem and recognition.[13]

The viscountess

The future Lady Clementina Hawarden was born in 1822, the daughter of Admiral Charles Elphinstone Fleeming and Catalina Alessandro, a Spanish beauty a quarter century younger than her husband.[14] Hawarden's ascendance into the wealthier aristocracy came about through her marriage to Cornwallis Maude, Viscount Hawarden, in 1845. A wealthy woman upon her marriage, with servants to attend to her housework and childcare duties, Hawarden was physically taxed in producing, for the 20 years of her married life, a child nearly every other year. Whatever her feelings about these many pregnancies, and regardless of support from household staff, the physical strain of being constantly pregnant and repeatedly giving birth cannot have been a luxurious experience for her.[15] Hawarden was known in her social circle as a "great baby lover," so it seems she translated the experience of repeated pregnancies into a socially accepted and perhaps personally satisfying myth of maternal grace.[16]

And yet, by the late 1850s, she was apparently looking for something to do beyond producing babies, as she began taking photographs using a stereoscopic camera around 1857.[17] Despite giving birth to three more children after she began to pursue photography, Hawarden produced a large and apparently intensely sought oeuvre of photographs between 1857 and 1864. Decisively, the family's move to 5 Princes Garden at the end of the 1850s provided Hawarden with what became her photography studio. It appears that she sequestered the entire first floor of the home as her space in which to make photographs.[18] She and her eldest girls must have devoted significant amounts of time to the project, in that producing 800 photographs with wet plate collodion process would have been a labor-intensive accomplishment. The photographs also evince a "fingerprint" in that nothing looks like a Hawarden photograph but a Hawarden photograph – a moody, enigmatic, and evocative admixture of nubile daughters' beauty, Victorian costume, and hauntingly spare, light-saturated architectural interiors. Through the photographs, Hawarden belies the docility of her aristocratic matron life. The images often suggest extraordinary tensions between the beauty of the home and the girls and the cage formed by this beautiful space.

As Figures 1.1 and 1.2 show, Hawarden used her daughters Isabella and Clementina to create double figures, posing the girls so that they faced each other as if one were a mirror image of the other. In Figure 1.1, the door through which the

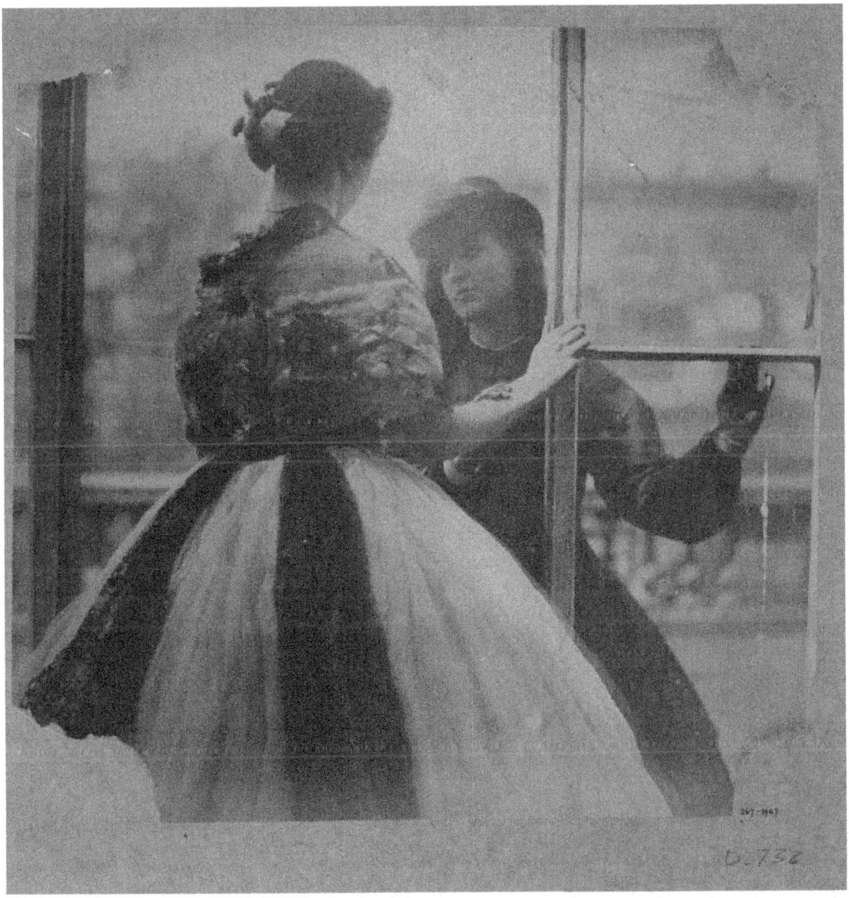

FIGURE 1.1 Clementina Hawarden, *Studies from Life or Photographic Study; Isabella Grace and Clementina Maude, 5 Princes Gardens*, circa 1864, albumen print from wet collodion on glass negative, 23.5 × 24.8 cm. © Victoria and Albert Museum, London.

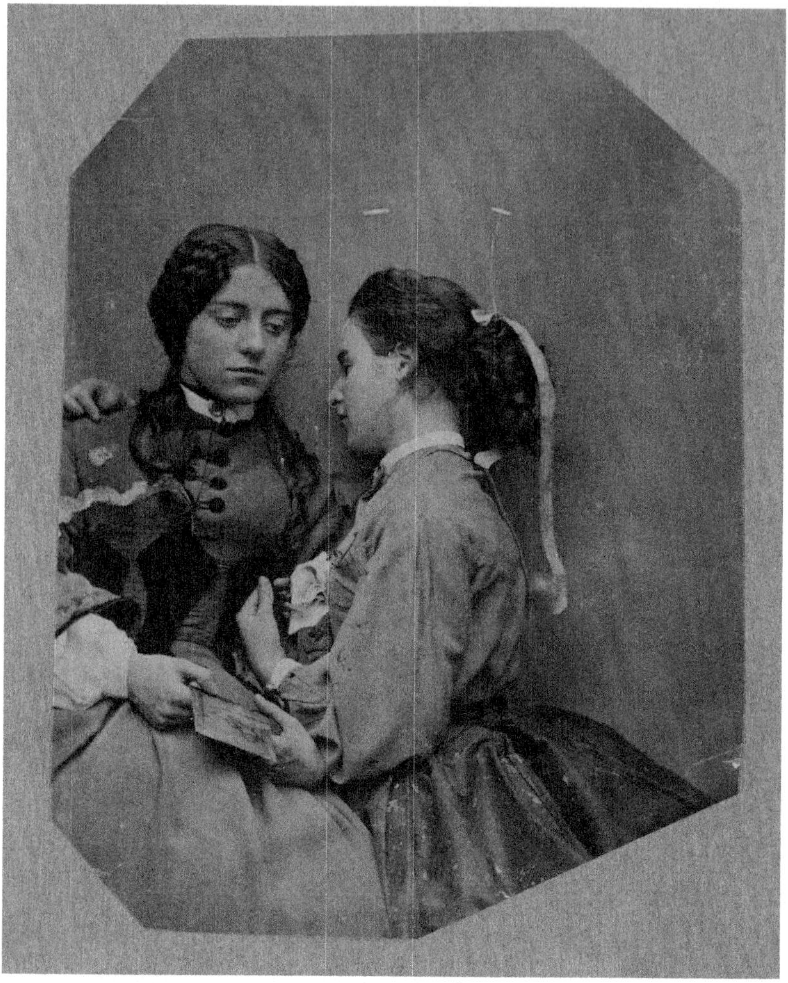

FIGURE 1.2 Clementina Hawarden, *Isabella Grace and Clementina Maude, 5 Princes Gardens; Photographic Study*, circa 1861–1862, albumen process, 9.7 × 7.5 cm. ©Victoria and Albert Museum, London.

girls face each other behaves like a mirror, which exits and entrances frequently do in her photographs. Here, Isabella, who stands within the room, turns her back to the viewer while Clementina, who is suggestively touching her sister's arm, looks obliquely past the viewer, her gaze on her sister. Clementina is standing not actually outside the house but on the enclosed veranda and yet, wearing riding clothes, she seems to be beseeching her sister to come away with her. The opening of the house here is poignantly illusory – one cannot leave the house by the veranda – and so this sense of enclosure together with the trope of a well-lit open door gives a feeling of intense longing to the photograph. Eve Kosofsky Sedgwick chose this photograph for the cover image of *Novel Gazing: Queer Readings in Fiction*, and this interpretation of lesbian longing in the picture is not out of bounds with the image's force of intensely felt desire.[19] And yet what makes the image so potent is that it does not close down the possible vistas of interpretation – it could be expressing lesbian longing, yes, but it could also express the desire to leave the room, to leave the claustral space of the house owned by the girls' father. The tension of the photograph plays especially around the door, which acts as a membrane suffused with emotion: a mirror so the girls' body positions echo each other, and an opening that does not seem capable of allowing the turned figure of Isabella to walk through it. The aperture of the door is also a cognate for Hawarden's camera, which offers a way out of the domestic and yet also never leaves that space. In this way, the opening of the house is as much a force in the photograph as is Clementina's look of longing and her hand tenderly touching her sister's arm.

Hawarden's work, as Alison Chapman rightly suggests, is full of uncanny apertures.[20] In addition, in her photographs actual mirrors abound, presenting structural and luminous forms, apertures that yet offer no way out of the domestic space. The window that acts as a door, the mirror that acts as a window, the door that acts as a mirror all make light a transfiguring and uncanny element, thereby allowing it to perform a way of entering, exiting, and exciting the always enclosed space in which the photographs are made. That Hawarden created most of her best-known work in this one large, beautiful room gives her oeuvre a feeling of claustrophobia. One could say that is only happenstance that the photographs were made in this one singular space (for of course Hawarden and her daughters could leave their home). And yet Hawarden clearly felt powerful and comfortable taking photographs in this room: I say that because after 1859 she took most of her photographs there, and the photographs evince a control and virtuosity that suggest she hit her stride in this context. The social constraints against Hawarden leaving the studio that she had created for herself in order to photograph in public – like the social constraints against her paying models as opposed to using her progeny to model – motivate the images in positive and negative ways. Even as she submitted to decorum by not soliciting photographic subjects outside her domestic parameter, Hawarden created images that crackle with energy drawn from constraint and its resistance.

The sense of deep enclosure that haunts Hawarden's work is incidental – she just happened to have her studio in one stripped and elegant room – and of great import. As an aristocratic woman in Victorian England, a woman who went through pregnancies while creating her photographic oeuvre, Hawarden was very confined in her sphere of power. Her photographs elegantly and poignantly explore the parameters of such "soft" confinement and its gendered contours. Indeed, if Hawarden's husband had so chosen he could have forbidden her to create her studio in the house that by law belonged to him. It seems to me that Hawarden's photographs show the edges of what Abigail Solomon-Godeau (referring to Francesca Woodman's work) calls "the nightmare of femininity," a trope of delicate enclosure.[21] Hawarden's images are tightly controlled and formal, enigmatic and elegant, and their mood is immensely melancholy as the two beautiful teenage daughters gaze past each other, or look into mirrors, or look through doors. Never is there a sense that the girls can walk out the doors, for the edges of the room also delimit the power of their mother, whose photographic eye follows them through every step in this space.[22] Hawarden's gaze ended at the edges of her beautiful and enclosed room – if we define gaze as does Christian Metz, that is, looking with a valence of social power.[23] And indeed, given the social constraints of the Victorian aristocracy, not only did her power to create the photographs as she envisioned them end at the limits of that beautiful room but so did her sole power over her daughters. The photographs are her message of resistance, her refusal to accept the soft eclipse of proper aristocratic Victorian marriage and maternity.

The great wealth that Hawarden enjoyed matters for these photographs. Not only did she need money to take photographs that were not remunerative, but also each image showcases a house that only the very wealthy could afford. Costumes, furniture, and the glowingly healthy daughters evince a moneyed life. Even so, money does not undo the gendered oppressions that also governed Hawarden's life,

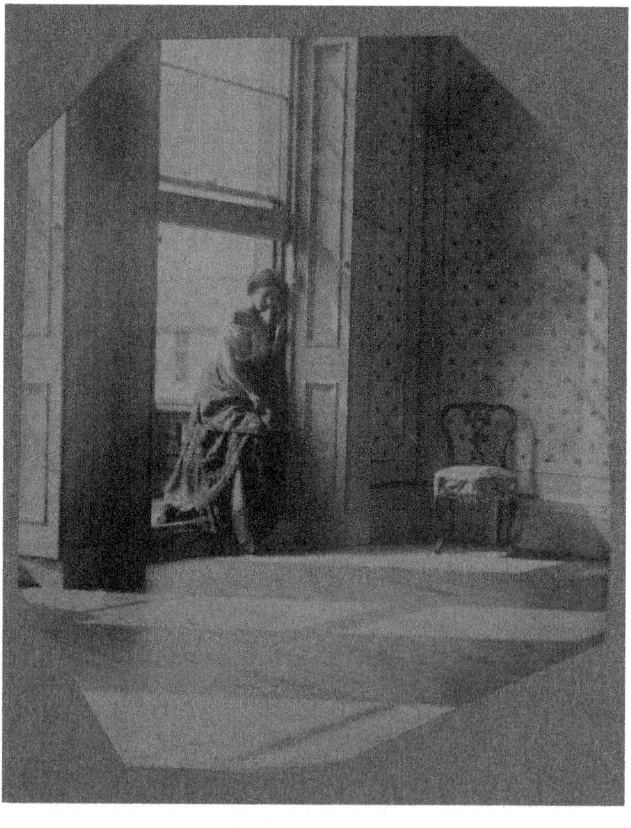

FIGURE 1.3 Clementina Hawarden, *Clementina Maude, 5 Princes Gardens; Photographic Study*, circa 1862, albumen print from wet collodion negative, 10.6 × 8.8 cm. ©Victoria and Albert Museum, London.

the oppressions of which her photographs are visually eloquent. The fact that she adhered to the feminine constraints of Victorian culture doesn't necessarily mean she was unhappy, yet Hawarden's photographs do not so much adhere to those constraints as dramatize and deconstruct them. The daughter posed at the window stands as if supplicant – head bowed, a strikingly odd gesture – seeking to move neither toward nor through the window and yet showing respect, almost devotion, to the window. The slightly erotic slipping of the girl's undergarment top suggests an accessibility, as if the mother were offering her to the viewer.[24] In this case, the

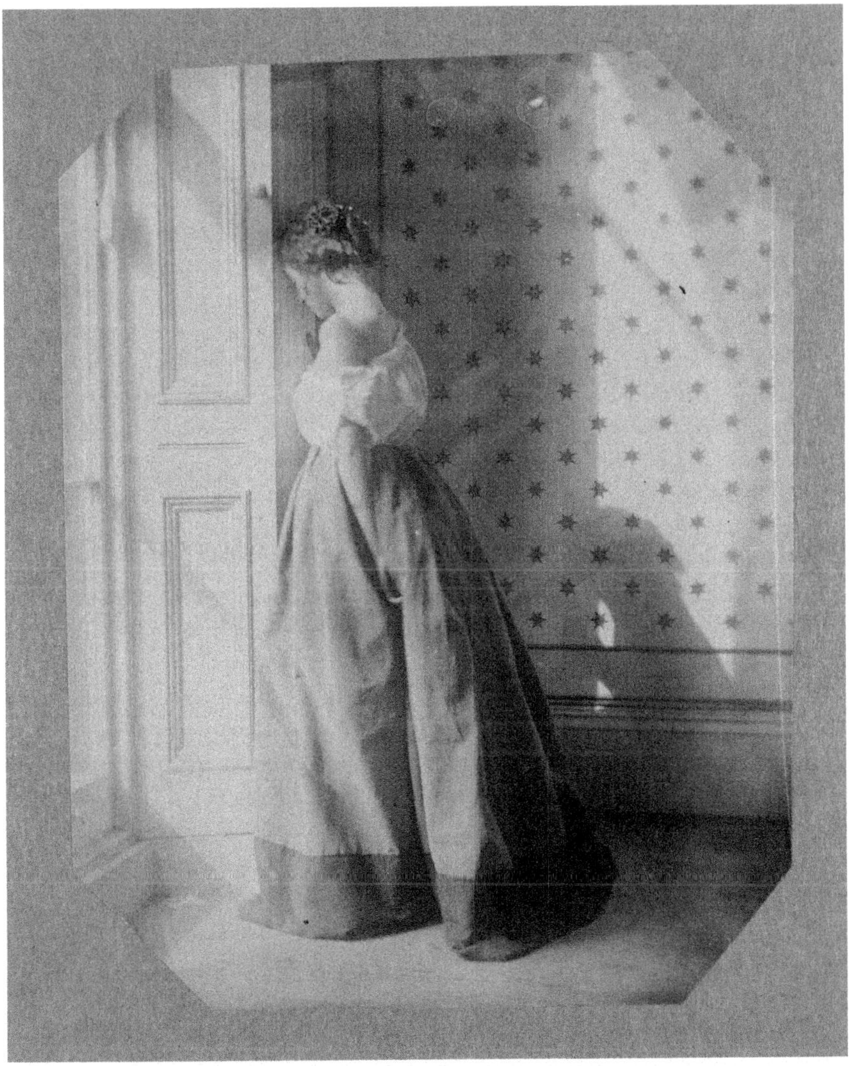

FIGURE 1.4 Clementina Hawarden, *5 Princes Garden, Clementina Maude*, circa 1862, albumen print from wet collodion negative, 23.1 × 20.3 cm. © Victoria and Albert Museum, London.

viewer was only Hawarden herself, as this particular photograph was not one of the small handful shown publicly during her lifetime. The offering of the girl's naked shoulder, the supplicatory gesture before reaching the window, are granted to the mother's gaze. Still, this almost illicit play of motherly, erotic desire is hardly the strangest force in the image.[25] That force is rather the image's conjuring of entrapment and longing juxtaposed with a strict and formal architecture, a beautiful place that the girl cannot leave, which impels the viewer into the image. Other photographs show a daughter pulling on the drapery as if taking apart the house, even as the drapery appears unified with her own gown, as if she were unmaking the house that is also her body.

Many of Hawarden's subtly mournful, valedictory photographs place daughters Isabella or Clementina before a mirror. This placement sets up an uncanny play of light and a scene of simultaneous self-recognition and loss of self (as the figure is absorbed by the glass), thereby suggesting a manifestation and evacuation of the visual. In the photograph where Clementina and Isabella stand on the veranda looking back to their mother who is photographing them, they seem to step toward the twentieth century, almost but never quite beyond their mother's gaze. Hawarden frequently creates what Barthes (not writing specifically of Hawarden's work) calls the "pensive image," the image that "makes us think."[26] There is no written evidence that Hawarden's politics were anything other than in line with the traditional and predominant patriarchy of her time, and she was known to be a devout Roman Catholic. Yet her photographs advocate feminism because they pull the viewer into the melancholy created by the particular system of sexist oppression under which the wealthy Hawarden lived.

The melancholic vistas of the images, the structural motif of always approaching but never passing through doors, the repeated act of gathering light through enormous windows into an almost empty room, and the erotic doubling of daughters all display a kind of stunned entrapment. The images mourn the thresholds that closed against the young women and the solitary vacancy that accompanied wealthy Victorian women's lives – lives hemmed in and limited in their compass.[27] The images also suggest a deep desire on the part of each girl to stay with her sister and mother as well as an erotic desire for the female body that contours the way the women look at each other, a desire that traditional patriarchy seeks to curtail. Hawarden's photographs refuse this curtailment, this patriarchal separation of girls whose bodies upon marriage will be no longer for each other but for a male spouse. Her images mournfully insist on staying in the place of the boundary: at the window, at the door, at the mirror. Those spaces are where the desirable body of the young woman is not given away to a man but instead echoed and returned to herself through the figure of her reflection or her sister.

Hawarden's photographs of her daughters refuse to perform feminine decorousness-as-effacement and instead meditate on the daughters' faces, their individuality, and the expressiveness of their shoulders and arms. In the architecture of their father's beautiful house at 5 Princes Garden, Hawarden's daughters refuse to leave their aesthetic play, their love and even desire for each other, and their mother's gaze. In these photographs (unlike the history of their lived lives), Hawarden's daughters refuse to become wives, refuse the aggressive finality of that role in nineteenth-century aristocratic Britain. Hawarden's photographs plumb the enclosure of gender and the space of women who are not permitted full participation in the polis, and the images protest this enclosure precisely by evoking a painful beauty at its limits. The grace of the architecture of the husband and father's house; the sparseness of the rooms' furnishings; the overwhelming light that moves through windows and against mirrors; and the daughters' smooth, corseted curves and expressive adolescent faces build an image-world that tells us of entrapment and the intimacy it creates among women. But the photographs also create an image-world that refuses to cede the beautiful female body to male possession and instead claims the pleasure of the gaze for the mother and sisters. The photographs show the daughters' thoughts when they are alone together and with their mother; their intimacy shows their personalities in ways unlikely to be recorded by male photographers.[28] Hawarden's daughters are not guarded as they pose together for their mother's camera. The enigma of their intimacy stands as feminist in its insistence on the richness and complexity of women's interior lives (that is, psychological and cognitive), a radical revelation in Hawarden's day.

Julia Margaret Cameron

The similarity between Clementina Hawarden and Julia Margaret Cameron does not extend far beyond their contemporaneity, their privileged social status, and their use of cultural myth to frame their production of photographic oeuvres. Julia Margaret Cameron (1815–1879) saw her photographs as the work of an artist; that is, she aimed toward and claimed the place of *Art* for her work, pointedly placing it in conversation with that of painters and poets. She is known for her characteristic soft focus, an approach that emphasized form and shading, a kind of sculpting of the image, as opposed to the crystalline clarity of which silver colloid photographs are excellently capable (a clarity at which Hawarden excelled).[29] Of her soft focus technique, Cameron made clear that she created blurred images on purpose, not because of a lack of skill:

> My first successes in my out-of-focus pictures were a fluke. That is to say, that when focusing and coming to something which, to my eye, was very beautiful, I stopped there instead of screwing on the lens to the more definite focus which all other photographers insist upon.[30]

Cameron's thoughts on her photography are preserved not only in her unfinished memoir but also in numerous letters that she sent to men such as scientist John Herschel, from whom she learned much of her early handling of photographic chemicals. In addition to sending Herschel letters describing her art, Cameron also prepared albums of photographs for him to demonstrate the progress she had made in creating photography that was, in her opinion, fine art.

Of photographing what she called male genius, Cameron claimed, "When I have had such men before my camera my whole soul has endeavored to do its duty towards them in recording faithfully the greatness of the inner as well as the features of the outer man."[31] In a brilliantly canny approach, Cameron asked powerful men to favor her photographs with the accolade *great art* in exchange for her extolling the men's transcendent greatness. I am not saying that Cameron's use of these mythical terms *art* and *genius* was not sincere, but it was very savvy of her to coax powerful men to call her photographs examples of photographic genius by claiming to capture in her photographs these men as embodied images of genius.

Cameron's tactics of self-presentation were clearly more forceful and unorthodox than Hawarden's. But in this book I focus on the photographs, the images themselves, and bring forward the argument that the images advocate feminism, or show a feminist aesthetic, rather than the photographers. How shall we, then, interpret Cameron's photographs of putative male geniuses as feminist images? A surface argument, although not an inconsequential one, would be to point out that by capturing the images of powerful men, Cameron slyly turns the tables of gender stereotypes. She becomes the active party, the one who wields the camera and captures the subject, while the men are set still in her gaze. I say this argument is somewhat superficial because it is very debatable that one can read, conclusively and only from seeing the images, the gender of the photographer who took Cameron's portraits of Herschel, Carlyle, Tennyson, and Watts. We know that the photographer was Cameron, but an aesthetic reading of the image asks what is legible in the image and so must transcend historicity. I suggest that the photographer's gender is not legible or only barely legible in Cameron's portraits of great men; instead, the photographs humanize the men. They subtly suggest that these men are actually not greater than human but are all too human insofar as their faces show care, wear, and damage. By focusing on qualities that are human, fallible, and not gendered, she decenters their status as male. Cameron is a great portraitist because of the ambiguity of her images, which suggest both the power and the fragility of the sitters. As Barthes (not specifically discussing Cameron's photographs) argues, the photograph turns its subject into an object.[32] Even so, Cameron's portraits of famous men objectify them, even as she avows no such diminution.

Of greater interest from a feminist perspective are Cameron's many photographs of girls and women. Notably, Cameron photographed men who were middle age and older, men with white hair and gray beards, Victorian sages. Yet her images of females rarely include a woman over age 30.[33] Cameron chose her female models for their beauty, not their personal accomplishments. In other words, her approach to photographing men differs in clear and troubling ways from her approach to photographing women. She frequently photographed her maids Mary Hillier and Mary Ryan, young women whose economic position was profoundly disempowered in contrast to Cameron's relative wealth. (For an aristocrat, Cameron was not wealthy, but nevertheless she was far more well-to-do than the working-class women she employed.) Cameron also chose to photograph her young niece, Julia Jackson (who later, as Julia Stephens, became the mother of Virginia Woolf), celebrating the classical features for which her niece was famed. Moreover, Cameron very often, although not always, posed the women she photographed as types – mythical or cultural figures such as the goddess Pomona, Shakespeare's Ophelia, the great lyric poet Sappho, the androgynous angel at Christ's tomb, and the Madonna – eliding the name and personal history of the models.

In that her oeuvre appears to support the idea that women are interchangeable and valuable for their youth and beauty, while men are unique and valuable for their accomplishments and wisdom, in what ways are Cameron's photographs feminist? Moreover, given Cameron's frequent use of her maids – that is, of women who depended on her for their economic welfare – as models, how can we see Cameron's photographic practice as supporting women's empowerment? Indeed, it seems clear that the empowerment Cameron's photographic practice supported was mainly her own. She voiced herself as an artist while her female models remain silenced, and she was an exacting photographer for whom to pose.

And yet, asking whether the images advocate feminism is not the same as asking whether Cameron herself, in her life and artistic practice, lived by feminist ideals of equality and empowerment for all women. To answer the first question, one must consider the images in contrast to and in relation to contemporary representations of women, for instance, paintings by the nearly contemporaneous Pre-Raphaelites. The mid-nineteenth-century Pre-Raphaelite Brotherhood, a group that included the painters John Everett Millais and Dante Gabriel Rossetti, emphasized an almost hyperreal clarity of representation, with lushly detailed brushstrokes and heavy color saturation combined with ornate symbols. The group produced several paintings of women that we can interpret through the lens of feminist theory.[34] Millais and Rossetti depict women by emphasizing their female beauty, delicately eroticizing their subjects while not showing them to be engaging in thought, their eyes half closed or blankly staring. By contrast, one is struck by how dignified Cameron's women look, whether Julia Jackson as herself or Mary Hillier as Sappho.[35] Their eyes are turned away from the viewer as if they did not need or seek the viewer's approval. By putting them in profile, Cameron sets the women as if stamped on coins, absolutely unconcerned with seeking the favor of the viewer. She establishes in many of her photographs of women the strong sense that her subjects have an internal, psychic life of memory, thought, and feeling – a life that is powerful and even sacred and to which the viewer consequently is not given full access. In this way, her photographs of women, even as they cohere to societal norms for her time (and, sadly, for ours) by presenting women as valuable for their youth and beauty, also display the idea that women have intelligent, complex inner lives and are not focused always on the erotic. The inner lives that Cameron reveals photographically create a gravity and power that subtly overturn the discourse of eroticized female vulnerability dominant in the nineteenth-century West.

Ophelia and *Alice in Wonderland*

Cameron's photographs titled *Ophelia* and *Pomona* (Figures 1.5 and 1.6) also subvert the paradigms of sexist oppression of their historical era. Her representations of the terrain of the ruined girl, Ophelia, and of the goddess of fertility and the harvest, Pomona, deconstruct and argue against more well-known male representations of the same figures. To begin, Ophelia was a trope of fascination for Victorian England, a figure representing the idea that women were inherently mentally fragile, vulnerable to madness and to hysteria.[36] Pre-Raphaelite painter John Everett Millais's *Ophelia* (1851–1852) depicts Elizabeth Siddal, Dante Gabriel Rossetti's mistress and muse, floating in a stream at the brink of death, about to be submerged in the water that will drown her. The girl's open hands, open mouth, and half-closed vacant eyes suggest a fusion of the erotic with the deathly that was the coin of the realm for feminine beauty in that era.[37] Millais's *Ophelia* suggests no inner life in the dying girl, but instead it depicts a delicate-boned young woman who is opening herself in erotic abandon. The frothy waters, at one with her pale dress, consume her.

By contrast, Cameron's *Ophelia* (Study #2, 1867) shows a young woman who sits dry and upright. Although Cameron's photographic technique somewhat blurs her eyes, they are open and alert. Her face looks pained and also thoughtful. She is not erotically posed, and she is looking somewhat away from the viewer, as if looking into herself or her own suffering. Cameron's *Ophelia* is thoughtful and suffering mental anguish, whereas the mind of Millais's *Ophelia* is vacant. Cameron's seems to be positioned in time before the young woman's suicide; Millais pictures the suicide. Cameron's photograph, then, implies the possibility that Ophelia might somehow survive; she has not yet moved to cause her own death but instead meditates on her distress. Millais's image disallows the possibility of Ophelia's survival. Cameron works in the paradigm of her day, thereby choosing the image of Ophelia for the way that it connects with Victorian suppositions regarding the beauty and romance of a young woman's erotic madness. But the photographer then subverts that paradigm by showing the young woman as a contemplative, if pained, subject. In this way, Cameron's *Ophelia* advocates feminism by showing that a young woman whose very name represents madness and lack of reason actually has the capacity to think and reason and to contemplate her distress. Cameron's *Ophelia* (Figure 1.5) refuses the eroticized trope of female madness.

Cameron's *Pomona* (Figure 1.6), modeled by Alice Liddell, performs an intertextual work of another kind, one that is equally subversive in its way. As a child, Alice Liddell modeled for Lewis Carroll (Charles Dodgson), whose images of her some have interpreted as erotic. She apparently inspired the writing of *Alice in Wonderland*, a book that itself has been read as coded erotica.[38] The question of whether Carroll was a pedophile who took erotic pleasure in touching, kissing, and photographing very young girls is debatable; he is certainly known to have kissed and photographed very young girls, but we don't know if he felt erotic pleasure in so doing.[39] Without question, a grown man with high social standing has more power than prepubescent girls left in his care, and in the photographs that Carroll produced of

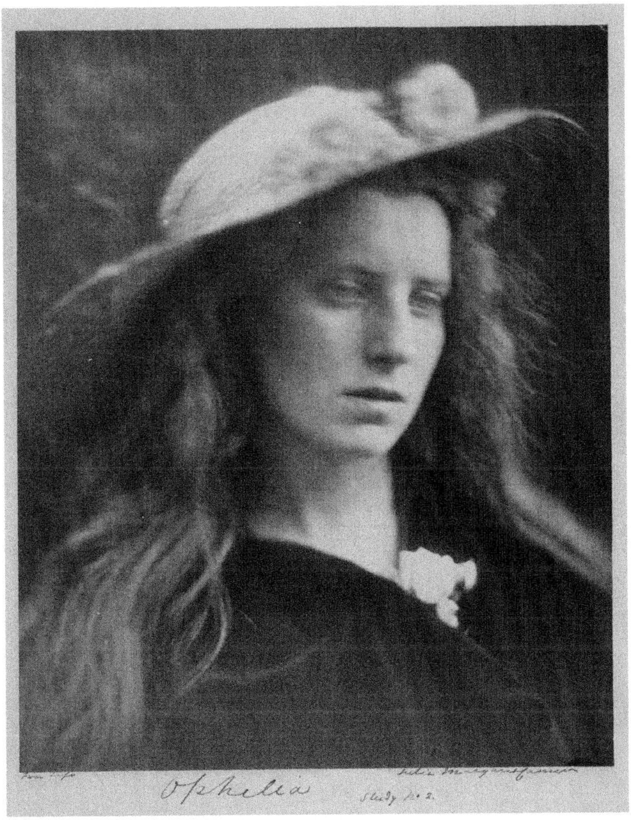

FIGURE 1.5 Julia Margaret Cameron, *Ophelia, Study No. 2*, 1867, albumen print, 33.0 × 27.1 cm. George Eastman Museum, Rochester, NY.

the little girls, this power imbalance seems eroticized. Eroticized power imbalance is not quite the same as actual molestation, but it moves in that direction. My point is that whether or not Carroll molested Liddell, he certainly posed her in photographs that emphasize a power difference between herself and the photographer. In 1858, as a prepubescent child, Liddell posed as a little beggar maid for Carroll, and Julia Margaret Cameron seems to visually quote Carroll's image in her 1872 *Pomona*; in both photographs, Liddell has a hand on her hip and gazes directly at the camera.[40]

And yet, Cameron's image is strikingly different from Carroll's. In *Pomona*, Liddell squares her hips and shoulders and stares face on at the viewer. I read the look of stoicism, anger, and strength in her face and the suggestion of muscularity in her neck and shoulders as Alice Liddell's (and Julia Margaret Cameron's) photographic reply to Lewis Carroll. For whereas in Carroll's photographs of her Liddell is tiny, winsome, and eroticized, in *Pomona* she looks fierce, self-possessed, tall, and strong, partly because Cameron photographs her at a very slight upward tilt. Although Carroll may have lost interest in Liddell once she became a woman (as would be the case were he a pedophile), Cameron celebrates her in a stance of powerful

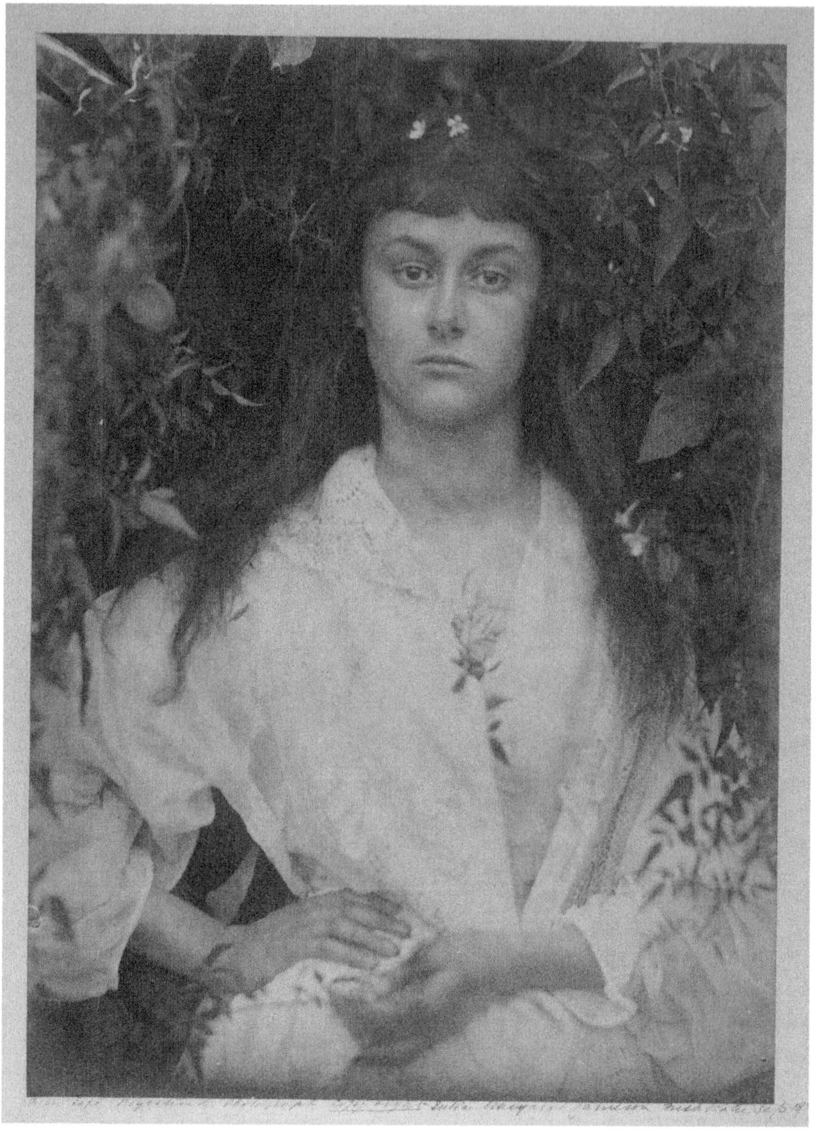

FIGURE 1.6 Julia Margaret Cameron, *Pomona*, 1872, albumen silver print from glass negative, 36.4 × 26.3 cm. Metropolitan Museum of Art (David Hunter McAlpin Fund, 1963), New York.

womanliness and has her personify a Roman goddess, a trope of female power and fertility. Intertextually, Cameron takes the eroticized little girl subject of Carroll's fascination and remakes her as a powerful woman. The photograph of Liddell as Pomona performs a subversion of the terms of femininity – docility, childishness, girlishness, and erotic availability – that formed some aspects of sexist oppression in nineteenth-century Britain. Cameron shows us Alice Liddell surpassing the male gaze, fiercely staring it down, not docile, childish, or erotic.

Feminist looks

Cameron and Hawarden, Victorian matrons who did not count themselves as supporters of the nascent nineteenth-century feminist movement, created photographs that subtly and powerfully suggest new ways to see women, hence, new ways to conceptualize being female. Born in a country and in an era when women could not independently own property and could not vote and when women were considered biologically incapable of serious intellectual accomplishment, Cameron and Hawarden created photographs that insist on a rich, complicated, and self-possessed inner cognitive life for the women who appear in them. This rearranging of the sensible shows women not as men's erotic possessions or fatally fragile responsibilities but as independent from men and carrying forward personal narratives of intellectual and emotional force, as deeply compelling in these photographic representations.

Notes

1 Carol Mavor, *Becoming* (Durham, NC: Duke University Press, 1999), xvi. Hawarden's work was recognized as the product of a gifted amateur during her lifetime, and the Royal Photographic Society awarded it a medal. But her photography has a clearly different stature vis-à-vis the art world now than it did during her lifetime.
2 Mark Haworth-Booth, "What the Lady Saw," *Bonhams Magazine* 34 (2013): 52.
3 See Linda Nochlin's classic essay on the concept of genius, "Why Have There Been No Great Women Artists?" in her *Women, Art, and Power* (New York: Harper and Row, 1989): 146–157. See also Liz Heron and Val Williams, *Illuminations: Women Writing on Photography from 1850 to the Present* (Durham, NC: Duke University Press, 1996), 8–13.
4 Victoria Olsen, *From Life: Julia Margaret Cameron and Victorian Photography* (London: Palgrave, 2003), 63.
5 Griselda Pollock and Rozsika Parker, *Old Mistresses: Women, Art, and Ideology* (London: I.B.Tauris, 2013).
6 See Roland Barthes, *Mythologies* (New York: Farrar, Straus and Giroux, 1972).
7 Carol Mavor, *Becoming: The Photographs of Clementina, Viscountess Hawarden* (Durham, NC: Duke University Press, 1999).
8 Geoffrey Batchen, *Burning with Desire: The Conception of Photography* (Cambridge, MA: MIT Press, 1999), 5.
9 Beaumont Newhall, *The History of Photography* (New York: Museum of Modern Art, 1983); Batchen, *Burning with Desire*, 22–50.
10 Olsen, *From Life*, 3.
11 On wet plate collodion photography, see Richard Benson, *The Printed Picture* (New York: Museum of Modern Art, 2008).
12 Mavor, *Becoming*, 44–71.
13 I use the term "relative lack" very precisely here, comparing Hawarden and Cameron's social positions as practitioners of art with the positions of dominant male artists of the era. I do not mean that Hawarden and Cameron received no recognition. Rather, they received less support and recognition than male artists of their time.
14 See Virginia Dodier, *Studies from Life* (New York: Aperture, 1999).
15 Repeated pregnancies and childbirth would have been exhausting, even with household help. Having gone through only two pregnancies, one of which led to a home birth, I am

exhausted just to imagine that multiplied by five. One must also factor in the excessively high rates of maternal (not to mention infant) mortality in nineteenth-century Britain; despite her wealth, Hawarden was not immune to these risks and lost two children in earliest infancy. See Geoffrey Chamberlain, "British Maternal Mortality in the 19th and Early 20th Century," *Journal of the Royal Society of Medicine* 99, no. 11 (2006): 559–63.

16 Dodier, *Studies from Life*.

17 Ibid.

18 Ibid.

19 Eve Kosofsky Sedgwick, *Novel Gazing: Queer Readings in Fiction* (Durham, NC: Duke University Press, 1997).

20 Alison Chapman, "Mary Elizabeth Coleridge, Literary Influence, and Technologies of the Uncanny," in *Victorian Gothic: Literary and Cultural Manifestations in the Nineteenth Century*, ed. Ruth Robbins and Julian Wolfreys (London: Palgrave, 2000): 109–128.

21 Strikingly, Oscar Rejlander, Hawarden's near contemporary and an eminent photographer, described Hawarden as being like a "clasp," suggesting something about the visual rhythm of enclosures that echoes through her photographic works. See also Haworth-Booth, "What the Lady Saw."

22 Mavor, *Becoming*.

23 Christian Metz, *Film Language: A Semiotics of Cinema*, trans. Michael Taylor (Chicago: Chicago University Press, 1974).

24 Ibid.

25 Carol Mavor's interpretation in *Becoming* of Hawarden's work is strongly focused on what Mavor sees as the lesbian erotic underpinnings of Hawarden's gaze onto her daughters, reflected principally in the ways that she poses the girls.

26 Roland Barthes, *Camera Lucida: Reflections on Photography* (New York: Macmillan, 1981), 64.

27 Lydia Murdoch, *Daily Life of Victorian Women* (London: Greenwood, 2013).

28 For example, if one compares Hawarden's handling of the female form and face with that of Oscar Rejlander, the difference is stark. Hawarden's daughters brim with freshness and privacy that surely stems from their comfort and trust in posing for their mother's camera.

29 Lindsay Smith, *The Politics of Focus* (Manchester, UK: Manchester University Press, 1998).

30 Beaumont Newhall, *Photography, Essays, and Images* (New York: Museum of Modern Art, 1980), 135–9.

31 Ibid.

32 Barthes, *Camera Lucida*, 9.

33 See Sylvia Wolf, *Julia Margaret Cameron's Women* (New Haven, CT: Yale University Press, 1998).

34 Elizabeth Prettejohn, *The Art of the Pre-Raphaelites* (Princeton, NJ: Princeton University Press, 2000).

35 See the following paintings of Dante Gabriel Rossetti: *Beata Beatrix*, *Lips That Have Been Kissed*, and *The Lady Lilith*.

36 Lisa Appignanesi, *Mad, Bad, and Sad: A History of Women and the Mind Doctors from 1800 to the Present* (London: Virago Press, 2008).

37 Elisabeth Bronfen, *Over Her Dead Body* (Manchester, UK: Manchester University Press, 1994).

38 Lewis Carroll's photograph *The Beggar Maid* and Cameron's *Pomona* are housed in the collection of the Metropolitan Museum of Art in New York City.

39 See Lorena Munoz Alonso, "Was Lewis Carroll a Pedophile? His Photographs Suggest So," *Art Net News*, January 30, 2015, https://news.artnet.com/art-world/was-lewis-carroll-a-pedophile-his-photographs-suggest-so-237222.

40 It is possible that Cameron did not know this particular image, but it seems likely that she did. Lewis Carroll was critical of Cameron's soft focus (that is, her use of a lens flaw to create this effect), and she was keenly aware of her detractors as well as supporters;

moreover, Carroll and Cameron ran in the same social circle. Using a model who once modeled for Carroll, Cameron is likely to have had in her mind's eye his earlier work with the same girl. See Ksenya A. Gurshtein, "The Mountain and the Mole-Hill: Julia Margaret Cameron's Allegories," *University of Michigan Museums of Art and Archeology Bulletin* 17 (2007): 5–25; see also Dave Oliphant, ed., *Gendered Territory: Photographs of Women by Julia Margaret Cameron* (Austin, TX: Harry Ransom Humanities Research, 1996).

2

AFTER AND IN THE FRACTURE

Claude Cahun, Lee Miller, and surrealism

The fracture between the nineteenth and twentieth centuries, a break opened wider by World War I, brought profound changes in European culture and in the aesthetics of its photography and fine art. Such changes were radical shifts in the idea not only of what an image should look like but also what an image should *do*. In the West, the interwar phenomenon of surrealism captured and also created this shift; its idea of convulsive beauty was a rejection of earlier notions of grace and containment in aesthetics. Claude Cahun (1894–1954) and Lee Miller (1907–1977) are associated with surrealism, although during their lifetimes both photographers were pushed into fairly peripheral roles in the movement. Twenty-first-century retrospective interpretations of surrealism increasingly give Cahun and Miller a central role, but I emphasize two points. Their accomplishments earn them this newly found centrality. And, while Cahun and Miller were alive, the male surrealists, including André Breton who dominated the movement, did not consider them essential artists.[1] The terms of their insider-outsider status differ sharply. Miller was photographer Man Ray's student as well as his mistress and muse. Cahun, a lesbian who frequently dressed as a man and considered herself to occupy a third sex, played the role of peripheral figure and literate commentator on the movement.[2] Notably, the photographs for which Cahun is now best known, her autoportraits (self-portraits of a kind), were not shown in public during her lifetime but became known decades after her death. Miller's photography – although successful as commercial photography that male surrealists saw and that *Vogue* magazine circulated during her lifetime – was not accorded critical acclaim until late in the twentieth century when her son began circulating it years after her death.[3] Indeed, Miller has become increasingly popular, and twenty-first-century feminist critics focus on her much as late-twentieth-century feminist critics "discovered" Cahun.[4] Taken together, Cahun and Miller reshape and redefine the boundaries of what constitutes surrealism.

Even so, recognizing the peripheral status that Cahun and Miller inhabited while they were producing their work helps us understand what it meant for them to create their oeuvres from a professional identity of near invisibility. Both thematize gendered trauma in their visual work, thus echoing and altering surrealism's interaction with the traumatic aftermath of World War I, and both experienced the trauma of not gaining substantial recognition for their work while they were alive. What is the cost to a woman or, in Cahun's case, a member of neither and both genders, whose artistic production remains largely invisible to the powerful (and almost entirely male) artists of her milieu and her era?[5] I argue that even as critics often interpret Miller through the lens of her early childhood trauma and read Cahun's work for its gender nonconformity, the trauma of invisibility and the social space inside that would draw together these photographers' very different oeuvres. For photographers as gifted as Miller and Cahun, this trauma may have been a force comparable to and connected with that of being pressured to occupy the position of the traditional feminine. It may have been a force even comparable to surviving sexual objectification. Surrealism as a movement inspired their art, but during their lives it did relatively little to succor and nurture Miller and Cahun themselves.

Convulsive beauty, personal trauma

The largely European surrealist movement of the early twenty-first century rejects eighteenth- and nineteenth-century Western ideals of beauty. Instead, it seeks a convulsive beauty and the aesthetics of *l'informe* – that is, the unformed, the grotesque, the emergent, and often the violently emergent. It tears apart inherited, Romantic notions of the continuity of self, nature, the meaning of perception, and the experience of looking.[6] The surrealist movement responds to World War I by creating the art of fracture; the surrealists draw on the dreamscape to dislocate the day-to-day world, reflecting the historical reality that the war had torn apart Europe's day-to-day world.[7] For the surrealists, the dreamworld or the psyche fed convulsive beauty and the aesthetic of *l'informe*.[8]

To access this dream space, the surrealists developed a practice of automatic writing, a technique by which the writer-artist reaches his or her subconscious thoughts by writing down unexpurgated all thoughts and images that come to mind, using words as shovels by which to delve into the interior psyche. Cahun's practice of autoportrait – a skillfully parodic, intensely searching, decades-long series of self-portraits – clearly resonates with this idea of automatic writing. However, her images also problematize and trouble suppositions about the relationship between surface and depth in identity. In Cahun's autoportraits, she is questioning the idea of the subconscious, in very formal and conceptual terms questioning how the camera structures and alters the gaze, in particular the gaze of the self onto the self. She queries the relationship between the gaze and the subconscious, ultimately using photographs as masks that disavow the reality of any substratum that could be said to sustain a stable self. The very play of the subterranean and surface meanings of identity as elusive to and also revealed by the camera keeps Cahun's autoportraits tense, questioning, and singular.[9] Whereas critics have compared her to Cindy Sherman, only Sherman's earliest work in the *Film Stills* warrants this comparison.[10] For what makes Cahun's autoportraits so searing is the very sense of immediacy, a wild and automatic authentication not of self but of the desire to see the fragments that make up the mask of self. Sherman's later works, by contrast, are predictably staged and without surprise, returning to the cliché of a very unary legibility. But Cahun's work remains true to the raw aesthetics of surrealism in its constant urging toward revelation; the fabricated masks of her autoportraits mask the unknown parts of the self even while revealing fragments of identity as if by echo.

Man Ray, arguably the best-known surrealist photographer, was inspired by the work of Eugene Atget, a Parisian photographer who did not see himself as belonging to any artistic movement and who created many of his images to sell to painters to aid their work.[11] His images of Paris shops in particular influenced the surrealist aesthetic of the random and painful shock of meaning's loss in a capitalist, war-scarred culture. Atget photographed shop mannequins, a trope that Man Ray disturbingly applied in his photography of Lee Miller, turning her classical beauty into atomized mannequin views. As Man Ray's student and lover, Miller might also have been his true protégé had their relationship not soured in ways that seem to have prevented him from supporting her efforts to become a fully developed artist. When she appeared as a young woman at Man Ray's café table asking him to teach her photography, her beauty may have been her leverage with him (since Man Ray was not at that time a teacher). But her gift for the medium was readily apparent, and she did learn photography during their relationship. Indeed, as his darkroom assistant, Miller arguably should be credited with creating the technique of solarization that critics strongly associate with Man Ray's oeuvre.[12] Claude Cahun, as I will explain, was not willing to make herself an acolyte of any kind to the male surrealists.

The third sex: Claude Cahun's autoportraits

Claude Cahun (born Lucy Schwob in 1894) lived and worked in Paris and the island of Jersey. During her life, she was known mostly as a writer, publishing her masterwork, *Aveux non Avenus*, in 1930.[13] Assuming the gender-neutral name Claude Cahun while still in her twenties, she lived openly as a lesbian with Marcel Moore (née Suzanne Malherbe), her lifelong partner. Cahun's interactions with the surrealists were primarily social, but she was part of the avant-garde Parisian milieu. Her publications, particularly *Aveux non Avenus*, emphasize a reenvisioning of the idea of the self. The posthumous, late-twentieth-century popularity of her autoportraits – images that question and break down gender binaries – coincides with Judith Butler's attention to these themes in *Gender Trouble*.[14] But the more interesting and compelling aspect of Cahun's work is not merely her refusal to remain in one gendered role but indeed her refusal to remain in one holistic, stable self. Her consummate exploration of this instability using the heuristic of her camera resulted in a body of work that is formally and conceptually extraordinary.

Cahun's autoportraits not only explore the photographer as a man and as a woman but also relentlessly suggest that the idea of the self – regardless and apart from gender – is a fabrication. Her photographs put forward the idea that the photographic self-portrait is a kind of mask that paradoxically reveals ways that the self is always a version of a mask.

The photographic self-portrait is one of the earliest uses of the camera. Robert Cornelius, an American, and Hippolyte Bayard, who was French, both created photographic self-portraits in the first years after Louis Daguerre announced his invention. (Bayard uses his own direct positive method of photography to portray himself as a man drowned by Daguerre's preemptive invention, but Cornelius photographs himself using daguerreotype.)[15]

The camera's gaze turned on the self is different from the painterly self-portrait. With the camera, the gaze is not introspective but retrospective, the photograph always looking back in time from the moment the image is shot. A photographic self-portrait definitively marks a body in time. For Cahun's autoportrait project, each instance of the self marked in time is discrete and noncontiguous. In her autoportraits, Cahun repeatedly creates a set of masks or costumes that are not so much expressions of self-identity as rather steely inoculations against the trope of self that anchors a Western conceit, namely the "right" to dominate the other. As the Western empire – the aggressions of Great Britain, France, and Spain in colonizing India, North Africa, and South America – began to collapse during World War I, surrealism reconceives the self as amorphous, fleeting, masked, insubstantial. Arguably, Cahun's autoportrait work brings forward this surrealist shift in the notion of self more searchingly than the work of any male surrealist photographer. Despite and possibly because of their sharpness of vision, Cahun's photographs were not publicly circulated until the late 1980s, decades after she made the images and decades after her death.

In *Que me veux-tu*, Cahun combines two negatives to create the image of Cahun questioning Cahun. One shot shows her face tilted with her gaze angled but engaged; the other shot shows her in profile with her gaze largely obscured by the angle of the shot. It is as if the full-face image of Cahun is questioning the profile image of Cahun, and the profile image, with eyes heavily outlined in kohl and lips deeply lipsticked, says to her interlocutor, "What do you want of me?" At the same time, the audience is also invoked, for here Cahun, with her head shaven, presents a somewhat androgynous figure. The frontal shot reveals that she is apparently female, with a delicate chin, a slender neck that lacks a visible Adam's apple, and large eyes that look vulnerable and almost beseeching. The profile image, by contrast, conceals gender: even though here Cahun is wearing makeup, kohl on her eyes, and lipstick on her lips, she is angled so as to obscure the neck and chest areas that in similar photographs suggest décolletage. *Que me veux-tu*, then, poses Cahun as a differently androgynous figure facing and turning from herself. The image asks the audience why we might need Cahun to choose a gender and stay in its prescribed boundaries. More globally, it asks the audience what do we want of the sitter, why do we want to look at her, and to what gendered and cultural constraints do we expect her to conform?

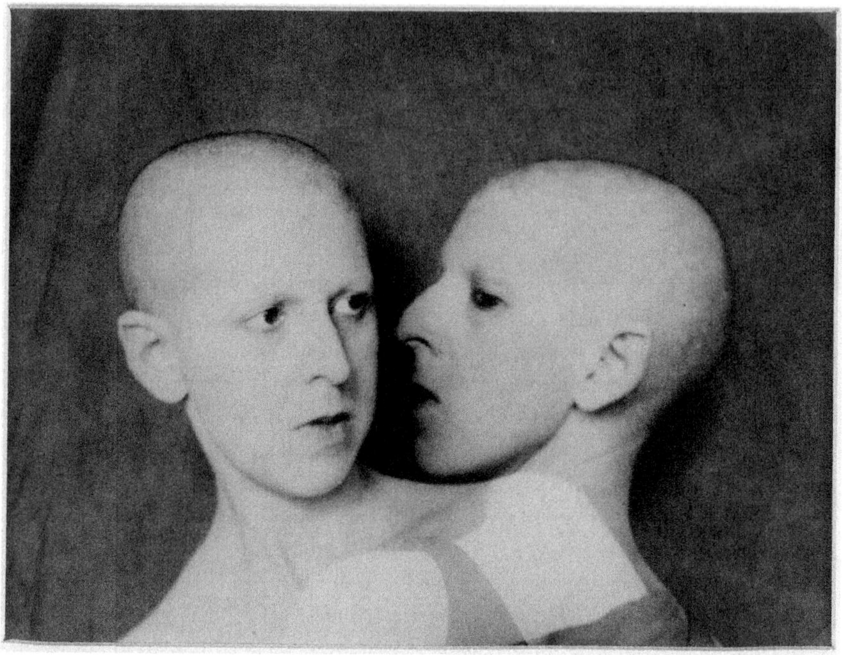

FIGURE 2.1 Claude Cahun, *Que me veux-tu?*, 1928, gelatin silver print, 18 × 23 cm. Musée d'Art Moderne, Paris. Photo credit: Eric Emo/Parisienne de Photographie. © Claude Cahun.

Beyond skewing gender expectations, *Que me veux-tu* raises poignant and painful questions about the self as a fragile, vulnerable, embodied entity. Not only does Cahun's shaven head evoke fragility, but the material history of Cahun's work also bespeaks Cahun's vulnerable social situation. Cahun created her autoportraits with a standard amateur camera and had the images printed at her local apothecary.[16] The images often remained in their drugstore envelopes, and when they made their way to the Jersey Heritage Museum following Moore's suicide in 1972, their nonarchival and physically fragile status could hardly have been more pronounced. In this sense, Cahun's photographs materially express the fragility of self, which, along with the mutability of self, is a major theme of her work. She took her images cheaply without expert equipment, and – not in their formal contours but in the actual quality of the prints – they echo the amateur. Then she left the photographs not with collectors but in a house that Moore, who later committed suicide, inherited after Cahun's death in 1954. The trauma of nonrecognition, then, plays through not only the thematics of her work but also the materiality of her images, including Cahun's photographs' vulnerability as material objects left in a less-than-secure situation.

Cahun's autoportraits draw from the surrealist exploration of the psyche by an oblique angle, the camera in her work standing in as interlocutor. Brilliantly, her autoportraits do not so much limn the internal psyche as the field of social powers that create the mask called the psyche. Her fidelity to the concept of the mask – not as that which covers the true self but as that which produces what we believe is the self – holds throughout her decades-long series of autoportraits. The mask is the external system of meaning that Cahun tracks in all its elusions and feints and in its ultimate unreality and reality.

The autoportrait showing Cahun dressed as a doll and splayed on the shelf of an enormous wardrobe exemplifies her photographic explorations of herself as a chameleon, a wearer of masks. As frequently as Cahun dressed as a man and photographed herself as such, she also donned feminine costume and played out various feminine roles before the camera. In other words, her abiding interest is not in "being" either male or female but in showing how illusory these turns of subjectivity are and also, importantly, how impactful gendered masks are in creating the apparent substance of self. Cahun dressed as a doll plays through not only her biological sex and petite size but also her role as the daughter of a wealthy family, upon whose wealth she drew for material sustenance for most of her adult life. However fiercely independent Cahun's art and practice of self are – and this ferocity is without question – her economic mode of life was that of an unmarried daughter of a wealthy family. In the self-portrait as a doll, Cahun displays the economic conditions in which she lives, the daughter on the paternal shelf. Earlier, she photographed herself as in the mode of a young rabbinical student, looking entirely boyish, serious, and austere. In this image, Cahun represents herself inhabiting a role that in life, in France in the 1920s, she could not really live: she could be part of the lesbian demi-monde of her era, but she could not be a rabbinical student. The poignancy of her self-portraits as masks, then, inheres not only in their invocation of the insight that the self is a mask but also in their revelation of the way that such masks are not all chosen. They fasten on the skin of the self, as it were, in profound, material, and often damaging ways.

Rosalind Krauss has written persuasively about the role of Jewish identity in Cahun's oeuvre and life.[17] She argues that for Lucy Schwob to choose the Jewish surname Cahun (which means temple priest) is to step away from her very secularized, assimilated, and wealthy family to reclaim an unmistakably Jewish identity. Krauss also argues – rightly – that given the political climate in Europe leading up to World War II, it was more provocative and risky for Cahun to choose a name that clearly identified her as Jewish than to take a gender-neutral first name, Claude.[18] Cahun's brave activism against the invading Germans ultimately led the Nazis to imprison her at the end of World War II.[19] Gen Doy argues that Cahun's photographs are a "sensual politics," thereby interpreting the autoportraits and Cahun's literary works published during her lifetime as political acts of resistance. Such resistance was not merely to performative gender conformity. It was also resistance to the patriarchal structures that uphold social structures of oppression, and resistance to the kind of patriarchy that expressed itself as fascism in Germany during the Third Reich.

Cahun's images also resist their own invisibility. Despite not gaining – or, apparently, very clamorously seeking – recognition from dominant male surrealists, Cahun continued to create autoportraits from the 1920s through the 1940s.[20] Each photograph implies a performative resistance to the erasure of Cahun's vision. Her dedication to the work of taking the image of herself refuses the rather silenced place of the muse-model-lover that male surrealists seem to have envisioned as the main role for women.[21] Instead, she becomes muse and model to herself while working in conjunction with her female lover. Marcel Moore's role in the creation of the autoportraits is absolutely central. Cahun created the shots and posed in them, but Moore snapped the shutter and, together with Cahun, created the conversation that the photographs evince and that surely went on beyond the photographs. In this sense, whereas Cahun is the artist, and we see her vision in the autoportraits, Moore is a collaborator of great importance without whom the images could not have been made.

By playing her own model and her own muse, Cahun created a body of work that refuses traditional gender delineation, but this refusal to inhabit a stable identity should not be confused with a decision to become male. Some of her most beautiful images are erotic and display the feminine figure as such – for the lover's gaze, for Moore's gaze. In one such image, Cahun masks herself, blinding herself, while posing naked for the camera Moore wields. Only by folding her legs inward does Cahun avert this sensual photograph from becoming a spread eagle. The vulnerability of the image, the blindness, and the almost pornographic self-revelation swirl, like the swirls of the image's quilt, stretches to the very boundaries of the notion of a contained, "I"-identified self. Here, the body of the self is presented for the beloved other. Throughout her body of work, Cahun refuses the constrictive claims of the fixed and stable self, thus (a) poignantly marking a self that passes through time and vanishes and (b) showing the terms of this mortal transfiguration repeatedly as she shows the mask of self in radically differential and fractured terms.

Cahun's work both proves and complicates the provocative case Peggy Phelan has made that invisibility is powerful for women artists.[22] In *Unmarked*, Phelan argues that visibility can be dangerous for women, that indeed for a woman to be seen is often to be consumed and conscripted by the male gaze, something Cahun refused. She was able to make this refusal partly because she was financially independent (although, as noted, dependent on her family money) but, more important, because she was artistically independent. Cahun created autoportraits that pushed the boundaries of surrealist aesthetics, and she did so by not attempting – in any way – to please the eyes of Breton and Man Ray. The result of this refusal was indeed a kind of invisibility, in that her greatest photographic works, her autoportraits, remained unknown during her lifetime.

By remaining in the unmarked zone of private artistic creation, Cahun remained in control of the subject matter and creation of her artistic oeuvre. (In this she was uncannily similar to Clementina Hawarden, with whom she would seem to have little else in common.) And yet she also risked its erasure. It is something of a matter of chance that after Moore's suicide Cahun's photographs found their way to the Jersey Heritage Trust. And it was another matter of chance that cultural and art critics discovered them there and began to write about them. The risk of invisibility is not merely that one's artistic creations might not be seen but, also that the photographer will during her lifetime lack the cultural power and status of an established and well-regarded artist. Whereas Claude Cahun's autoportraits are miraculous in their piercing and at times painful elocution of the absent core and constructed nature of the self, the materiality of her work tells the story another way. The social conditions of her work were far from empowered, even as her conceptual and formal brilliance ultimately carried that work to the wide viewership and critical appreciation that they now claim.

Lee Miller's wars

The ascendant critical reputation of Lee Miller is encapsulated in an early twenty-first-century article about her that claims for her work a distinctly gendered "female sublime."[23] Both the concept of the sublime and feminist reinterpretation of the sublime have long histories. Immanuel Kant (1724–1804) and Edmund Burke (1729–1797) placed the sublime in the intellectual foreground with their respective works, *The Critique of Judgment* (1790) and *A Philosophical Enquiry into the Origin of Our Ideas of the Beautiful and the Sublime* (1757). Feminist theorist Julia Kristeva critiques the gendering of the sublime in *Powers of Horror* (1984), with Barbara Claire Freeman carrying forward this critique in *The Feminine Sublime* (1997). My book, *Francesca Woodman and the Kantian Sublime* (2010), draws from this feminist tradition. Outside of feminist interpretations, theories of the sublime have numerous permutations, including Jean-Francois Lyotard's important *Lessons on the Analytic of the Sublime* (1994), and I simply sketch a framework here for this concept.[24]

Burke's and Kant's formulations differ substantially. For Burke, the sublime has to do with the emotion of fear, and an image is sublime if it invokes terror but does not directly threaten harm to the viewer.[25] (By image, I mean simply a scene that is seen, not necessarily a painted image; there were no photographs when Burke and Kant wrote.) Burke's sublime carries more than a whiff of sadism: in his view, to see someone else suffer grave bodily risk or even harm could be a sublime experience provided one were assuredly protected from also suffering this harm. Hence, watching a tidal wave wash away a shore village, if one were safely protected in a castle above, could be a sublime vision in Burke's terms. As Debra Walker King points out, racism and the practice of kidnapping and enslaving Africans, which was prevalent when Burke wrote *A Philosophical Enquiry*, shape and inform his version of the sublime. Burke's version includes a racialized view, both violent and horrific, with social parameters that today are very offensive.[26] By contrast, Immanuel Kant's theory of the sublime does not directly invoke themes of bodily harm and physical horror. Instead, he argues that the sublime is an event that occurs when sensuous information in an image calls the viewer's faculty of reason and rational thinking to respond. That is, the sublime occurs when, in a sensed, visual event, the eyes alone cannot take in the import of the image and so the faculty of reason moves to comprehend it. This strain, a kind of merging of perception and intellect, causes pain in the viewer as it pushes the faculty of reason to its limit, and the sublime emerges from this intense pain.[27]

For Kant, the sublime is definitively an occurrence in the mind of the viewer, and there is no such thing as a scene sublime in itself. Instead, specific aesthetic properties cause the sublime, properties that cannot formally be determined in advance but that are known by their effect in the viewer's mind.[28] Kristeva and Freeman critique Burke by arguing that he presents the female body as a source of sublime terror and fear. They say that in Kant's *Critique*, the notion of the sublime depends on an implicit construction of the female as grotesque.[29] By contrast, I argue that the Kantian sublime contains, in its essence, an explosive and chaotic force that dismantles gender rather than reinforces its constraints. In this sense, Kant's work is useful for feminist artists, such as Francesca Woodman, whose photographic work often dwells on the edge of pain and sublimity.[30] Miller's work confronts violence explicitly and so connects to aspects of Burke's sublime. But Miller's work also importantly structures the gaze so as to push the viewer toward an encounter with the limits of her faculty of reason. It pushes her to the place where the sensual faculty of sight calls on the rational faculty to comprehend the image. In this act of intense interpretation, the sublime event occurs in the mind of the viewer.

I have titled this section Lee Miller's Wars because I focus on Miller's extraordinary photographs taken in the immediate aftermath of World War II, when she worked as a photographer for *Vogue* magazine. The sublime, as applied to Miller's war photographs, allows us to access the images' fine balance between the horrific and the painfully beautiful. Although, to interpret these images, one must also consider her earlier work and in particular trace its connections with surrealist aesthetics.[31] When Miller asked Man Ray to become her photography instructor, she was already well known as a fashion model. The impetus to be something other than a beauty at whom others gazed may have arisen from the traumatic forms of gazing to which Miller had been subjected. Before becoming a fashion model, she had already experienced the dissociative relationship to one's image that models necessarily develop as their images circulate as signs of desire in appetitive capitalist exchange. When she was a child, her father regularly photographed her in the nude, continuing this disturbing practice well into Miller's adolescence.[32] She also survived rape as a prepubescent: a family friend sexually assaulted her, an experience from which she contracted venereal disease.[33] Her experience as an object of desire, a body sexually consumed by men much older and more powerful than she, runs as a damaging and traumatic thread from her childhood rape through her role as Man Ray's model and muse. But the knowledge of photography that Miller gained from Man Ray allowed her to structure modes of seeing rather than merely being seen. However, seeing and being seen are interconnected, and what makes Miller's work a kind of sublime – suffused with a sense of dissociation and fear – is that her images engage deeply with both the power of seeing and the relationship between the seer and the seen. In her work, that relationship is imbricated by force, danger, submission, and often transcendence.

Miller's beauty allowed her to connect with virtually any man she might wish to draw. That fact and her traumatic history of suffering childhood rape seem to have strongly affected her personal life for many years. She moved from man to man, and – until she photographed the aftermath of the war for *Vogue* – her photography emerged historically through the places she encountered as a man's mistress, model, or wife. Her early photograph *Exploding Hand* is a deft configuration of surrealist detail and reveals her immersion in the aesthetics of surrealism as Man Ray's student. Here, Miller captures a visual pun: the glass door has been subtly scratched by many hands turning the metal knob, and when Miller's camera captures the way light refracts, angled, off these scratches, the hand on the knob seems to be exploding into light. This image bears out the surrealist idea of convulsive beauty – the hand dissociated from the body and the sense of a slow explosion that takes place over time make the image not only clever but also poignant. The glass door's reflection of trees echoes Atget's skill in capturing the still and pensive details of the world reflected by glass, a *mise en abyme* of photography, wherein the glass acts as a camera and the image made by Miller's actual camera contains this camera. Her untitled photograph of rat tails (1930) similarly follows a surrealist trope of creating aesthetic order and beauty from substance that would have been considered improper in nineteenth- and turn-of-the-twentieth-century art photography. In this, Miller's image of rat tails presages her war photography, which mixes gruesome or unsettling physical fact with aesthetic crispness and precision.

Miller's photographs from Egypt, taken when she was married to Egyptian businessman Aziz Eloui Bey, carry forward surrealist interest in the odd juxtapositions of the everyday world and the uncanny in the physically real. They also open toward her own concerns with vista and with interrogating colonialism and imperialism. This interrogation of the colonial gaze connects strongly to a feminist point of view. Miller's photographs *Portrait of Space* and *From the Top of the Great Pyramid* subvert the Western imperialist gaze that had long been turned on Egypt and "the Orient" by contending with the Egyptian landscape from the point of view of the desert itself.[34] She creates images that are not of a person watching the desert or regarding the Great Pyramid of Giza but rather of the desert regarding itself and the Great Pyramid regarding all that lies beneath it. This reversal of the conventional tourist photograph point of view can be understood as Miller's feminist rebuttal to Western patriarchal claims of domination over the non-Western "Other."[35] But this reversal can also be understood as Miller's connection – empathic and implicit – with that which is objectified and made into an "Other." Her history, not only as a student who had sex with her teacher but also as a child who was raped, plays through her photography in Egypt.

In Egypt, her instinctive redrawing of the boundaries of watcher and watched creates photographs like *Portrait of Space* that derealize and make uncanny the space of the photographic. Not only do these images make us question what it means to have or to be subjected to the imperialist gaze as embodied by the tourist photograph, but they also make us aware of the uncanny properties of photographic space, of its possible revelations of the power structures inherent in gazing. *Portrait of Space* works through several self-conscious framing devices, the frame of the photographic image, the torn screen, the mirror, all leading the viewer into an uncanny encounter with space as vision and a loss of self as the watcher is immersed in the act of gazing. This sense of being lost and also of seeing differently permeates Miller's photographs taken in Egypt.

The photographs Miller took for *Vogue* magazine in the immediate aftermath of World War II are now her best-known work. These documentary images seem to depart from her earlier surrealist work, but they also deploy surrealist turns by shifting the vantage so that we are brought into the emotional experience of facing not only concentration camps just after liberation but also suicided Germans in *The Burgermeister's daughter (Regina Lisso), Town Hall, Leipzig, Germany 1945* and *Dead SS Guard floating in canal, Dachau, Germany 1945*.

Miller's work photographing these desolate scenes of war and its aftermath immersed her in a realm of trauma with which she was, in some ways, already familiar because she knew how violation felt. Drawing on the aesthetic of *l'informe*,

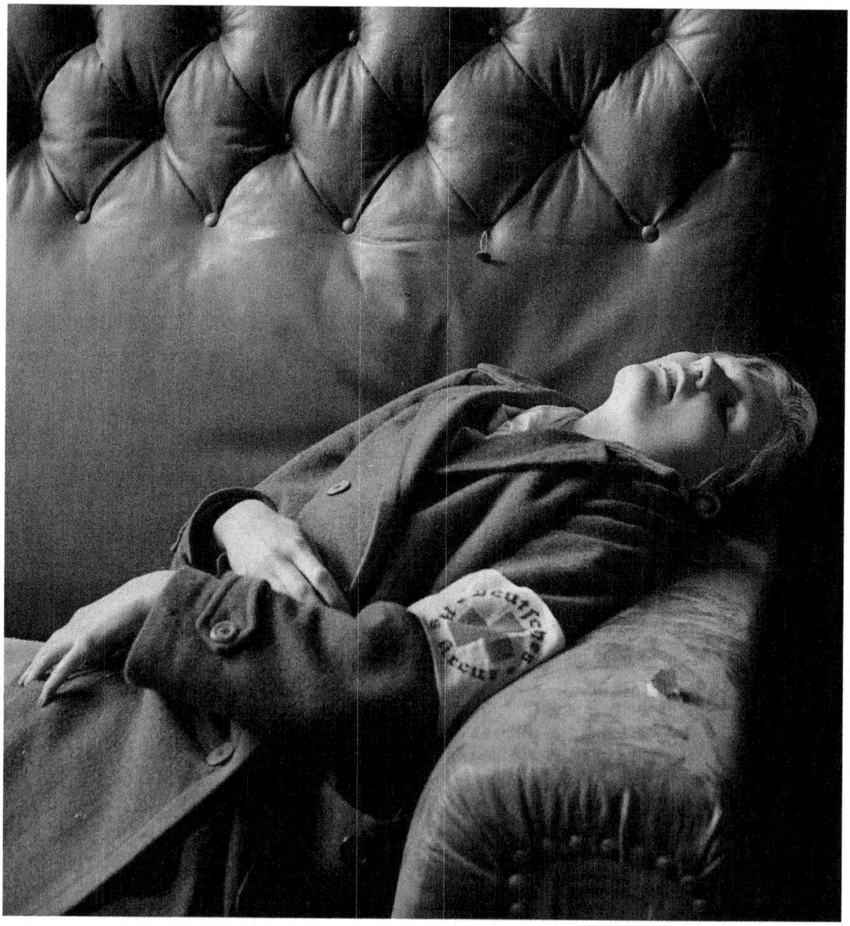

FIGURE 2.2 Lee Miller, *The Burgermeister's daughter (Regna Lisso), Town Hall, Leipzig, Germany 1945*. www.leemiller.co.uk.

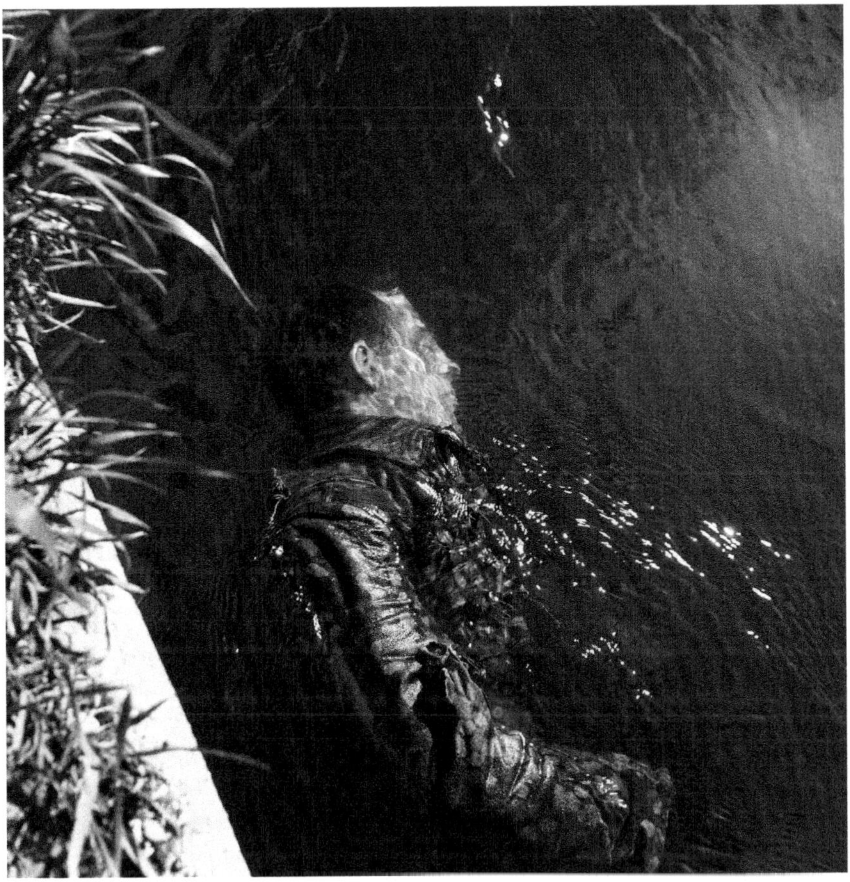

FIGURE 2.3 Lee Miller, *Dead SS Guard floating in canal, Dachau, Germany 1945*.

Miller photographs the chaos of the war's very immediate aftermath. She seems, also, to have been drawn to suffering and in particular to newly liberated concentration camps with large numbers of corpses, in part from some deep and untheorized connection between her trauma as a survivor of childhood rape and the trauma of the survivors and victims of the Nazis.[36] I do not suggest that such traumata are literally comparable but rather that trauma, as such, follows in these different cases similar interior, psychic contours.[37]

Miller did not avert her gaze from the ravaged victims and survivors of the Nazis because she saw in them a state of woundedness similar to her own childhood experience.[38] Her photographs of concentration camp victims take the idea of convulsive beauty and expose the limits of the avant-garde, interposing between surrealism and documentary photography Miller's empathic and frightening revelation of history. The Holocaust stands as one of the most barbaric acts of war in modernity, and Miller's presence, with her camera, as one of the very first Allied noncombatants to see the camps indicates the force of her personality. She was willing to see face-to-face and preserve what many cannot bear, even now, to look upon in photographs.[39]

Whether these war photographs are sublime depends on one's definition of the sublime. Using a Burkean sense, one could argue that Miller's photographs of carnage present an unsavory sublime that allows the pleasure of watching others suffer while we the viewers are safe.[40] But I argue that Miller's deeply empathetic sublimity inheres in the way her images pull the enormity of the suffering and pain of the Holocaust into formal contours, as it were a formalizing of *l'informe*.

The Kantian rather than Burkean sublime, then, offers a way of understanding the power of Miller's war images. Miller's photographs *Dead SS Guard floating in canal, Dachau, Germany 1945*; *The veiled Eiffel Tower from the Palais de Chaillot [Paris Under Snow], Paris, France 1944* (Figures 2.3 and 2.4); and *Dachau: Human Remains in a Cremation Furnace, 1945* engage our eyes in a painful double task. The images are formally acute records of devastation of different kinds. The photograph of Paris suggests the city's disappearance as snow renders spectral the allée reaching toward the Eiffel Tower (Figure 2.4). Among statues a lone man is walking with an umbrella, and the statues seem to regard him as like them – both present and absent, at the edge of survival. *Dead SS Guard floating in canal, Dachau, Germany 1945* shows a young and strong-looking man curled in the fetal position in a shallow river (Figure 2.3). The image has uncanny connections to Andreas Gursky's much later photo-painting *Rhein II* in that both contend with Germany's pastoral and Romantic ideal. In *Dead SS Guard floating in canal, Dachau, Germany 1945*, the bucolic river doubles as a scene of probable suicide, as SS guards killed themselves in the advent of Germany's defeat. The young man, then, represents and is a defeated soldier. This knowledge stands quite apart from the sinister and vicious public reputation of the SS guards, that organization (the *Schutzstaffel*, or Protection Squadron) in Germany that bore direct responsibility for enacting the so-called final solution – that is, the Holocaust.

Susan Sontag argues that a photograph can never give information but always needs information to be interpreted.[41] The idea that any visual image can stand alone without culture and knowledge feeding its interpretation is absurd; all visual art is always interpreted in and through a cultural matrix. That being the case, it is very fair to say that part of the sublimity of Miller's photograph is the juxtaposition of our cultural knowledge of the barbaric acts enacted by the SS with the youthfulness of his face and the eerie peacefulness of the posture in which Miller catches him. He is newly dead and the water barely covers him. The gentleness of the image shimmers painfully against our knowledge not only of this man or any man's death but also of his very likely participation in killing Jewish, Roma, and gay people during the Holocaust. The sublime power of the photograph inheres in this way that the photograph forces the visual field to carry knowledge and meaning that need the faculty of reason or thought to comprehend. The Holocaust cannot be comprehended except by thought; sustaining sense and feeling becomes impossible before its enormity of suffering.

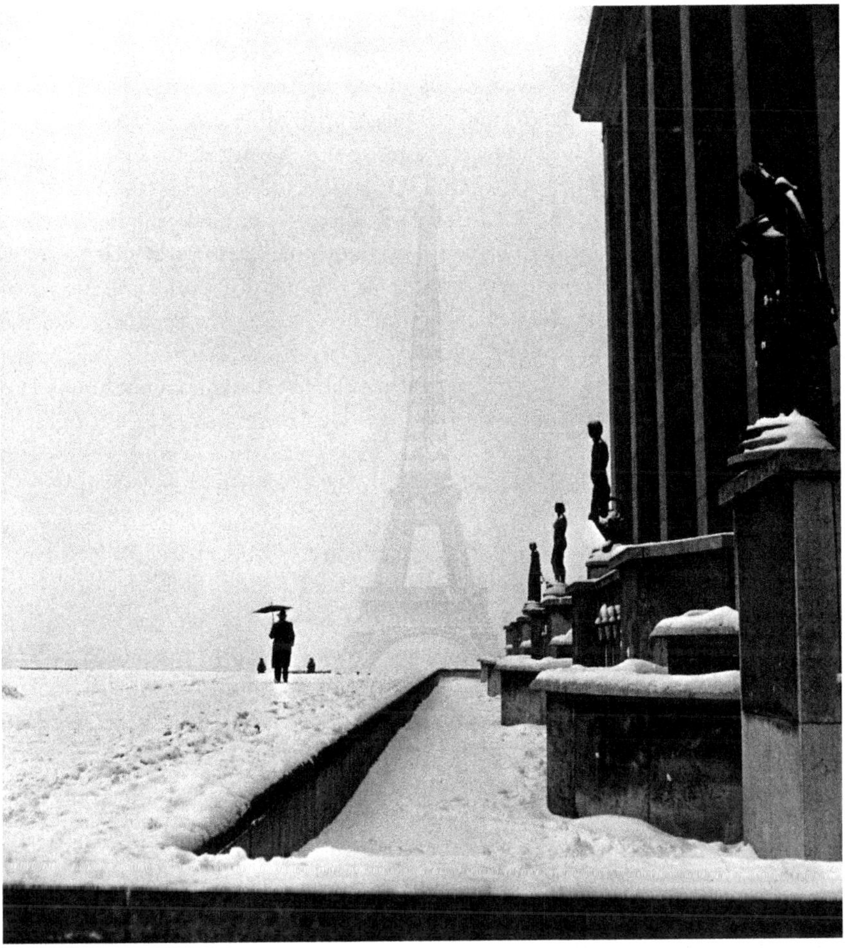

FIGURE 2.4 Lee Miller, *The veiled Eiffel Tower from the Palais de Chaillot [Paris Under Snow], Paris, France 1944.* www.leemiller.co.uk.

Miller's *Dachau: Human Remains in a Cremation Furnace, 1945* likewise draws on painful formal structures to convey a sense that the viewer is entering the furnace in which human beings were burned in the camp. The image's intense deployment of vanishing point and linear perspective jars against the gruesome and tragic subject and also reveals that subject: the furnace was long and deep and dark because it was created for violent use. In capturing the jarring, discordant notes of Germany's formal, efficient, grotesque, and barbaric mass killing of people who were not enemies and were not soldiers, Miller creates some of the most compelling images of the Holocaust. She carries this trauma through formal patterns in a sublime revelation of events too painful and overwhelming in their scope to be absorbed except intellectually. This process of compelling the intellect into the realm of the senses is the essence of the Kantian sublime.

In the years after the war and before her death, Miller put away her photographs of the war and, apparently, all of her photographs. They caused her too much pain. Her son, Antony Penrose, discovered the photographs after Miller's death, and he began to make a concerted effort to circulate his mother's work. The war photographs, then, have a doubly uncanny aspect. They are formally sublime images memorializing one of the cruelest human acts in recorded history, the Holocaust, and they are images that bear in their material history decades of invisibility. The situation in which Lee Miller's oeuvre now finds itself is one in which the photographer herself can play no active role. Being decades deceased, Lee Miller cannot now tell us how she would like to have her images circulated, curated, and reprinted. This ironic and painful femininity of position (that is, passive), Miller shares with her fellow surrealist photographer Claude Cahun, despite Cahun's vigorous personal rejection of all aspects of traditional femininity. Against this vanishing, Cahun and Miller's photographs are visual representations of feminism in the way that they resist settling into the invisibility (of artistic renown) that their contemporaries offered them.

And so I emphasize that the putative femininity of Miller's and Cahun's work inheres more in its reception than its aesthetics. And that is precisely what makes the work feminist – aesthetic resistance to oppressive terms of reception. Cahun's decades-long series of autoportraits never give us a sense of knowing Claude Cahun; instead, the images gaze at us, asking us to question how and even why we look at her. Similarly, Lee Miller's oeuvre never forms a neat whole. Instead, it is fractured and fragmentary, the broken and transfigured gaze that one could call "feminine" because it emanates from a photographer who survived several kinds of sexual objectification, including childhood rape. But this articulation raises the question of what we mean when we use the word *feminine*, illuminating the difficult and persistent connection between this word and pain and passivity. One must be very careful to untangle the history of oppression of what is culturally designated feminine from the work of art created from a perspective that is feminist.[42] They are not the same. Miller's work is feminist not because it sees and shows the world through the lens of someone who has been damaged by patriarchal oppression but because her work sees through that lens – yes, her photographs look beyond it – to force a reckoning.

Notes

1 Consider the following retrospectives: *Angels of Anarchy: Women Artists and Surrealism* at the Manchester Art Gallery in Great Britain, September 2009–January 2010; *In Wonderland: The Surrealist Adventures of Women Artists* at the Los Angeles County Museum of Art, January 29–May 6, 2012; *Cherchez La Femme: Women and Surrealism* at Sotheby's London, Fall 2015. See also Rosalind Krauss, *Bachelors* (Cambridge, MA: MIT, 2000); André Breton, *The Manifesto of Surrealism*, trans. Richard Seaver and Helen Lane (Ann Arbor, MI: University of Michigan Press, 1969).

2 Alice Gambrell, *Women Intellectuals, Modernism, and Difference* (Cambridge, UK: Cambridge University Press, 1997); see also, Natalya Lusty, *Surrealism, Feminism, Psychoanalysis*

(London: Ashgate, 2010); Gen Doy, *Claude Cahun: A Sensual Politics* (London: I.B. Tauris, 2006).

3 See Hilary Roberts and Antony Penrose, *Lee Miller: A Woman's War* (New York: Thames and Hudson, 2015) and Carolyn Burke, *Lee Miller: A Life* (Chicago: University of Chicago Press, 2007).

4 See Anna Hanreich, Klaus Schroder, and Walter Moser, *Lee Miller* (Ostfildern, Germany: Hatje Cantz, 2015); Jui-Chi Liu, "Beholding the Feminine Sublime: Lee Miller's War Photography," *Signs: A Journal of Women in Culture and Society* 40, no. 2 (Winter 2015): 318; Becky Conekin, *Lee Miller in Fashion* (New York: Monacelli Press, 2013); Laura Bailey and Lizzie Thynne, "Beyond Representation: Claude Cahun's Monstrous Mischief Making," *History of Photography* 29, no. 2 (2005): 135–48; Jennifer Blessing, "Claude Cahun: Dandy Provocateuse," in *Dandies: Fashion and Finesse in Art and Culture*, ed. Susan Fillin-Yeh (New York: New York University Press, 2001), 185–97.

5 Cahun was not intersex biologically; instead, as a person born biologically female, she experienced herself as both male and female, dressing as a man and as a woman at different times. To my mind, it is beside the point whether Cahun, had she been born in the late twentieth rather than the late nineteenth century, would have transitioned and become a transman. She lived her life between genders, fiercely defending her right to both femininity and masculinity. On intersex identity, see Anne Fausto-Sterling, *Sexing the Body: Gender Politics and the Construction of Sexuality* (New York: Basic Books, 2000).

6 André Breton, *Manifestos of Surrealism*, trans. Richard Seaver and Helen Lane (Ann Arbor, MI: University of Michigan Press, 1969).

7 The war approached 40 million casualties in total. See Samuel Dumas, *Losses of Life Caused by War* (Oxford, UK: Oxford University Press, 1923); and Michel Huber, *La Population de la France pendant la guerre* (Paris: Les Presses universitaires de France, 1931).

8 The concept of *l'informe* roughly means the formless. Georges Bataille, who originated the concept, argues, "formless is not only an adjective having a given meaning, but a term that serves to bring things down in the world, generally requiring that each thing have its form. What it designates has no rights in any sense and gets itself squashed everywhere, like a spider or an earthworm . . . affirming that the universe resembles nothing and is only formless amounts to saying that the universe is something like a spider or spit." Please see Georges Bataille, *Vision of Excess: Selected Writings, 1927–1939*, trans. Alan Stoekl (Minneapolis, MN: University of Minnesota Press, 1986), 31.

9 There are clear points of connection between Cahun's autoportrait practice as a kind of automatic photography – that is, photography that pulls on the depths of the psyche precisely by staying on the surface, the level of the mask – and Walter Benjamin's theory of the "optical unconscious." See Walter Benjamin, *On Photography*, ed. and trans. Esther Leslie (1931, rpt., London: Reaktion Books, 2015). It is the optical unconscious that Cahun reveals through her long practice of photographing herself in various masks and guises.

10 See Krauss, *Bachelors*, 101–61.

11 Eugene Atget created the definitive body of work responding to the fracture between the old and the new, the nineteenth and the twentieth centuries, photographing hauntingly clear and depopulated scenes of Paris and its environs. Andreas Krase and Hans Adam, *Eugene Atget's Paris* (Cologne, Germany: Taschen, 2001); see also, Susan Laxton, *Paris as Gameboard: Man Ray's Atgets* (New York: Columbia University Press, 2002).

12 Philip Prodger and Lynda Harigan, *Man Ray/Lee Miller: Partners in Surrealism* (London: Merrell Publishers, 2011).

13 Susan Muth titled her translation *Disavowals: Or Cancelled Confessions* (Cambridge, MA: MIT Press, 2008).

14 Judith Butler, *Gender Trouble: Feminism and the Subversion of Identity* (Abingdon, UK: Routledge, 1990).

15 See Jeffrey Batchen, *Burning with Desire* (Cambridge, MA: MIT Press, 1999).

16 Gen Doy, *Claude Cahun: A Sensual Politics* (London: I.B. Tauris, 2007).

17 Krauss, *Bachelors*, 1–51.

18 This in itself is a more complicated claim than Krauss avows, inasmuch as the situation of Jews in France changed significantly from the first two decades of the twentieth century, a time during which there was relatively little anti-Semitism in the country, to the late 1930s, when anti-Semitism burgeoned. Cahun chose her name during a relatively halcyon time.
19 Doy, *Claude Cahun.*
20 Ibid., 90.
21 Much ink has been spilled either lambasting the male surrealists for being sexist or alternately for arguing that they were not sexist. See Mary Ann Caws, *Surrealism and Women* (Cambridge, MA: MIT Press, 1991); Rudolf Kuenzli, "Surrealism and Misogyny," *Dada/ Surrealism* 18 (1990): 17–26; David Bate, *Photography and Surrealism, Sexuality, Colonialism and Social Dissent* (London: I.B. Tauris, 2004); and Kraus, *Bachelors*.
22 Peggy Phelan, *Unmarked: The Politics of Performance* (London: Routledge, 1993).
23 See Liu, "Beholding the Feminine Sublime," 308.
24 Jean-Francois Lyotard, *Lessons on the Analytic of the Sublime* (Stanford: Stanford University Press, 1991).
25 Edmund Burke, *A Philosophical Enquiry into the Origin of Our Ideas of the Sublime and Beautiful*, www.gutenberg.org/files/15043/15043-h/15043-h.htm.
26 See Debra Walker King, *African Americans and the Culture of Pain* (Charlottesville, VA: University of Virginia Press, 2008).
27 See Claire Raymond, *Francesca Woodman and the Kantian Sublime* (Aldershot, UK: Ashgate, 2010).
28 Immanuel Kant, *The Critique of Judgment* (1792, rpt. Oxford, UK: Oxford University Press, 2009).
29 Here, I offer very shorthand glosses of tremendously sophisticated works. See Julia Kristeva, *Powers of Horror* (New York: Columbia University Press, 1984) and Barbara Claire Freeman, *The Feminine Sublime* (Berkeley, CA: University of California Press, 1997).
30 Raymond, *Francesca Woodman.*
31 Caitlin Davis, "Lee Miller's Revenge on Culture," *Woman's Art Journal* 27, no. 1 (Spring/ Summer 2006): 3–9; see also Sharon Sliwinski, "Visual Testimony: Lee Miller's Dachau," *Journal of Visual Culture* 9, no. 3 (2010): 389–408.
32 Burke, *Lee Miller*, 16.
33 Ibid., 17.
34 Paula Salvio, "Uncanny Exposures: A Study of the Wartime Photojournalism of Lee Miller," *Curriculum Inquiry* 39, no. 4 (2009): 521–36; see also, Patricia Allmer, *Lee Miller: Photography, Surrealism, and Beyond* (Manchester, UK: Manchester University Press, 2016).
35 Edward Said, *Orientalism* (New York: Vintage, 1979), xviii.
36 Sliwinski "Visual Testimony: Lee Miller's Dachau." See also Barbara Zelizer, *Remembering to Forget: Holocaust Memory through the Camera's Eye* (Chicago: University of Chicago Press, 1998).
37 Cathy Caruth, *Unclaimed Experience: Trauma, Narrative, and History* (Baltimore, MD: Johns Hopkins University Press, 1996).
38 See Emmanuel Levinas, "Useless Suffering," *The Problem of Evil: A Reader*, ed. Mark Larrimore (London: Wiley-Blackwell, 2000): 371–380. Levinas argues that it is from the place of one's own suffering – one's own woundedness – that one is able to understand and empathically connect with the suffering of the other.
39 The experience apparently left her with a form of post-traumatic stress disorder, as she later stated that she could "never get the stench of Auschwitz out of [her] nostrils." See Burke, *Lee Miller*, 284.
40 Frances Guerin and Roger Hallas, eds., *The Image and the Witness: Trauma, Memory, and Visual Culture* (London: Wallflower Press, 2007).
41 Susan Sontag, *On Photography* (London: Picador, 1977).
42 See Helene Cixous, "The Laugh of the Medusa" (1975). Trans. Keith Cohen and Paula Cohen. *Signs* Vol. 1, No. 4 (Summer 1976): 875–893.

3

TRUTH IN PHOTOGRAPHY

Dorothea Lange and Imogen Cunningham

In *The Truth in Painting*, philosopher Jacques Derrida argues that the frame of the image – the parergon – is the place of comparison, the space where the image mediates with the not-seen. Derrida claims that

> the external never remains outside. What's at stake here is a decision about the frame, about what separates the internal from the external, with a border which is itself double in its trait, and joins together what it splits. At stake are all the interests caught up in the trial of this split.[1]

In looking at the work of American photographers Imogen Cunningham (1883–1976) and Dorothea Lange (1895–1965), I want to examine the concepts of "pure photography" and "documentary photography" with which their work, respectively, is so deeply connected.[2] Cunningham, as a founding member of Group f/64, and Lange, as a documentary photographer employed by the Farm Security Administration (FSA), gave their entire faith and effort to the idea that photography was uniquely capable of showing "truth." As a practitioner and proponent of "pure photography," Cunningham believed that photographs were capable of showing the visible world more precisely, accurately, and completely than other arts. For Lange, the "truth" that photography could reveal was social reality, and she aimed to show the real lives of the dispossessed, the ghosts of America. Her work during the Great Depression testifies not only to Lange's intense desire to capture and record human suffering and perseverance but also to her belief that the photograph was the correct and best medium by which to show what was happening, what was "real."

In discussing Lange and Cunningham, I have placed the words "truth" and "real" in quotation marks to indicate that these concepts, in which the photographers placed such intense faith, are more correctly understood as aspects of belief. The belief that documentary photography shows reality is a conceit, and one that later theorists, such as John Tagg and Allan Sekula, have argued to be an inaccurate way of thinking about photography.[3] These theorists argue that to believe that a photograph shows us simply what is there is to be deluded by the photograph's performative (and suspect) claims of authenticity. And yet, Derrida's theorization of the role of the parergon is essential to understanding Cunningham's and Lange's use of the camera as a tool of truth, for the photograph is defined not as true or false but rather *by* its frame (that is, what it excludes from the image) and the frame's relationship to its referent (what it shows). The photograph is defined by recording and also by being part of the physical world that unfolds in time. Derrida's understanding of the frame – the place where the work is limited by, at the boundary of, and extensive into the world – carries with it a nuanced theory of the work of art as, by definition, not self-sufficient. That is, the work of art exists always between the act of representation and the force of the aesthetic that moves to cut off the work from the quotidian world. This constant movement, never resolved, between the image and the act of representation is especially relevant to the goals of documentary and pure photography, which aspire to show a truth that they actually create. What is at stake, then, are ideologies that mask cultural power as well as the photograph's ability to transmit these ideologies and also, perhaps, to unmask them.

Group f/64 and pure photography

Group f/64, the West Coast group of photographers that Imogen Cunningham helped found, was named after the aperture stop that, at the time the group formed, was the smallest on a large-format camera and hence yielded the greatest clarity across the image. The group can be associated with landscape photography, but in fact the photographers were drawn not only to photographing landscapes but also to making all subjects a landscape, as one sees in Cunningham's work.[4] That is, Cunningham's close-up photographs of calla lilies, for example, and also her image *Magnolia Blossom, Tower of Jewels* show in crystalline and minute detail the interior of a flower, thus making the flower a landscape that the camera reveals. Cunningham's images of industrial buildings such as gas tanks also develop from the photograph's inimitable ability to create typologies: the camera can show forms in exact detail and thereby also reveal minute differences in similar structures. For Cunningham, this capacity of the camera to show clearly the form of the physical world acts as prescription and catalyst, the basis of her rejection of pictorialist aesthetics.[5]

Beginning in the 1920s and throughout the rest of her career, Cunningham sought in her work to use the camera's unique capacity to show clearly and accurately the forms of the visible world, producing modestly sized silver gelatin prints of flowers, nude women, and industrial objects.[6] Her work visually affirms the fundamental beliefs of Group f/64, as expressed in the group's manifesto:

> Pure photography is defined as possessing no qualities of technique, composition or idea, derivative of any other art form. The production of the "Pictorialist," on the other hand, indicates a devotion to principles of art

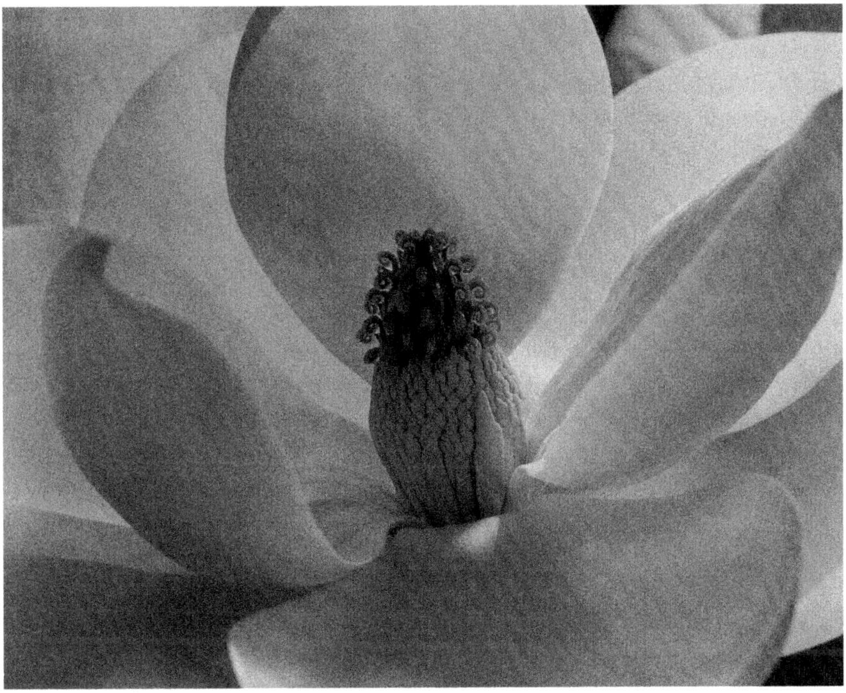

FIGURE 3.1 Imogen Cunningham, *Magnolia Blossom, Tower of Jewels*, 1925 (printed 1971), gelatin silver print, 22.2 × 27.9 cm. Norton Simon Museum, Gift of the Artist to the Blue Four Galka Scheyer Collection.

> which are directly related to painting and the graphic arts. . . . The members of Group f/64 believe that photography, as an art form, must develop along lines defined by the actualities and limitations of the photographic medium, and must always remain independent of ideological conventions of art and aesthetics that are reminiscent of a period and culture antedating the growth of the medium itself.[7]

The word *pure* has complicated connotations. Group f/64 used it to convey that which emerges directly from the use of the camera. And yet this word also carries what Derrida calls "trace meanings,"[8] connotations imbued by its path through common English language usage. Purity connotes a status as something separate, sanctified, and, indeed, approaching the holy.

There are, then, deeply problematic ideological aspects embedded in this notion of purity. Yet Cunningham's photographs of nude women and of the interior parts of flowers manage with éclat to at once suggest and deconstruct paradoxical aspects of the idea of visual purity and, hence, of pure photography. That is, Cunningham's photography suggests and deconstructs the problematic ideological aspects of the word *purity*. Her close-ups of the interiors of flowers echo and fall into conversation with

Georgia O'Keeffe's paintings of flowers' reproductive parts.[9] Cunningham's emphasis on the feminine – the flower, the nude girl – is radicalized by her shift in angle of approach. Her flower interiors take the unthreateningly pretty form of the flower and make it frightening and monumental (in relative scale). Here, I do not mean that her photographs of flowers are large in print size. Rather, they make the flower's interior commanding, large to the eye, and architectural, as Cunningham's title *Magnolia Blossom, Tower of Jewels* suggests.

As I have noted, Cunningham's flower imagery bears comparison to the flower paintings of Georgia O'Keefe, which are often discussed in terms of their evocation of vaginal imagery. The history and substance of the question whether and, if so, how images that evoke female genitalia are "feminist" is vexed.[10] On the one hand, one can argue that imagery of the female body created by women artists liberates that body from its traditional position as the muse and model for the male artist and the object for the male gaze.[11] On the other hand, problematic assumptions are enfolded into the argument (a) that to show something is tantamount to liberating it and (b) that a photograph of a nude woman or of a flower representing female genitalia, if created by a woman photographer, is legibly different from a photograph of a nude woman or of a flower representing female genitalia taken by a male photographer. Also, the question hovers at the edge of such imagery as to whether – and, if so, how – female genitalia correlate to being a woman, which is a cultural identity. As I pointed out in the previous chapter, Peggy Phelan argues that at times invisibility may be a greater source of power than visibility.[12] I find her argument incomplete because nonpresence – or that-which-is-not-represented – risks complete erasure, however tactical a maneuver some instances of invisibility may be. But Phelan makes the very good point that just showing one's body – in particular if one inhabits a body that has for centuries been considered a marker for sexual powerlessness and a site of sexual conquest – does not necessarily place one in a position of power. There is also the fundamental question of whether having a biologically female body structures subjectivity and, hence, seeing: simply having female genitalia has no inherent meaning until that genitalia – and possessing it – are given social meaning. Cunningham's flowers, however, evince an oblique reply to stereotypes of femininity. Her gendered typologies of flowers, with their cool, slant vision, acknowledge the fabricated nature of the feminine while relishing the oblique, the strange, and the impenetrable place where actuality abrades myth. Photographs are great reservoirs and purveyors of social myth. In this, Cunningham the "pure" photographer lucidly plays with and subverts social myth – the myth of femininity and the myth of flower – changing these topoi into an aloof geometric and structural aesthetic.

Likewise and differently, Cunningham's photographs of nude young women make of their bodies architectural and geometric forms. She gave these images titles such as *Triangles* to make this approach explicit. In Cunningham's nudes, the women are rendered untouchable statuary.[13] And yet, departing from tradition, Cunningham takes the visual emphasis off representation of women as objects of desire or as mystical sources of comfort. Instead, her geometrical nudes are, for all their bare skin rendered textural, remote. Cunningham emphasizes their angularity rather than their curves, but they are not women who look masculine. She shows in these nudes the absurdity of ascribing to femininity the attributes of softness and curves when many women are angular. Her nudes have a look of freshness, almost a century after they were made, because they deconstruct the male gaze that acquires the feminine body as its property. Cunningham's nudes become form, angle, and geometry; they are not fragmented in the manner of cubism but instead are seen from a different angle, arguably a woman's angle. Here I do not mean "point of view" in the social sense of viewpoint but vision in the transcendent sense. Cunningham sees her nudes from what could be understood as a feminine point of view, arresting and resting in their complex embodied humanness. One would not say she does not eroticize her female nudes, for indeed they are, in their way, erotic. In any case, feminist photographers, including Claude Cahun, represent the female body in erotic ways. Instead, the feminist difference visible in Cunningham's nudes is the way she makes of her female models something both de-naturalized and unreachable, thus admiring and eroticizing the female body and never humiliating it.

Grab a hunk of lightning

As Dorothea Lange well understood, the documentary photograph does not simply show the truth. "A documentary photograph is not a factual photograph per se," she said. "It is a photograph which carries the full meaning of the episode."[14] This idea of an episode that is held in the still image correlates with Lange's notion that to take a great documentary photograph is to "grab a hunk of lightning,"[15] to capture in an instantaneous moment a durational truth, an episode, or even an era. Indeed, Lange's best work is visually synonymous with the Great Depression in the United States. Her photographs of migrant farm workers (taken while she was employed by the FSA) are not blunt instruments of fact but subtle documents, condensing into singular images information about the photographic subject's position in history. Querying Lange's most famous photograph, *Migrant Mother*, or, *Destitute pea pickers in California. Mother of seven children. Age thirty-two. Nipomo, California* (Figure 3.2), I will focus on this image and on the series of images from which it emerges as exemplifying some aspects of Lange's genius for documentary portraiture.

Florence Thompson

The photograph that by custom has come to be called *Migrant Mother*, Lange originally captioned "Destitute pea pickers in California. Mother of seven children. Age thirty-two. Nipomo, California. February 1936" (Figure 3.2).[16]

Lange, then, saw the photograph as an exemplary document, an image that showed an economic situation – namely the dire poverty of the Great Depression. Even so, Lange's early training and background as a photographer was in portraiture, and it is as portraiture that her documentary photographs excel. That said, in making her an icon, the portrait of Florence Thompson somewhat effaces the woman

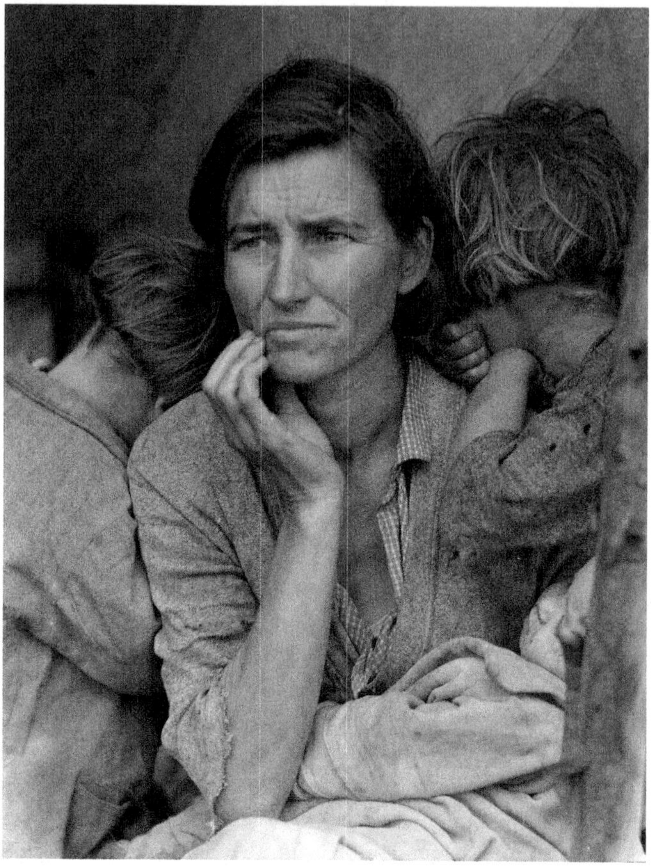

FIGURE 3.2 Dorothea Lange, *Migrant Mother*, also titled *Destitute pea pickers in California. Mother of seven children. Age thirty-two. Nipomo, California*, 1936.

herself. In describing the making of the photograph, Lange as much as admits that she made no effort to get to know her most famous photographic subject:

> I saw and approached the hungry and desperate mother, as if drawn by a magnet. I do not remember how I explained my presence or my camera to her, but I do remember she asked me no questions. I made five exposures, working closer and closer from the same direction. I did not ask her name or her history. She told me her age, that she was thirty-two. She said that they had been living on frozen vegetables from the surrounding fields, and birds that the children killed. She had just sold the tires from her car to buy food. There she sat in that lean-to tent with her children huddled around her, and seemed to know that my pictures might help her, and so she helped me. There was a sort of equality about it.[17]

The "sort of equality" that Lange infers between the two women was apparently not something Florence Thompson felt. Thompson was angered by the photographs (*Migrant Mother* is only one image from this series), which she felt shamed her by revealing her to be in dire straits, and angered too by the fact that she never got money for posing. Indeed, it seems clear that being in Lange's famous photograph did not materially help Thompson, although toward the end of her life, she apparently reconciled herself to the image (Figure 3.2).[18] Moreover, although Thompson was a migrant farmworker, destitute, and a 32-year-old mother of seven children, the way that Lange's photograph presented Thompson to the American public was inaccurate in some respects. For one thing, Lange erased Thompson's Native American heritage and presented her as a white woman.[19] Lange herself seems not to have been aware that Thompson was Native American because she did not engage her sitter in conversation.[20] Instead, Thompson became the putative Mona Lisa of the Dustbowl; Lange's boss at the FSA, Roy Stryker, commented that "you can see anything you want to in her. She is immortal."[21] Thompson becomes an image and in so becoming feels she has lost herself. She does not feel the equality that Lange suggests in her description of the photograph's creation, and equality between women is surely as important an aspect of feminism as is equality between genders.

And yet, by reading *through* Thompson's sense of distress, rather than eliding her rage at the photograph's co-opting of her identity, there is a space in which the equality that Lange felt – the women coming together to create this iconic image – works in the image itself. Florence Thompson's feeling that Lange's photograph purloined her identity is entirely accurate. The photograph moves away from the complicated realities of Thompson's life: it does not show all of her children; it cannot show her deceased first husband; it does not show the man who fathered the baby she holds; and it does not indicate the complicated and brutal history of Native American displacement. (To my understanding, Thompson descended from the Southeastern tribes of Georgia and North Carolina, and so the very fact that she is not only destitute and impoverished but in California is testimony to the violent terms of Native American displacement, dispossession, and diaspora.) The photograph instead shows a young but careworn woman alone with two small children and a nursing infant, the family group apparently residing in a makeshift tent.

Migrant Mother has been compared, usefully, to Renaissance paintings of the Madonna, but the grouping of children in the photograph actually suggests Renaissance and later paintings of the Virgin, Christ, Saint Anne, and John the Baptist. The clustering of the children's heads with their mother's, and even the slight tilt of Thompson's face, uncannily suggest Leonardo da Vinci's *Madonna and Child with St. Anne and the Young St. John* (1507–1508).[22] I suggest that Lange's feeling of community between women gathers into her handling of her photographic subject, and this feeling of community between women felt on the photographer's part creates the visual echo of the Madonna with Saint Anne. By contrast, the typical presentation of the Madonna is of a woman alone with her child. Lange's photograph implies some communal connection between women: the very connection that Lange (but decidedly not Thompson) felt when taking a series of photographs that sodden afternoon in 1936.

Lange's own sense of connection with the impoverished mother she photographed may have been personal in that Lange had been forced to board out her two sons so that she could work and earn a living.[23] It is clear from Thompson's later comments that she did not find the experience of being photographed by Lange helpful or supportive. And yet, she did allow the photographs to be made. In the images we do not see a woman walking away or battling the photographer. Instead, we see a woman who is extremely tired and who perhaps lacks the energy to object. The always possible violence of photography – that it flattens its subjects to fit a two-dimensional image – hovers at the frame of the *Migrant Mother*.

The tent over the mother and children acts as a frame porously incapable of keeping the outside out. Likewise, the photographs in this series are frames that evince the mother's inability to keep the outside out: a stranger is not only intently watching but photographing her nursing her baby. (When I think of my own experience nursing an infant, I remember so strongly wanting privacy.) Her makeshift home is open to the elements, and Lange's camera records its own act of visually penetrating Thompson's porous and unstably framed home. It is in the nature of photographs to invade, to make of the subject an object. In this sense the frame that defines a photograph is always about permeable and violated boundaries, but photographs also have the capacity to take the pain of invasion and make its images into formal meanings, albeit oblique to and always intermediary to the situation shown. The photograph can mediate between imagination and blunt fact, between representation as act and as vision, and in Lange's photographs of Thompson – originally circulated as photographic "truth" – we see some facts (the tent, the earth, the clothes) and also very prominently we see Lange's imagined encounter with a woman to whom she felt drawn like a magnet. The encounter is imagined because Thompson did not reciprocate Lange's feelings of connection, but Lange imagined this intense connection, and that imagined empathic link – "a kind of equality" as Lange describes it – gives the photograph series its power. It also gives the close-up of Thompson's face its peculiar ability to collect in one image the pain of the Depression, the pain of motherhood, and sorrow imbued with dignity because Thompson is neither a contented nor defeated photographic subject.

Florence Thompson's face looks not at the viewers but past us (also past Lange), and her children's faces are turned away so that we see only their hair. (Apparently the children were giggling and Lange told them to turn their heads so the photograph would not show their smiles.) Thompson's face, her children's heads, the sleeping baby, all in close-range focus, move into our emotions much the way Roland Barthes (not writing on Lange's work specifically) describes as the effect of the photographic "punctum," the arrow that flies from the image and strikes the viewer with the power of a painful affective experience that can only be described as aesthetic.[24] The affective power of Lange's images of Thompson, and particularly the photograph known as *Migrant Mother*, at once belies and carries with it

Thompson's actual suffering. It belies her suffering in that it effaces her Native American heritage, effaces her between-marriages status, and effaces even her children's giggles despite their hunger. But the image carries all these with it: that is, the image has a "punctum" because despite Lange's decision not to hear, or possibly not to remember or record, the real story of Thompson's life, her photograph testifies to the pain of silencing and carries with it the melancholy force of its own violence. That is, the violation of the subject is also the revelation of the subject. We "feel for" Florence Thompson not because we interpret her in falsified terms as a "pure" married white woman but because a message without a code is caught – apparently without Lange's conscious knowledge – in the photographs.[25] The images contain the unreadable and yet palpable knowledge of displacement (not just the displacements of the Depression but those of Thompson's cultural and familial history), the unreadable and yet visceral knowledge of a young husband's death and a young woman left with several children who then becomes pregnant by another man, and the obliquely legible disregard in which Thompson holds Lange by not refusing her but not condoning her.

It is precisely Thompson's reaction to Lange – woman to woman – that shows Thompson's dignity. And I would argue that despite all Lange's failings in not bringing forward the grave situation of Native Americans during the Great Depression and despite Thompson's anger against Lange's appropriation of her image, Lange does create feminist photography in her representation of Thompson. The image's capacity to show what it seems to hide – Thompson's strength of personality, her formidability, her refusal of the white woman's gaze – the paradoxical position of disempowerment in which Thompson finds herself and even the humiliation of being caught in Lange's gaze and lens all come into play in the complex textures of the photographs that Lange took of Thompson. Women humiliating other women is not and should not be part of feminism, but Lange's photography makes of Thompson the face of dignity in adversity. In other words, the sense of shame that Thompson felt so strongly in the aftermath of the photograph is part of what gives the photograph its power, but the image would not have this visual power – its iconicity – if it did not contain a powerful movement away from shame and into a transcendent dignity and beauty. It is the way the image overcomes itself, overcomes its own cliché, that pulls forward and makes visible the woman's ability to handle and overcome her adverse circumstances and makes of the photograph an image that resonates.

The damages of photography

Lange's 1936 photograph *Damaged Child, Shacktown, Elm Grove, Oklahoma* (Figure 3.3) presents further complications in its ethics of creation. Lange's photograph of the developmentally challenged child immediately raises the issue of how the girl could possibly have understood her position as photographic subject sufficiently well to meaningfully give consent for Lange to take her image and for the FSA to circulate it and, as it happens, circulate it far beyond this originally planned media. In Lange's portrait, the girl's vulnerability is palpable and painful. She stands before

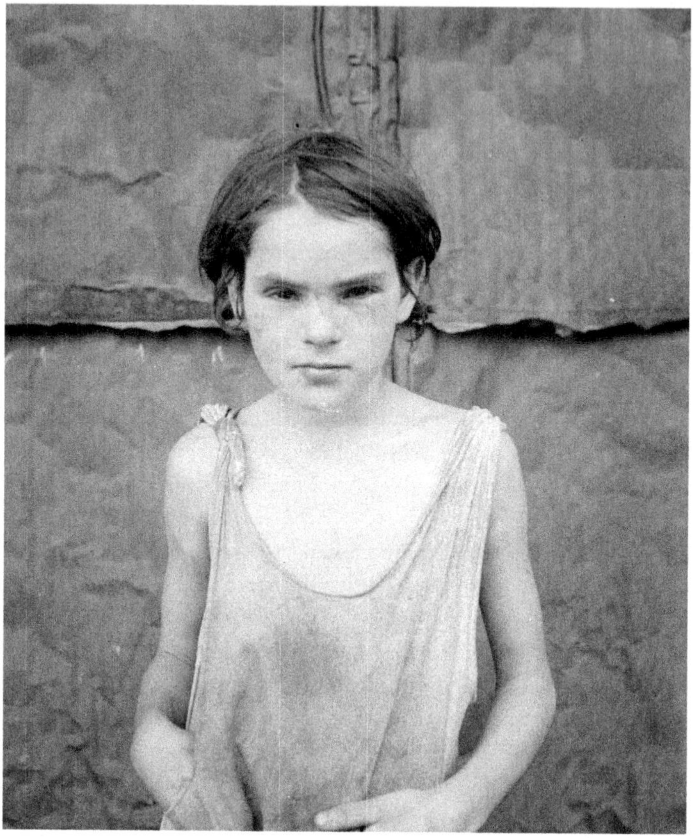

FIGURE 3.3 Dorothea Lange, *Damaged Child, Shacktown, Elm Grove, Oklahoma*, 1936.

a door that appears to be made of metal plates soldered together and hence marked with a kind of cross where the metal plates have been roughly soldered. Her face is marred by the scar left from an agricultural accident. The child is wary (Lange recalled that she had been teased and treated cruelly by other children) and is very poorly dressed, in a shirt made of gunnysack and tied rather than sewn.

Lange's photograph transforms the vulnerable, injured girl into a symbol of the Depression: the damaged future of the United States. But the photograph itself damages the child. It flattens the visual field in which the child appears, as if the metal door behind her were moving toward her, literally flattening her. The damaged wall, with its ridge of solder, fills the frame and echoes the child's face misshapen by her scar. The whole photograph is a scar – the scar of the moment in which Lange snapped the shot. This photograph is the scar of the violence of seeing photographically. The metal door that is created by soldering panels into a cross to form a scar; the child whose face has been scarred by accident; and the photograph that is the scar of light, silver, and emulsion cohere to create a figure of blight – a personification of the Depression.

But the photograph also shows the child's alertness to the complex matrix from which her image will emerge. She sees, emotionally, that Lange is making use of her. She also sees Lange's apparent sorrow at her plight (years later, when describing the encounter with this child, Lange wept), and possibly she also sees Lange's intention to use the photograph as evidence. The evidentiary force of this photograph is its turn, the way that it takes violence – the violence done to the child by other people, by time, by fate, and by the process of photography itself – and makes of these forces of violence an image that condemns violence and that acts as a witness for the violated and the oppressed. This turn, such a narrow difference, is what makes Lange's portrait of the girl feminist. It clarifies the wrongness of oppression and envisions or imagines hence another society in which the child would not be damaged. What the photograph tells us is she was not born this way; the world did this to her. Whatever is true about the child, the photographer, the Depression, and its multiple causes does not matter to (and cannot be known entirely from) the image. The photograph frames pain of harm and also the vision for a world in which oppression and damage could be eradicated. That vision of the possibility of something else – precisely at the edge or as the sliver in the scar of what is – constitutes Lange's feminist aesthetic.

Suppression after the depression: internment camps

Although Lange arguably created her best-known work while she was employed by the FSA, a few years after she lost that job she undertook a project that bears particular discussion.[26] During World War II, Lange accepted another government job, this time taking photographs of Japanese Americans in internment camps. The internment of Japanese Americans during World War II is a scandalous chapter in American history, occurring when the United States government decided to punitively herd American citizens of known Japanese descent into what amounted to concentration camps, following the gravely erroneous assumption that such Americans were likely to be secretly spying for or supporting Japan's army. (The United States government later officially apologized to descendants of the interned and paid some reparations.) The government hired Lange to take photographs to prove that Japanese Americans were not suffering as a result of the internment, but her photographs showed just the opposite. When government officials saw the photographs, they fired her and suppressed her images. The internment photographs came into general circulation only in the twenty-first century.[27]

Lange's photograph of a grocery store that the Japanese American owner had been forced to abandon when he was interned shows the tension Lange felt in recording these images. On the one hand, it is an extremely careful and quiet image, showing a typical American street corner (13th and Franklin in San Francisco) in what looks to be midday light. But the grocery store is eerie for its emptiness, and across the upper windows is a large sign in block letters: "I AM AN AMERICAN."[28] The sign rebukes the government's decision to intern the grocery store owner, and Lange's photograph centering on this sign magnifies the sentiment. The photograph itself points not so much to the physical fact of the abandoned store but rather uplifts and exposes the subtext of the store's abandonment.[29] The store acts as a double sign, evincing both the absent body of the proprietor and his protest. The photograph magnifies the sign, making it a message that crosses space and time, protesting even now to the mistreatment of Americans who are forced by racist prejudice to make a painful case for their own inclusion in the nation, revealing racist ideology at the heart of exclusionary definitions of citizenship.

Lange's resistance to the patriarchal racism that led to the internment of innocent Japanese Americans during World War II remained invisible for many years because the government suppressed the photographs that she took. The force of the photographs' power inheres in this contrast between Lange's carefully formal, well-controlled compositions and the chaos of human life and the violence human beings do to each other, as revealed by these photographs. She traces history in human form with the machine of seeing, the camera that does not show transparent truth but can allow an image to reconfigure and thereby refuse dangerously false ways of seeing. In its rearrangement of the sensible, Lange's documentary photography shows us how to see the poor, the dispossessed, and the victims of racism and capitalism run amuck. The photographs do so not through the false ideology of compassion but straight through the nature of chance and the capacity for dignity that Lange's subjects have despite their hard fates. That is, her best photographs teach us to see ourselves in others. Lange draws on her strength as a portrait photographer and her skill for balance in composition. The images she creates tell a truth that is not literal, not factual, about her subjects but that moves through the frame (of the image, of time, and of history) to mark her viewers with a knowledge of experience of the widest and deepest kind. Her work is feminist because it does not look away from visual sources of knowledge, the very sights that tell us not how but where to begin to change oppressive structures of power in society.

Notes

1 Jacques Derrida, *The Truth in Painting*, trans. Geoff Bennington and Ian McLeod (Chicago: University of Chicago Press, 1987), 331.
2 Mary Street Alinder, *Group F.64: Edward Weston, Ansel Adams, Imogen Cunningham, and the Community of Artists Who Revolutionized American Photography* (New York: Bloomsbury, 2014).
3 John Tagg, *The Disciplinary Frame: Photographic Truths and the Capture of Meaning* (Minneapolis, MN: University of Minnesota Press, 2009); Allan Seukula, "The Traffic in Photographs," *Art Journal* 41, no. 1 (Spring 1981): 15–25. See also the introduction to Stephen Shore, *The Nature of Photographs* (London: Phaidon, 2007). Shore does not discount photographic pretense to truth with the rigor of Tagg and Sekula, but instead he discusses the relativity of the "truths" it might offer – conceptual and symbolic, but never literal. Philosopher Jean Baudrillard makes the case that the more "real" a photograph appears, the more it obscures reality: "It is precisely when it appears most truthful, most faithful and most in conformity to reality that the image is most diabolical." See Jean Baudrillard, *The Evil Demon of Images* (St. Louis: Left Bank Books, 1987).
4 James Curtis, *Mind's Eye, Mind's Truth: FSA Photography Reconsidered* (Philadelphia, PA: Temple University Press, 1989). See also Deborah Bright, "Of Mother Nature and Marlboro Men: An Inquiry into the Cultural Meanings of Landscape Photography," in *The Contest of Meaning*, ed. Richard Bolton (Cambridge, MA: MIT Press, 1990): 125–145.

5 Almuth Spiegler, "Blumen im tiefschlaf," *ART: Das Kunstmagazin* 8 (2013): 105.
6 Richard Lorenz, *Imogen Cunningham, 1883–1976*, ed. Manfred Heiting (New York: Taschen, 2001).
7 Paul Karlstrom, ed., *On the Edge of America: California Modernist Art 1900–1950* (Berkeley, CA: University of California Press, 1996), 257.
8 Jacques Derrida, *Speech and Phenomena: And Other Essays on Husserl's Theory of Signs*, trans. David Allison (Evanston, IL: Northwestern University Press, 1973), 141.
9 Nicholas Calloway, *Georgia O'Keeffe: One Hundred Flowers* (London: Phaidon, 1990).
10 Amelia Jones, *Sexual Politics: Judy Chicago's Dinner Party in Feminist Art History* (Berkeley, CA: University of California Press, 1996); see also Judy Chicago, *Beyond the Flower: The Autobiography of a Feminist Artist* (New York: Penguin, 1997).
11 See Linda S. Klinger, "Where's the Artist? Feminist Practice and Poststructural Theories of Authorship," *Feminist Art Criticism* 2, no. 50 (1991): 39–47; see also Amelia Jones, *Body Art/Performing the Subject* (Minneapolis, MN: University of Minnesota Press, 1998).
12 Peggy Phelan, *Unmarked: The Politics of Performance* (London: Routledge, 1993).
13 Victor Stoichità, "Photography/Sculpture," in *The Pygmalion Effect: From Ovid to Hitchcock*, trans. Alison Anderson (Chicago: University of Chicago Press, 2008): 161–181.
14 *Dorothea Lange: The Making of a Documentary Photographer*, an interview by Suzanne Riess for the Regional Oral History Office of the University of California Bancroft Library, Berkeley, in 1960–1961, published in 1968, http://bancroft.berkeley.edu/ROHO/narrators/lange_dorothea.html.
15 See Elizabeth Partridge, *Dorothea Lange: Grab a Hunk of Lightning* (San Francisco, CA: Chronicle Books, 2013).
16 See www.loc.gov/pictures/item/fsa1998021539/PP/ [accessed January 18, 2017].
17 Ibid. Much of even this small amount of information was incorrect, according to Florence Thompson's later testimony, indicating either that Lange made up the details, or, much more likely, forgot from which peapicker she had heard which story and thus applied someone else's story to Florence Thompson. See, Robert Hariman and John Louis Lucaites, *No Caption Needed: Iconic Photographs, Public Culture, and Liberal Democracy* (Chicago: University of Chicago Press, 2007).
18 Ann Whiston Spim, *Daring to Look: Dorothea Lange's Photographs and Reports from the Field* (Chicago: University of Chicago Press, 2009); see also Wendy Kozol, "Madonnas of the Fields: Photography, Gender, and 1930s Farm Relief," *Genders* 2 (1988): 2–11.
19 "What Does the 'New Deal' Mean to This Mother and Her Children?" *San Francisco News*, March 11, 1936.
20 Sally Stein, "Passing Likeness: Dorothea Lange's 'Migrant Mother' and the Paradox of Iconicity," in *Only Skin Deep: Changing Visions of the American Self*, ed. Coco Fusco and Brian Wallis (New York: Abrams, 2003), 345–6.
21 Robert Hariman and John Louis Lucaites, *No Caption Needed: Iconic Photographs, Public Culture, and Liberal Democracy* (Chicago: University of Chicago Press, 2007), 53–5.
22 *Madonna and Child with St. Anne and the Young St. John*, 1507–1508, Leonardo Da Vinci.
23 Linda Gordon, *Dorothea Lange: A Life Beyond Limits* (New York: W.W. Norton, 2009). Whether Lange boarded out her young sons because of ambition – wanting to keep working – or poverty – needing to keep working – or a combination of these factors, her sense of the tensions, difficulties, and poignancy of mothering children under uneasy conditions permeates many of her photographs, most notably the series of images of Florence Thompson.
24 Roland Barthes, *Camera Lucida: Reflections on Photography* (New York: Macmillan, 1981), 28. The effect of Barthes's punctum can only be described as aesthetic because, although he gives it emotional power, the punctum originates strictly from something seen and more precisely from a photographic image – not from real life or lived life but instead from an image.
25 Ibid., 90.
26 Linda Gordon, "Dorothea Lange: Photographer as Agricultural Sociologist," *Journal of American History* 93, no. 3 (2006): 698–717.

27 Christina M. Smith, "Theorizing Circulation in Visual Rhetoric through Dorothea Lange's Images of Japanese American Internment," *Journal of Visual Literacy* 31, no. 2 (2012): 71–89.
28 Lange's photographs of the interned surfaced where they had been stored, in the National Archives, www.archives.gov/exhibits/picturing_the_century/portfolios/port_lange.html.
29 Roland Barthes discusses the photograph's capacity to act as a multilayered sign, or, as he argues, a message without a code; photographs convey information beneath and between direct linguistic signification. See *Mythologies* (New York: Farrar, Straus and Giroux, 1972).

4

ROUGH STREET

Diane Arbus and Vivian Maier

If documentary photography seeks – or believes it seeks – to document the real as reality looks back, returning the gaze, street photography turns on the conceit that it can show what happens on the street as it takes place, depicting subjects unaware or only tangentially aware of the photographer. Although street photography can be associated with the male gaze through the work of Garry Winogrand, Robert Frank, Lee Friedlander, and to some degree Larry Clark, photographers Diane Arbus (1923–1971) and Vivian Maier (1926–2009) take the practice of street photography in another direction. Here, what I mean by the term *male gaze* is somewhat related to Laura Mulvey's work, but I am using the term more expansively and loosely to describe a kind of unquestioned claim on the presumed – and taken – right to look at other people without offering them anything in return.[1] As I will discuss further, one may say that in the work of photographers such as Frank and Winogrand, the camera acts as a prosthetic extension of the male body in social space: the camera is allowed to view, visually touch, and assume claim over the photographed subject. By contrast, Arbus and Maier – who also incontestably do lay claim to vision and to seeing – create photographs that evince an exchange of some kind between the viewer and the viewed. This exchange is not gentle and loving, but it does track a mutual acknowledgment that stems, I argue, from the differential social meaning of a woman photographer's looking, watching, and touching with her eyes her subject.

Arbus photographed people on the street, yes; but also she frequently photographed people, whom she had met on the street, in other settings, people with whom she had fallen into conversation and who then had invited her deeper into their lives.[2] If Winogrand perfected the street snapshot, Arbus took the always somewhat invasive premise of street photography (capturing the images of people who never intended to be photographic subjects when they left home that morning) and altered the terms of this invasion, turning it into something between a seduction of and a collaboration with her subjects. Arbus's subjects rarely if ever appear to be taken by surprise in a temporal fashion. Instead, the surprise is what she makes of the intimacy that she achieves by talking with and working her way into camaraderie with her subjects. By contrast, Arbus's near-contemporary Vivian Maier never took the same subject twice. Maier composed her photographs in her viewfinder camera so quickly that she developed a kind of genius for the surreptitious and off-the-cuff glance at the urban environment.

The photography of American Diane Arbus (1923–1971) and French American Vivian Maier (1926–2009) allows us to explore the putative male gaze that so haunts feminist theory. I do so by tracing (a) ways that these two photographers seize the gaze, thereby inhabiting the street as flâneurs or even voyeurs and (b) ways that they have sustained notable cultural punishment for looking – looking in public at what they did not have cultural permission or sanction to see.[3] Arbus, a suicide, was punished in the way that Susan Sontag wrote about her, in particular, in "America, Seen Through Photographs, Darkly."[4] Even Arthur Lubow, in his biography *Diane Arbus* that reveals apparent secrets about Arbus's personal life, strongly diverts attention from her work.[5] Maier's punishment came in the form of complete nonrecognition of her art during her lifetime. Maier lived a working-class life in which she was not recognized as an artist, and she died indigent and unknown. The camera as a prosthetic eye, a gaze made manifest, then, comes to the fore in Arbus's and Maier's unsettling images of mid-twentieth-century America as the photographers used the camera to access, to claim, and to make strange and revelatory public space and bodies in public. And in this work, Maier and Arbus resist the cordoning of feminine decorum of looking. By suggesting that they were punished for looking, I do not argue that they were literally arrested or legally condemned. Instead, I refer to the social facts of how Arbus's reputation was generated by some critics and biographers who viewed her as a woman who was extremely sexually promiscuous, spoiled, manipulative, and unstable as opposed to a woman who brought dogged determination and extraordinary discipline to her craft of photography. Meanwhile, Maier was simply not allowed socially – not granted cultural sanction – to live a public life as an artist.[6]

Arbus and Maier subvert the male gaze by using the camera and by using it in public, on the street in a way that commandeers for themselves that space, with its deep history of masculine prerogative. In their work, they also unmask the codes of privacy and surveillance that structure America's classed, gendered, and raced systems of domination. The mere fact of a woman holding a camera in public, although it is historically of interest, does not mean that the photographs she produces with that camera will be feminist. Still, Arbus and, in a very different way, Maier broke ground both in laying claim to the street and in the photographs created through that visual claim.[7]

The scandal of being Diane Arbus

That Diane Arbus is one of the preeminent American photographers of the twentieth century is, from the vantage of the early twenty-first century, a social fact.

And yet, the terms of her canonicity have been debated to an extraordinary degree. In my discussion of her work, I focus on a small number of photographs, drawing forward the power of these specific images – their capacity to convey the form of an embodied reality that, in Arbus's photographs, seems always to move beneath the skin of any presumption. However, I want first to sketch the problematic history of Arbus's reception, as it bears upon the question of a feminist aesthetic, in photography, that is pursued in this book. If Susan Sontag's essay excoriating Diane Arbus as a person so as to condemn her art[8] did not shape the way all critics interpreted Arbus's work, then it certainly shaped the way that the photographer's estate responded to critics seeking to write about her photographs. Some 40 years later, Arthur Lubow's biography of Arbus, although praiseful of her photography, consigns Arbus to the role of madwoman – a nymphomaniac whose photographic works, suggests Lubow, cannot be fully differentiated from her sex life.[9] After Arbus committed suicide in 1971, her photographic work came to her eldest daughter, Doon Arbus, who was fiercely protective of her mother's work. In response to Sontag's denigrating treatment of Arbus's iconoclastic work, Doon began to very tightly control, and in general to refuse, permission for critics writing about Arbus's work to reprint her photographs.[10]

Sontag's argument in "America, Seen Through Photographs, Darkly" was that Diane Arbus took the expansive premise of Walt Whitman's joy in all aspects of American life and turned his democratic pleasure to a cruel circus of those whom Sontag deems the fringe.[11] Uncannily, Sontag's essay pivots on striking and insightful quotes from Arbus, as if Sontag were surreptitiously undercutting her own argument by allowing the condemned to speak: even as Sontag argues that we should not consider Arbus's photography as one of the most powerful bodies of work produced in the twentieth century, by quoting Arbus Sontag reveals just how very brilliant is her adversary.[12] These quotes, regarding "the flaw" and the risk that photography reveals and entails, pull us toward, rather than pushing us away from, Arbus's work.[13] Even the essay's title suggests the distinctly visionary aspects of Arbus's best work. Echoing Saint Paul and the Epistles,[14] the title suggests that Arbus's photographs show us the mortal world, the dark glass. And that is exactly what her work strives to do: to show us the risks, the beauty, the danger, and the astonishment of being human. Whereas I do interpret Sontag's essay as being an expression of lateral violence – that is, a woman attempting to silence the power and brilliance of another woman – it also has a subterranean and fascinating sense of convergence as Sontag repeatedly describes just how different Arbus is from her pictorialist and documentary predecessors. In trying to bury Arbus, Sontag gives us the essence of her genius: that she is entirely original, that her work is dark and uncompromisingly honest, that she indeed risked her social self to get that work done, and that her vision of mid-twentieth-century America as an unjust place is deeply accurate.

But revealing mid-twentieth-century America as a place of surreal contradictions and evasions and a place where the social norm condones and hides racism and sexism, not to mention the Cold War, is not necessarily a feminist aesthetic. What Arbus's photographs do is create a condition of stare – the camera's stare and also the stare of the photographic subject looking back and returning the gaze. This condition – *pace* Sontag – empowers Arbus's photographic subjects, who seem to stare straight into our souls. Her photographs of women are particularly adept at pulling away the mask of the cultural feminine, that historical accretion, and showing the thinking and suffering subject beneath. I will focus, then, on Arbus's photographs of feminine subjects.

Young Brooklyn Mother

Arbus's 1966 photograph *A young Brooklyn family going for a Sunday outing, N.Y.C.* (Figure 4.1) showcases her ability to reveal the pain of the misrecognition of the feminine position. By feminine position, I refer to bell hooks's definition of the feminine, discussed in my introduction, as the position of someone who is facing,

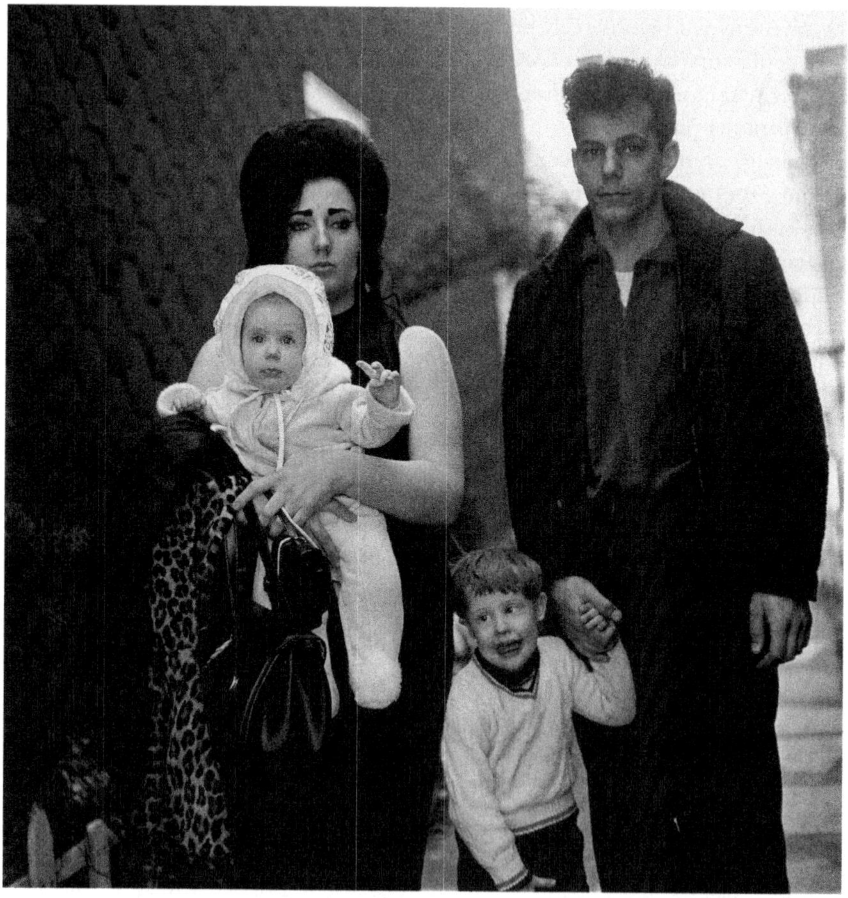

FIGURE 4.1 Diane Arbus, *A young Brooklyn family going for a Sunday outing, N.Y.C.*, 1966, gelatin silver print, 50.2 × 40.6 cm. © 1970 The Estate of Diane Arbus. Yale University Art Gallery, Stephen Carlton Clark, B.A. 1903, Fund and Henry S.F. Cooper, B.A. 1956, Contemporary Print Fund.

or has faced, masculinist oppression in the specific sense of being socially placed outside structures of masculine power. *A young Brooklyn family going for a Sunday outing, N.Y.C.* shows a young couple, apparently of European descent and in their early twenties, with a very young male child and an infant who seems to be dressed as a girl (and who in fact was the couple's daughter).[15] The young man's eyes suggest that he is not excited by the event of being photographed but is tolerating the situation. The young woman, by contrast, appears excited to be photographed, and she is very heavily made up, with fantastically overdarkened eyebrows. She carries herself in an approximation of a fashion model's stance. As an accoutrement, she carries not an expensive cloche but a baby girl, and beside her the son, to whom she gave birth when she was a teenager, stands barely controlled by his father.[16] From Arbus's notes, we learn that the little boy is cognitively disabled and that the very young mother believes she looks like Elizabeth Taylor.[17]

The photograph acts as a metaphor, a word Arbus used to describe why certain photographic subjects attracted her: people who appeared to Arbus to be walking metaphors.[18] The young parents caught by fate – caught by the fate of giving birth to a developmentally challenged child, caught by the fate of being very young when they became parents, caught by the fate of not being wealthy – stand as a metaphor for the trump of time. But Arbus also saw the young family as representing the essentially "creepy" quality of every family.[19] What she means here is somewhat enigmatic, but it could in part refer to the suppressions and repressions of mid-twentieth-century American family life. That is, in this realm that capitalism defined as "safe" and "private," economic systems hold women in oppressed positions and whiteness is reified through the destructive myth of the proper family that, in mid-twentieth-century America, by definition excluded nonwhite people.[20] Arbus's image exposes the fallacy of this construct.

Photography has the capacity to show what Arbus calls "the flaw," referring to the difference between the way a person thinks he appears and the way he really appears. Part of the power of *A young Brooklyn family going for a Sunday outing, N.Y.C.* inheres in the tender and tragic way that it shows the flaw of the young mother.[21] She poses herself in the belief that she is a dead ringer for Elizabeth Taylor, and yet what we see in the photograph is a young woman struggling against circumstances that have nothing in common with the movie star's lifelong fame and wealth. The family becomes a metaphor for mid-twentieth-century American nuclear families who aspire to somehow have a photographic life like movie stars – in this, the image uncannily predicts the Facebook culture in which we all now live our lives photographically – while being caught in circumstances that bind them economically and temporally. Arbus's photograph reveals a cruel pressure on the young woman to define herself as a beauty (like Elizabeth Taylor). Sontag may say that Arbus's photography is cruel, but I would counter that Arbus's work reveals subtle yet forceful social patterns of cruelty, such as the pressure on women to define themselves by their sexual allure. *A young Brooklyn family going for a Sunday outing, N.Y.C.* is not cruel: it reveals the cruelty of a culture that enforces the idea that beauty and sexual desirability are the trope of femininity. The mother in the young Brooklyn family can aspire only to look like Elizabeth Taylor – Taylor herself a product of manufactured feminine sexual allure. Other forms of personal success (such as professional accomplishment) are beyond her socially sanctioned purlieu.

A young Brooklyn family going for a Sunday outing, N.Y.C. shows the young mother's plight and also the existential scope of the family's position (Figure 4.1). Here Arbus also recognizes, I think, a photographic reality – what Roland Barthes calls the "family stock" aspect of photography – the way that photographs reveal the uncanny structural similarities between family members' faces that we do not usually notice face to face.[22] "Family," with its promise of generations and inheritance as counterweight to death and finite individuality, exemplifies the mortal and temporal bonds that contain all human beings. The poignancy of the family, then, is held in this temporal frame. For this reason I suggest that Arbus's photographs of various families (and in particular the family discussed here) – taken between 1956 and 1971 – superlatively showcase Barthes's argument that the photograph is a visual manifestation of the idea of time. The metaphor that Arbus seeks is the place where having human dreams intersects with coming to terms with what one actually *has*. (One does not actually look like Elizabeth Taylor, for example, and even if one did, this appearance would not bring one Taylor's wealth.) Sontag, among others, accused Arbus of prurient and cruel interest in the "freaks" whom she photographed: the word "freaks" here is Sontag's word; as for Diane Arbus, she did not refer to her photographic subjects by that word, with the exception of those who were active performers in carnivals that at the time went under the rubric of freak shows.[23] Arbus's work may not be conventionally pretty, but I see the photographs as stares that map out the intents of fate. Her work rejects the pictorialist and some earlier documentary traditions that might obscure the contours of individual fate in an effort to suggest a common family of man; instead, Arbus shows how the common denominator of being human is the singular relationship each of us has to fate. Barthes calls photographs "clocks for seeing,"[24] and Arbus's portraits carry this weight of time without striving to symbolically represent it. It is always evening at noontime in her photographs.

Uncanny doubles and debutantes

Diane Arbus's photographs take us away from what is safe, but they do so not by showing graphic violence or (not usually) sex but rather by showing the most ordinary aspects of twentieth-century American life and by pulling back the mask of custom to reveal the strangeness beneath. Sontag complains that, in addition to photographs of people whom Sontag calls "freaks," the majority of Arbus's photographs show so-called normal people as freakish.[25] This is Arbus's melancholy genius, to look impassively and dispassionately and with grace at people from whom we routinely look away, or at whom we look with horror. For example, consider her photographs *A Jewish giant at home with his parents in the Bronx, N.Y.* (1970) and *Russian midget friends in a living room on 100th Street, N.Y.C.* (1963). Arbus also shows just how uncanny is the structure of mid-twentieth-century American culture and what it considers normal. Her photography of people outside of what is considered normal has absolute overlap with her photographs of the putative parameters of the normal. This overlap is absolute precisely because her work seeks to unmask and to show the strangeness *within* what society condones and upholds as a desirable norm and, in parallel, to show the grace and humanity of those whom society seeks to expel from its gaze. By photographing people on the fringes of society with this dispassionate and respectful articulation of vision, Arbus questions, subverts, and effectively overturns social hierarchy, including that of gender.

Doubles

Her photograph *Identical twins, Roselle, N.J.* (1967) (Figure 4.2) uses Arbus's trademark square format, a frame that accentuates the impassive gaze by making literal an articulation of ratio and objectivity. Likewise, Arbus's black borders – indicating that she did not crop her images but framed them in her mind, her eye, and, of course,

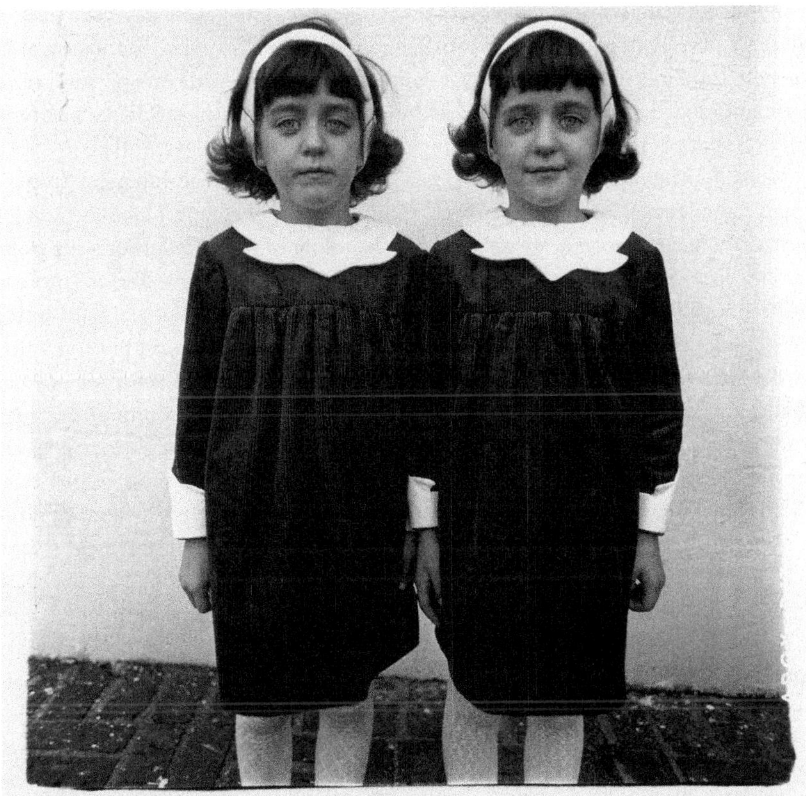

FIGURE 4.2 Diane Arbus, *Identical twins, Roselle, N.J.*, 1967, gelatin silver print, 50.2 × 40.6 cm. © 1970 The Estate of Diane Arbus. Yale University Art Gallery, Stephen Carlton Clark, B.A. 1903, Fund and Henry S.F. Cooper, B.A. 1956, Contemporary Print Fund.

her camera as she made the shot – make visual manifestation of her code of honesty. The black border authenticates that what we see in the image is what was there. Of course, it also articulates the frame, and the frame in turn indicates that what the photographer chose to show us is what we see.

The twins – Cathleen and Colleen, members of a twin club, in Roselle, New Jersey – are dressed identically, as was the custom for identical twin girls in mid-twentieth-century America. The disturbing connotation of marketing the cuteness of twin daughters extends to a popular advertisement for Doublemint chewing gum. Beginning in 1956, the Wrigley company used young women twins to advertise the product: "double your pleasure" was the tag line. When Arbus took her photograph of the little girl twins in Roselle, the reigning Doublemint twins were Terrie and Jennie Frankel, pretty young girls who dressed identically in the commercials and whose images thus "doubled the pleasure" of the consumer. Arbus's twins photograph, then, can be understood as an avant-garde critique of the force of sexism that associates all female bodies with possible sexual pleasure, as implied by the Wrigley advertising campaign for Doublemint. The voyeuristic gaze of sexually desiring girl twins is obvious: in imagining sex with twins, one is imagining precisely the objectified body, not a sustained relationship with one person but the automatic rejection of the other's personhood. The marketing of pretty girl twins, then, was part of the sexist oppression of the era in which Arbus worked.

Identical twins, Roselle, N.J. (1967) counterpunches the commercial trope of sexualized identical girl twins. Arbus's twins are prepubescent, but that does not necessarily mean that they are asexual. Her handling of the girls subverts the popular sexualization of identical girl twins. Her twins, as Stanley Kubrick's homage to the photograph indicates, are not there for our titillation, but they are instead frightening, uncanny. The twins' father reportedly disliked Arbus's photograph of his daughters, and Arbus's intention, I suggest, is to evoke this sense of unease.[26] That is, she wants us to think critically about the pleasure of consuming the image of the female body – *double your pleasure*. Instead of doubling our (sexual) pleasure, her photograph atomizes it, thus causing us to rethink the cuteness of girl twins. The little girls are dressed identically and yet their facial expressions are opposite, as if one were a bad twin and one were a good twin. The oppositeness is subtle enough that the photograph does not become comical in its posing of antitheses, but instead it lays bare the ideology of the cute little girl as consumable object by showing the girls as individuals with disparate personalities. Some critics have argued that the photograph is all about identity and the concept of self, and that it questions how identity matches biology, suggesting strongly that identity does not tally to biology.[27] But I think the photograph goes beyond querying the metaphysical concept of the self and instead interrogates social structures of domination and how these structures create the self.

Arbus photographs the twins against a rough wall with a few paint chips at their feet, and this ordinary, slightly down-at-the-heels suburban setting with its absolutely spare and unvarnished look also acts to critique the fantasy of cute girl twins. Arbus's twins are shown without the pretty trappings of a commercial setting, their apparently homemade clothes are not terribly expensive (as Arbus, a former fashion photography shot designer, would have known well), and their setting is mundane and decidedly middle class.[28] The photograph offers no fantasy and no dream of sexual availability or capitalist allure. Instead, it is anti-fantasy. The twins stand as markers of the still somehow lurking uncanniness of the self and the body, the fact that one's embodied experience is always at a remove from one's perception. Arbus's photographs reveal a certain bodily strangeness – an estrangement – as her subjects pose for our consideration. The twins are minutely observed; they stare at us, and their stare reflects that the photographer who captures their likeness does not seek to make them look pretty, sweet, or alluring. Instead, she shows them as they fearfully are, or as we all fearfully are, mortal and not made for commercial use. Even though the twins' father did not like the photograph and even if the twins themselves did not like the photograph, the image does feminist work because it so radically deconstructs tropes of sexist oppression that accrue around ways of seeing girls.

The argument that cruelty is what we see in Diane Arbus's photographs is a deeply gendering way of reading her work.[29] By accepting gendered expectations that women are empathic and loving, we come to see a woman who produces photographs that are sharp, intense, cold, and disturbing as a bad woman (or, in the biographies of Arbus written by Patricia Bosworth and Arthur Lubow, a mentally ill woman).[30] In *Identical twins, Roselle, N.J.*, the twins do not appear to be shamed, humiliated, or offered as sexual aperitif; instead, they appear frightening and even spectral. Compared to the portrait work of Arbus's precursor in documentary photography, Walker Evans, her portraits leave no space for pity; they draw forward the stare between photographic subject and viewing audience so that we almost fear the people staring at us through her square, black-bordered frames. We do not fear them because they represent fringe identities but because Arbus's photographs create a feeling of uncanny permeability, transmissibility, and questioning of the boundaries of the self. That is, the photographs return and represent ourselves – our mortality and our stares.[31]

Debutante of the year

To photograph *Brenda Duff Frazier, 1938 Debutante of the Year, at home, Boston, Mass.* (1966), Arbus sought out the former debutante and socialite after Frazier had struggled for years with anorexia, bulimia, alcoholism, and addictions to pills (Figure 4.3). The former great beauty was living as something of a recluse. Arbus was working for *Esquire* when she took the photograph, but it is quintessential Arbus. One could argue the image is cruel in that it presents Frazier wearing, as she did at her debut, white makeup with heavily kohled eyes and lipsticked lips. Given the hard years between her debut at age 17 and when Arbus photographed her at age 45, Frazier looks notably cadaverous and derelict. Clearly, the photograph contrasts the dilapidated middle-age Frazier with her youthful beauty. (As a debutante, Frazier was frequently photographed, and hence, Arbus's image participates in an implicit series of

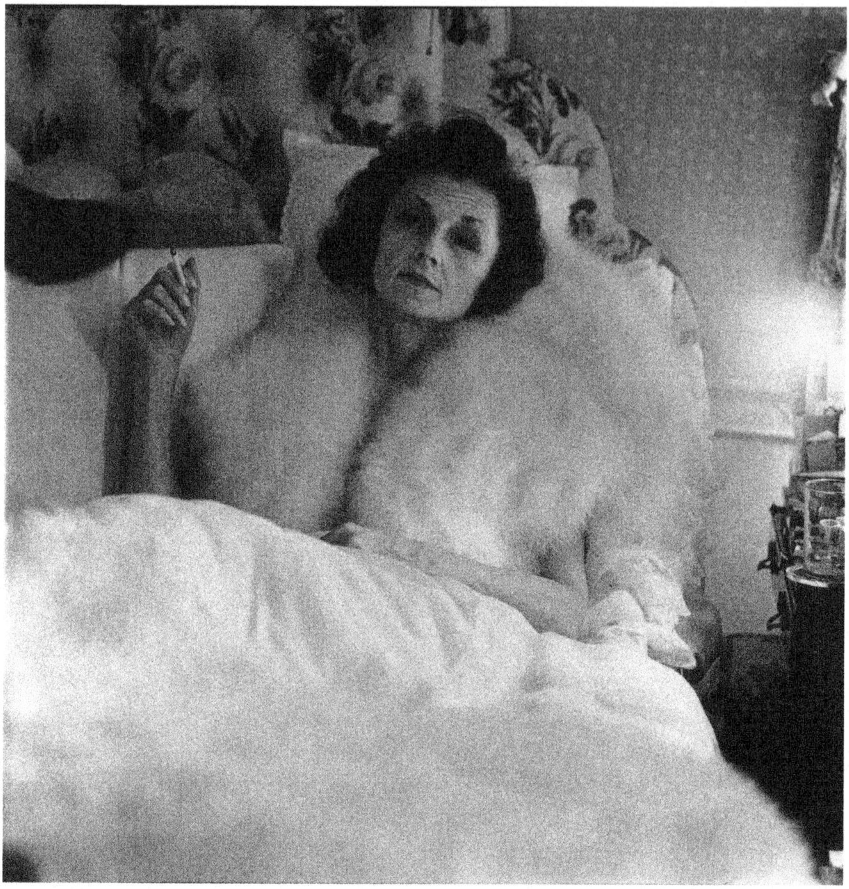

FIGURE 4.3 Diane Arbus, *Brenda Duff Frazier, 1938 Debutante of the Year, at home, Boston, Mass.*, 1966, gelatin silver print, 36.5 × 37.1 cm. © 1970 The Estate of Diane Arbus.

images of Frazier.) In Arbus's photograph, Frazier is still trying to look beautiful: her face is made up, she is wearing fur or faux fur, and she is surrounded by roses. Off to the side of the bed on which Frazier reclines, one sees many bottles of pills. The photograph's power inheres in its showing the flaw that is the gap between Frazier's circumstances – she is prematurely aged and looks deathly – and her self-image, her belief that somehow she is still able to appear as a stunning young woman, as long as she wears makeup and keeps her weight down. But it is precisely the makeup and the emaciation that make her look prematurely aged. Is there cruelty in Arbus's revelation of this gap between self-image and the camera's acute stare?[32]

The photograph, *Brenda Duff Frazier, 1938 Debutante of the Year, at home, Boston, Mass.* (1966), is not kind in the commonplace sense of the word: the photograph reveals her age, her misery, her ill health, and her delusion that there is value in trying to feign youthful beauty as opposed to just being a healthy middle-aged woman who looks middle aged. Arbus understood that the camera sees with a different eye and finds a different nature than we do when we look with our own eyes. (There is indeed a striking similarity between Walter Benjamin's argument in *A Short History of Photography* that "it is a different nature that the camera sees" and Diane Arbus's statement that "it hurts just a little to be photographed . . . because we are kinder to each other than the camera is.")[33] The photograph of Brenda Frazier sees a different nature; that is, it does not attempt to meld the surface cues of the woman's image – the makeup, the flowered background, the fur – and come up with the notion of style and class. On the contrary, Arbus deconstructs the punitive strictures of femininity in this photograph. Frazier as the quintessential beauty, the debutante of the year – that is, the girl considered most desirable – stands as a metaphor for the trap of traditional femininity.

Arbus's photograph makes visually manifest the idea that some forms of "feminine" behavior are deathly to the woman who tries to follow them: only because most of us do not starve ourselves to stay thin, and do not keep trying to look exactly as we did at age 17, and do not try to remain a pretty young thing but instead give up or refuse, do we thereby live. Frazier is shown as a woman who never refused to perform traditional femininity in every way. She appears fragile, passive, made-up, and tragic because her very adherence to the social code of the feminine has killed her. Arbus's revelation of this death, I argue, uses Frazier to tell us that the social desirability of being the perfect woman is a mask for the pressure to be a dead woman. In this image-message, Arbus is deeply ethical. Arbus arguably understood this pressure from the inside: she rebelled against her early role of loving wife and devoted mother, and she hailed from a social class not entirely unlike Frazier's. Arbus began taking photographs in the late 1950s, and by the time of her death by suicide in 1971, she had both refused certain traditionally feminine parameters (of mid-twentieth-century America) and convinced herself, somehow, that her own death was warranted as if in exchange for this radical departure from traditional femininity. In this sense, I would argue that Arbus, in taking this photograph of the former debutante of the year, is not so much cruel to Frazier as drawn to her. Arbus is drawn to see and show in order to deconstruct and ultimately dismantle the gendered oppression and sexism that clearly destroyed the 1938 Debutante of the Year and, maybe, also Diane Arbus.

Vivian Maier

Enigmatic Vivian Maier shares with Diane Arbus a general time period of photographic production: Maier's best photographs were taken in the mid-twentieth century and Arbus's were in the 1960s. They both photographed in urban America and could be called American photographers – even though Maier, born in New York City to European parents, spent much of her childhood in France. For Maier and Arbus, fame could properly be described as a posthumous phenomenon, and they both had an apparent allegiance to documentary photography. But unlike Diane Arbus, who received prestigious fellowships and had major gallery exhibitions during her lifetime, Vivian Maier was entirely unknown while she was alive. She earned her living as a nanny, taking photographs while caring for her charges and during her days off. The nature of Maier's drive to take photographs is somewhat obscure: she filled a terrifyingly large number of film rolls, printed very few images, and preserved her work in a storage facility even when in old age she became so impoverished that she had no money for a place to live. Her devotion to photography was a very private worship and one she zealously maintained.[34] A former employer recalled Maier filling her living quarters with so many photographic supplies that the floor began to buckle.

Maier, then, appears to be a woman dedicated exclusively to the moment when the camera frames the photograph, the moment when the image is articulated as image in the camera, rather than as printed object. She appears to have had little desire to place her photographs where others would see them, much less to try to gain a reputation as an established artist. In the 1950s, photography was not routinely considered a fine art, although it always had its champions. Maier may have simply loved the camera for what it could do in creating images in the viewfinder frame and may not have considered what the photographs she took could do for her professionally. Her story – or rather the story of her work – is chilling and inspiring. In the early twenty-first century, Chicago real estate developer John Maloof apparently accidentally purchased a box of Maier's photographic negatives, drawn from a storage facility in which she had kept her photography equipment and photographs and for which she had been unable to pay the rent.[35] In 2009, Maloof, who had no background in photography or the fine arts, began scanning her work and posting the images online; the photographs, thus digitally circulated, began attracting attention.

Here, the position of Maier is one of passivity: she comes to us as a woman always already dead, in the sense that the actions of others manufactured her fame, her reputation, her "career" – as opposed to the photographs she took. And as it happens, those others are male. That does not mean that we cannot experience and interpret the photographs as images that Maier created – that is, that her gaze instigated and that her camera captured – but the men who bought her photographs from the abandoned storage unit created Maier as a public phenomenon when she was unknown and unable to say or do anything about it or to be any part of it. None of the purchasers of her photographs ever met Maier, who died in 2009, several months after suffering a serious head trauma. She was apparently still alive when Maloof first started circulating her photographs online, but Maier, severely injured and indigent, would have died unaware that her photographs had been discovered. This passivity I link to her large number of images to suggest a kind of contained, even stymied, power that reflects her social position as a woman who was never the beneficiary of forms of social power such as being male, wealthy, or even middle class. The story of the way Maier's photographs became known is not the same as the story of the photographs, as such, and yet it is also not entirely separate. History entwines her reception with the social position that she occupied, which in turn informs and produces the images she created.

It is crucial to understand Vivian Maier's photographic work, her life, and how her work came to the public in the context of capitalism and class-based oppression in mid-twentieth-century America. Capitalism is imbricated with gendered terms of domination, and in many ways Vivian Maier's fate exemplifies the effect of those interlocking modes of domination. Born to a working-class, emigrant mother, Maier's social class and her access to structures of power in America differed from Diane Arbus's. The fact that Maier worked her entire adult life as a nanny[36] means that she, a working-class woman, provided a very gendered form of labor for wealthy people. Women hired to care for other women's children, to live in the home of their employer, and to therefore be available to fulfill the needs and demands of the employer nearly all the time exemplify the ways that capitalism and sexist oppression interlock. A nanny is paid to give nurture, traditionally a feminine role. There could, theoretically, be nannies who enjoy giving this care, and there could, theoretically, be families who are kind and generous to the women they employ for childcare (of course, live-in childcare providers could be male, but they very rarely are), but the structure of economic domination is absolutely in place in the relationship between a family that hires a nanny and the nanny.

Folded into the terms of economic domination are gendered expectations that deepen class-based domination, for a nanny is expected to perform femininity of a very traditional and, I would argue, restrictive kind.[37] The good nanny is expected to be warm and loving, to be giving and nurturing, and to give up her life and her desires for the sake of her charges. These are all traditional gendered expectations of good mothers. But, unlike the good mother, the good nanny is also required to leave once the children reach adolescence, reaping very little, if any, of the long-term expectation that the children for whom she has cared will in turn respect and care for her in old age. The nanny, then, is positioned in the wealthy home as a woman who provides womanliness on demand and then disappears when no longer needed.

Maier, as her former charges report, was not always the ideal nanny. She seems to have had a sharp temper and seems to have sometimes made choices that allowed her to take photographs at the expense of the happiness and safety of the children in her care.[38] It is only because Maier rebelled (in what must have been rather small ways, because she generally maintained employment) against gendered and class pressures to give up her desires and individuality to fit the class-based and gender-based mold of the "good" nanny that she produced her photographic oeuvre. Without this rebellion, there would be no "Vivian Maier"; that is, her apparent imperfections as a nanny – her unwillingness to behave as a docile servant – allowed her the psychic and temporal space to create her oeuvre.

Invisibility and its contents

As a nanny with young children, Maier had a kind of public invisibility. She apparently kept her camera with her while taking care of others' children, and she often sought out the fringes of the cities (Chicago and New York City) in which she worked, apparently seeking material to photograph. Her invisibility gave her many opportunities to snap the photographs that were her quest as a street photographer, using at times a Rolleiflex viewfinder camera. Maier's work is astonishingly repetitive: she took such a large number of shots (nearly 100,000 negatives and slides were found with her belongings in storage, and Maloof owns only some of them). Yet her work is also singular in that she rarely took photographs of the same scene or the same person twice. The physical reality of how Maier's work was preserved – in negatives and in slides, with only about 3 percent of her body of work printed during her lifetime – chimes with this theme of near invisibility. What are the "photographs" that Vivian Maier created? Most of them are nearly disembodied negatives that men who found her body of work printed and circulated after her death.[39]

And yet, within this social and material near invisibility, Maier strove to see and to create moments of vision. With her Rolleiflex, she worked very quickly, in street photographer mode, snapping shots when she saw a scene or person that drew her in. Unlike Arbus's work, Maier's photographs do not generally constitute studies in personality. Instead, they are interesting structurally, articulating similarity and structural resemblances between unlike things or people. One such image is the photograph that Maier took on September 26, 1959, in New York City. It shows a baby held by its grandfather after a visit to the zoo, with the balloon the baby was given at the zoo floating up so as to exactly obscure the old man's face.[40] Another is the photograph she took in 1955 (possibly in Chicago) showing an elaborately curving playground slide with children climbing up and going down as if in synchronized choreography. Maier's ability to see structural intersections and immediately snap the shot was certainly extraordinary, but the aspect of her work that I want to consider is its revelation of the dispossessed, those at the edge or outside the edge of class and race structures of power and domination. Maier's gift is not for depth of study but for showing, quickly and often painfully, the surface of lives as they are cast in their fated shapes of domination and resistance.

The photographs of the grandfather, the baby, and the balloon and of the slide and the children obliquely evoke revelations of class-based oppression. The former is also a photograph about race: the grandfather and infant are African American, and the photograph implies that people who are part of this (in 1959) oppressed and dominated group are effaced by their social position. Hence, the balloon effacing the grandfather's face conveys more than just a visual pun. Similarly and differently, the tall, curling slide with children climbing up and sliding down stands as a metaphor for the uncanny coil of Cold War triumphalism, space-age sleekness pitted against the children's vulnerable bodies. There is a coolness to Maier's photographic gaze. She has an ability to see social forms as they are expressed in moments of structural synchronicity and in a refusal to get to know the individuality of the subject. Instead, her work is deeply sociological, following the nearly contemporary dictum of sociologist C. Wright Mills that each individual is created by his or her social circumstances and has relatively little capacity to alter the fate that is productive of the self. Mills argues against the fallacy that we have complete or even considerable control over our own fates, arguing instead that most of what we experience in our lives derives from the social circumstances into which we were born and in which we often remain. (A prime example of this would be the experience of racism, or of class- or gender-based domination.) Writes Mills:

> The individual can understand his own fate only by locating himself within his historical period. . . . He can know his own chances in life only by becoming aware of those of all individuals in his circumstances. It is a magnificent and terrible lesson.[41]

Whereas that might not sound like feminism, Maier's photographs are feminist in that, often with startling clarity and sangfroid, they present the cruelty of circumstances into which people afflicted by racism or poverty find themselves cast. The first step of revolution is to see injustice. Maier's photographs of African American children are especially insightful and poignant.

The 1950 photograph of two very young African American boys, one wearing a Mickey Mouse hat, is a case in point. The black-and-white photograph shows the boys turning to face Maier as she wields her viewfinder camera. The image is interactive in the old-fashioned sense of the word: we see the boys interacting with Maier as she works her camera. We see the boys seeing Maier see them. In particular, the younger child regards Maier and her camera. He turns toward her with an expression that epitomizes innocence: his gaze is not studied, not practiced, and not conditioned to being a photographic subject. Instead, he regards the woman (who may have bent down to have her camera level with her subject) with hope and possibly with the expectation that she photographs him because of his hat, of which he is proud in the way that little children often are proud of talismanic objects through which they build a sense of self.[42] Maier's photograph does not make fun of the boys; it does not belittle them. Instead, the image can be interpreted as revealing structures of racism, in that it contrasts the younger child's complete innocence of regard with the slightly older child's already somewhat skeptical or mistrusting glance. The older child is already a little aware of how racism functions through the gaze and of the risks of being seen, and yet he still smiles, just a little, at Maier. In this contrast between the boys inheres the power of the photograph. Maier's position as a nanny is also interesting in the context of this photograph: here she photographs children who probably do not have a nanny to care for them, and she photographs them with a tenderness that possibly she did not always extend to the wealthy white children for whom she was paid money to care.[43]

Maier's 1954 photograph of an older African American boy riding a horse under elevated train tracks in New York (Figure 4.4) is a beautiful, structurally balanced "snapshot." It provides no explanation as to why he is riding the horse in this urban setting – he may work for a business that gives tourists rides in horse-drawn carts through part of the city – but he rides it so gracefully and with such dignity that he could have been cast in bronze. The solitary boy and horse against a mundane urban background and beneath the heavy weight of the train tracks that curtail and cut off the boy's horizon create a scene both strange and tragic. The photograph

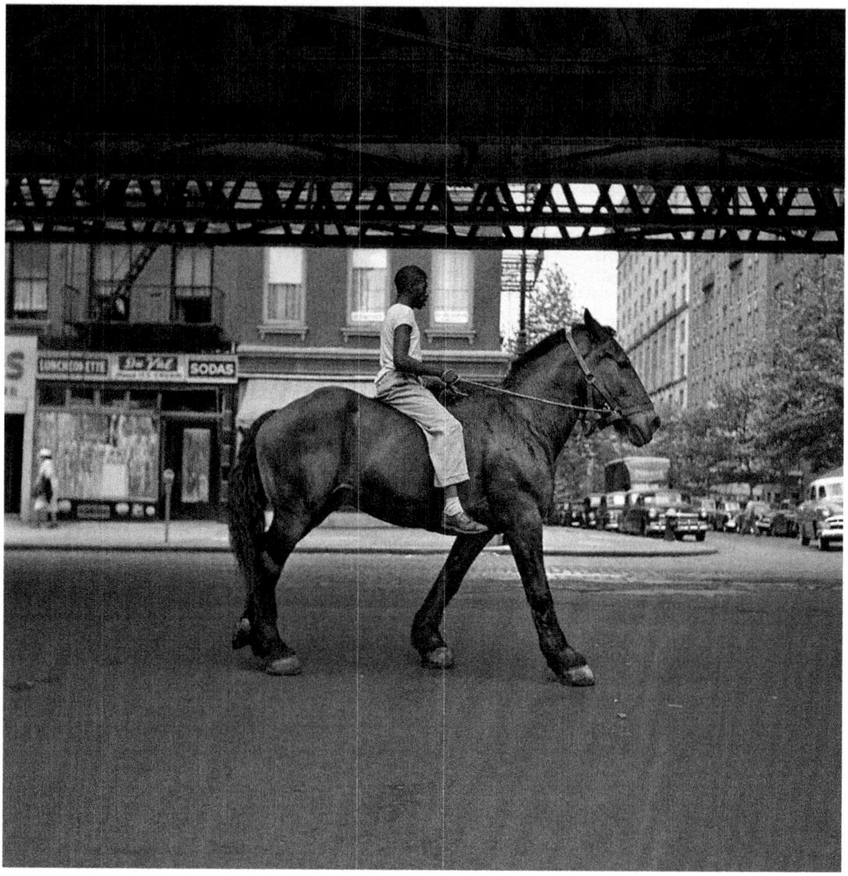

FIGURE 4.4 Vivian Maier, *Untitled*, (New York, NY, August 11, 1954), printed later, gelatin silver print, 12 × 12 inches (image size), 12 × 16 inches (paper size). ©Vivian Maier/Maloof Collection, Courtesy Howard Greenberg Gallery, New York.

almost suggests that if the boy could really ride away – ride out of the frame of the urban landscape into which he was born – he could transcend the terms of racism that deeply informed the experience of African Americans in the United States in the 1950s.

If I am arguing that Vivian Maier's work is feminist, why am I focusing on her representations of race and not focusing on how she represents women? As I have said in a previous chapter, the feminist movement is not, in essence, about sex or even about gender but about structures of power, domination, and oppression, including racism, and how they form and are formed by the gaze. Maier, caught in the economics of serving others by performing traditionally feminine labor for money, turns her photographic gaze on manifestations of social structures of oppression in photographs that are deeply responsive to the vagaries of what we might call "fate" and how it affects human beings. When I use the phrase "what we might call 'fate,'" I do not mean that which the stars decree but instead what French philosopher Michel Foucault called "subjectivation," that is, the way social structures of power form the subject.[44] Foucault was well aware of the difficulty, sometimes bordering on impossibility, of transcending the terms by which social spirals of power form what we think of as ourselves.[45] And yet Foucault also argued that in each person there is that space and capacity to know and hence to be something outside of these structures of domination and dispossession. Maier's photography seeks toward the pleasure of seeing as it sees through structures of dispossession and gains possession of vision at the edge of the agentic self. In this sense, the fate of her photographs exemplifies the philosophy of art through which she produced them: she saw what she saw; she framed it as image, as aesthetic space; and then she moved on to create the next image, always privileging her ability to see over the social act of telling others what she saw.

Notes

1 Laura Mulvey, "Visual Pleasure and Narrative Cinema," *Screen* 16, no. 3 (Autumn 1975): 6–18.
2 Arthur Lubow, *Diane Arbus: Portrait of a Photographer* (New York: Ecco, 2016).
3 Mulvey's essay, "Visual Pleasure and Narrative Cinema," may be the ground zero of this concept of the male gaze, but it gets plenty of play in the work of Tania Modleski and Mary Ann Doane and also in the *Killing Us Softly* films. See also Tania Modleski, *The Women Who Knew Too Much: Hitchcock and Feminist Theory* (London: Routledge, 2005); Mary Ann Doane, *Femmes Fatales: Feminism, Film Theory, Psychoanalysis* (London: Routledge, 1991). See also the films of Margaret Lazarus, Renner Wunderlich, Patricia Stallone, and Joseph Vitagliano, *Killing Us Softly: Advertising's Image of Women* (1979) and *Killing Us Softly IV* (2010). See also Terri D. Conley and Laura R. Ramsey, "Killing Us Softly? Investigating Portrayals of Women and Men in Contemporary Magazine Advertisements," *Psychology of Women Quarterly* 35, no. 3 (2011): 469–78.
4 Susan Sontag, "America, Seen through Photographs, Darkly," in *On Photography* (New York: Picador, 2001): 27–51.
5 Lubow, *Diane Arbus*.
6 As I discuss later in the chapter, Catherine Lord's essay, "What Becomes a Legend Most: The Short Sad Career of Diane Arbus," stands out for its welcome emphasis on Arbus's seriousness and determination and rigorous discipline as she navigated the work of fine art photographer and commercial photographer.
7 The argument that Arbus's photographs are feminist is contentious. To frame this debate, see Arthur Lubow, "How Diane Arbus Became 'Arbus,'" *New York Times*, May 26, 2016, and Catherine Lord, "What Becomes a Legend Most: The Short, Sad Career of Diane Arbus," in *The Contest of Meaning: Critical Histories of Photography*, ed. Richard Bolton (Cambridge, MA: MIT Press, 1992), 111–25.
8 Sontag, "America, Seen Through Photographs, Darkly."
9 Lubow's massive biography makes sincere and repeated attempts to contend with Arbus's photography. And yet, the biography discusses at length the supposed facts that Arbus had sex, as an adult, with her brother, and with many of her photographic subjects. Lubow's decision to include this material – which is necessarily conjectural, given that Arbus and her brother Howard Nemerov are deceased – emphasizes an inability to conceive of Arbus outside of the highly eroticized terms so often reserved for women in our culture. See Lubow, *Diane Arbus*.
10 Lord, "What Becomes a Legend Most," 115.
11 Sontag, "America, Seen through a Glass, Darkly."

12 Lisa A. Baird, "Susan Sontag and Diane Arbus: The Siamese Twins of Photographic Art," *Women's Studies* 37, no. 8 (2008): 971–86.
13 Sontag, *On Photography*, 41.
14 See 1 Cor. 13:12 (KJV).
15 Mary Warner Marien, ed., *Singular Images* (New York: Aperture, 2006): 67–76.
16 Jeanne Wolff Bernstein, "Unlocking Diane Arbus," *Studies in Gender and Sexuality* 8, no. 4 (2007): 334.
17 Donna Bassin, "Picturing Herself: On Diane Arbus's Revelations," *Studies in Gender and Sexuality* 8, no. 4 (2007): 337–9.
18 Fran Bartlkowski, "Stricken with Good Fortune," *Studies in Gender and Sexuality* 8, no. 4 (2007): 349–52.
19 Anthony W. Lee and John Pultz, *Diane Arbus: Family Albums* (New Haven, CT: Yale University Press, 2003).
20 Theorist and cultural critic Debra Walker King develops the theory of America as a conceptually "white nation" that defines itself as that which is not black in *African Americans and the Culture of Pain* (Charlottesville, VA: University of Virginia Press, 2008).
21 Wayne Koestenbaum, "Diane Arbus and Humiliation," *Studies in Gender and Sexuality* 8, no. 4 (2007): 345–7.
22 Roland Barthes, *Camera Lucida: Reflections on Photography* (New York: Macmillan, 1981), 105.
23 Here, it is essential to be aware of the historical reality that, in America, well into the twentieth century, there were carnival sideshows that were called "freak shows," so that this word was not a metaphor but rather a descriptive term in the same way that "Disney character" is now a recognizable descriptive term. For more in-depth discussion about Arbus's early work, please see Gregory Gibson, *Hubert's Freaks: The Rare-Book Dealer, the Times Square Talker, and the Lost Photos of Diane Arbus* (Orlando, FL: Harcourt, 2008).
24 Barthes, *Camera Lucida*, 11.
25 Robin Blyn, *Freak-Garde: Extraordinary Bodies and Revolutionary Art in America* (Minneapolis, MN: University of Minnesota Press, 2013).
26 David Segal, "Double Exposure: A Moment with Diane Arbus Created a Lasting Impression," *Washington Post*, May 12, 2005.
27 Frederick Gross, *Diane Arbus's 1960s: Auguries of Experience* (Minneapolis, MN: University of Minnesota Press, 2012).
28 Bernstein, "Unlocking Diane Arbus," 333–6.
29 Garry L Hagberg, ed., *Art and Ethical Criticism* (Hoboken, NJ: Wiley-Blackwell, 2010).
30 Patricia Bosworth, *Diane Arbus: A Biography* (New York: Norton, 1987); Lubow, *Diane Arbus*.
31 As Robin Blyn argues in *Freak-garde*, "These photographs are actively engaged in the intellectual and political ferment of the sixties, and particularly in the anxious efforts of leftist dissidents to generate a viable alternative to what they perceive as the repressed subject of liberal capitalism. . . . Biology in *Diane Arbus* is immanent to capitalism, yet it is endowed with the potential to liberate the subject from the repressive system. Biology, in the Deleuzian terms . . . is a virtual dimension of liberal capitalism" (152–4).
32 David Davies, "Susan Sontag, Diane Arbus, and the Ethical Dimensions of Photography," in *Art and Ethical Criticism*, ed. Garry L. Hagberg (Oxford, UK: Blackwell, 2008): 211–229.
33 Walter Benjamin, "A Short History of Photography," *Screen* 13, no. 1 (1972): 5–26.
34 Ben Merriman and Andrew Seeder, "Introduction: Vivian Maier," *Chicago Review* 57, nos. 3 and 4 (2013): 102–3.
35 Kerri MacDonald, "Digging Deeper into Vivian Maier's Past," *The New York Times*, January 12, 2016, http://lens.blogs.nytimes.com/2016/01/12/digging-deeper-into-vivian-maiers-past/?_r=0.
36 Richard Cahan and Michael Williams, *Vivian Maier: Out of the Shadows* (Chicago: City-files Books, 2012).
37 See Barbara Ehrenreich and Arlie Hochschild, eds., *Global Women: Nannies, Maids, and Sex Workers in the New Economy* (New York: Holt, 2004).

38 Vivian Maier, John Maloof, and Geoff Dyer, *Vivian Maier: Street Photographer* (Brooklyn: PowerHouse, 2011).

39 A series of men acquired, circulated, publicized, and sold Maier's photographs, and Maloof is the one who ended up with the majority of her work and the lion's share of the press. See MacDonald, "Digging Deeper into Vivian Maier's Past."

40 All of Vivian Maier's photographs are untitled in the sense that she did not title, publish, or display them during her lifetime. Others will only be able to establish a definitive *catalogue raisonné* after disputes regarding the rights to Maier's photographs are resolved.

41 C. Wright Mills, *The Sociological Imagination* (Oxford, UK: Oxford University Press, 2000), 5.

42 Maier used a Rolleiflex camera that allowed her to maintain eye contact with her subjects; even so, this child is so young that to bring her camera level with him she may have needed to kneel.

43 Inger Raymond, to whom Maier was nanny, has claimed that Maier was physically and psychologically abusive to her as a child, and other former charges have mentioned her quick temper. See Susanna Rustin, "Our Nanny, the Photographer Vivian Maier," *The Guardian*, July 19, 2014; see also Rose Lichter-Marck, "Vivian Maier and the Problem of Difficult Women," *The New Yorker*, May 9, 2014.

44 Echoes of C. Wright Mills' social theory of subject formation are present, if unexpected, in Foucault's theory of subjectivization. The difference is that Foucault, with greater debt to Romanticism, ultimately envisions a space of self that even by its negative cast is implicitly beyond the reach of social power.

45 On this notion of pleasure, see Michel Foucault, *Histoire de la sexualité*, vol. 2, *L'Usage des plaisirs* (Paris: Gallimard, 1984), 256.

5

AFTERIMAGES

Ana Mendieta and Francesca Woodman

Photographer Francesca Woodman and photographer and earthworks and body artist Ana Mendieta share the unhappy fate of being artists who did not get the chance to develop their work over the course of a long life; Woodman died at 22 and Mendieta at 36. And yet, Mendieta's photographic recording of her earthworks and body performances shapes a multimedia oeuvre of great significance, while Francesca Woodman's enigmatic photographs constitute one of the most fascinating bodies of photographic work produced in the later twentieth century.[1] The question of whether the early deaths of these artists set the stage for interest in their art after their deaths is complicated. The cultural allure of the woman who dies while young is deeply entrenched in the Western aesthetic, glamorized in the mid-nineteenth century and manifested in the late-twentieth-century popularity of the ultrathin, brink-of-death waif look.[2] In a troubling way, Mendieta and Woodman seem to gain artistic stature by dying horrible and early deaths, and yet these artists' photographic works also predict, exploit, and subvert our culture's desire for the sacrificial figure of the deathly, beautiful woman. For Woodman and Mendieta do not directly owe their current reputations as artists to their scandalous deaths. Instead, their art stages, confronts, rebuts, and overturns the valorization of the deathly, passive feminine, even as the terms of this cultural feminine haunt the reception of their work.

Born 10 years apart, Ana Mendieta (1948–1985) and Francesca Woodman (1958–1981) participated in very different ways in the feminist art of the 1970s. In the late 1970s, Mendieta was active in the A.I.R. gallery, an all-woman feminist collective in Manhattan. Her photographed earthworks and body works present a fusion of cultural feminist bodily representation with broader sculptural interest in earthworks. During this time, Woodman was a student at the Rhode Island School of Design (RISD) who expressed the feminist art zeitgeist by creating a large number of photographs of herself nude.[3] Both Mendieta and Woodman gesture obliquely but unmistakably to feminist performance art of the 1970s – art that laid claim to and celebrated woman's embodied experience.[4] Carolee Schneeman, Judy Chicago, and Miriam Schapiro emphasized in their work aspects of female embodiment that had hitherto been considered taboo, improper for fine art.[5] Mendieta and Woodman, then, are of the same era in American art even as their personal backgrounds are very different. Both focus a significant portion of their work on tracing, representing, and photographing the female body. Mendieta creates the temporally expansive *Silueta Series*, and Woodman creates an oeuvre of small black-and-white photographs, including the *House*, *Space*, *Space²*, and *Angels* series, several notable diazotypes, and her much larger masterwork, *Blueprint for a Temple*.[6]

Although Mendieta and Woodman emerge from the body-oriented feminist art movement of the 1970s, they diverge from artists such as Carolee Schneeman, Mary Beth Edelson and Hannah Wilke by creating works that formally (that is, through a skewing of form) trouble and swerve from the represented presence of the female body. They show that body as trace, echo, and blur, and they predict the feminism of the late twentieth century in that their depictions of the female body show its elusion. Mendieta's and Woodman's photographs, though, push far beyond the truisms of deconstructivist feminism. They engage the female body as a template for exploring the mark of time, mortality, citizenship, and ontology – that is, the meaning of being. They explore the embodiment of fate – gender as fate – in their photographic works. By invoking the term *fate*, I do not mean that Mendieta and Woodman were passive and helpless in their art. I mean that their art predicts and shows the limitations of poststructuralist feminist theory that postulates gender as a series of performative gestures. Pushing beyond notions of the performative, the two artists show gender as a form of haunting, a fate that catches or marks the subject despite and even against her own choices and will.[7] Their art does not advocate acceptance of this fate. Indeed, it is exactly in the depth and the power with which they show gender as fate that inheres their refusal of its terms. Fate is the circumstance that catches the subject unprepared; gender, as explored visually in Woodman's and Mendieta's work, surfaces as a force that catches the subject unprepared. Their work visually iterates the struggle and force of returning to substance, as the self is caught in the matrix of materiality. In visually evoking the tactile, haptic, and textural, their art stages extraordinary resistance to superficial theories of gender as performance and also to the bitterly entrenched ways that a woman becomes a woman because of how she is culturally seen. The violence of their work breaks apart received ways of seeing and opens new opportunities to comprehend not only gender but also exile, earth, space, mortality, and time.

Ana Mendieta's Invisible Photographs

Ana Mendieta was active until the mid-1980s.[8] I write about her photographic works because photographs and a not-insignificant collection of films are what is principally left of her oeuvre. That said, Mendieta is generally regarded as an earthworks and body artist.[9] Mendieta's career indeed shows an uncanny aspect of

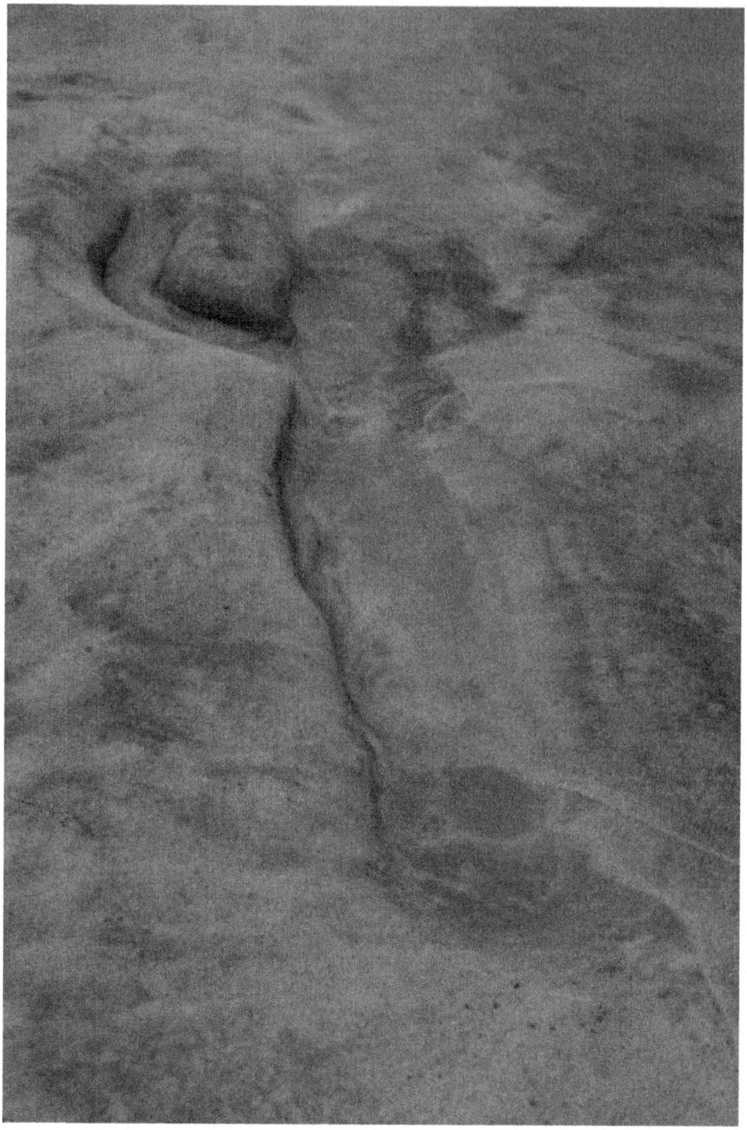

FIGURE 5.1 Ana Mendieta, *Untitled: Silueta Series*, 1976, earth/bodywork, Mexico, 35mm color slides. © The Estate of Ana Mendieta Collection, L.L.C., Courtesy Galerie Lelong, New York.

photography, its ability to consume and transpose different art forms. She produced hundreds of photographs, mainly slides, documenting and recording her earthworks performances, and I will focus on the ones from her *Silueta Series*.[10] While Mendieta was alive and producing her art, she considered her photographs to be documents of her earthworks and body works; even so, I suggest that her photographs are a

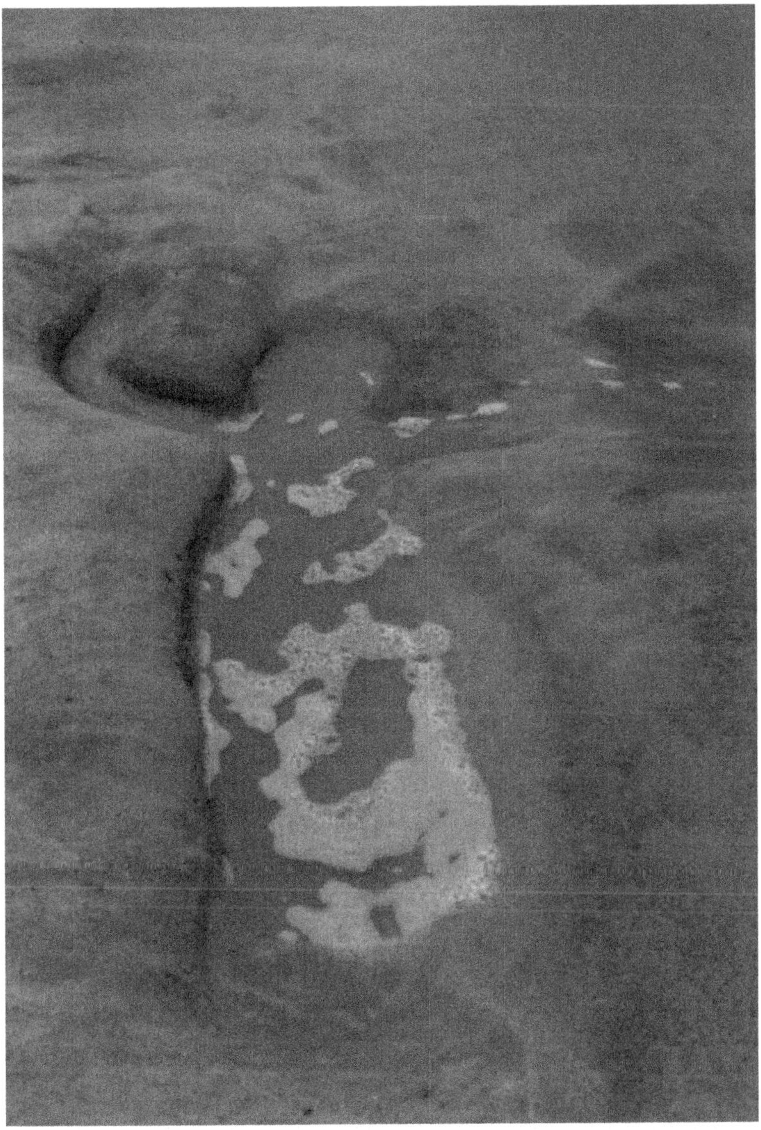

FIGURE 5.2 Ana Mendieta, *Untitled: Silueta Series*, 1976, earth/bodywork, Mexico, 35mm color slides. © The Estate of Ana Mendieta Collection, L.L.C., Courtesy Galerie Lelong, New York.

primary artistic legacy.[11] Roland Barthes's argument that we perceive the image rather than the photograph – "it is not it that we see" – is especially true of Ana Mendieta's body of work.[12] She continues to be widely interpreted as an earthworks and body artist even as her fame has ascended exponentially after her death, a fame that largely rests on the photographic images she created. A respected artist

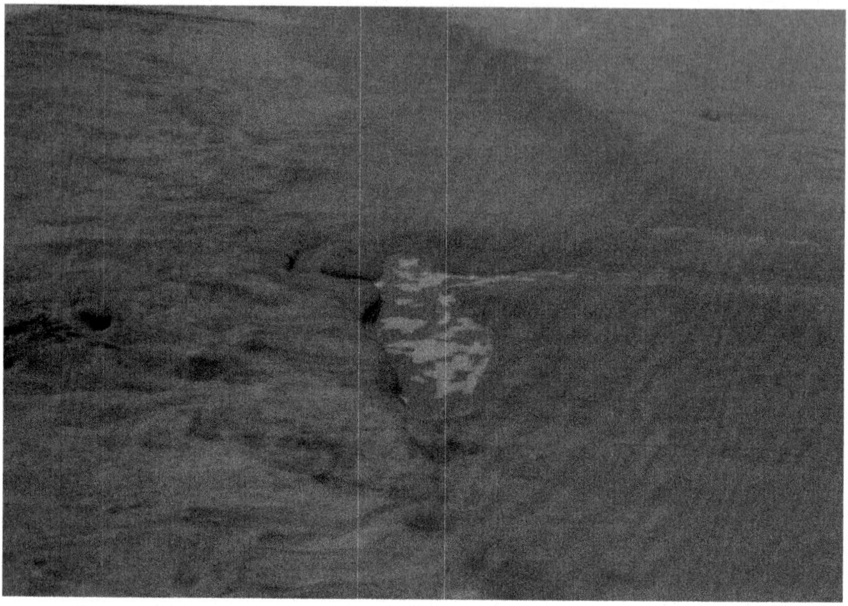

FIGURE 5.3 Ana Mendieta, *Untitled: Silueta Series*, 1976, earth/bodywork, Mexico, 35mm color slides. © The Estate of Ana Mendieta Collection, L.L.C., Courtesy Galerie Lelong, New York.

before her death, Mendieta yet struggled for major gallery and museum representation.[13] After her death, her photographs and other works are represented by the prestigious Galerie LeLong, and her work has been displayed in New York City's Solomon R. Guggenheim Museum and London's Southbank Centre. I mention these facts not to suggest that having one's work shown in well-regarded galleries and museums has aesthetic meaning in itself – it does not – but instead to make clear that Mendieta's reputation as an artist has grown significantly stronger in the decades after her death.[14] Since she is no longer alive to perform earthworks and body works, one must conclude that her ascent in reputation is based in part on the photographs that document her earthworks and body works. Many of these were slides, created to be shown with a projector. The materiality of photographic slides aligns with Mendieta's somewhat uncanny oeuvre: slides are too tiny to view accurately with the naked eye, but when projected the image will fill a wall as a kind of phantasmagoric monument. On this wall, it has an immaterial quality, entirely projected light and image. Yet it also has the force of a large work, filling the wall. Mendieta seems to have chosen slides for their convenience as documentation of her earthworks, but it is worth considering how the uncanny materiality of slides supports the haunting discourse of her oeuvre, its thematics of exile and trace, presence in absence.

Mendieta was born in Cuba into a wealthy and politically powerful family that fell from favor when Castro came to power. In an effort to save their children, her

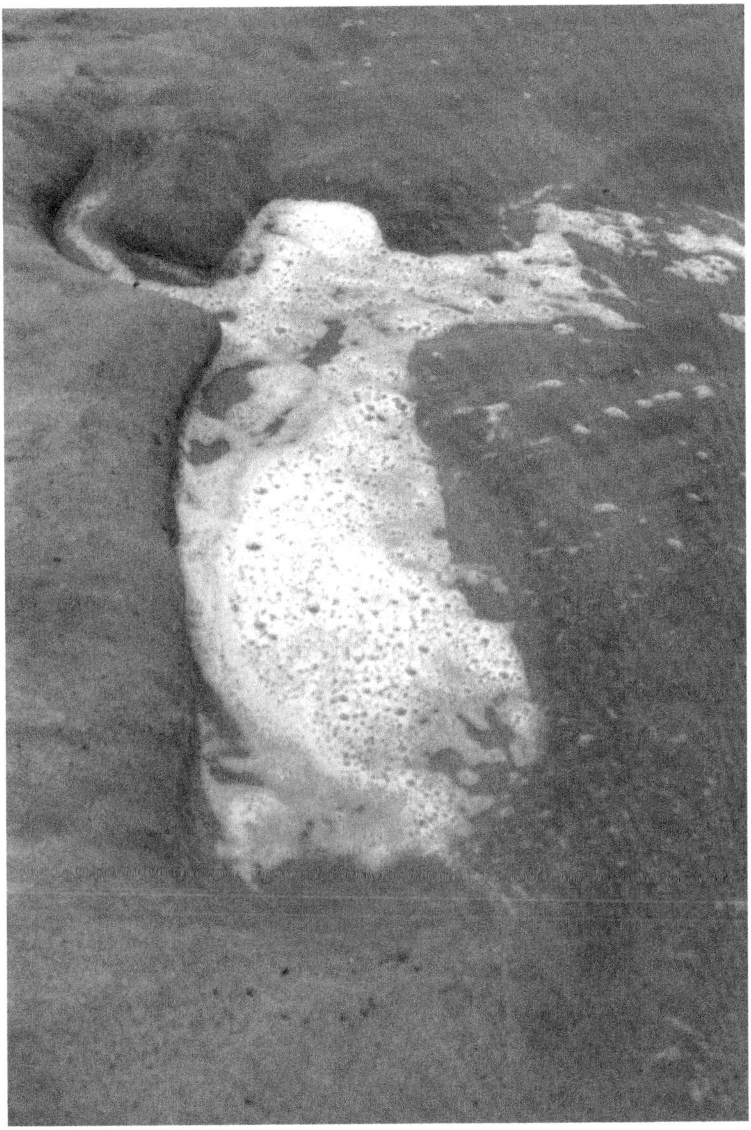

FIGURE 5.4 Ana Mendieta, *Untitled: Silueta Series*, 1976, earth/bodywork, Mexico, 35mm color slides. © The Estate of Ana Mendieta Collection, L.L.C., Courtesy Galerie Lelong, New York.

parents sent Ana, then age 12, and her elder sister, Raquelin, to the United States through Operation Peter Pan, and they entered foster care in Iowa.[15] The state proved a cruel place for Mendieta, because it was rife with racism. She later remembered being called the "little whore" by her Iowa classmates, simply because of the color of her skin.[16] At the University of Iowa, Mendieta enrolled in the master of arts program, where she met Hans Breder, a teacher who became her lover. Traveling

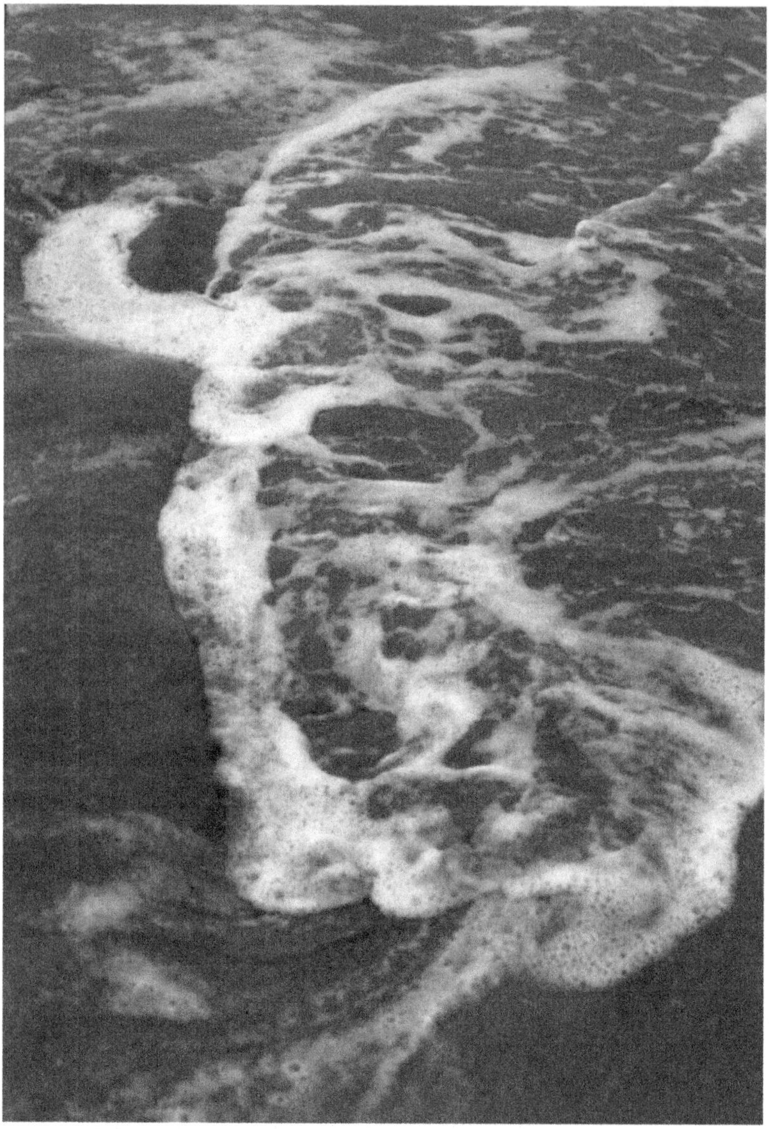

FIGURE 5.5 Ana Mendieta, *Untitled: Silueta Series*, 1976, earth/bodywork, Mexico, 35mm color slides. © The Estate of Ana Mendieta Collection, L.L.C., Courtesy Galerie Lelong, New York.

with Breder to Mexico, Mendieta began to create her numerically massive *Silueta Series* in the early 1970s. While Breder was photographing Mendieta nude at La Ventosa, Mendieta was creating some of the most striking images in this series.

The *Silueta* images that Mendieta created at Salina Cruz (1976) are among the most powerful in the larger series of images that she called *Siluetas* (Figures 5.1–5.9).[17]

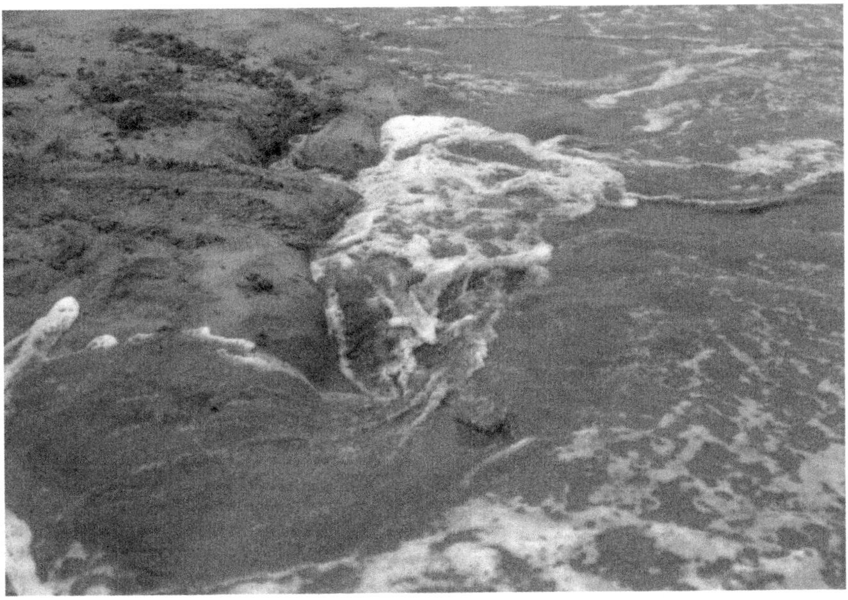

FIGURE 5.6 Ana Mendieta, *Untitled: Silueta Series*, 1976, earth/bodywork, Mexico, 35mm color slides. © The Estate of Ana Mendieta Collection, L.L.C., Courtesy Galerie Lelong, New York.

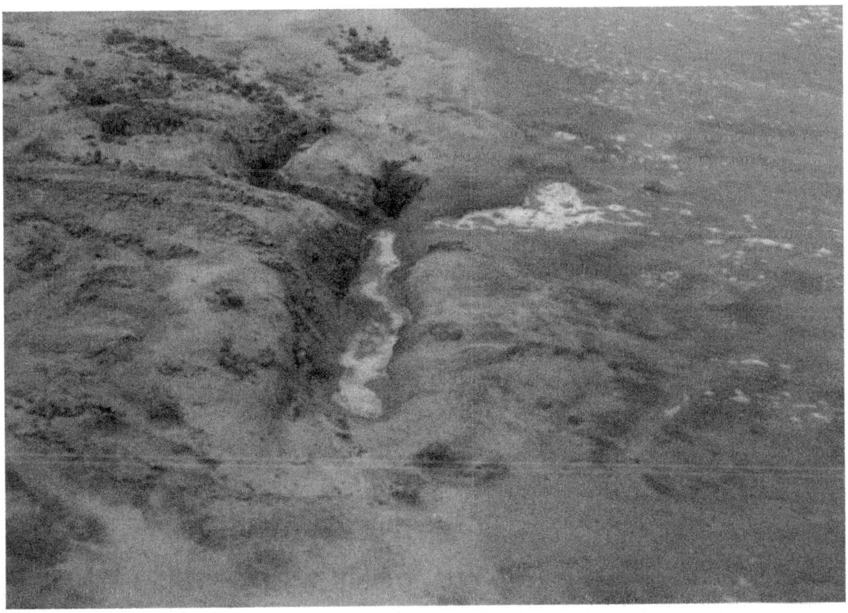

FIGURE 5.7 Ana Mendieta, *Untitled: Silueta Series*, 1976, earth/bodywork, Mexico, 35mm color slides. © The Estate of Ana Mendieta Collection, L.L.C., Courtesy Galerie Lelong, New York.

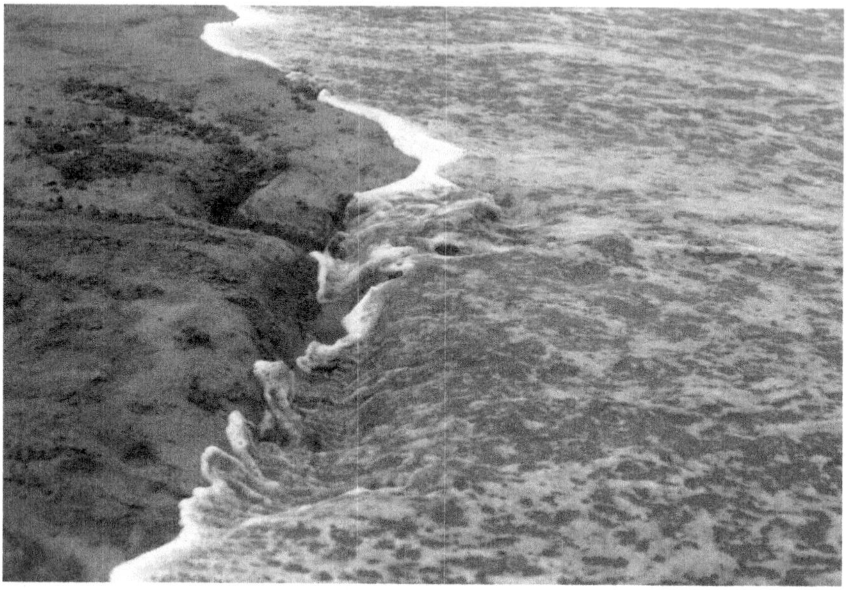

FIGURE 5.8 Ana Mendieta, *Untitled: Silueta Series*, 1976, earth/bodywork, Mexico, 35mm color slides. © The Estate of Ana Mendieta Collection, L.L.C., Courtesy Galerie Lelong, New York.

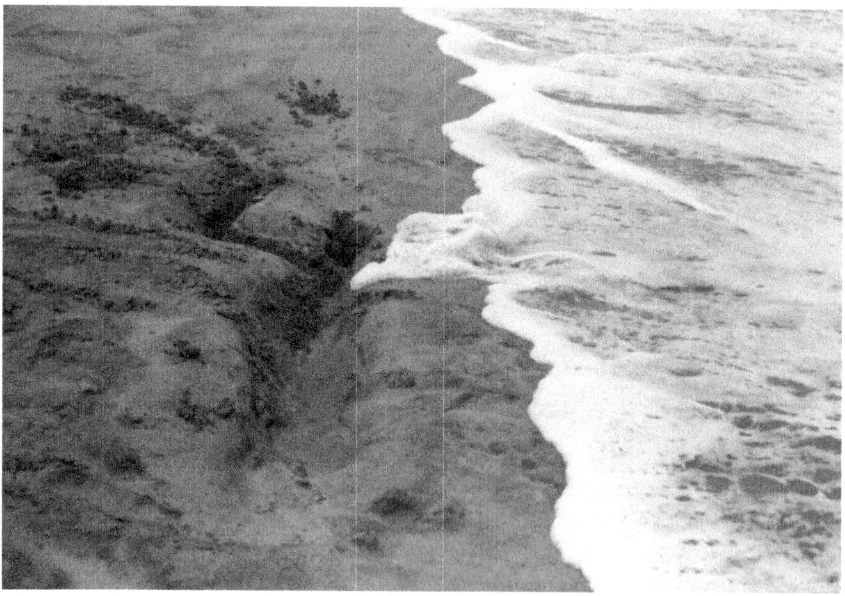

FIGURE 5.9 Ana Mendieta, *Untitled: Silueta Series*, 1976, earth/bodywork, Mexico, 35mm color slides. © The Estate of Ana Mendieta Collection, L.L.C., Courtesy Galerie Lelong, New York.

Focusing my discussion on this very small subset of images drawn from the enormous *Silueta Series*, I choose images that stand out as exemplary. And yet, to begin to grasp Mendieta's work, one must view as many of the *Siluetas* as possible. Only such viewing of this massive series that Mendieta continued to develop until her death reveals the obsessive force with which Mendieta approached and worked through the problem of how to represent, in photographs, the pain of exile. The *Silueta Series* is a work that, in the years when she was creating it, Mendieta claimed would have no end. The images photographed at Salina Cruz show the outline of a woman's body that Mendieta traced in the sand near the boundary of the ocean. Along the traced outline, she has placed red pigment. As the ocean tide rises, it progressively sweeps the figure into the water (Figures 5.1–5.9). Mendieta shot the photographs low and at close frame so that nothing could be seen apart from the essential elements of the earthworks performance: the sand, the ocean, the outline of the woman's form, and the red tinge. The close frame gives a sense of intimacy and sparseness to the image. There are no people, just a feminine outline that is eroded by the waves. There is no sky, just water, sand, and red. The sense of desolation is palpable.

But to say that Mendieta is creating images of disappearance is a false reading. Instead, she is marking the earth with the female body's outline and the red pigment. The way the ocean slowly erodes the contours of this mark is expressed photographically as a series: Mendieta photographs the erosion of the outline she has made. The photographs then become a more permanent mark and in this sense double the *Silueta*, thus standing as a record of the marks Mendieta has made on the earth. Never the story of disappearance, her photographs documenting earthworks and body performance insist on the artist's capacity to make her mark even as the images profoundly evoke the sense of personal anguish that comes with exile and loss of one's homeland.

The elements of the color red and the ocean suggest Santería, an Afro-Caribbean religion that incorporates elements of Roman Catholicism. Mendieta was well versed in Santería, although she was raised Roman Catholic.[18] In the Salina Cruz series of *Silueta*, Mendieta conjures Yemaya, the mother-goddess who lives in the ocean, whereas the red set by the feminine outline suggests blood. The images, though, supersede and can be read without knowledge of Santería. They show a profound dispossession and express the condition of exile and loss: a small feminine outline eroded and cast adrift into the ocean. But the idea that Mendieta is simply staging feminine erasure in the *Silueta Series* does not begin to limn how instead the images show dissolution and return: what goes into the ocean does *not* disappear but becomes part of the ocean, circling with the currents and insistently returning to shore. The back-and-forth motion of the waves skew temporal readings of the photographs so that there is no exact moment at which the mark of the outline is effaced but rather several scenes of formal interaction between the ocean and the woman's outline, as gradually the ocean and the outline merge.

Mendieta traces her personal and political experience of exile in these images by elegantly limned symbolic form. The rise of her reputation as an artist in the twenty-first century rests on the unique power of her photographic work to simultaneously evoke the experience of exile, orphanhood, *and* the claiming of place or the making of one's mark no matter how fate conspires to cause one's silence. Her *Silueta* photographs explore with power and persistence the condition of exile and loss and the longing for return to a homeland that Mendieta uses as a metaphor for womb-like and maternal.[19] Their power is to set a claim on a place, no matter how dispossessed one is.[20]

The dissolution of the figure of the feminine that Mendieta repeatedly stages in her haunting *Silueta* photographs is not a personal confession of her desire to not exist. Instead, the *Siluetas* call the viewer to contend with her own lost places and her own claim on place, especially her claim on spaces from which she has been cast out. Mendieta stamps the earth with her *Silueta* earthworks, and the voluminous body of photographs that document her *Silueta Series* stands as one of the most important interventions in feminist art of the late twentieth century. I say this because Mendieta's photographic work contends with issues of exile and the lost condition of the human in ways that go beneath and beyond the obsession with costumery and performativity made popular in the late twentieth century by Judith Butler and Cindy Sherman. In the twenty-first century, the problem of displaced persons, exiles, and refugees is epidemic. Mendieta's oeuvre, and especially her photography, addresses this problem of exile. Mendieta is an important photographer because the fearless and brilliant works that she created show the orphanhood of existence – the state of exile – which is more and more common in our twenty-first-century world. Her work evokes the necessity of claiming one's place even in this fragile and shifting terrain. This ability of Mendieta's *Silueta* photographs to evoke the state of the exile and to shape a visceral facing of it makes her work of increasing importance and concern in the twenty-first century.

Francesca Woodman's *House*

Born in Boulder, Colorado, in 1958, Francesca Woodman was something of a photography prodigy. She began taking striking and memorable photographs as a young teen. By the time she was in her late teens and early twenties, she was already producing a body of work that ultimately would place her among the more interesting, evocative, and debated photographers of the late twentieth century. Although Woodman created her photographs from the early 1970s until her death by suicide in 1981, her reputation as a photographer is largely a twenty-first-century phenomenon. Some six years after her death, Woodman's mother, the ceramic artist Betty Woodman, engineered a small exhibition of Francesca Woodman photographs at Wellesley College Museum in Wellesley, Massachusetts. The exhibit featured catalog essays by prominent feminist art historians, notably including Abigail Solomon-Godeau, whose essay "Just Like a Woman" is a classic feminist analysis of Woodman's work.[21] In 1998, Fondation Cartier mounted an exhibit in Paris, and Scalo Publishers brought out an important book of Woodman's photographs, featuring essays by the likes of philosopher Philippe Sollers.[22] In 2004, the

Marian Goodman Gallery in New York City featured Woodman's work, and the photographer's reputation began to gather steam. In 2006, Phaidon Press brought out a splendid collection of her photographs.[23] In 2010, the first full-length monograph on Woodman's work appeared.[24] In 2011 and 2012, her work was shown at the Metropolitan Museum of Art and the Guggenheim Museum in New York City and at the San Francisco Museum of Modern Art.[25] Thirty years after her death, the photography prodigy had arrived.[26]

But this posthumous reputation created Francesca Woodman as a kind of cult phenomenon, a photographer adored by some outside of the art world and debated or even disparaged within it. Art historian Carol Armstrong writes that a male colleague responded dismissively to her article on Francesca Woodman by questioning her attention to the achievement of an adolescent: opines Armstrong, "I think he may have meant an adolescent *girl's* achievement."[27] Woodman's status as a very young woman when she created her photographic oeuvre erects a barrier to her work being taken seriously. Despite the power of her photographs and despite the fact that major museums have exhibited and purchased her work, art historians who write on Woodman are almost always women writing feminist theory. That does not misrepresent Woodman's photography – her work draws powerfully on themes of gender – but it does reflect the excessive gendering of Woodman's corpus. She is not a photographer about whom esteemed male art historians seem to care to spend their time studying and writing (David Levi Strauss and Benjamin Buchloh being significant exceptions). Even so, Francesca Woodman attracts a kind of popular adulation that only the Internet age could measure. She is tweeted and blogged about, and digital versions of her photographs circulate widely. Not only is her posthumous fame something that occurred in the twenty-first century, but also the viewing habits of the twenty-first century seem matched to her enigmatic, quixotic work. Each time we look at a Francesca Woodman photograph online, we see an image the artist did not intend to take up space on the gallery or museum wall – unlike the work of many professional photographers. Instead, her work reads like a secret door into a mystery, uncannily appropriate to float randomly up through the flotsam and jetsam of the Internet. The reason Woodman's work was not intended to fill a gallery wall is that she died before she was invited to have gallery representation. Near the end of her life, Woodman did display the work *Blueprint for a Temple* in Manhattan's Alternative Museum.

Her later works in diazotype are large, most notably the *Blueprint for a Temple*, which is 15 feet high and originally (when Woodman showed the work shortly before her death) filled two walls of the Alternative Museum, whereas her earlier black and white photographs are quite tiny, 5 inches by 7 inches or smaller. Despite her later turn toward a monumental scale, Woodman's work has been called diaristic, that is, like diary pictures. But on the contrary, her enigmatic photographs confess nothing personal – thematizing instead time, space, mortality, and embodiment.

Woodman's photograph *My House* and her *House* and *Space^2* series (1975–1976) present the photograph as a kind of fate, something that seals an event in its ineluctable *that-has-been-ness*, "a fugitive but certain testimony."[28] These images are not necessarily the most important and substantial of Woodman's work – her later diazotypes fill this role – but these series represent Woodman's quintessential work, that by which most audiences, if they know her, recognize her.[29] In these photographs, this testimony of gender as fate works at a slant to late-twentieth-century theories of gender as an apparent garment effected by language, discourse, sign.[30] In Woodman's photographs, gender is a sign that, in its very excessiveness, returns and wounds the subject, becoming fate.

Even as the *House* and *Space²* images showcase temporal distortions (Figures 5.10 and 5.11), in these images Woodman's affinities with the feminist performance art of her era are striking. Her work elides the boundaries between genres, thus coming to rest as photography not so much in its inception as in its reception.[31] I do not mean that Woodman did not conceive of herself as a photographer: clearly she did. But the genius of Woodman's work is the scene, the symbolic torque. Her power is oneiric and her work has the aura of fate. In this, she deploys the photograph as a

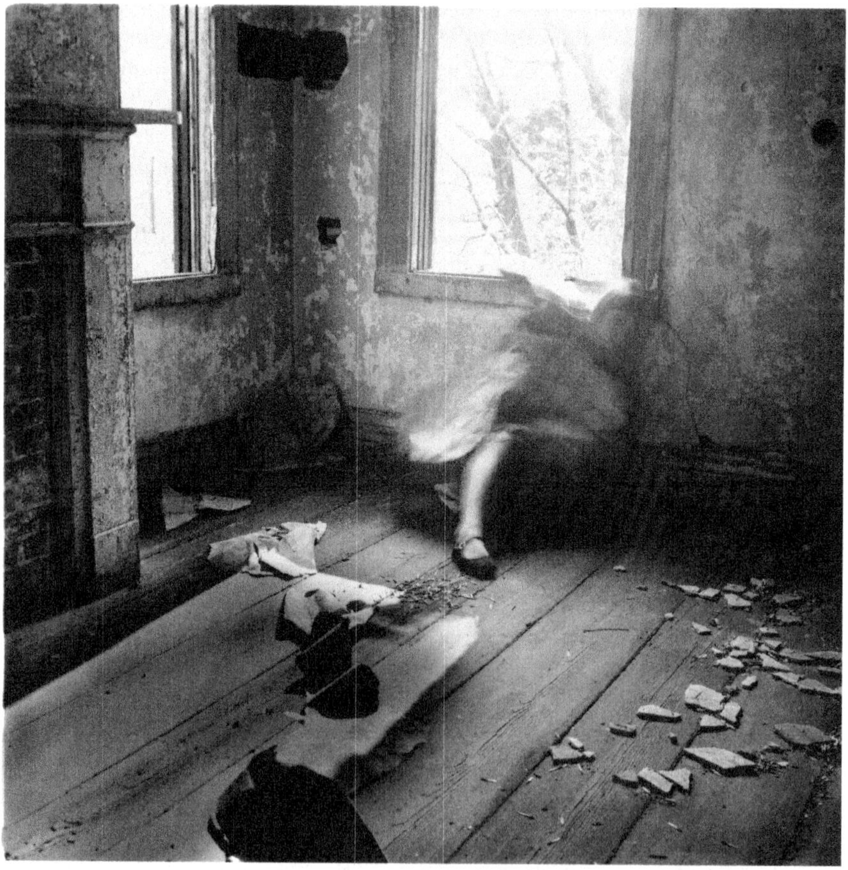

FIGURE 5.10 Francesca Woodman, *House #3*, Providence, Rhode Island, 1976, 2⅜ × 6⁷⁄₁₆ in. Courtesy George and Betty Woodman.

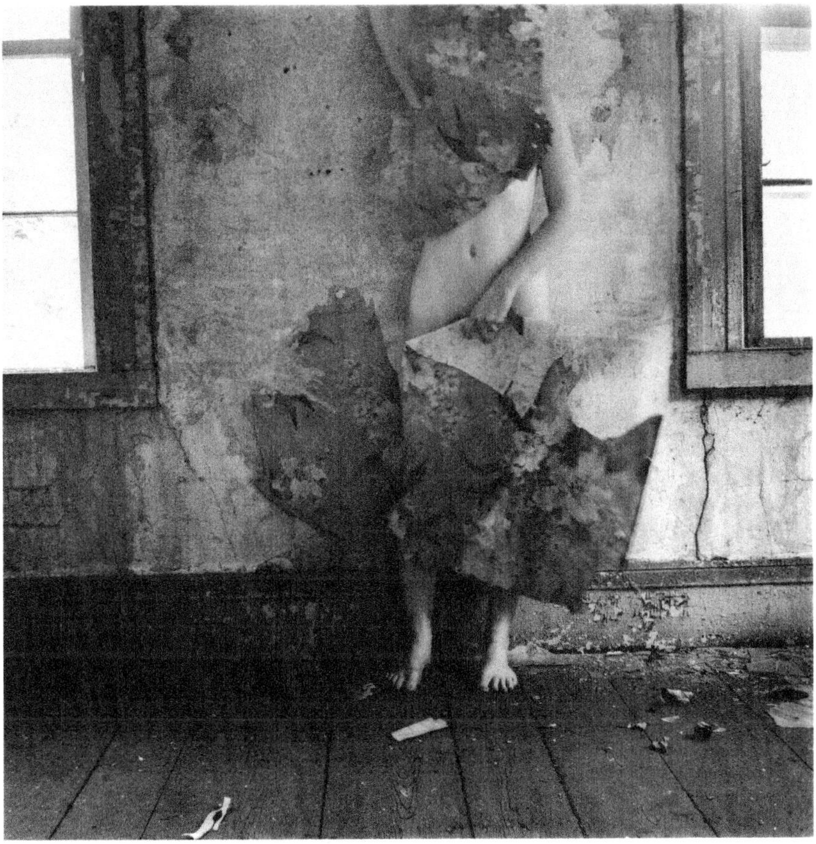

FIGURE 5.11 Francesca Woodman, *From Space²*, Providence, Rhode Island, 1976, gelatin silver print, 2⅜ × 6⁷⁄₁₆ in. Courtesy George and Betty Woodman.

sign of fate – never an actual truth but an encoding of image that appears as truth – that which is written for us. The photographs of the *House* and *Space²* series and the image, *My House*, stage a young woman, Woodman herself, as the double of dilapidated interiors rich with visual rhymes that reveal formal consanguinities between the ruined architectural spaces and the young woman inhabiting them (Figures 5.10, 5.11, and 5.12). As Chris Townsend rightly points out, Woodman diverges from the Pictures Generation, which emphasized pastiche and repetition of stock images and with which she is contemporaneous, in that her photographs visually quote from the history of European art, not commercial images.[32] Importantly, I would add, they carry a sense of depth that is an always indicated, never revealed intimacy and expanse.

Woodman's abandoned house images are hauntingly real, even as they were entirely staged.[33] Woodman went to abandoned spaces, moved in props, and photographed herself amid very carefully planned and constructed scenes. Meaghan Thurston has elegantly described Woodman's photographic use of the body in domestic space.[34] I have articulated this theme as Woodman's relationship to

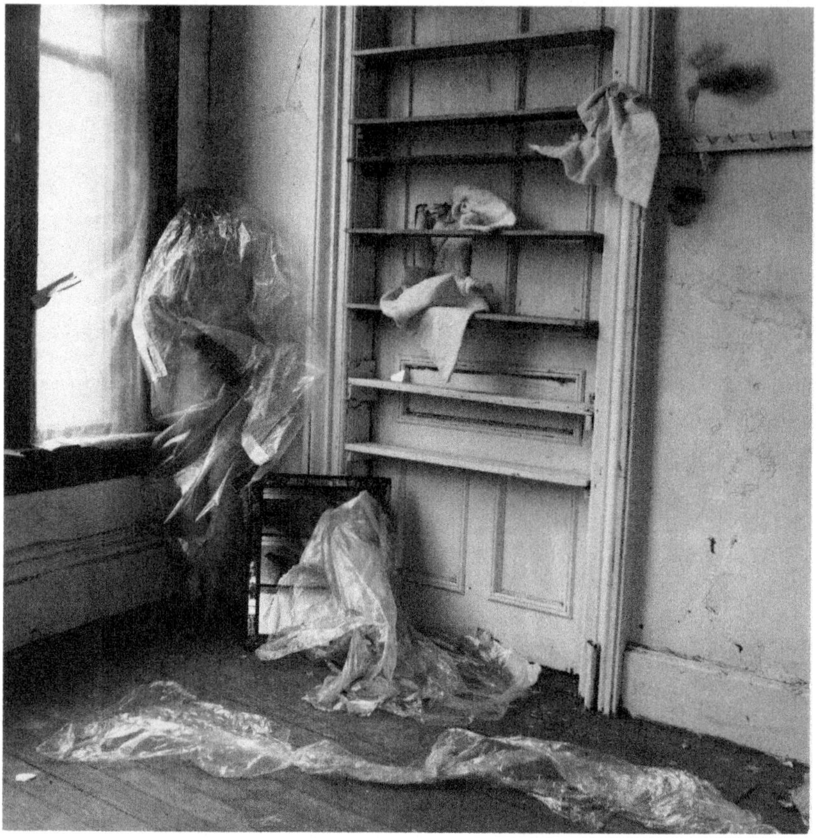

FIGURE 5.12 Francesca Woodman, *My House*, Providence, Rhode Island, 1976, 5¾ × 5⅝ in. Courtesy George and Betty Woodman.

architecture, to built space.[35] In the *House* and *Space*[2] photographs, Woodman's body is the formal symbol that carries present time through the time-as-the-past space of the abandoned house (Figure 5.10 and 5.11). Here, the fate of the gendered subject is invoked through melancholy reflection. Photographs, as Barthes argues, are tied to time, and the *eidos* of the photograph is time, its passage, and its mortal light.[36] Woodman's photographs exemplify this photographic idea of the passage of time – the body's vulnerability to time. They achieve this transformation by invoking gender with the young female body becoming in Woodman's work the eloquent descriptor of fate: what happens no matter how hard we try not to let it happen. Here, I want to emphasize that I do not mean that Woodman takes photographs of her actual fate; rather, I mean that her photographs exemplify that quality in photography that presents the past – any past – as if it were the only possible path. A sense of the inevitable attends Woodman's images even as they protest that end. In this sense, they are rigorously honest images of gender as a force that often eludes the subject's attempts to escape its domain. And yet precisely by showing this tight space of gender-as-fate, Woodman protests it and opens for her viewers possibilities of transcendence and transformation that are beyond restrictive codes of the gendered self and of the self as such.

Domain

With the disembodied and denaturalized fecundity of photography, Francesca Woodman's series in abandoned houses is pensive in the sense that Barthes describes – the pensive image causes one to think because it cannot be easily read.[37] Her black-and-white photographs from this era are typically very small prints; in this sense they seem private and demand concentrated, close-up viewing. For the *House* and *Space²* series, Woodman comes to the abandoned house, that house where no housework has been done for years, and increases its disarray. She peels already peeling wallpaper further from walls, brings scavenged ruined objects into the house, and scatters plaster on the already dirty floors.[38] She exaggerates – makes excessive – the melancholy of an abandoned house. Woodman undoes the cover of domesticity in the abandoned spaces she photographs, marking them as her own by performing the opposite of housework. Instead of hiding time's marks, Woodman exaggerates time's marks in abandoned spaces wherein time's marks are already well shown. Having thus prepared the scenes, she takes her photographs. Instead of erasing the marks of time, Woodman causes those marks to pose, to hold still. Not erasing the mark of time as fate, Woodman slows it, stills it. In these two series, she poses the house at its ruinous edge where it will no longer offer safety to inhabitants but instead will show us our fragility, our need for cover, and the limits of that cover (Figures 5.10–5.12).

The pose, as Barthes argues, is the essence of the photograph: a photographic image forces the physical and visible world to hold still.[39] In her *House* and *Space²* series and in the image *My House*, Woodman poses as the singular union of housewife, housekeeper, and vestal daughter, whose insoluble grief, or rage, opens the disarray of the house to sight. More than simply a rebellion against the terms of femininity – although these photographs do act rebelliously – the pose of Woodman, the woman who freezes time rather than removes it, is not so much an anti-housewife as a repudiating claim on the house. Woodman instates a scene of pain at the origin: the ersatz familial house.

Woodman's poses in the decrepit, abandoned domestic space play on well-established tropes of gender. The hearth, which traditionally suggests the vestal daughter, is central to some of the images. The diaphanous garments of torn paper, the Mary Jane shoes, and the plastic wrap used as clothing (Figures 5.10–5.12) all strike home by conveying concentric circles of gendered inscriptions. Woodman allows the garment of light to pose across her and across the rooms, in uncanny technique, poised between performance and the negation of performance. Her visual domain is the image that constitutes the edge of claim. In the photograph *My House* and in the *House* and *Space²* series, the formal symbol of the daughter Woodman portrays returns to a house that cannot protect her from fate. Instead, this entirely photographic house can only perform fate.

Gender as fate

Ana Mendieta theorized and conceptualized her work's relationship to gender, describing her earthworks as an attempt to connect with the womb of the earth,[40] but Francesca Woodman did not write about feminism in a theorized way. Although seeming to agree with its tenets, Woodman apparently felt that feminism was not of much practical use.[41] For Mendieta, the inscription of gender as fate came to appear overdetermined after her death: it seems that her husband, Carl Andre, may have caused her death.[42] Even so, Mendieta's fidelity to representing the female figure, in her *Silueta Series* and in several other performance pieces, creates a dialogue around the gendered figure that subverts notions of gender as costume and frames the seriousness (and pain) of gendered fate.[43] In Woodman's work, gender is played through and visually theorized: her art contemplates links among gender, fate, visuality, and photography. The risk of such work is that Woodman deploys this category of fate as an embodied force, a problem to solve visually in photographs that push the nude female figure to the edge. Woodman's typical refusal to show the face of her

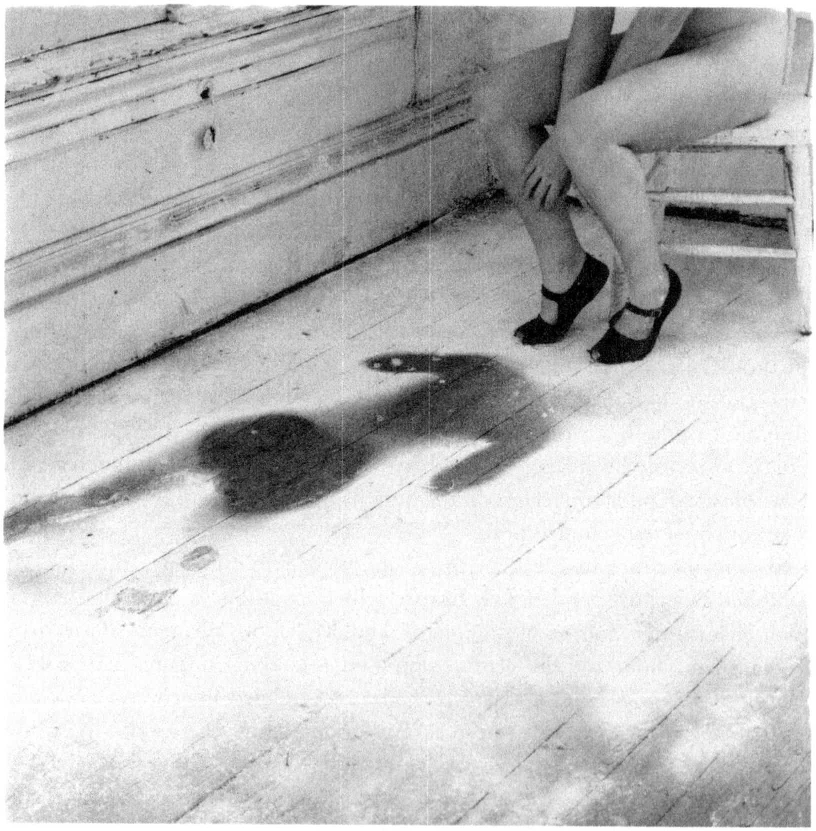

FIGURE 5.13 Francesca Woodman, *Untitled*, Providence, Rhode Island, 1976, gelatin silver print, 5½ × 5½ in. Courtesy George and Betty Woodman.

photographed subject – many of her photographs are images of Woodman herself – makes of the female body an iconic rather than a personal mark, not unlike Mendieta's outlines of the feminine figure in her *Siluetas* (Figure 5.13). In this image, Woodman poses above the outline of her body traced in flour on the floor (Figure 5.13). In an ingenious combination of wry humor and pathos, she stages the body's outline and its evanescence, even as she figurally envisions herself, nude but for her Mary Janes, in a chair looking down at what appears to be the mark of her own vanishing. The outline, here, evokes traditional police use of an outline to mark the fallen body of a victim, and yet Woodman's very young and healthy living body perched above the outline not only visually skews the formal shape of the image but also symbolically alters the work to be not about vanishing or a desire to vanish but rather the intelligence and the will to stand apart – in ecstasy and enlightenment – and see the transience of one's physical self. Her photographs work against acceptance of the fate of gender even as they mourn the way gender stakes its claim on the subject in advance of the subject's efforts to reinscribe a self.

Whom do I haunt?

Going to abandoned houses, Francesca Woodman investigates the posture of the revenant. The houses haunt her, and through her photographs of abandoned domestic spaces, Woodman troubles us. Whereas Carol Armstrong argues that Woodman is a ghost in the house of the woman artist, and Katherine Conley locates Woodman as a surrealist ghost, I suggest that Woodman, no ghost, is intent on photographing the house of the visible and the relationship of time to this house.[44] She uses her body as a symbol of the risk of both claiming and refusing to inhabit a house if the terms of this house degrade one. As stated by the title of her photograph *My House*, Woodman does *not* imagine herself inhabiting someone else's house, but instead claims her own place: the house is hers. Her house is more expansive and far rougher than that of the polished grande dame.

Woodman's *House* and *Space*[2] photographs, however, do have a clear relationship to a precursor work of feminist art: *Womanhouse*.[45] Woodman is likely to have been aware of California Institute of the Arts Feminist Art Program's *Womanhouse* given the prominence of Judy Chicago and Miriam Shapiro, who spearheaded the performance and exhibition, and given *Womanhouse*'s near proximity in time to Woodman's own work. The influence of *Womanhouse* is fateful in Woodman's photographs. Like the creators of *Womanhouse*, Woodman seeks an abandoned house in which to create her work. But if *Womanhouse* is a kind of public protest art, Woodman takes a turn to the interior in her housework. Through the work of photographing a house, Woodman creates the melancholy, private images of material fate that is a form of return.

By performing for her own camera in an abandoned house, Woodman points to the damning cultural narrative that merges woman with house, that makes the house an imprimatur – as Barthes would define the word, a *myth* – of the cultural interpretation that a woman goes into a house to be somehow contained within it, that a woman's relationship to a house is one of submission, even by dint of being protected, rather than of ownership.[46] Instead, Woodman claims the house as her own and accepts the risks of its rough edge. Denying herself a comforting domestic, she reaches past protest to a kind of sublimity that is a rapprochement with self-denial. Beyond the abandoned house photographs, she shows the place of fate also by her use of doubling and the visual rhymes that make up the subtext of many of her photographs. The divided and echoed subject is both on the floor and standing above her double (Figure 5.13), and in other photographs the structural parallels between Woodman's body and a bird wing, a fish skeleton, a taxidermy fox, and eels are played through in further structural parallels with the architecture that contains the woman's body. This use of doubling, wherein the house that is falling apart is coded to stand with the woman who inhabits the house, poses photographic fate. The figure of the house's inhabitant is marked by light, effaced by light, and preserved by light in the photograph's persistence. She is the double of time: torn wallpaper is her garment, oversaturated with light, and then light is her garment, almost swallowing the figure (Figure 5.10).

Melancholy of photography

Barthes defines the *punctum* as the place in the photograph that marks the viewer, the place where the photograph establishes itself as part of the viewer's fate, as it were specific to her.[47] The punctum of photography then is its melancholy or, as Barthes writes, its "tyche," the place where the reality of time touches the viewer. Working along similarly oblique lines, Jacques Derrida asks "Whom do I haunt?" as a constitutive question, going on to posit that those whom "I" haunt are those who are wounded, painfully or pleasurably, by me; I am formed by those whom I haunt.[48] Conversely, those who haunt me are my fate. Francesca Woodman's photographs in an abandoned house invoke her audience because the photographs show Woodman as one who is haunted by the visual terms of gender, implicated in the mortal gaze of the photograph: she is not a ghost in anyone's house but instead a purveyor of the cultural force – through photographic images – of haunting. Woodman's images employ and embody the melancholy of fate that is woman's figural conscription at (and as) the site of this repetition of gender. Woodman's photographs prick us with the fate of being gendered, released from that fate only if also cast out of the house.

The fatedness of gender is evident also in the way that Woodman's abandoned house photographs show her staying in the house through the process of its desolation and destruction.[49] To paraphrase Philippe Sollers, Francesca Woodman is more *risked* than anyone, at least in the visual lexicon of her photographs. Woodman's photographs pose a melancholy effect of gender as repetition of fate, poised not *at* the boundary but *in* the boundary: her photographs stage transcendence as risk. Rather than confronting sexist oppression directly in the way of its predecessor *Womanhouse*, Woodman's *House* and *Space*[2] series perform as melancholy photography. They are images that say gender codes will not change in bright unity, but in the severe task of changing form, often in ulterior psychic spaces, and at personal risk. Woodman's *House* and *Space*^{2} series come after the early 1970s performance space *Womanhouse* not just in time but in *telos* (or goal); her photographs aim to express the melancholy recognition that *mutatis mutandis* (despite changes, the main point stays the same); despite feminism, a woman whose art goes against the grain is a woman at risk.

In these images, Francesca Woodman is haunted by her precursors – the house of the woman artist was already filled with ghosts long before Woodman came on the scene.[50] Woodman's house shows a space where writing, reinscription, will not reach: the photograph as the space of fate cannot be rewritten, the photograph cannot be transformed once it is made. In its essence, a photograph cannot be transformed, only manipulated. (Consider photomontage and composite photography, and photo-shop, not as transformative of the photographic image itself, however much they may be transformative for works of art.) But for just this reason Woodman's photographs have the traction that opens to transformation. The uncanny and displaced positions that Woodman creates in her photographs speak to a kind of social violence entailed in a woman's efforts to create a self, and they shape a haunted space wherein the young woman is engaged in an immense struggle with the house. The fate of the house is photographic image, that is, space swallowed by time. Although one may interpret Woodman's use of blur in some of the *House* and *Space* photographs as importing ghostliness to the images, here blur articulates her struggle with her house – of inheritance, of future, of self-as-artist, and of the always enigmatic otherness of the figural in time (Figure 5.10). For Woodman, blur is necessary for this housework of alterity: she is fighting for her place in space and time, making a rough chrysalis of the abandoned house that she claims as her own.[51]

Francesca Woodman's Zen

In *Photography Degree Zero*, Jay Prosser writes persuasively about the Buddhist strand in Barthes's *Camera Lucida*, arguing that here, in his last book, Barthes the semiotician confronts or is forced to come up against the limits of words.[52] Prosser emphasizes what he sees as the photograph's connection to trauma, a connection that Prosser argues is inherent to Barthes's theory of the photograph as memento mori. This trauma Prosser does not interpret along the lines of contemporary Western trauma theory but instead along the lines of Buddhist notions of the fleeting emptiness of the physical world, the illusion of stability that surrounds those things that occupy time and space.

Francesca Woodman's images in an abandoned house and her *Angels* series of images occupy time and space with a visceral code of risk or pain. Critics have interpreted her photographs as containing her own trauma.[53] And yet, no one can say with exact specificity what Woodman's particular personal trauma might be, other than the eventuation of her act of committing suicide. Needless to say, she had not yet completed that act at the time she made her photographs: it was not a foregone conclusion to the images. To read Woodman's images as messages of a personal history of trauma is to miss what photography can do. Woodman might have had a personally traumatic history; it is certainly possible that she did. And yet that does not matter to her photographs. Instead, their quality of what Barthes calls "thus-goneness" carries the ontological curve of the hollowing spatial real. Hollowness and lightness are the codes by which one might read both the images from Woodman's photographs in an abandoned house and her *Angels*.

In the *Angels*, and related *On Being an Angel*, photographs, the body of the girl (who is Woodman) depicts a quality of near disembodiment, with the flourish at the edges of the body as detritus. If Prosser posits the unbearable loss of Barthes's mother as the engine of Barthes's need for photography to provide the path of death that words cannot provide, then Woodman creates images that provide the path of nullity for reasons that remain powerfully latent in the images. Instead of offering personal confession, the images are deeply informed by the privative code of the photographic as such. As Sloan Rankin suggests in her commentaries on Woodman's history, when Woodman was making the photographs on which her reputation now rests, she was not depressed but healthy and even joyous.[54] The slant and precarious beauty of the images expresses this delicate space of joy and recognizes the emptiness of the physical and temporal world not as a pathological state but as an enlightened state. Woodman was not a student of Zen in the sense of studying Buddhism, but her work exemplifies a careful and serious encounter with the ephemeral contours of embodiment, an encounter that Woodman repeatedly stages in photographs that repeat and exhaust embodiment.

In that Woodman's reception history had a decidedly gendered slant, her work's meditative intellectual energy has been somewhat overlooked, in favor of readings that contend with an assumption that some form of gendered pathology inspired her work.[55] There are sharp and painful explorations of gender in her work – not just a nightmare of the feminine but also the illusion of objects in time and space is exposed in the delicate and frightening imagery of Woodman's photographs. Importantly, Woodman titled photographs *Space* and *Space*^{2} (Providence, Rhode Island, 1975–1978), thus indicating that the images interact with space itself and render space in the flat plane of the photograph (Figure 5.11).

In *House #3* (Figure 5.10), Woodman looks as if she had just crashed through the window. The fractured lines of light seem to emanate from the shoulders of the figure of the girl crouched beneath the windowsill. The blurred figure suggests not a ghostly figure but more directly a figure without weight, or one whose weight is of a different quality and force than we usually accord with the human body. The room seems to sway with a kind of wind, as if the figure of the girl, falling in, shaped the room into a hollow. Each echo of this hollow is articulated and embellished by the photograph's implicit gestures of counter-comparison: the damaged wall, the fracture line of the wall, the overly bright (overexposed) light of the trees, the trees as fracture lines, the girl both overexposed and blurred (because of a long exposure time during which Woodman moved), and the floor covered with detritus as if the building were emptying itself. This ascesis is Woodman's enlightenment, her coming to terms with the illusory nature of the physical world by photographing its limits, photographing the places where home is not, in fact, home and cannot protect or sustain us. Similarly, Woodman's *Angels* (Rome, Italy, 1977) questions the boundary of flesh and illusion and of the unseen seen. In the image from an abandoned factory in Rome, Woodman seems to be trying to levitate, but the fey joke of the image is the impossibility of flight for the body in gravity. And yet this picture also abounds with the pun of the illusion of materiality, the present absence of the body as it attempts, comically, to transcend gravity to gain control of its own illusory field. The place where it happens is marked by the photograph as a wound of time. The nubile body half-stripped tries to jump out of its skin, out of its social position, or, more straightforwardly, out of its materiality and its illusory secured place in space and time.

The photograph as illusion that leads to truth, the way of the dead, is particularly relevant to Woodman's *Angels*. She creates the most obvious and banal illusion, the image of the angel in a postlapsarian space, and infuses it with awareness of its falsity that becomes exemplification of its truth. The camera opens the path of the dead through its proscenium function, its ability to create a stage. The stage she uses is carefully set and also vacuous, inhabited by a problematic shift of gravity. In an image from the *Angels*, the gravity of partial nudity marks the angelic body that tries to lift itself above earth in a partial escape. The action is echoed by the clumsy wing-like sheets draped above the jumping figure, toward which the figure gestures. The young girl's partial nudity, her thin arms, and her long hair that attempt to reach the sky signify in graphic detail the impossibility of flight, but the photograph as the path of the dead signifies its own domain here, as Woodman stages the facing of the immaterial through the material and stages the invisible through the visible. The angle of the shot forces us to look up through the impossibility of her path, through the narrow gauge of light that is the impossible domain of her trajectory. The photograph becomes the way of the dead not because Woodman has a death wish but because she is true to the medium of photography. She is true to photography's capacity not to stop time but to show the fractionary gait of time, the mortal divisions of depth that imbricate the body in time that is almost light.

Polka dot oneiric

The camera-produced image, the photograph, may not invite or even permit the viewer's act of imagination, argues Jean Baudrillard: the hyperreal instead stays above the mortal and dreaming world, a kind of final, fatal Platonic form that forces out the negotiations of thought.[56] Here Baudrillard extends, perhaps, Theodor Adorno's thesis that diabolical popular culture actively deprives the proletariat of the space of dreams, imagination, and aesthetic force.[57] Woodman's series of near-self-portraits oscillate between popular culture – a cult following of a sort – and fine art – they have been displayed at the Tate Modern in London, the Guggenheim Museum in San Francisco and in New York City, and the Metropolitan Museum of Art in New York City. Most attempts to explain the power of her images come up short – we venerate the cult of the dead girl, or we see her links to surrealism, and maybe her inchoate feminism, but cannot explain why any of that matters. And yet, I think another way to read the power of Woodman's photographs – perhaps an eccentric reading but one not antithetical to my earlier readings of her work as contending with the Kantian sublime – is by tracing the force of the oneiric as it pulses through the images' striking constellations of the nude female body, damaged architecture, and frames of violence implicit and obscure.[58] The shapes of things as they emerge in understanding rather than in fact form the visual game of some of Woodman's images.

Consider the photograph *Polka Dots* (Figure 5.14), one of the two images chosen for the poster of the popular culture film *The Woodmans*.[59] The image from *Polka Dots* pulls the eye to multiple fractionary darknesses in the frame: the polka dots, the damaged walls pitted with dark marks and gaps, the girl's eyes, and most

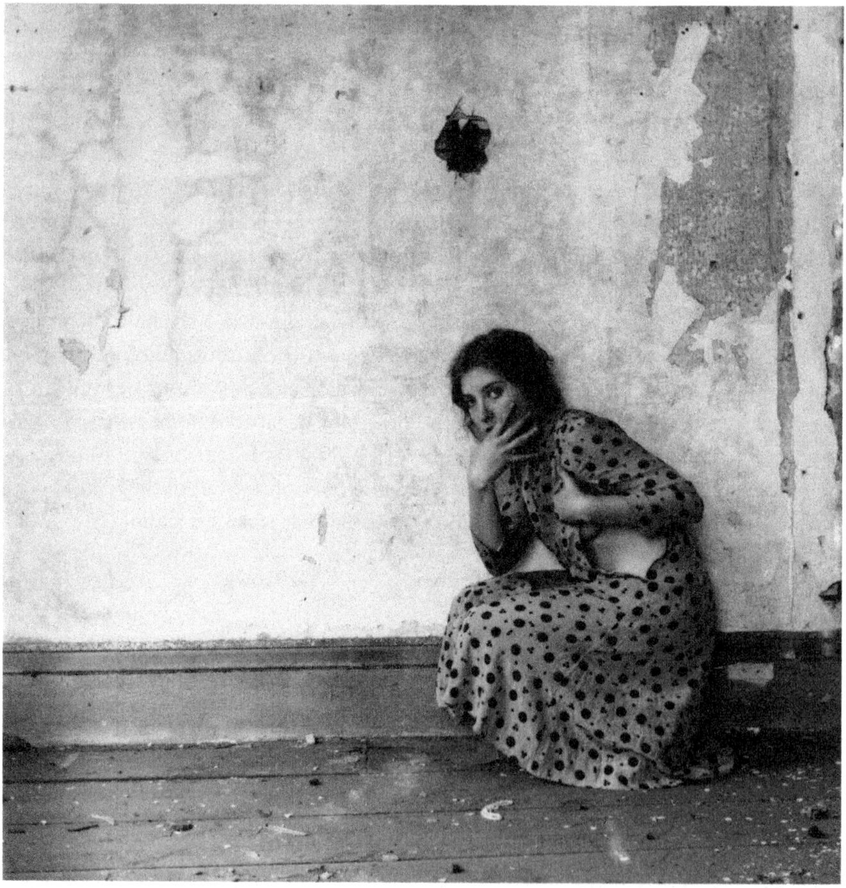

FIGURE 5.14 Francesca Woodman, *From Polka Dots*, Providence, Rhode Island, 1976, gelatin silver print, 5⅛ × 5⅛ in. Courtesy George and Betty Woodman.

saliently the girl's body, which is shown as a shadow beneath and within her partly opened dress. As if she were showing a wound, or the way the body is a site of wounding, and as if she were her own doubting Thomas, Woodman places – and invites the viewer to place – a hand in the wound of the open dress. This wound is the weighted gape manifest not as the female body but rather as the mortal body overwritten by gendered codes of fragility. The girl in the picture looks not only vulnerable but also terrifying, as if crouched to take flight, her crouched form echoing the large black spot on the wall above her, with its wing-like irregularities.

The image invites us deeper inward, even as the form – the photograph – is the essence of surface, the definitive superficial. As Baudrillard argues, the photograph is a realm without depth, or as Woodman put it, the photographic image is flattened to fit paper. This play on the premise of depth in the visual scape of superficiality arrests the image and traps it in its own performance. This entrapment is much as we experience dreams as a concatenation of images and symbols that are so compressed, or pressed together, as to impress us with a sense of the impossibility of resolving them into translatable meaning. This tractive quality of resisting translation makes some of Woodman's photographs almost inexplicably powerful. That is, given her social place – a privileged child whose subject matter can superficially appear to be meditation on the end or edge of childhood's privilege – we might not expect the images to carry such heft. But they do carry a disturbing and penetrating force: training a gaze looking always into rooms whose inaccessibility manifests as cognate with the limits of language, Woodman's photographs force their claim to inhabit and sustain an untranslatable visual realm.

But are Woodman's photographic images evil demons in the Baudrillardian sense? Woodman's photographs do not negate the imaginary; rather, they propel the imaginary so far forward as to compel our acceptance of the blank space around the photograph, that is, compel us to reach and see the end of the photograph, what Barthes calls its blind field.[60] In the same way that Agamben shows that the poem is always about its own ending, so also Woodman's most accomplished photographs tell us to look away.[61]

In the *Polka Dots* (Figure 5.14) photograph, Woodman's thumb is in her mouth, partly a play on infantile regression but also a literal play on words: the thumb suppressing speech forces us to look to the open dress, with its wound-like turn of flesh. Language moves from words to code, here, from the words the thumb suppresses in the mouth to the code of geometrically regressive interiority by which the image stakes its claim. This interiority is not manifestly sexual but rather ontological, an interiority of the wound of the eye, the wound of the embodied gaze. The palpable metaphor for the eye here is the polka dots themselves.

The wound that is the eye, the image tells us, grants and also is risked by the force of sight, the room we do not choose to inhabit is the room we most clearly see. As in dreams, we inhabit not the spaces of the demonic but spaces of force when we look at Woodman's more successful images. Whereas one could interpret this "eye" along Georges Bataille's sexualized terms, the challenge in reading Woodman's photography is that to see the force of the images is to divest oneself of the pathologizing gaze of looking at Woodman as the troubled teen, a bad or crazed girl.[62] It is harder but more tallied to the images to see in Woodman's best photographs the tension of the forms' harness of mortal time and fate as space, the body as space in space, an easeless and terrifying emergence.

Notes

1 See Olga M.Viso, *Ana Mendieta: Earth Body* (Berlin: Hatje Cantz, 2004) and Olga M.Viso, *Unseen Mendieta: The Unpublished Works of Ana Mendieta* (London: Prestel, 2008); see also Claire Raymond, *Francesca Woodman and the Kantian Sublime* (Burlington, VT: Ashgate, 2010).

2 See Elisabeth Bronfen, *Over Her Dead Body: Death, Femininity, and the Aesthetic* (Manchester, UK: Manchester University Press, 1992); see also Claire Raymond, *The Posthumous Voice in Women's Writing* (Aldershot, UK: Ashgate, 2006) and Debra Ferrday, "A Waif's Progress: Kate Moss and the Feminine Uncanny," *Feminist Media Studies* 14, no. 5 (2014): 791–805.

3 Jane Simon, "An Intimate Mode of Looking: Francesca Woodman's Photographs," *Emotion, Space and Society* 3, no. 1 (2010): 28–35.

4 Carolee Schneeman, "Regarding Ana Mendieta," *Women and Performance: A Journal of Feminist Theory* 21, no. 2 (July 2011): 183–90.

5 Judy Chicago's *Menstruation Bathroom* in the performance and exhibition *Womanhouse* (1972) and her better-known work *The Dinner Party* (1979) illustrate a rather direct and graphic invocation of the female body, as was popular in the era's feminist art practices.

6 The photographs that speak to the visual concept of the angelic include *On Being an Angel* (1976), *From Angel series* (1977), *From a series on Angels* (1977), and *Angels* (1977–78). See Del Valle-Cordero, "Ana Mendieta: Performance in the Way of the Primitive," *Arte Individua y Sociedad* 26, no. 1 (2014): 67–82; see also Anca Cristofovici, "Performing Corpo-Realities," *Consciousness, Literature and the Arts* 19 (January 2009): 157–91.

7 By using the term "haunting," I do not mean that Mendieta and Woodman invoke the spectral, the shadowy, the insubstantial; there are important differences between haunting, which implies power and the return of the oppressed, and spectrality, which suggests ethereality. On this argument, see Avery Gordon, *Ghostly Matters* (Minneapolis, MN: University of Minnesota Press, 1999). That said, many scholars who write on Woodman describe her as a ghost: see Prema Purigali Prabhakar, "Invoking the Spectral Body: A Study of Potential Corporealities in the Work of Marina Abramovic and Francesca Woodman," *Excursions* 1, no. 1 (2010): 91–101; and see also Katharine Conley, *Surrealist Ghostliness* (Lincoln, NE: University of Nebraska Press, 2013).

8 Clara Escoda Agusti, "'I Carve Myself into My Hands: The Body Experienced from Within in Ana Mendieta's Work and Migdalia Cruz's 'Miriam Flowers,'" *Hispanic Review* 75, no. 3 (Summer 2007): 289–311.

9 Any consideration of Ana Mendieta's work should begin with Olga M.Viso's incomparable studies of the artist. Please see Viso, *Ana Mendieta: Earth Body*.

10 See Viso, *Unseen Mendieta*.

11 Claire Raymond, "Roland Barthes, Ana Mendieta, and the Orphaned Image," *The Conversant: Interview Projects, Talk Poetry, Embodied Inquiry*, September, 2014, http://theconversant.org/?p=7854.

12 Roland Barthes, *Camera Lucida: Reflections on Photography* (New York: Macmillan, 1981), 6.

13 Before her death, Mendieta received the Prix de Rome and was a respected artist. See Joyce Wadler, "A Death in Art," *New York*, December 16, 1985, 38.

14 Cuban American artist Coco Fusco included Ana Mendieta in her brilliant performance installation *Better Yet When Dead* at the Festival Internacional de Arte de Medellin in Colombia in 1997, which commented on Mendieta's ascension in the art world after her death.

15 Jane Blocker, *Where Is Ana Mendieta*? (Durham, NC: Duke University Press 1999).
16 Ibid., 52–53.
17 *Silueta Series*, performance photographed in a series of 35 mm color slides, 1976.
18 Stephanie Rosenthal, Adrian Heathfield, and Julia Bryan-Wilson, *Ana Mendieta: Traces* (London: Hayward Publishing, 2013).
19 Commenting on her own work, Mendieta stated: "I have been carrying out a dialogue between the landscape and the female body. . . . I believe this has been a direct result of my having been torn from [Cuba]. . . . My art is the way I re-establish the bonds that unite me to the universe. It is a return to the maternal source. Through my earth/body sculptures I become one with the earth. . . . I become an extension of nature and nature becomes an extension of my body. This obsessive act of reasserting my ties with the earth is really the reactivation of primaeval beliefs . . . [in] an omnipresent female force, the after-image of being encompassed within the womb." See Petra Barreras del Rio and John Perreault, *Ana Mendieta: A Retrospective* (New York: New Museum of Contemporary Art, 1988), 10.
20 Although Mendieta made a hundred silhouettes, she took thousands of slides archiving them. See Susan Best, "The Serial Spaces of Ana Mendieta," *Art History* 30, no. 1 (February 2007): 57–82.
21 Ann Gabhart, ed., *Francesca Woodman: Photographic Work* (Wellesley, MA: Wellesley College Museum/Hunter College Art Gallery, 1989).
22 Hervé Chandès, ed., *Francesca Woodman* (Zurich: Scalo, 1998).
23 Chris Townsend, *Francesca Woodman* (London: Phaidon, 2006).
24 Claire Raymond, *Francesca Woodman and the Kantian Sublime* (Aldershot, UK: Ashgate, 2010).
25 Corey Keller, Julia Bryan-Wilson, and Jennifer Blessing, *Francesca Woodman* (San Francisco, CA: San Francisco Museum of Modern Art, 2013).
26 Woodman also exhibited at the Sammlung Verbund Gallery, in 2014. See Betsey Berne, Gabriele Schor, and Elisabeth Bronfen, eds., *Francesca Woodman: Works from the Sammlung Verbund* (Kologne: Verlag der Buchhandlung Walther Koenig and New York, New York: Distributed Arts Publishers, 2014).
27 Carol Armstrong, "Francesca Woodman: A Ghost in the House," in *Women Artists at the Millennium*, ed. Catherine de Zegher and Carol Armstrong (Cambridge, MA: MIT Press, 2006), 351.
28 Barthes, *Camera Lucida*, 93–4.
29 On Woodman's *Blueprint for a Temple* and other diazotypes, see Claire Raymond, *Francesca Woodman's Dark Gaze* (London: Routledge, 2016); see also Harriet Riches, "Projecting Touch: Francesca Woodman's Late 'Blueprints,'" *Photographies* 5, no. 2 (2012): 135–57.
30 Butler, *Gender Trouble* (London: Routledge, 1990) 129–49.
31 Townsend, *Francesca Woodman*.
32 Ibid.
33 Elisabeth Bronfen, "Leaving an Imprint: Francesca Woodman's Photographic Tableaux Vivants," in *Francesca Woodman: Works from the Sammlung Verbund*, ed. Betsey Berne, Gabriele Schor, and Elisabeth Bronfen (Kologne, Germany: Verlag der Buchhandlung Walther Koenig and New York: Distributed Arts Publishers, 2014), 11–30.
34 Meaghan Thurston, "'At Home in Dust': Francesca Woodman's *House Series*, Revisited," *FORUM: University of Edinburgh Postgraduate Journal of Culture and the Arts* 11 (Autumn 2010): 2–13.
35 Raymond, *Woodman and the Kantian Sublime*.
36 Barthes, *Camera Lucida*, 15.
37 Ibid., 74.
38 Sloane Rankin, "Peach Mumble – Ideas Cooking," in *Francesca Woodman*, ed. Hervé Chandès (Zurich: Scalo, 1998): 34–35.
39 Barthes, *Camera Lucida*, 31.
40 Blocker, *Where Is Ana Mendieta?*

41 Woodman's spoken opinion on feminism was ambivalent, and this ambiguity is visible in her works. See Berne, Schor, and Bronfen, *Francesca Woodman*. See also Elisabete Lopes, "Francesca Woodman's Journey into the Gothic Wonderland," in *Women and the Arts: Dialogues in Female Creativity*, ed. Diana V. Almeida (Bern, Switzerland: Peter Lang, 2013), 71–84. See also Peggy Phelan, "Francesca Woodman's Photography: Death and the Image One More Time," *Signs: A Journal of Women in Culture and Society* 27, no. 4 (Summer 2002): 979–1004; and see also, Harriet Riches, "A Disappearing Act: Francesca Woodman's Portrait of a Reputations," *Oxford Art Journal* 27, no. 1 (2004): 95–113.

42 Whether Andre killed Mendieta or whether she accidentally fell during an argument is a question that only Andre can answer. He was twice tried, and twice acquitted, of her murder. See Vincent Patrick, "A Death in the Art World," *New York Times*, June 10, 1990.

43 Mendieta photographed all of the *Silueta Series* images in which she did not appear, which means that she was the photographer for almost the whole series. Other people photographed the performance works in which she did physically appear. For this reason, I limit myself to discussing her *Silueta Series*.

44 Armstrong, "Francesca Woodman: A Ghost in the House"; see also Conley, *Surrealist Ghostliness*.

45 See Johanna Demetrakas's documentary film *Womanhouse*, 1974, www.wmm.com/film catalog/pages/c324.shtml. See also http://womanhouse.net.

46 Roland Barthes, *Mythologies*, trans. Annette Lavers (New York: Farrar, Straus, Giroux, 1972).

47 Barthes, *Camera Lucida*, 79.

48 Jacques Derrida, *Specters of Marx* (London: Routledge, 2006), 132.

49 Woodman created the abandoned house images in Providence, Rhode Island, while a student at RISD, photographing in abandoned spaces, implicitly those buildings ignored by the government. Providence was later the scene of one of the largest class-action lawsuits for lead poisoning of young children in substandard housing. See Jenna Berman, "Rhode Island's Childhood Lead Poisoning Crisis Remains Painted Thickly on the Wall after *State v. Lead Industries Association*," *Villanova Environmental Law Journal* 20, no. 2 (2009): 217.

50 Avery Gordon describes ways that the social figure of the ghost encodes her own process of being haunted by cultural terms of violence and silencing. See Gordon, *Ghostly Matters: Haunting and the Sociological Imagination* (Minneapolis, MN: University of Minnesota Press, 1999), 140–1.

51 I developed the next two sections of this chapter, "Francesca Woodman's Zen" and "Polka Dot Oneiric," from blog posts that originally appeared on my website, www.claireraymond.org.

52 Jay Prosser, "Buddha Barthes: What Barthes Saw in Photography (That He Didn't in Literature)," in *Photography Degree Zero: Reflections on Roland Barthes's Camera Lucida*, ed. Geoffrey Batchen (Cambridge, MA: MIT Press, 2009), 91–105.

53 While there is significant nuance in the way that different theorists approach and interpret the question of Francesca Woodman's state of mental health – and I regret very much that there is not the space in this chapter to offer detailed readings and interpretations of these various theorists, all very valuable in what they bring to discussion of her work – my point is simply that the very fact of Woodman's mental health being emphasized in scholarship arguably can have the effect of pulling attention away from the photographic work. See Phelan, "Francesca Woodman's Photography: Death and the Image One More Time"; Adele Tutter, "Metamorphosis and the Aesthetics of Loss: II. Lady of the Woods – the Transformative Lens of Francesca Woodman," *International Journal of Psychoanalysis* 92, no. 6 (December 2011): 1517–39; see also Anna C. Chave, "Normal Ills: On Embodiment, Victimization and the Origins of Feminist Art," in *Trauma and Visuality in Modernity*, ed. Lisa Saltzman and Eric Rosenberg (Hanover, NH: Dartmouth College Press, 2006), 138.

54 Scott Willis, *The Woodmans*, C. Scott Films, 2011.

55 Phelan, "Francesca Woodman's Photography: Death and the Image One More Time." See also Jui Ch'i Lui, "Woodman's Self Images: Transforming Bodies in the Space of Femininity," *Woman's Art Journal* 25 (Spring–Summer 2004): 26–31; Tutter, "Metamorphosis and the Aesthetics of Loss: II"; Amy Sherlock, "Multiple Exposures: Identity and Alterity in the 'Self-Portraits' of Francesca Woodman," *Paragraph* 36, no. 3 (November 2013): 376–91.

56 Jean Baudrillard, *Simulations and Simulacra*, trans. Sheila Glaser (Ann Arbor, MI: Michigan University Press, 1994).

57 Theodor Adorno, "The Culture Industry: Enlightenment as Mass Deception," in *Dialectic of Enlightenment*, ed. Max Horkheimer and Theodor Adorno (Redwood City, CA: Stanford University Press, 2002): 94–137.

58 Raymond, *Francesca Woodman and the Kantian Sublime*.

59 Willis, *The Woodmans*.

60 Barthes, *Camera Lucida*, 57.

61 Giorgio Agamben, *The End of the Poem: Studies in Poetics* (Redwood City, CA: Stanford University Press, 1999).

62 Georges Bataille, *Story of the Eye*, trans. Joachim Neugroschal (London: Penguin Modern Classics, 2001).

6

PERFORMANCES

Nan Goldin, Nikki Lee, Catherine Opie, and Zackary Drucker

Photographers Nan Goldin (born 1953) and Catherine Opie (born 1961) and the performance and multimedia artists Nikki Lee (born 1970) and Zackary Drucker (born 1983) have created works in the 1980s, 1990s, and early 2000s that reflect and fall into conversation with cultural trends that emphasize the idea of a performative self – that is, a self produced not by an inherent truth of one's soul but instead by cultural forces. Of course, Goldin, Opie, Lee, and Drucker, all active in the United States, are not just reflecting the cultural zeitgeist in their photographic works but creating and shaping the visual culture into which their art emerges as singular and formative work. To understand the idea of identity as social performance, one turns to the work of philosopher and historian Michel Foucault, who published several books from the late 1960s to the early 1980s that laid the foundation for the cultural movement away from belief in a stable and essential identity of self.[1] Foucault's theories of identity formation have worked their way so deeply into segments of Western culture that one need not have read his work to be influenced by the echo effect of some aspects of the philosopher's arguments regarding the transience and mutability of subject formation and how that formation is inextricably imbricated with culture. That said, an understanding of Foucault's pivotal arguments regarding Western history and culture will illuminate the zeitgeist that his work reflects and furthers.

Foucault's work on the concept of sexuality influenced feminism at the end of the twentieth century, a development that is in some ways curious and even ironic, for Foucault was largely unconcerned with questions of feminism, women's rights, and even gender. But through his minute, carefully detailed examinations of historical facts – using a reading method he called archeology – he explored how the modern era ushered in tropes of enforced development and containment of a heavily monitored self. Foucault argued that the self was a product that emerged from forms of capitalist and quasi-Christian power and domination. Foucault's argument that various forms of cultural belief (for example, notions of biological destiny) only masquerade as knowledge or truth, offered feminists ways of rethinking what it meant to be called a woman. In his three-volume work *The History of Sexuality*, Foucault argued that the idea of a stable sexual identity (e.g., a gay man) was a creation of modern systems of capitalist nation formation. Foucault argued, then, that the idea of a pathological sexuality inherent in men attracted to men was not a stable fact but instead a transient effect produced by the needs of capitalist states to control the reproduction of citizens who the states value primarily as consumers. Foucault expanded this very specific and in some ways rather narrow idea – that cultures produced and framed forms of sexuality as pathological to uphold forms of capitalistic state power – to a much broader and possibly revolutionary idea. That broader concept suggests that not only did a false consciousness underlie capitalist production and consumption but also that the very idea of a true kernel of self that *precedes* the shaping of desires manifested by capitalist state urging (via cultural production that creates the images of desire's fulfillment) is suspect. Foucault argues that we, in capitalist modernity, have lost the path of our desire. Instead, what he calls power-knowledge – that is, capitalist-supported state interests that in turn shape identity and hence longing – is implanted in us and shapes our wishes and thoughts before we recognize that we are being shaped this way. And so Foucault develops the counternotion of pleasure as opposed to desire, pleasure that we feel in our bodies as the only space still untouched by capitalism and therefore still open for the creation and formation of a genuine self.

For feminists, Foucault's idea of the near lack of a stable stratum of self that precedes cultural structures of power-knowledge provided a way to counter the belief that people society calls women were biologically predestined to serve specific roles. And yet, Foucault argues that embodiment can be experienced as a counterforce to capitalism. While Foucault does argue that the oppressive hyperfeminine notion of being female is culturally produced in the service of modern capitalism, in many ways feminist co-opting of Foucault's work is a misprision of his argument.[2] And yet to some degree it has been a productive misreading. For Nan Goldin, Catherine Opie, Nikki Lee, and Zackary Drucker, the idea that the biological female self need not be feminine and the biological male self need not be masculine opened an approach to photographic work that made the feminist gaze central.[3] This is not to say that these four artists produced photographic works that look similar to each other. Their work can be dissimilar in form, and when they do look similar it has more to do with the self-referential development of documentary photography and less to do with formal similarity between their works. Rather, their work shares the expanse of possibility that comes with a greater certainty of claim, the sense that unlike, say, Clementina Hawarden, these photographers did not think of themselves as seeing the way women see. Instead, they conceived of themselves as possessing a gaze detached from biology that is elusively, or fluidly, defined culturally. Even as they developed work that I will argue shows a feminist aesthetic, Goldin, Lee, Opie, and Drucker also created work that is very much radically questioning of what it might mean to see with a woman's eyes.

A radiant eye

Sarah Ruddy took her friend Nan Goldin's phrase as the title of her 2009 essay "A Radiant Eye Yearns from Me."[4] In it, Ruddy emphasizes that Goldin claims to take photographs because of love, not expressly love for the camera or for art but love for the people whom she photographs.[5] Goldin's work in some ways prefigures the era of Facebook, in that the photographs for which she is best known chronicle the lives of her friends and lovers, though her pungent and intense work could never be mistaken for typical Facebook material. These include the exhibits, series, and books *The Ballad of Sexual Dependency*, *I'll Be Your Mirror*, and the *Cookie Portfolio*, as well as the exhibit *Witnesses: Against Our Vanishing*, in collaboration with David Wojnarowicz. In this chapter, I will focus on the images that became *The Ballad of Sexual Dependency*. I do so because these photographs were the force that propelled Goldin, who struggled for years with chemical dependency, from the demi-monde – tending bar and attending parties always with her camera in tow – into galleries and museums. They are the photographs that made her famous. I want to query why. What is the force of these images – so personal as to arguably have no relevance to anyone outside of Goldin's immediate social circle – that translates them into the concern and desire of outsiders? And how can this propulsive force, away from or beyond the people of whom the photographs were made, be understood as part of a feminist aesthetic? These questions interlock.

Goldin originally showed these photographs as slides in performances set to music for the friends whom she had photographed in 35-millimeter roll film.[6] In this sense, Ruddy's descriptions of the photographs as having a snapshot aesthetic – or, as she perceptively frames it, affective documentary – are accurate.[7] Goldin's photographs, in their subject matter and instantaneous, almost always not-posed aesthetic, are a cousin of street photography. They are also a hybrid with that domain of traditional feminine photography: the mother who photographs and thereby chronicles her children's lives. Here the unposed (street) image merges with the vernacularly (snapshot) posed. However, Goldin's subjects are not her blood kin, much less her descendants, but her friends who share the demi-monde of intravenous drugs, queer sexuality, and dressing in drag.[8] The intimate and loving photographs that she creates chronicle her friends at parties, taking drugs, just before and after having sex, in the nude, and in party clothes.[9] She photographs parties where she is not an onlooker but part of the party; she is there getting stoned and having sex and carrying her camera.[10] What Ruddy means by affective documentary is that Goldin takes photographs of her friends not as someone who is judging them or even in a sense watching them but as someone who is with them, of them, and whose love for these people makes her want to commemorate the moments through which they, and she, live.[11]

To my mind (although I very much like and value Ruddy's insights into Goldin's work), the translucent and transient materiality of slide shows marks Goldin's aesthetic not so much as a snapshot aesthetic or even affective documentary. Rather, Goldin's aesthetic is one of almost vanishing and yet not vanishing, as the photographic image is cast up against the disappearance of the self. The very voluminousness of Goldin's output, hundreds of thousands of images still wait to be cataloged, gives insight into and exemplifies this slideshow aesthetic: her photographs are always true to the slideshow concept, as the idea that motivates the photographs is transience and the beauty of the fleeting body moved by love. Goldin's work has been printed in color and framed, it hangs in galleries and museums (for example, the National Museum of Women in the Arts, Washington, DC; the Art Institute of Chicago; the North Carolina Museum of the Arts, Raleigh), and it has also been published in books (*The Ballad of Sexual Dependency* [New York: Aperture, 2005], for example, presents in book form a tiny fraction of the images that made up the slideshow *The Ballad of Sexual Dependency*): yet the essential aesthetic of the photographs is the slideshow. They capture moments that echo their intended presentation as images that only last a minute – a slideshow clicking from image to image. And the intense color saturation that shows so well against blank walls, as if revivifying ghosts, is the fingerprint of Goldin's photographic style. She creates slideshows, and even though the photographs have been circulated in the art-world public mainly as framed prints on walls, their primary characteristics are of slides, images created to shimmer with quick and very often painful insight and bright, drenched colors and then move away, out of the gaze and into the mind's eye. This quality of being intensely and almost instantaneously memorable sets apart Goldin's photographs.

Goldin takes a traditional feminine point of view – loving her family – and shifts it very much in the direction that anthropologist and feminist Kath Weston suggests in *Families We Chose* (here, I am not arguing that Goldin has read Weston; instead, I tender an interpretation of Goldin in light of Weston's work).[12] The family members that Goldin chooses are men and women, most of them gay or bisexual and drug users, who have left their biological families but not to create new, traditional families made up of biological mother, father, and children. Goldin's feminist vision, then, inheres partly in her invocation of the family one chooses, as opposed to the traditional biological model whereby a woman socially mothers those children to whom she bodily gives birth.

That said, there is some room to question whether Goldin's vision of the family she chooses moves far enough away from certain tropes of the traditional feminine. The most obvious question would be, if women can escape the biological determinism of being biological mothers who spend their lives nurturing their offspring, is it really that big an improvement – for personal self-determination – to become the "mother" of a family one has chosen, that is, a group of loved ones who are not biologically connected to you? If you are still providing nurturance and care that is not fully reciprocated (the traditional power imbalance for the biological family), then how feminist is this change? The answer to this question surely appears in Goldin's photographs, which shake loose the pain of love and make of this pain, in several instances, gorgeous revelatory works of art. Goldin may – or may not – be providing maternal care with the love of her radiant eye (her camera), but in return for this loving eye she gets a body of work that memorably and with painful truth shows the "eggshell" fragility – to quote writer and critic Luc Sante – of not just

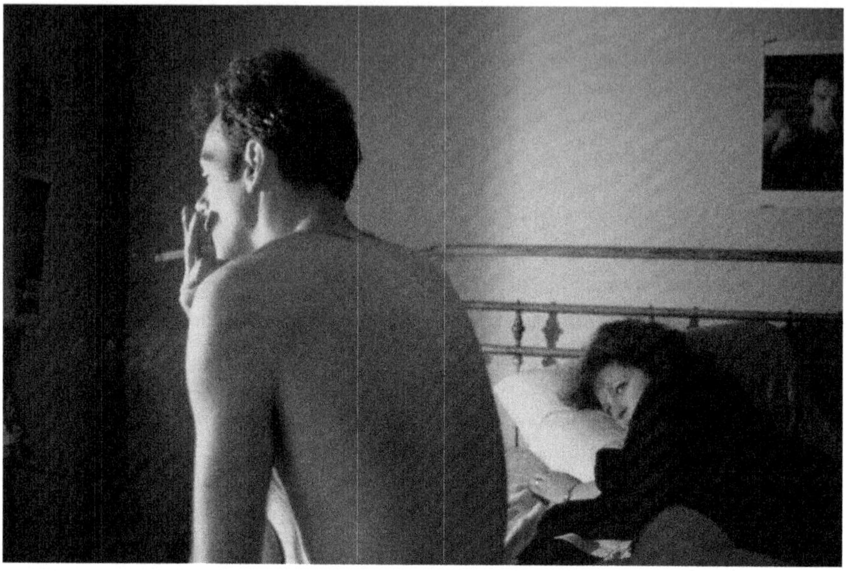

FIGURE 6.1 Nan Goldin, *Nan and Brian in bed, NYC*, 1983. © Nan Goldin, Courtesy Matthew Marks Gallery.

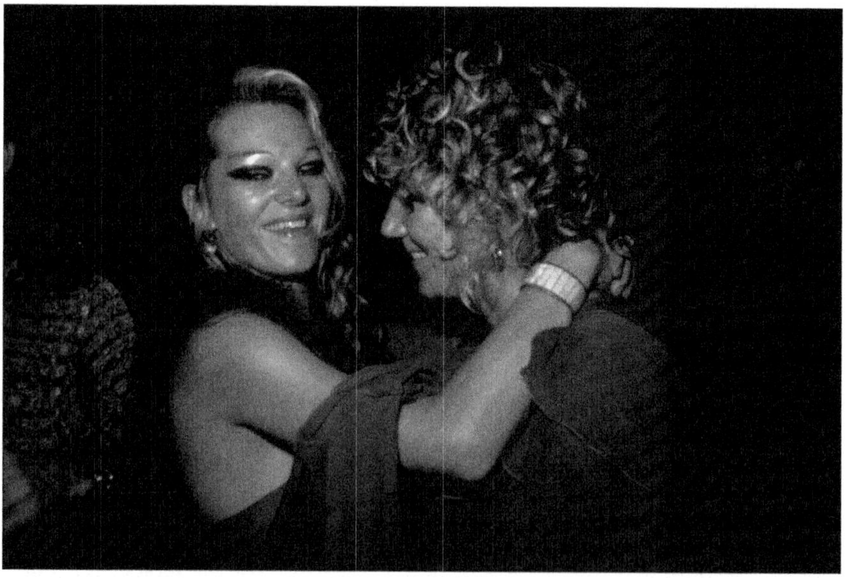

FIGURE 6.2 Nan Goldin, *Cookie and Sharon dancing in the Back Room, Provincetown*, 1976. © Nan Goldin, Courtesy Matthew Marks Gallery.

the demi-monde but by implication of all human beings.[13] Goldin's photographs of late-night desolation as a party winds down (*Trixie on the cot*, 1979); the eerie post-coital pull between lovers (*Nan and Brian in bed, NYC*, 1983); the color-saturated embrace of two women in love (*Cookie and Sharon dancing in the Back Room,*

Provincetown, 1976); the transfiguring, uncanny shadow cast as a man and a woman embrace (*The Hug*, 1980), this shadow suggesting the bodies violently becoming one form; and even her own face after being savagely beaten by her ex-boyfriend, Brian (*Nan one month after being battered*, 1984) pull her audience into a rich visual world in which we care for those Nan loves (Figures 6.1, 6.2, 6.3). She can share her radiant eye with viewers of her photographs because she is so skilled at finding the moment that reveals a social fact in aesthetic form. But this capacity to show the real does not entirely explain the feminist power of Goldin's work. That is a more complicated function.

For the link between femininity and pain is a potential problem in Goldin's work. *Nan one month after being battered* is prefigured by the earlier photograph *Heart shaped bruise* (1980), in which a bruise on a woman's thigh stands as a symbol for love as pain. But, as I hope to show, Goldin's battered face in *Nan one month after being battered* (Figure 6.3) undoes rather than repeats this fusion of love and pain. The self-portrait photograph that Goldin took after her boyfriend Brian savagely beat her, to remind herself to never go back to him, does not present the bruises as a sign of love but as a sign of love gone wrong. The photograph employs that very central and essential trope of photography – the stare – to stare down, to look straight at the transfiguring pain of desire and dependency. A complex network of signifiers, cultural and visual, achieves the gendering of the photograph *Nan one month after being battered*.

Although it (Figure 6.3) records how Goldin's face looked after Brian beat her, nothing in the photograph necessarily tells us that a man beat the battered woman

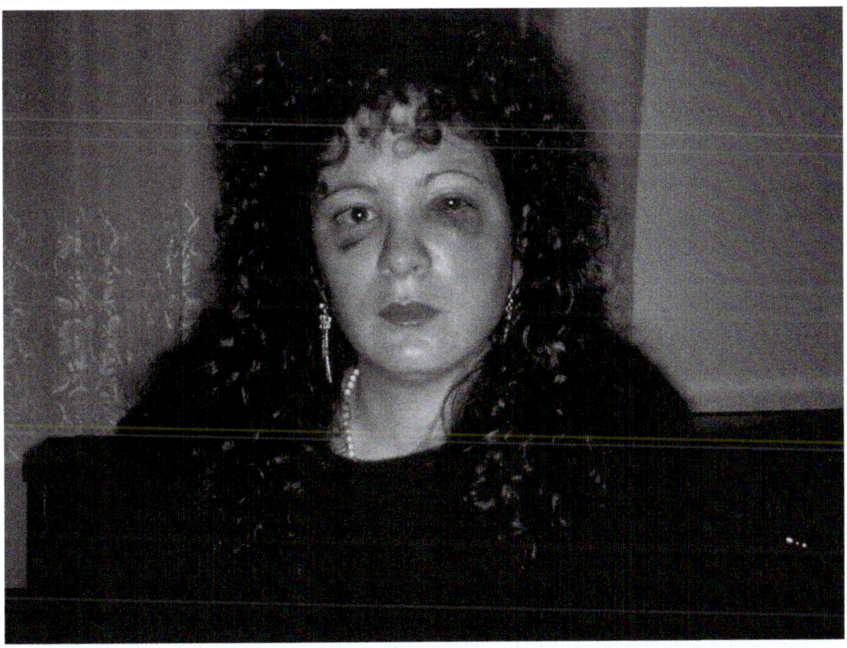

FIGURE 6.3 Nan Goldin, *Nan one month after being battered*, 1984. © Nan Goldin, Courtesy Matthew Marks Gallery.

shown in the image. And yet the statistical reality in the United States is that when intimate partner abuse rises to the level of severe battery, it is almost always a man who does the battering. (Other, lesser forms of intimate partner violence may have more gender parity, although even that could be debated.) And so in the social context of late twentieth-century and early twenty-first-century America, if we see a woman's battered face and assume that a man caused the damage, we are usually correct.[14] The photograph also cues us that this woman's damaged face tells a story of gendered power dynamics: the face, although horribly injured, is made up with lipstick and eyeliner; the lush and longish hair is curled and carefully coiffed; the sitter wears earrings and a delicately luminous necklace. She has made an effort to look pretty in a fairly traditional feminine way: eye make-up, lipstick, earrings, necklace, and carefully managed long hair. In this sense the sitter presents herself as traditionally feminine, and a traditionally feminine appearance in its turn cannot but evoke traditional gender dynamics. Women try to look pretty for men because men have social power; a man can choose whether he wants to share that power with a given woman if her appearance pleases him. In other words, looking pretty in a traditionally feminine way is a visual and social cognate for conveying one's subservient position. Of course, one could imagine – at least theoretically – that women might want to look attractive to men just to have sex with them, but that attractiveness would not need to include the placating and self-effacing gestures of make-up – especially not of make-up placed over wounds.

Here is how Goldin's self-portrait after being battered becomes iconic: it shows the violent harm and desire of compulsory heterosexuality, the make-up applied over the wound. The photograph does not romanticize male-on-female violence (Goldin never went back to Brian). Instead, it stares head-on at this violence, staring at it from the place of pain where the watcher is both the violated one and the one who turns to face the terms of her own violation. It is an extraordinary visual performance going to the deepest place of the gaze, where the self confronts the self not in some fatuous selfie mode but in an effort to get at and create a marker of death against death. The marker is the death of the self through violation (by being beaten by a man) and the self's refusal to accept this annihilation, a refusal that is performed by locating the edge where the annihilation has almost – but not yet wholly – occurred. The place and time of day of the photograph are significant. Virtually all of the images in *The Ballad of Sexual Dependency* are nighttime, indoor images. And yet *Nan one month after being battered* suggests daylight behind the ultrafeminine white lace curtains. The curtains suggest a window, which suggests an outdoors, a way out. Likewise in its signifiers of over-the-top femininity – lipstick, pearls, gold-tinted curls, lace curtains – the photograph is anchored as a female space. This is a place unlike the bed Nan shared with Brian and a place unlike the decor of all the interiors in which Nan photographed Brian, showcasing him as the masculine other to her camera's desirously feminine gaze. The about-face that Goldin performs in *Nan one month after being battered* is possible because all along, in all her photographs, she has been performing this gaze that aspires to love and nurture the subjects her camera captures.

Yet that gaze is also immensely sharp and clear, seeing with an eye that may be loving but also is – always – unsparing and accurate.

Cookie Mueller

Goldin's *Cookie Portfolio* exemplifies the feminine gaze of love that Goldin claims typifies her photographs with the very important torque that Goldin's loving (traditionally feminine in caring about other people and in its immersion in the social world) is focused here not on her biological children and not on a man, but on a woman whom she loves (Figures 6.1–6.3). An actress, writer, and personality, Cookie Mueller was Goldin's friend, not her lover (both Goldin and Mueller had sexual relationships with men and with women but apparently not with each other). Goldin photographed Mueller frequently beginning in the late 1970s. Goldin did not plan all the images in the *Cookie Portfolio* as a series but rather compiled them after Mueller died of AIDS in 1989, attempting with the photographs to arrest her loss of loved ones to this disease. Indeed, Goldin claims she originally picked up photography after the death by suicide of her beloved sister, Barbara. Goldin said she felt if she took photographs of those whom she loved, then she would never lose them in the way that she so utterly lost her sister. Later, after the AIDS epidemic took many of her friends, Goldin revised this idea, saying that she had come to realize that taking photographs of people does not keep the people with you after their death.[15] Even so, the emotional energy of Goldin's photographs stems from this immense need to capture not simply the moment but the person photographed. The force of this desire makes her find those moments when someone's personality and history is visually revealed, and that gives the photographs – arguably – a feminist torque. Those moments show not so much maternal care but something much fiercer and more aggressive performing a visual claiming and understanding of the person photographed.[16]

Nan Goldin's photographs have a feeling of being not so much images as territories, to borrow from Felix Delueze and Gilles Guitarri; she de-territorializes the landscape of the feminine family snapshot and wrests it into a terrain in which her camera commands a vision of the soul (damaged, plaintive, longing) of the sitter.[17] For example, Goldin's photograph of *Cookie in Tin Pan Alley, NYC* (Figure 6.4), captures her friend's face and shoulders in eerie visual rhyme with the figures on the wall behind her. Cookie is already becoming-image in this plaintive, elegiac photograph. The stoicism of the woman, the hardness of what she is facing, here, become metaphors for the pull of identity as the real: the embodied self that can perform in various guises but is also tied to mortality, exhaustion, thirst (glasses throng the table where Cookie leans forward on her elbows.) Cookie's beautifully structured face is not traditionally pretty but already seeming to be sculpted in some harder material, and Goldin articulates this structure of stricture, of containment and longing as the keys of vision, in the portrait of a meditative, exhausted Cookie (Figure 6.4).

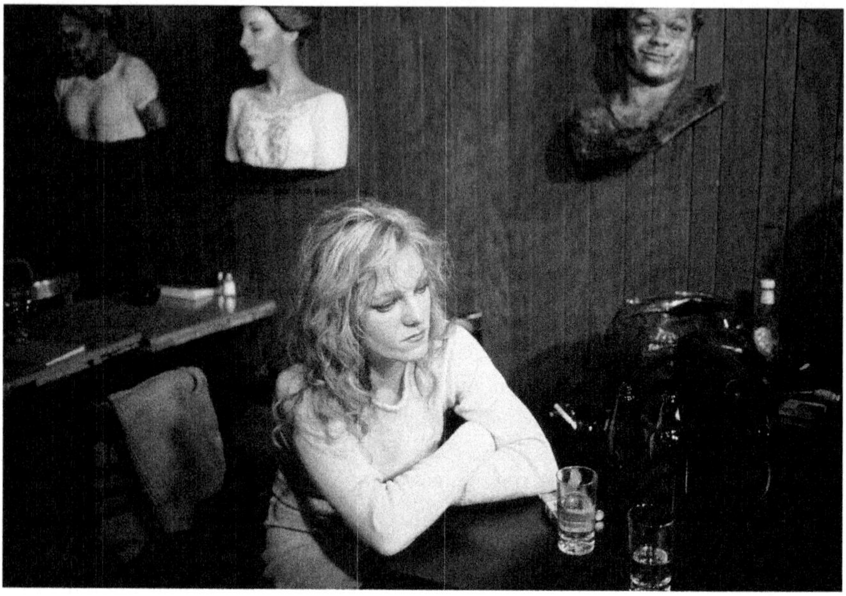

FIGURE 6.4 Nan Goldin, *Cookie in Tin Pan Alley, NYC*, 1983. © Nan Goldin, Courtesy Matthew Marks Gallery.

Goldin, then, powerfully shifts the feminine terrain of family building through photographs from the traditional biological mother collecting photographs of her progeny. And in the *Cookie Portfolio*, she does something even more radically feminist: she honors a woman whom she loves not because she has sex with her but because she loves her as a fabulous human being. Goldin's photographic devotion to Cookie Mueller was not intended as a chronicle of a woman who died young of AIDS. Mueller did not have AIDS, and no one in their social circle had heard of the disease when Goldin began photographing Mueller dancing with her girlfriend Sharon, sitting with her son, and standing close with Goldin at parties. But certainly the way that Goldin photographed Cookie as she descended toward death from AIDS is an extraordinary achievement of empathetic and feminist vision. She photographs Cookie, ill with AIDS, at Cookie's wedding to the HIV-positive Vittorio, and then she photographs Cookie standing at Vittorio's open casket, and then she photographs Cookie lying in bed, near death, being taken care of by her former lover, Sharon.

The images of Cookie use several coincidental visual tropes to bring home not only Cookie's grief and pain but also Sharon's and Goldin's in relation to Cookie's too-early death. The color saturation of the photograph *Sharon with Cookie on the bed, Provincetown* (1989) uncannily parallels the color scheme of Goldin's much earlier photograph of the pair dancing in the back room (Figures 6.2 and 6.5). In the 1976 photograph, *Cookie and Sharon dancing in the Back Room*, the women's lavender and purple dresses merge as they lean together in their dance, one part of Cookie's (or Sharon's? the women press so close together you cannot see where one dress ends and the next begins) garment draped over the shoulder of her lover. The joy in the young women's faces is palpable and surely shared with the photographer who catches their joy (Figure 6.2). Darkness surrounds the women, so that we see no other dancers clearly. And the women who are so in love with each other are set against a lush, velvety background that gives the photograph a painted feel. Cookie's gaze is fey, clever, heavily made up, and alluring, although not in a come-hither way but rather expressing astuteness and self-awareness – avowedly sexual. Sharon looks overjoyed and even a little awed that she is Cookie's partner.

The photograph that Nan takes as Cookie lies dying and Sharon cares for her, some 15 years later, displays the same color scheme: Sharon and Cookie wait on a bed and before a wall patterned in deep purples and lavenders and black (Figure 6.5). The pattern of the wallpaper and bedclothes is identical, making the scene slightly vertiginous and echoing the way that the women's garments merged in the earlier, happy photograph of them dancing. In the later photograph, Sharon is wearing purple, while Cookie's garments cannot be seen. The photograph seems part of a tragic diptych, the other half being the much earlier image of the women. Sharon and Cookie's eyes in the later photograph are haunting, especially in contrast to the earlier one. In the later photograph, Cookie still looks astute: just as she knew she was incredibly sexy in the earlier photograph, in the later photograph she knows she is dying. Her eyes still look heavily darkened, but this is not make-up, not eye shadow and liner, but death, exhaustion, illness, and emaciation that darken her eyes.

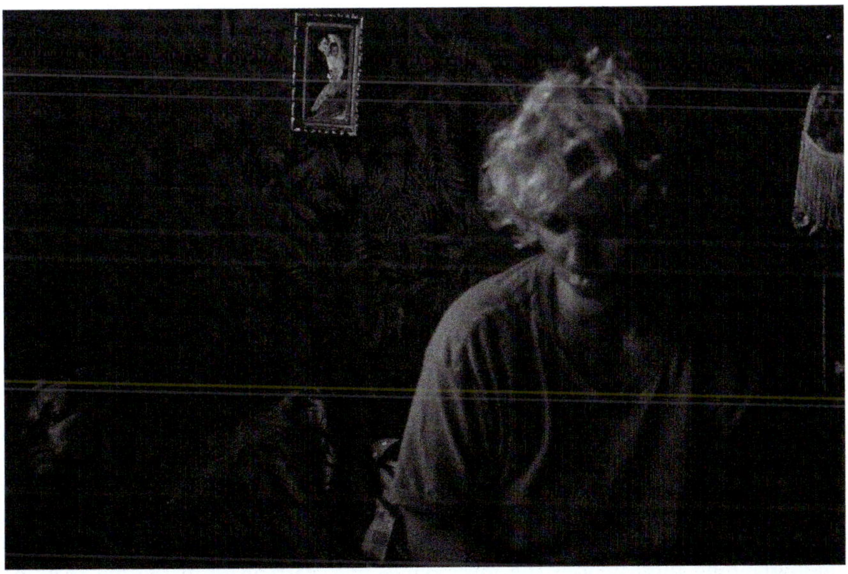

6.5 Nan Goldin, *Sharon with Cookie on the bed, Provincetown*, 1989. © Nan Goldin, Courtesy Matthew Marks Gallery.

Sharon, as in the earlier photograph, is more subdued. In the earlier photograph, Sharon has something of an expression that says, "I can't believe my good luck," and is amazed to be with a woman as vibrantly sexual as Cookie. Yet in the later photograph, she still looks surprised by fate – now by her fate of being the one who is still there, who still loves Cookie, and who will nurse her through her final illness. Sharon looks physically strong, emotionally exhausted, already bereaved, as on the wall between the heads of the two women (recumbent Cookie and upright Sharon) is set the wedding photograph that Goldin took of Cookie and Vittorio (Figure 6.5). Although one could say that photograph shows how Cookie's marriage came between Sharon and Cookie, I suggest that the photograph stands instead as a sign for the weakness and ineffectuality of compulsory heterosexual love compared to the depth of love between Cookie and Sharon. Vittorio is just a small image, a moment in Cookie's life. Sharon is real, large (because she is closer to the camera than Cookie), and unframed (she sits in the photograph at an angle, at the edge of the frame). In this sense, the photograph does not so much comment on the irony of the wedding to Vittorio standing between Cookie and Sharon as rather comment on the relative meaninglessness of Cookie's marriage to this man (a barely legible image in the background) in comparison to the depth of love between Cookie and Sharon and also between Cookie and Goldin, who is at Cookie's side as she suffers. Goldin is there with her camera not to watch Cookie but to be with Cookie, to share her bodily presence with Cookie – to share her eye, her gaze, and her camera. In the deeply feminist space of the photograph, Cookie and Sharon's love is merged with Goldin's love. It is a love honored and valued and given meaning above that of Cookie's quick marriage to a man. Even Cookie's son, her biological progeny, who shows up in many of the photographs of the portfolio, is absent from this deathbed scene.

Whereas one could argue that finding femininity in the deathly is regressive and repressive (Elisabeth Bronfen has persuasively made this argument), I suggest that here Goldin is using photography at its most powerful, acknowledging the always elegiac force of the photograph as such.[18] And the subject of her elegy is the meaning of this woman, Cookie, not as biological mother or heterosexual partner but as she is loved by women, including the photographer. The force and power of the photographer's desire ultimately draw together Goldin's work as feminist. Her photographs claim their territory of night, and their revelations cause us to feel we know the people in the photographs and make the images revelations not of specific people's specific histories but of the mortal coil, the eggshell fragility of being human, of living in a body, and of loving those who are embodied.

Nikki Lee's transformations

If Goldin represents one of the greatest performances of photographic sincerity – photographing those whom she loves while they participate in the life that she shares with them, including drugs and sex, and always at nighttime with her camera around her neck as a sign of her authenticity – then performance and multimedia artist Nikki Lee inherits the terrain Goldin established and estranges that terrain. For Lee's photographic series appear to be snapshots of Lee among those with whom she lives and loves; however, Lee does not consider herself a photographer. She only used the camera in these works for its usefulness in carrying out the extended experimental performance pieces that make up her series.[19] But, as becomes clear from seeing her projects in conjunction with each other, these images are all of Lee in costume hanging out with people whom she has known for only a month or less. The series, as a group, urgently questions the camera's capacity to lie by seeming to tell the truth, and by transfiguring Nikki Lee, who is Korean by birth and has Korean parents, it also raises questions about racism and the social invisibility that falls on Asian American women. Lee functions in the series as a kind of cipher, disappearing into performance not as a faux movie starlet à la Cindy Sherman but rather as a member of distinctly varied social groups. Lee's work torques the idea of the social self and queries the camera's role in the creation and formation of social roles that Lee's renditions reveal to be eerily performative.[20]

In the late 1990s and through the turn of the twenty-first century, New York City art student and performance artist Nikki Lee began a series of photographic projects in which she very carefully followed a prescribed set of social acts, each culminating in a photograph that she collected.[21] For each of these projects, Lee would befriend a group of people who others classified according to certain typologies: Hispanics, lesbians, yuppies, strippers, Japanese Americans, hip-hop devotees, Ohioans, senior citizens, and Korean schoolgirls, to list several of her more significant projects. Then, after spending no more than a month insinuated into each of these social worlds, Lee would ask members of the social group, or one of her friends from art school, or sometimes a passerby, to take photographs of her in her new group.[22] These photographs documented the project that constituted a kind of radical performance art.

Her *Exotic Dancers Project* (2000) makes clear the radical nature of Lee's performative strategy. For this series of photographs, Lee got a job working as a stripper. During the month in which she worked the job, she befriended the other strippers and asked others at the striptease club to photograph her in this milieu. In other words, she did not go to photograph strippers; Lee was a stripper, for this one month. In the *Exotic Dancers Project* she looks like a stripper because she lives among strippers and works as a stripper. In this sense, her desire to sound out social codes performatively seems fairly high risk; that is, she evinces a willingness to risk her own boundaries to get the results she wants from her project. Either that or the projects prove her point that since one never really has an identity one never really has boundaries. Whereas Susan Meiselas's pioneering photographic documentation of the lives of carnival strippers (1976) is gritty and real and harsh and very earnestly feminist, thus exposing sexist oppression as a war, Lee's work is full of play and feint. Looking at Meiselas's photographs, one feels queasy: the world revealed in the photographs is so unremittingly harsh as to seem insolvable, and one responds with nausea to Meiselas's carnival stripper photographs because the world they present is so dire and so unjust. What is the way out for these women, or for any woman, in such a world? But some 20 years later, Lee suggests that we can adopt and discard our different selves and float at the surface, feint, and dodge the heaviness of our social placement.[23] Lee deploys the snapshot aesthetic as a statement of philosophy, an ontology: it is all snapshot, nothing is permanent, we shift from character to character and as such we are not much more than images.

Lee's *The Lesbian Project* is similarly daring (Figure 6.6). Lee, not known to be lesbian, lives among lesbians and has a relationship of some kind with a lesbian, for

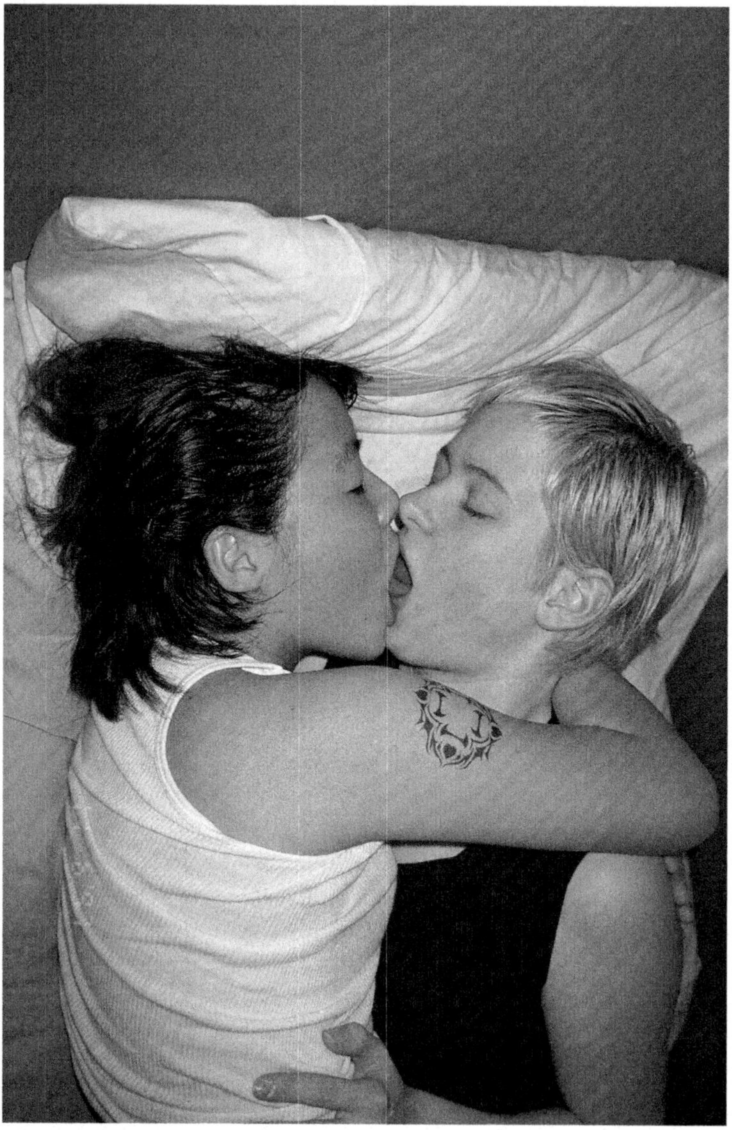

FIGURE 6.6 Nikki Lee, *The Lesbian Project (14)*, 1997, color print. © Nikki S. Lee, courtesy of Sikkema Jenkins & Co., New York.

the month of this project. On the one hand, she seems to be proving the point made by Judith Butler and Kath Weston, that one can choose the kind of family or social group with which one becomes intimate: this intimacy creates the tenets of selfhood. But Lee is only performing intimacy and not in the sense that Weston discusses intimacy and Butler defines performativity.[24] Lee's performance is actual performance: visual and conceptual art. And her intimacy is performative. With the *The Lesbian Project*, as with all her other projects in this series of works, Lee only remains with the group for one month (Figure 6.6). After that, she is done, lest she become too attached to the people involved. In an odd way, Lee is like a spy for the world of art; although she does not divulge information about the people in her projects, she moves into the social circle and convinces her new acquaintances that she belongs with them. She does so even as she tells them that she is working on a project of performance art. Her projects are brilliant and disturbing works that get beneath or behind the weft of the American social fabric and show how superficial and in many cases discriminatory is that weave. Her images are plaintive and show Lee's skill in staging – in choosing moments of revelation – not unlike Nan Goldin's utterly sincere works in aesthetic motivation. Looking at Lee and Goldin together, one realizes the fragile revelatory capacity of the snapshot – the photograph that takes up the visual cue of the instant and turns it into aesthetic resonance can be so real it is fake.

Time the Avenger

To show and to evade authenticity in her snapshots, Lee deploys a trope typical of vernacular photographs from the turn of the twenty-first century: date stamps. Photographs taken with 35-millimeter roll film in the late 1990s and early twenty-first century often had the date printed in pale numbers at the base of the developed photographic image. These vernacular photographs stand as signs, grave marks, of the last of analog photography. Time is the trauma of photography: the markings of time are the markings of the moment that will not return. Lee uses fake date stamps on her images both to authenticate them – so that they look like real snapshots – and to alert the careful viewer that her images are fakes. But it is the question of how they are fakes that opens the brilliance of Lee's photographic projects. Because the photographs are real photographs, technically they are just as authentic as any other photograph that is not photoshopped or digitally manipulated. What is fake about Lee's projects is also what is real and authentic about them: the photographs show that often those identities that we consider essential to ourselves may be fabricated and ephemeral. For most of us, identity is not in practice transient because we are constrained by economic forces to repeat whatever tropes of self have thus far permitted our survival, and of course many people feel that the gender, race, ethnicity, nationality, or even religion, into which they are born are deeply stable and meaningful. But Lee's work pushes through these boundaries of identity to the melancholy of meaninglessness. So in Lee's fakeness is a revelation of a real that is disturbing: none of us are really who we and others think we are. That is both frightening and liberating for women as an oppressed class.

Lee's work is an embodiment of existentialist philosophy: the project that is at the heart of the existentialist conceptualization of being human. The existentialist idea of a project is that because life has no given meaning, one must create one's own meaning by forging one's life project.[25] Lee takes this existentialist idea – that because of nothingness one must create projects to ground oneself – and reflects it in fragments: her projects are ephemeral, and they show us how ephemeral are the things that we believe to be essential to our selves. And yet the photographs that record her projects have staying power. That traditional meanings of gender and race are utterly taken apart in her subtle photographs is a given, but what really makes the projects important is the way they make of gender a mark of the surface, a form of nothingness. Lee's work has no earnestness, and that is its gift; she shows us that even the recourse to deconstruct gender, or "undo" gender as Judith Butler puts it, is a trap. Lee's projects show us that gender was never there and also, more depressingly, that it lingers despite its nonentity quality. She shows us ghosts in the everyday world of stereotypes, and she performs as the ghost, the one in the picture who will not stay (who will be gone soon, to inhabit another milieu). In this sense, Lee's feminist vision is one of constant renunciation and shifting and of moving away from gendered constraints – not through direct rebuttal or even irony (as Cindy Sherman does) but through a sublime ability to mirror what is not there and the nothing that is.

Madonna, Pervert: Catherine Opie

Catherine Opie, whose photographs explore social landscapes as they mark human bodies, came to prominence with a self-portrait that is formal and evokes comparisons to the Northern Renaissance masters, Hans Holbein the Younger in particular, and that presents Opie masked and clad in leather as a participant in sadism and masochism (S&M) lesbian sexual practices.[26] The most striking part of this photograph is the word "pervert" written by scarification in blood on Opie's bare chest; pervert referring to her pleasure in S&M and possibly also to her being lesbian.[27] Whether the self-portrait is actually self-revelatory, or an image created to show an aspect of lesbian life that was not (and is not) as widely circulated as other representations of lesbians, is not legible in the photograph.[28] That is, whether the image is bare sincerity or a calculated risk of self-representation – one that paid off in that this photograph, *Pervert* (1995), brought Opie's work into the public eye in ways that her earlier photographs had not – is ambiguous in the image itself.[29] The self-portrait shows a very stylized emblem of identity. The sitter is a self-proclaimed pervert not because of any sexual act that she does in front of the camera but because of the word that she has cut into her skin and the leather mask and arm needles with which she has adorned herself before sitting formally before a brocade cloth and taking the photograph. This self-portrait from her series *Portraits* (1993–1997) emerges as a striking part of Opie's lifelong work and interest in chronicling social worlds. Although she also has photographed landscapes, a presidential inauguration, and football players, her fame rests on the photographs of various segments of the lesbian, gay, bisexual, and transgender (LGBT) community.[30] Opie's origin story as a photographer turns on her desire to create photographs like Lewis Hine's – that is, documentary photographs that carry forward social realism and activism – and her work has been compared to August Sander's – photography as sociology, with an emphasis on brilliantly revelatory portraiture. And indeed Opie's work, like Hine's and like Sander's, contends not just with the social world but also with the social world as a site of pain and trauma, a space in which the photograph is offered as transformation and revelation.

The most obvious way in which Opie's photography could be called feminist is its vision for alternate performances of self for women: Opie shows us women who are butch, who look like men, and who look like whatever they want to look like. She shows us that the concept of two genders, male and female, is not enough to encompass what is actually in the world. In so doing, she shows us the way that we, however much we might think we are male or female, are also something else, something between, and are always possibly undecided. Whereas the vistas of LGBT life and embodiment that emerge in Opie's photography often are inflected by trauma, by a sense of either physical pain (scars and tattoos and eyes that look unaccustomed to the acceptance offered by Opie's encompassing gaze) or by a physical placement somehow at the edge of society (by roadsides, literally), these photographs also body forth the social contours of joy and pleasure in difference.

Opie's self-portrait nursing her son (*Self-Portrait/Nursing*, 2004, Figure 6.7) epitomizes this sense of freedom and capacity in people who are biologically female. In the photograph, Opie is bare-chested, as is convenient when nursing an infant, and reveals an ample bosom. She has short hair and her solid arms look very strong as they cradle the infant, who looks well past newborn and actually rather heavy. One could say there is nothing feminine about this image – no hourglass waist and slim neck, no long flowing hair, no lipstick or pearls. But that assessment would be to trade on notions of the feminine that are enforced by male domination; that is, notions of femininity that include physical delicacy, smallness of size, a certain incapacity to stand alone, and a desire to please the male gaze. Instead, Opie shows femininity rather directly: the word *feminine* is derived from the Latin "to suckle, to give suck," to feed at the breast. That is exactly what Opie is doing. The fact that she is also large and has a thick, strong body does not make the photographic subject masculine; rather, it refutes and alters oppressive notions of the feminine.

Opie's self-portrait nursing can be discussed in its obvious reference to Renaissance paintings of the Madonna, paintings that usually (although not always) occlude the breasts of the Virgin. But the rich, red cloth draped behind mother and child echoes the florid skin of Opie and her healthy son, in contrast to the Virgin's traditional cerulean blue. It is important to note that Renaissance paintings of the Madonna have as their reference point Eastern Orthodox icons of the Theotokos (literally, bearer of God), images that in Egypt, Ethiopia, Greece, and Armenia are among the earliest Christian imagery. These icons typically do not project a dainty, pretty Theotokos. Instead, she is shown as stern and fierce. In this sense, Opie's photograph of herself nursing her son is not so much thumbing its nose at Renaissance

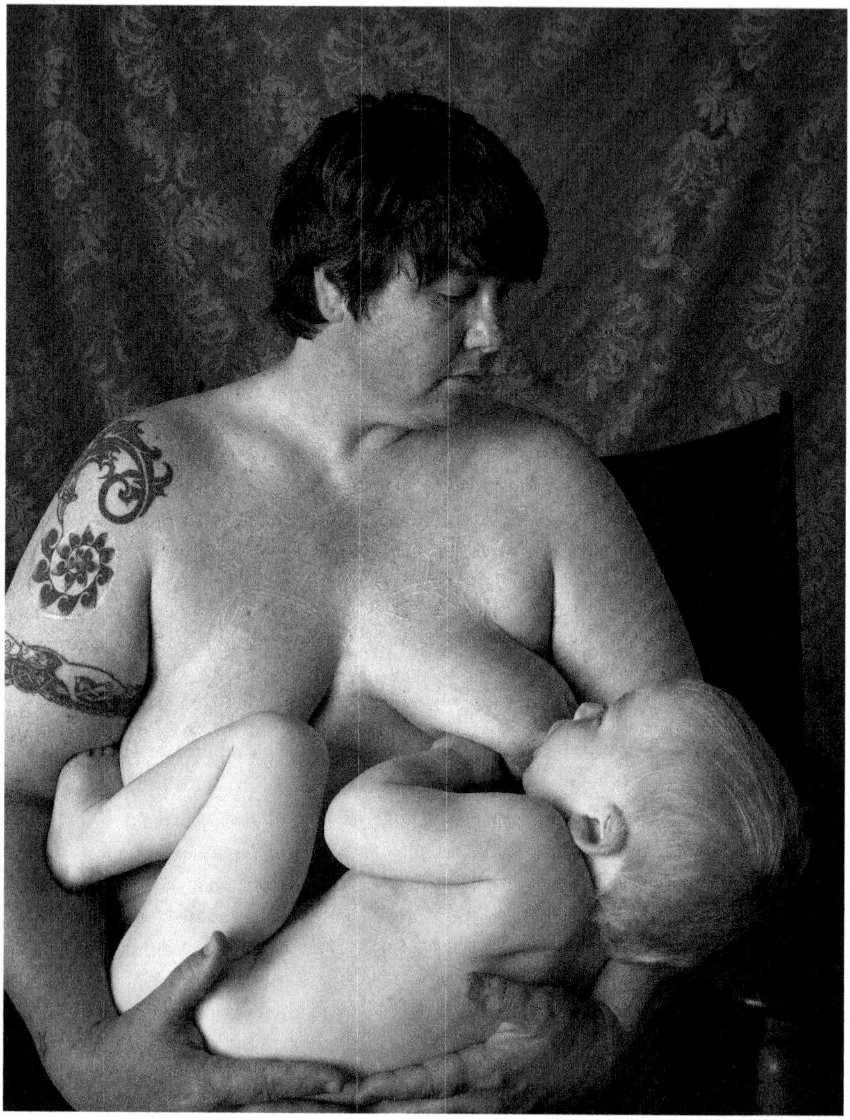

FIGURE 6.7 Catherine Opie, *Self-Portrait/Nursing*, 2004, chromogenic print, 40 × 31 in. Solomon R. Guggenheim Museum, New York. Purchased with funds contributed by the International Director's Council and Executive Committee Members: Ruth Baum, Edythe Broad, Elaine Terner Cooper, Dimitris Daskalopoulos, Harry David, Gail May Engelberg, Shirley Fiterman, Nicki Harris, Dakis Joannou, Rachel Lehmann, Linda Macklowe, Peter Norton, Tonino Perna, Elizabeth Richebourg Rea, Mortimer D.A. Sackler, Simonetta Seragnoli, David Teiger, Ginny Williams, and Elliot K. Wolk, and Sustaining Members: Tiqui Atencio, Linda Fischbach, Beatrice Habermann, and Cargill and Donna MacMillan, 2005. © Catherine Opie 2005. Courtesy Regen Projects, Los Angeles.

paintings of the Madonna as rather opening the field of the visual feminine to a more expansive, substantial, and long-standing discourse. What is a woman, what is a mother? In Catherine Opie's photography, a woman is large, strong, capable, and scarred. A woman breaks apart the constraints of delicacy and the need to visually please straight men. A woman is someone who pleases herself, who seeks pleasure, even by what others deem perversity (as the text of her earlier scarification is visible, faintly but clearly, in the self-portrait nursing her son).

And yet at the edge of this pleasure of being what one is, Opie's photographs carry a distinctive mark of pain. The cutting photographs for which she is known (that is, photographs of her self-mutilated skin from the 1990s) also typify her aesthetic in that they merge a direct signifying function (the word or sign cut in blood on the body) with the more enigmatic and spacious signification of the photograph. Opie's photographs of her cut skin – the self-portrait as a pervert being paradigmatic in this regard – forge a space for ulterior codes and dressing of womanliness but also show the pain of forging new social worlds. The cuts on the body of the photographer, then, are not only direct signs of pain but also indirect signs, thereby signifying that to change the codes of the traditional feminine is both necessary and never superficial, always involving cuts on the body of the (social) subject.

Opie shows us what women could be if we dared more than anything else to please ourselves. Even so, the problem of the delicate feminine, this subject in submissiveness, lingers outside the perimeter of Opie's photographic orbit. It does so inasmuch as her photographic representations of queer embodiment are posited as a kind of rebuttal to or refusal of traditional images of gender and inasmuch as the signifiers of pain – representations of bodily cuts and S&M that act as conduits between the traditional gendering of the subject and subject's rejection of traditional gender codes. As it happens, this problem of the feminine has been taken up by a visual artist whose womanliness renegotiates the meanings of performance and self.

Little Bo-Peep's sheep

Photographer, artist, and transwoman Zackary Drucker presents in her work either the logical extension of Opie's photography documenting LGBT communities or its flip side. Where Opie photographs drag kings and butch lesbians, Drucker rose to fame working with her partner, Rhys Ernst, in the collaborative series *Relationship* (2008–2013), which chronicles the relationship between biologically male Drucker, who transitions to become a woman, and the biologically female Rhys Ernst, who is her lover and who is transitioning to become a man.[31] Drucker's work since that breakthrough series has focused on representations of Drucker as a very pretty girl in photographs that searingly question the terms in which we view the feminine in the contemporary West. For some of these photographs, Drucker returns to her childhood home and – working collaboratively with transman Amos Mac – poses as Little Bo-Peep (Figure 6.8) and mimics poses of 1970s calendar pinup girls (*Translady Fanzine*, 2011). She creates a doormat that showcases her conventionally

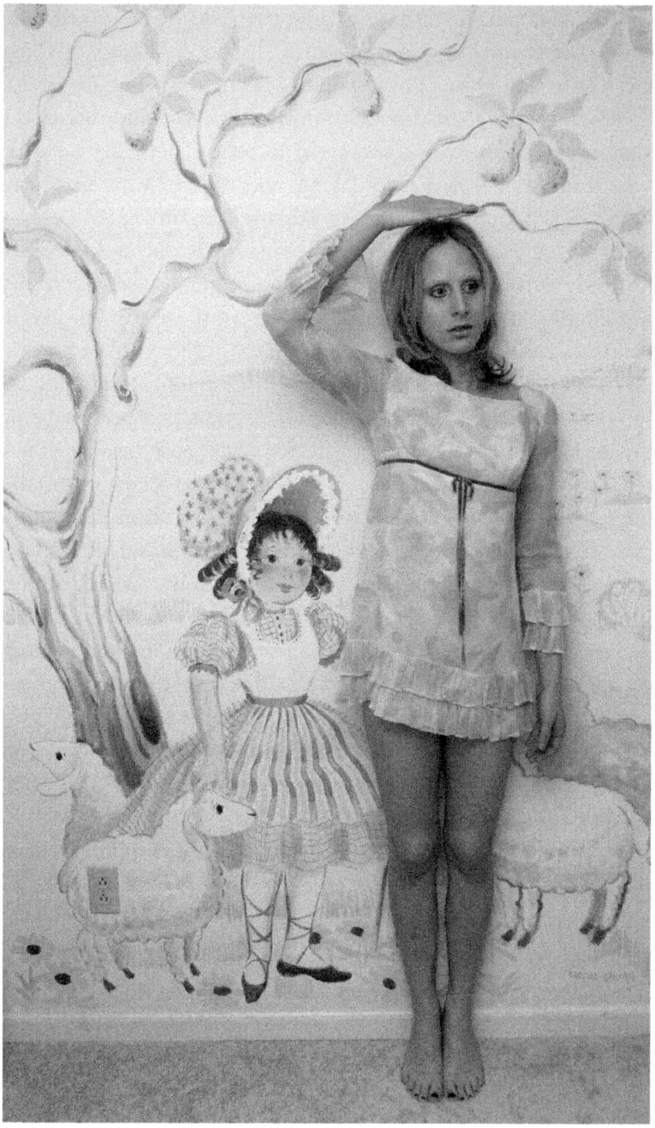

FIGURE 6.8 Zackary Drucker, in collaboration with Amos Mack, *Translady Fanzine* (Drucker poses as Little Bo-Peep). © 2011 Zackary Drucker and Amos Mac, courtesy of Luis De Jesus, Los Angeles.

beautiful face, ice-blonde hair, and pale blue eyes, and the doormat is sold with the icily ironic and haunting promise that the purchasers will be able to wipe their feet on Drucker's pretty face for the rest of their lives. This playful and also poignant gesture of being the very pretty girl whom others use as a doormat chimes with Drucker's earlier work, *Don't Look at Me Like That* (in collaboration with Manuel

Vason, 2010). Drucker's work pushes us to imagine the cultural place of the feminine – its vulnerability and the way that it intertwines with pleasure and consumption. Images from *Don't Look at Me Like That* present Drucker's exposed vagina (that is, an image drawn on one side of her leg as she sits spread-eagled in a metal chair, one bar of which covers her pubis) and show Drucker's apparently damaged skin as she lies naked on a rough table, surrounded by metal cutlery.

Drucker works through tropes of the feminine as a site of damage in images at once gorgeous, provocative, and dangerous. The images are dangerous in the sense that Drucker opens up and makes visible our deep cultural associations between femininity, damage, and vulnerability, but they are also provocative in that Drucker is clear that she was born biologically male.[32] In this sense, Drucker's photographs, combined with her performance art and personal activism, make a powerful feminist statement that the photographs viewed alone might risk losing. In many of the photographs of Drucker there is little to indicate that she is transgender, or the signs of her trans status are embedded in fairly arcane symbols. Here, I return to Susan Sontag's comment, in *On Photography*,[33] that a photograph cannot give you information; it is just a picture. And yet, pictures – photographs – can tell us about politics and change our politics, as I have argued throughout this book. Paradoxically, Drucker's photographic work, at the very times that it most searingly shows us the violence that our culture visits on the feminine body, veers the closest to covering up the escape routes from that violence. Her photographic work poses this very difficult question: are we in the West honest in our claims of gender equality? Drucker's work dares to show us that the feminist movement still has far to go.

In the photograph of Drucker standing before wallpaper with a Little Bo-Peep pattern (Figure 6.8), the surface of the image almost elides the photograph's symbolic play. The surface is fetching, sweet, and golden. Drucker – delicate, petite, and blonde – echoes and measures herself against harmless and childish images on the wallpaper, literally against the Little Bo-Peep version of femininity. The innocuous suburban interior and the figure of the small and pretty girl (Drucker, wearing a yellow baby-doll dress), standing as if beneath the golden pears printed on the wallpaper, all seem far from sinister. But with the literary motif of the yellow wallpaper[34] hovering in the cultural background of the image, and with the femininity of a delicate little girl – Little Bo-Peep – who loses things (her sheep) set forward as the model of femininity, Drucker's collaborative photograph takes a docile, domestic scene and uncovers something like terror. Drucker's *Translady Fanzine* image asks whether being a girl means fitting in with the wallpaper and losing the things that you guard (sheep, here, being symbolic for any desired or needed aspect of one's self).[35] Furthermore, if these conditions are placed on the object of femininity early and often, Drucker's image asks, then where is her home; that is, where will she not lose herself? To quote Drucker: "Distance is where your heart is, home is where you hang your heart," that is, home – in this era that is not anywhere near postfeminist in a real sense – is where you contend with the distance within yourself.[36]

Notes

1 Michel Foucault, *The Order of Things: An Archeology of the Human Sciences* (New York: Vintage, 1994); *The Birth of the Clinic: An Archeology of Medical Perception* (New York: Vintage, 1994); *Madness and Civilization: A History of Insanity in the Age of Reason* (New York: Vintage, 1988); *The History of Sexuality*, 3 vols. (New York: Vintage 1990); and *Discipline and Punish: The Birth of the Prison* (New York: Vintage, 1995). See also Roger-Paul Droit, *New York Times*, August 5, 1975, www.nytimes.com/books/00/12/17/specials/foucault-prisons.html.

2 Lois McNay, *Foucault and Feminism: Power, Gender and the Self* (Cambridge, UK: Polity Press, 1992).

3 Beyond Judith Butler's use of Foucaultian theory for possibly feminist purpose in *Bodies that Matter* (Abingdon, UK: Routledge, 1993) and in *Gender Trouble* (Abingdon, UK: Routledge, 1990), Judith/Jack Halberstam has influentially developed cultural theories of gender fluidity and indeterminancy. See Judith Halberstam, *Female Masculinity: Masculinity without Men* (Durham, NC: Duke University Press, 1998).

4 Sarah Ruddy, "'A Radiant Eye Yearns from Me': Figuring Documentary in the Photography of Nan Goldin," *Feminist Studies* 35, no. 2 (Summer 2009): 347–80.

5 Ibid., 352.

6 Chris Townsend, "Nan Goldin: Bohemian Ballads," in *Phototextualities: Intersections of Photography and Narrative*, ed. Alexa Hughes and Andrea Noble (Albuquerque: University of New Mexico Press): 103–15; Alison Dean, "Intimacy at Work: Nan Goldin and Rineke Dijkstra," *History of Photography* 39, no. 2 (May 2015): 177–93.

7 Ruddy, "A Radiant Eye," 347–78.

8 Oihana Garro-Larrañaga, "Art and Identity Construction: Reflections about Family Narratives with Nan Goldin," *Arte Individuo y Sociedad* 26, no. 2 (2014): 351–65.

9 Emma Wilson, "Nan Goldin, Self-Fiction and 'the Necessary Other,'" *Revue Critique de Fixion Française Contemporaine/Critical Review of Contemporary French Fixxion* 4 (2012): 26–37.

10 Martine Delvaux, *Nan Goldin: Guerrière Et Gorgone* (Montreal: Héliotrope, 2014).

11 Ruddy, "A Radiant Eye," 351.

12 Kath Weston, *Families We Choose: Lesbians, Gays, Kinship* (New York: Columbia University Press, 1997)

13 Ruddy, "A Radiant Eye," 351.

14 See Linda Gordon, *Heroes of their Own Lives: the Politics and History of Family Violence, Boston 1880–1960* (Champaign, IL: University of Illinois Press, 2002); Cheryl Albers, *Sociology of Families* (Thousand Oaks, CA: Pine Forge Press, 1999), 309; see also Elizabeth Schneider, *Battered Women and Feminist Lawmaking* (New Haven, CT: Yale University Press, 2002).

15 Ruddy, "A Radiant Eye," 353.

16 Walter Benjamin claimed, in his 1931 essay "A Short History of Photography," that sometimes a photograph can foreshadow the future, in that some photographs can – sometimes – reveal a truth about the sitter that he or she tries to conceal in the normal, nonphotographic discourse of life. See Esther Leslie's discussion of Walter Benjamin's concept of the predictive properties in photographs in Esther Leslie, *On Photography* (Chicago: University of Chicago Press, 2015).

17 Gilles Deleuze and Felix Guatarri, *Anti Oedipus: Schizophrenia and Capitalism* (Minneapolis, MN: University of Minnesota Press, 1983).

18 Elisabeth Bronfen, *Over Her Dead Body: Death, Femininity, and the Aesthetic* (Manchester, UK: Manchester University Press, 1992).

19 Phil Lee, "Indefinite 'Nikkis' in a World of Hyperreality: An Interview with Nikki S. Lee," *Chicago Art Journal* 18 (January 2008): 76–93.

20 Ibid., 78.

21 Mark Alice Durant, "Photography & Performance," *Aperture* 199 (Summer 2010): 32.

22 Louis Kaplan, *American Exposures: Photography and Community in the Twentieth Century* (Minneapolis, MN: University of Minnesota Press, 2005), 174.

23 Cherise Smith, *Enacting Others: Politics of Identity in Eleanor Antin, Nikki S. Lee, Adrian Piper, and Anna Deavere Smith* (Durham, NC: Duke University Press, 2011).
24 Eric Chenet, "Quand je est un autre: les multiples moi de Nikki S. Lee et Vibeke Tandberg/While I Is Someone Else: The Multiple Me's of Nikki S. Lee and Vibeke Tandberg," *Etc.* 81 (March 2008): 36–48.
25 Jean Paul Sartre, *Being and Nothingness: An Essay on Phenomenological Ontology*, trans. Hazel E. Barnes (London: Methuen, 1958).
26 Jean Dykstra, "Opie: The Community of Difference," *Art in America* 96, no. 11 (2008): 128–35.
27 Whereas clearly S&M has to do with finding one's place, and pleasure, in relationship to pain, and Opie's photographs of lesbian S&M subculture resonate with Robert Mapplethorpe's earlier photographs of gay S&M practitioners, I think it is reductive to argue that Opie's S&M photographs are only about pain. They instead face the viewer with her own fears of ostracism and threatened bodily integrity, and they become a form of facing, ethical tableaux in which the viewer must take apart and find again the limits of the human.
28 Alessandra Mondin, "Fighting Pain with Pain: Bob Flanafan/Sheree Rose and Catherine Opie," *Graduate Journal of Social Science* 12, no. 1 (2016): 40.
29 Avgi Saketopoulou, "Catherine Opie: American Photographer, American Pervert," *Studies in Gender and Sexuality* 14, no. 3 (2013): 245–52.
30 Orna Guralnik, "Being and Having an Identity: Catherine Opie," *Studies in Gender and Sexuality* 14, no. 3 (2013): 239–44.
31 Holland Cotter, "One Last Dance in the Old Place: 2014 Whitney Biennial Has New Faces and Interesting Choices," *New York Times*, March 6, 2014.
32 Tucker Neel, "Darling Zackary: An Interview with Zackary Drucker," *Artpulse* 3, no. 12 (Summer 2012).
33 Susan Sontag, *On Photography* (New York: Picador, 2001).
34 Charlotte Perkins Gilman, *The Yellow Wallpaper and Other Stories* (North Chelmsford, MA: Courier, 1997).
35 Please see, Jacques Lacan, *Écrits* (Paris: Éditions du Seuil, 1966)
36 Mel Mundell, "Sm{art}: Translady Fanzine," *Bitch Media*, March 7, 2012, https://bitchmedia.org/post/smart-translady-fanzine-feminist-magazine.

7

THE ORIGINAL EXPERIENCE

Carrie Mae Weems and Sally Mann

The "original experience," as philosopher Maurice Blanchot describes it, is the only source of work – work here meaning "work of art," which Blanchot differentiates from glossy, superficial, and consumable art. The true work, Blanchot argues, is essential, necessary, and risky (to the artist and possibly to her audience).[1] In Blanchot's theory, the only way for the artist to produce the work of art, as opposed to merely marketable art, is through willingness to risk the work, indeed to risk not completing the work and instead to stay in the place of error, repetition, and what Blanchot calls death – by which he means not the artist's physical death but rather the cultural space given to incompletion and nonbeing.[2] For Blanchot, "in art's milieu there is a pact contracted with death, with repetition, and with failure."[3]

Taking Blanchot's notion of "original experience" as that which is shattering but also constitutive, I apply his idea to the broad matrix of the culture of the American South and argue that photographers Carrie Mae Weems (born 1953) and Sally Mann (born 1951) – nearly contemporaneous – both create significant bodies of work that contend with the violence of the American South: the enslavement of African Americans, and the expulsion of Southeastern Native American tribes. In my reading of these photographers' work, I argue that Weems and Mann often respond to similar cultural histories but respond to them very differently, through the lens of African American and white experience, respectively. Indeed, the titles of some of their works invite comparison: Weems's *Family Pictures and Stories* (1980) appeared a decade before Mann's *Immediate Family* (1992); Weems's *The Louisiana Project* (2003) appears roughly at the same time as Mann's *Deep South* (2005) series. Both Weems and Mann are controversial photographers, even as the national media focus on Mann's purported transgressions indicate an embedded discourse of race in which whiteness and childhood stand as symbols for that which is intrinsically worthy of protection.[4]

In this chapter, I interpret the late twentieth-century and early twenty-first-century works of photographer Carrie Mae Weems (born 1953) as a form of "original experience," that is, a repetition at the origin. In particular, I read the series *From Here I Saw What Happened and I Cried* (1995), *The Hampton Project* (2000), and *The Louisiana Project* (2003) as works that immerse the photographer in the United States' crucible origins, the histories of African enslavement and Indigenous American oppression that form the heart of the American national experience, even as American national discourse and myth elide this history.[5] In the series *From Here I Saw What Happened and I Cried*, Weems rephotographs photographs of African Americans under enslavement and Jim Crow, and in *The Hampton Project*, she rephotographs Frances Benjamin Johnston's Hampton Institute photographs. Both series interpose verbal text with rephotographed images to create kaleidoscopic critiques of earlier ways of seeing race. *The Louisiana Project*, a work both hauntingly personal and sharply political, acts as Weems's immersion in the landscape of the Deep South. I interpret the work of Sally Mann (born 1951) as an exploration of a similar but differently viewed origin; in the series *Immediate Family*, Mann depicts an enclosed and somewhat protected world of whiteness – her own children in the landscape of the American South – and translates this world into a myth of origin, imbuing it with a nostalgia edged with violence, a violence never visually situated outside the naked bodies of Mann's very young children. While I will suggest that Mann's work may not go far enough in revealing its own origins in the violent privilege of whiteness, I yet argue that Weems and Mann can be read in conversation by tracing the way their work is imbricated by the crucible of southeastern United States culture.[6]

By looking at Weems and Mann in contrast and in conversation, I highlight the way their work is deeply American and revelatory of the codes of race that play through American culture, particularly in the American southeast, where, as Blanchot says, "the irremediable takes the form of an endless repetition, where the same is posed in the dizziness of redoubling."[7] As I have argued in previous chapters, what racial oppression has to do with gendered oppression, and hence with feminist theory, is *everything*. As Amelia Jones argues, "seeing differently" is a mode of seeing and producing art that emerges from the embodied subjectivity of the artist. Every artist has an embodied subjectivity, and her term "seeing differently" is Jones's resistance against interpretations of art that attempt to obscure the reality of subjectively embodied experience, in particular as race, gender, and sexuality encode and inform that experience.[8] The original experience to which Blanchot refers when he argues that true works of art emerge from the artist's visitation to the depths is not a gendered or raced premise prima facie. And yet, the photographs of Carrie Mae Weems hauntingly stage repeated moments of historical depth and vision. However, Sally Mann's photographs perform a kind of looking aside that evokes the violence of the traditional South not by showing who, historically, was violated or oppressed but instead by creating trompe l'oeil in which her young children frequently appear to be harmed and are exposed, often naked before the camera, or, in the series *What Remains*, showing corpses that in some oblique sense stand in as figures for the violence of the region's history.

Weems and Mann in their work often contend with the history of the formation of the American South. Both photographers confront the violence of that region's history. But Weems's late twentieth-century and early twenty-first-century work stages and performs vistas of reckoning. Mann's work, of the same era, proffers a series of substitutions and envisions the vulnerability of the naked young child's body, the architectural ruins of the antebellum South, and corpses, as markers for historical violence otherwise invisible in her work.[9] Family grounds the work of Weems and Mann, and yet Weems's photographic "family" comes to encompass all African Americans as her work becomes progressively more expansive and searching.[10] By contrast, although Mann's family is also a core of her work (decades after photographing her young children, she embarked on a moving series of photographs of her ailing husband), this white family is insular and at times frighteningly claustrophobic, thus hinting at a violence it never brings itself to disclose but instead echoes. Although the work often skates on the surface of the sentimental – the adorable child (*Immediate Family*), the beautiful ruin (*Deep South*), even the Gothic (*What Remains*) – Mann's photographs suggest that things always take a turn for the worse. Developing from the Southern Gothic literature, Mann's death-haunted landscape of images is never fully cashed out for its relationship to the privilege of the photographer's status as wealthy and white.

Carrie Mae Weems's original experience

Weems's somewhat late arrival to eminence reflects the controversial turns of her work. Born in 1953 in Portland, Oregon, to parents who had recently moved west from Mississippi, Weems began producing notable work in the early 1980s with her series *Family Pictures and Stories*. Despite steady and brilliant production of photographic and multimedia works – including the series *Ain't Jokin'*, *Kitchen Table Series*, *Hampton Project*, *The Louisiana Project*, and *Roaming* – Weems was not recognized with a major retrospective until 2012 when the Frist Center for the Visual Arts in Nashville, Tennessee, brought out *Carrie Mae Weems: Three Decades of Photography and Video*, a show that moved to the Guggenheim in New York City in 2014.[11] In 2013, Weems was named a MacArthur Fellow, receiving one of what are popularly known as genius grants.

Although early on her work habits may have been born of the necessity to keep producing art for three decades in the face of less-than-instantaneous acclaim, I apply to her immersion in work Blanchot's persuasive view. He suggests that such immersion is a visitation to the depths – that is, an immersion in the conditions of fear and risk that attend connecting with the real – and must take precedence over producing marketable art.[12] Several of Weems's deeply conceptualized photographic series and, later, films perform exactly this Blanchotian visitation to the depths for its own sake, that is, for the original experience. Indeed, Weems suggests this typography when she says of herself that she does not consider herself a great artist, but she does strive to be a "serious" artist.[13] Combining photography with words, film, and other pastiche techniques, Weems delves into the subterranean currents of European architecture of empire and conquest (*Roaming*, 2006) and American racist jokes (*Ain't Jokin*, 1987–1988). I use Blanchot's idea of a visitation to the realm of death, to nonbeing, as a way to understand Weems's repeated soundings of American culture, in particular her photographic critique of racist and sexist paradigms of suppression and oppression.

In this chapter's discussion, I focus on Weems's late twentieth-century and early twenty-first-century photographic series, yet Weems also has created multimedia works, series, and conceptual projects using photographs in conjunction with original written text. These include *Family Pictures and Stories* (1979–1980), which lovingly focuses on Weems's family of origin: working-class African Americans.[14] She undertook the series in response to the Moynihan Report, which then Assistant Secretary of Labor Daniel Patrick Moynihan conducted in the 1960s.[15] The report scandalously decreed that African American women were at fault for creating so-called pathological family structures. It is well known that Moynihan's study was controversial, and I do not have room here to plumb the reasons for controversy, but it is important to note that Moynihan – who served as U.S. Senator from New York from 1976–2000 – argued that African American women emasculated their men, thus creating families that were fatherless and, hence, often destitute. Needless

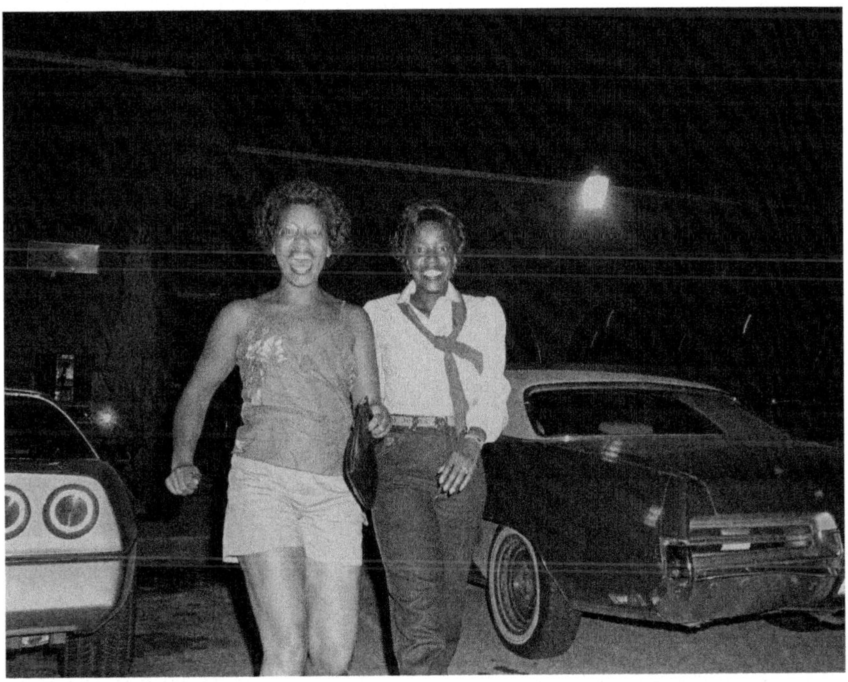

FIGURE 7.1 Carrie Mae Weems, *Welcome Home*, 1978–1984, vintage gelatin silver print with text, 8½ × 13 in. © Carrie Mae Weems. Courtesy of the artist and Jack Shainman Gallery, New York.

to say, Moynihan's interpretation was sexist, but it was also racist in that his study did not fully take into account the role of racist paradigms in generating and sustaining intergenerational poverty. Weems responds, with her photographs from the late 1970s, to Moynihan's 1965 report because that report set the tone for years and even decades to come, in terms of the federal government's response to African Americans living in poverty.

Weems's photographs of her immediate family show some struggle and a little chaos, but they mostly show a great deal of love. She takes them from an insider's perspective, a view that makes all the difference, as the photographic subjects – her family members – relax before her camera. She photographs busy young mothers; beautiful, pensive women; and women absolutely overjoyed to welcome home the photographer, who is their sister (Figure 7.1). The kind of joy Weems captures in these images stems in part from love for the photographer and as such could not be created by an

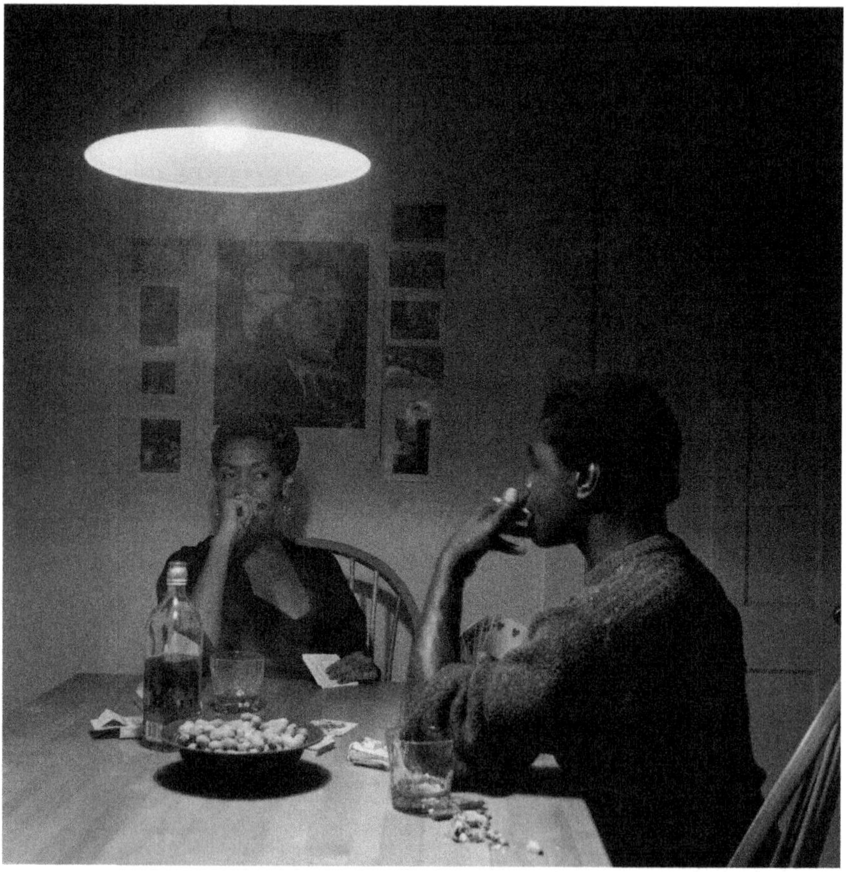

FIGURE 7.2 Carrie Mae Weems, *Untitled (Man Smoking)*, 1990, gelatin silver print, 28¼ × 28⅛ in. © Carrie Mae Weems. Courtesy of the artist and Jack Shainman Gallery, New York.

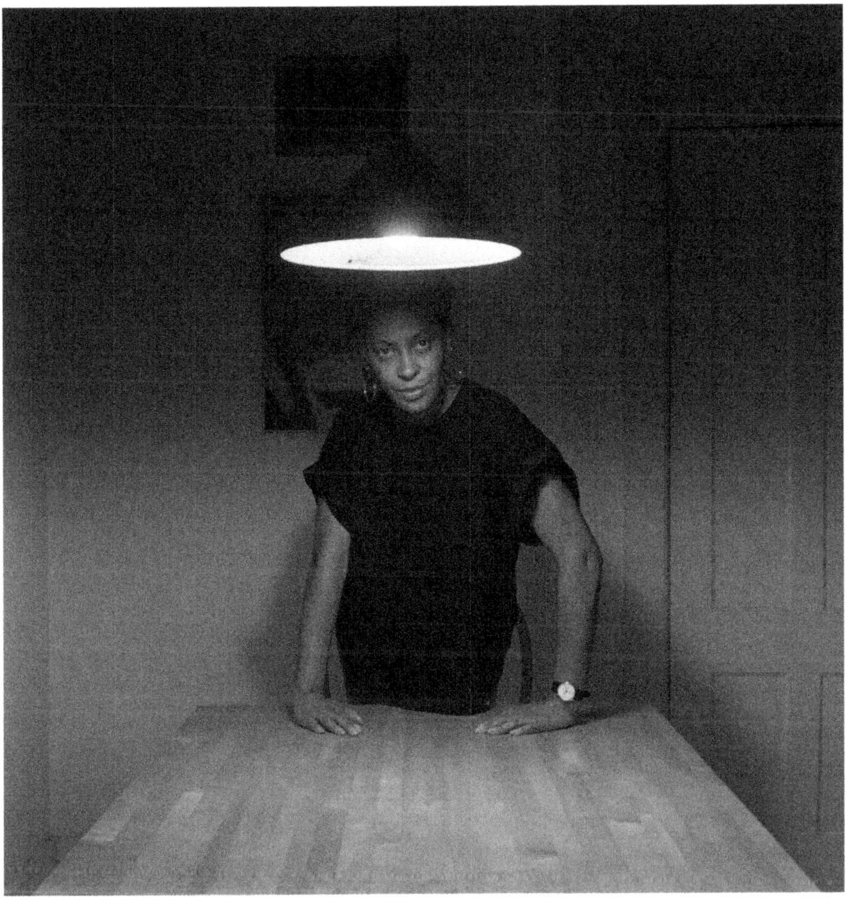

FIGURE 7.3 Carrie Mae Weems, *Untitled (Women Standing Alone)*, from the *Kitchen Table Series*, 1990, gelatin silver print, 28¼ × 28¼ in. © Carrie Mae Weems. Courtesy of the artist and Jack Shainman Gallery, New York.

outsider. She places the photographs with verbal narratives that serve as a counterpoint, thus expanding and complicating the visual information of the photographs.

Weems's work in the 1980s and early 1990s focused more trenchantly on race, and her *Ain't Jokin'* and *American Icons* play on the idea of the joke and the instantly recognizable stereotype to argue that racism in the post–Jim Crow, post–Civil Rights era is far from eradicated in America. She conceived her *Kitchen Table Series*[16] to rebut Laura Mulvey's theory of a "male gaze."[17] In this series, Weems presents photographs from a woman's point of view, imagining the scenes and narratives of the series as counterparts to jazz music (Figures 7.2 and 7.3). She makes visual and, elliptically, verbal arguments that the camera does not necessarily represent a male point of view when wielded by a black woman.[18] As bell hooks argues, the "oppositional gaze" that black women have the capacity to develop stems ironically from their invisibility as objects of (white) male desire.[19] She writes:

> Black female spectators have had to develop looking relations within a cinematic context that constructs our presence as absence, that denies the 'body' of the black female so as to perpetuate white supremacy and with it a phallocentric spectatorship where the woman to be looked at and desired is white.[20]

Weems's interpretation of this oppositional gaze evokes romance, sexuality, family, and time itself as a game of chance that a woman plays for herself and in her own way. Two images in particular from the *Kitchen Table Series* emphasize a different female gaze. When Weems poses herself and her male paramour at the table playing cards, she frames the image such that the viewer sees the man's hand of cards, while Weems's card hand is kept secret (Figure 7.2). Here, her paramour is played by a model, as indeed the "family" members in Weems's *Kitchen Table Series* are all models, not her spouse and not her children. By this choice of using models, Weems distances her work from document and conveys an expansive, conceptual field of family. Her gaze is figurally doubled with that of Malcolm X, in a photographic poster just above her. The male and female gaze, as configured in this photograph, subvert the idea that men powerfully look at women's passivity: instead, here, the woman holds all the cards and her gaze is sutured to that of a radical activist. Similarly, Weems's portrait of the woman (herself) at her kitchen table standing alone makes clear the nature of her gaze: she stares a powerful stare at the viewer as if to interrogate her audience (Figure 7.3). The gaze is Weems's own, but in this series her gaze also represents a decentering of white ways of constructing seeing and a centering of African American femininity as formal vision.

Not only does the *Kitchen Table Series* instates a gaze that is neither male nor white, but also the series begins to open up one of Weems's most important vistas: an expansive sense of family. For her *Kitchen Table Series* begins with a similar premise to her earlier *Family Pictures and Stories* – a domestic canvas – but it expands beyond the immediate, personal, biological family to encompass a more far-reaching family, one of African American identity intertwined with female identity, and incorporating visually the aesthetic of jazz music. All of these concepts are brilliantly played around the central signifier of the kitchen table, that from which most Americans – rich, poor, white, black, Hispanic, Asian – eat. This expansive sense of family as not only one's own personal, immediate family but instead as a sweeping conceptualization of history becomes Weems's genius in the early years of the twenty-first century as she creates *The Hampton Project* and *The Louisiana Project*.

Mann's sense of family is very much bound up in her experience of embodied maternity and spousal devotion, enclosed by white privilege with a narrow sense of family, and it is one that always hints at some unseen threat, a photography pervasively laced with foreboding of the mortal. By contrast, Weems unfolds an expansive and yet still very domestically inflected vision of family – embracing all African Americans – seen in her woman photographer's photographic lens.

In her series *Colored People* (1989–1990), Weems gathers under the rubric of this racialized title several loving portraits of people who are not her biological family but who are part of what she creates with her photographs: the family of African American identity. *Colored People* lays bare racist ways of interpreting African Americans according to skin tone by taking these photographic portraits and tinting them colors like bright yellow, purple, and indigo blue. Her installation of the images counterposed the tinted photographs with blocks of color. But the brilliance of this installation is not just its conceptualization of "color" as something very different from skin tone. The portraits themselves show Weems's abiding embrace of her subjects. *Golden Yella Girl*, a portrait of a girl on the cusp of adolescence, shows in profile a cherubic smiling girl (Figure 7.4).

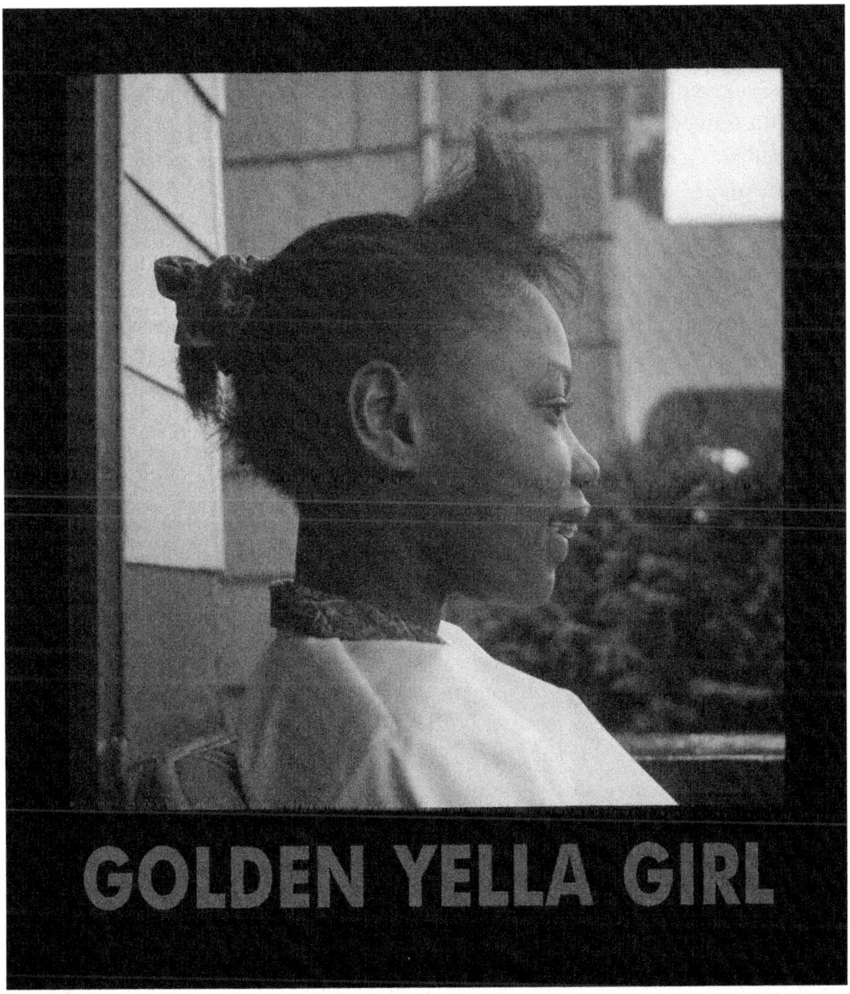

FIGURE 7.4 Carrie Mae Weems, *Golden Yella Girl*, 1997, silver print with text on mat, 30 × 39 in. image with mat. © Carrie Mae Weems. Courtesy of the artist and Jack Shainman Gallery, New York.

The gold tint around the girl's face almost has a halo effect, as Weems's camera at once creates a critique of racialized ways of seeing skin and also brings forward in a respectful and loving way the girl's personality as she moves into adolescence.

The depths

Weems's public reputation in many ways echoes the vibrant and strong persona that she projects in the *Kitchen Table Series*. Yet I am interested in pursuing where she takes that force in the 10 years between the mid-1990s and the early twenty-first century. In *From Here I Saw What Happened and I Cried* (1995), she responds to Weston Naef's invitation to contribute to the 1995 exhibition *Hidden Witness* photographs that perform as witnesses for African American life.[21] Weems compiles a set of 33 images (photographs from the nineteenth and early twentieth centuries that show enslaved African Americans and African Americans in positions of oppression) and rephotographs them (a postmodern strategy), tints them, sets them in rondo frames behind glass, and inscribes the glass with sandblasted text. The trenchant and biting text underscores the history of racism and racial violence that African Americans have survived.

This 1995 series begins Weems's immersion in the depths of America's origin story. She has stated that she cannot "live with" these images, a statement that is at once literal – she finds the series too painful to display in her house where she would see it every day – and also metaphorical, in that it describes the original experience she faced when she created, culled, and rearranged these haunting and disturbing images.[22] Michelle Obama, then First Lady of the United States, described the work as one of the most powerful pieces she had seen on America's history of enslaving West Africans. Because of its disturbing repetition of images of humiliation, *From Here I Saw What Happened and I Cried* has held a controversial place for African American intellectuals, as I have discussed at some length in *Witnessing Sadism in Texts of the American South*.[23] The series is a plaintive and painful act of witnessing images that reveal African Americans suffering under enslavement. It functions as an American *Guernica*, witnessing the tearing apart of the social fabric of many African American lives that is a tear in the meaning of self and community. Whereas sociologist Ron Eyerman argues that African Americans suffer a cultural and collective trauma because of the history of enslavement and racism, I see Weems's *From Here I Saw What Happened and I Cried* as a work that has meaning not only for African Americans.[24] It condenses and reveals the fractionary and violent history of the formation of the United States.

The Hampton Project (2000) and *The Louisiana Project* (2003) similarly emerge from the artist's steeping herself in history. Indeed, Weems has been called "history's ghost."[25] She received commissions to commemorate centennial and bicentennial celebrations in Hampton, Virginia, and New Orleans, Louisiana, respectively. *The Hampton Project* is a kind of bridge between *From Here I Saw What Happened and I Cried* and *The Louisiana Project*, in that for *The Hampton Project* she rephotographs images created at the turn of the twentieth century. In this gesture, Weems exposes the racist ideology that generated America's long-standing practice of sending Native American youth to special schools, such as the Hampton Institute, where they would be taught to dress, talk, and work in the white world. The phrase "Kill the Indian, and Save the Man" epitomizes this earlier era's ideological belief that Native Americans should cease to think of themselves as indigenous and instead should be forcibly merged into white American culture.[26] Weems's poignant rephotographing of Native American youth forced to leave their homes and assimilate into whiteness at the Hampton Institute is the powerful backbone of this series. Weems's work offended Hampton University, which had commissioned the work, and the school chose not to display it.[27]

She found a better reception at Tulane University in New Orleans, which commissioned her 2003 *Louisiana Project*, a multimedia work that includes written text and silhouettes. My comments here, however, focus on her photographs. This compelling series uses architectural photography to launch a critique of the deeply and disturbingly embedded racism in the architecture of the twenty-first-century American South. Eerily and presciently, Weems's *Louisiana Project* reveals fault lines of poverty and racial oppression that Hurricane Katrina laid bare two years later.

The photographs in *The Louisiana Project* (a multimedia work including photographs, a few of which are Figures 7.5–7.8) must be viewed as a series because the work is built conceptually through the implicit contrast of antebellum mansions scrupulously preserved as museums or bed-and-breakfasts with the industrial and impoverished neighborhoods that house many of the city's African Americans.[28] Weems constructs this implicit contrast by using her own image, costumed in garments that evoke a nineteenth-century woman, standing in witness of each architectural scene photographed. This figure functions like a ghost, or an embodied revenant, as she moves from image to image wearing the same anachronistic dress. The scene that Weems constructs in these elegant, spare, and devastating photographs is that of an enslaved African American woman returning not only to haunt but, more significantly, to *witness* the entrenched racism of New Orleans and, by implication, of the traditional South in the twenty-first century. Confronting the architecturally articulated structures of race and class hierarchy in and around twenty-first century New Orleans, Weems as witness stands quietly and elegantly in this series of photographs. Her back is usually turned to the camera, and in some images she faces the plantation architecture that has been so carefully and expensively preserved. In other photographs, the same witness figure or ghost figure stands and faces New Orleans industrial landscapes, a housing project, and an impoverished neighborhood with a garish billboard encouraging African American men to drink liquor. The stillness of the witness merges with the stillness of architectural photography, so that the series makes its case against racism by laying bare what is already there and plain to see, although we usually ignore it.

This feeling of sustained revelation is common in Weems's work. The elegance of her vision carries the pain that her camera reveals: cultural patterns of dispossession that Weems calls herself to see, making her camera's work of witnessing an experience of American origins. Not only is Weems history's ghost, but also her images have the extreme force of a bad dream, or, as Barthes would call it, a punctum.[29] Her photographs thematize the way that racial oppression haunts America, and in turn Weems's images haunt the viewer. *The Louisiana Project* stands as witness to unspeakable history – she puts away her self in these images as she performatively absorbs the suffering of American history in her art.

From *The Louisiana Project*, the photograph titled *In the Abyss* and the photograph showing a woman walking on train tracks form a kind of conceptual diptych (Figures 7.5 and 7.6). By considering the presentation in *In the Abyss* of the image of the first housing project built in New Orleans in parallel with the image of a woman walking down the center of railroad tracks in the industrial edge of New Orleans (Figures 7.5 and 7.6), we are able to witness the hinge where ulterior and exterior landscapes of desolation are joined. That is, both images structurally show a kind of abyss, a vanishing into the depths, with the photograph *In the Abyss*

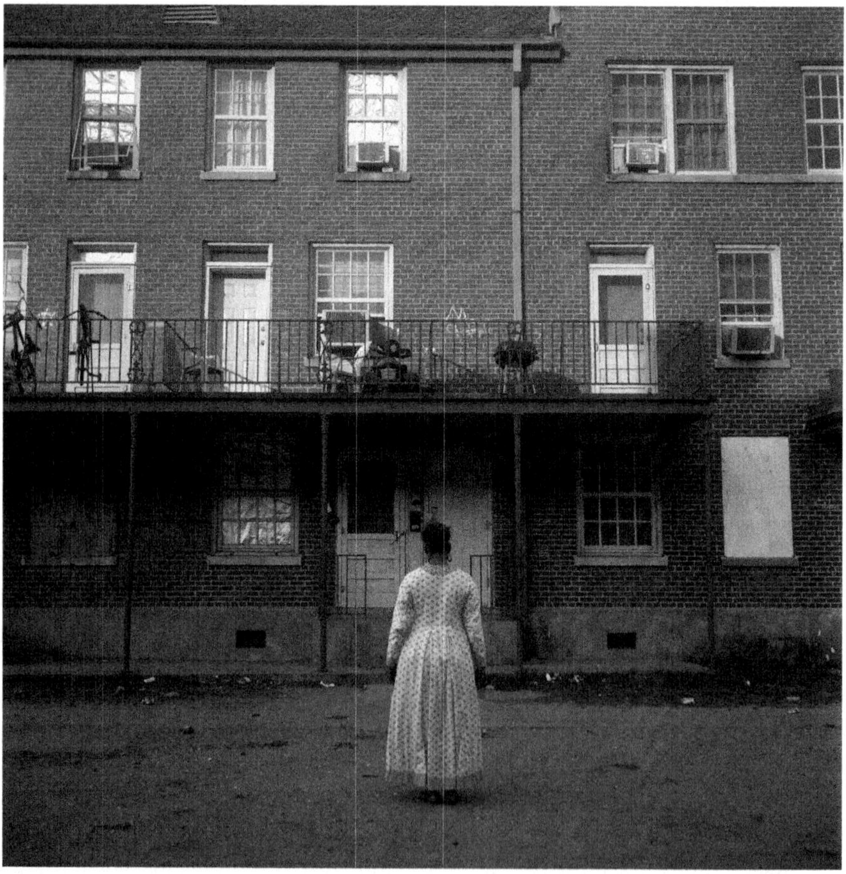

FIGURE 7.5 Carrie Mae Weems, *In the Abyss*, 2003, pigment ink print, 20 × 20 in. © Carrie Mae Weems. Courtesy of the artist and Jack Shainman Gallery, New York.

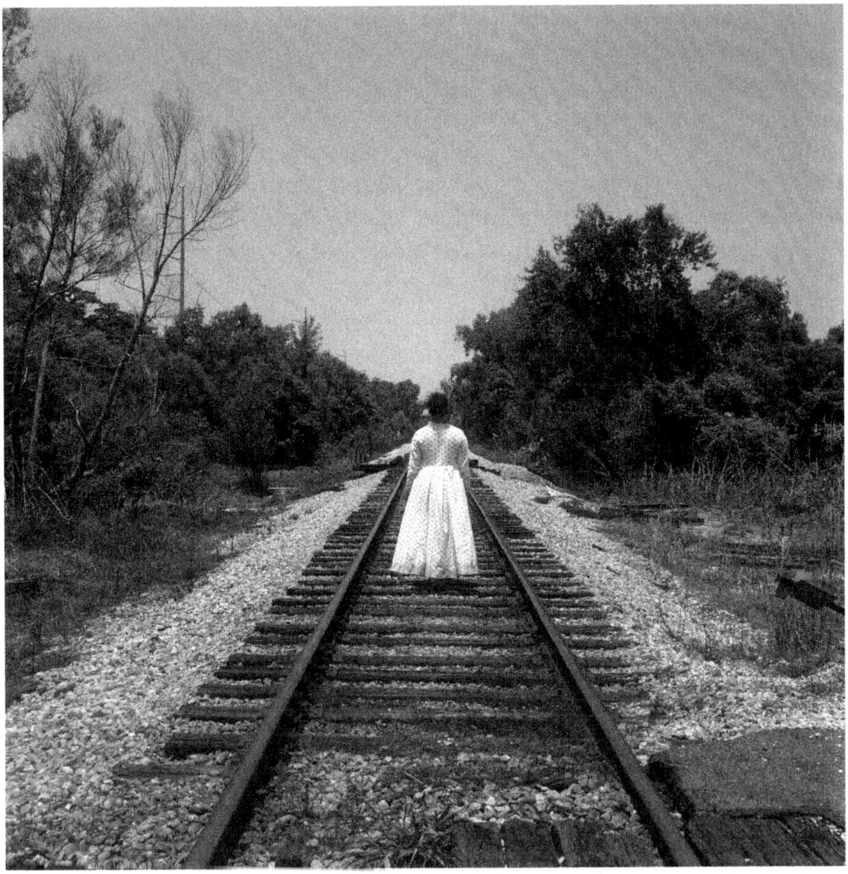

FIGURE 7.6 Carrie Mae Weems, *Untitled (standing on the tracks)*, 2003, gelatin silver print, 20 × 20 in. © Carrie Mae Weems. Courtesy of the artist and Jack Shainman Gallery, New York.

describing visually the way that cycles of oppression embed families in substandard housing for generations and with the image of the woman on the railroad tracks making a visual metaphor out of the clear presentation of the vanishing point. As the woman standing on the railroad tracks appears to be walking into the vanishing point, her feet, occluded by the rail ties, cannot be seen. She appears to be a ghostly figure, haunting the industrial periphery of the city (Figure 7.6). She is the ghost whose form witnesses the violence of the "cancer alley" industrialization of the Gulf Coast, and the way that environmental racism affects the lives of African Americans.[30] This same ghostly figure (portrayed by Weems) appears in *In the Abyss* and in several other photographs in *The Louisiana Project* (Figure 7.5). With her back to the audience, she stares at the housing project. This act of witnessing is emphasized as Weems's photograph is framed so that we see nothing beyond the housing project. We see no sky, no trees – we see only the dilapidated housing itself that seems to swallow us. We see an abyss of time and space, a visual meditation on the long and deep impact of racism and the painful history of racialized codes of domination.

Weems's emphasis in some of her works on race should be considered a form of feminism. If one is locked in Judith Butler's frame of gender as performativity, then Weems's intense emphasis on history and race could seem outside the scope of feminist enquiry. But if the feminist movement is, as bell hooks argues, a movement to end sexist oppression, then feminism should clearly concern itself with confluences between racism and sexism and their impact on African American women.[31] That is not to suggest that Weems's work does not contend with poststructuralist theory; rather, it is to point out that Weems deploys the figure of the witness, that she portrays herself *witnessing* in her photographs, in a way that trips up the facile arguments of performativity. Weems's performance as history's ghost is grave and serious, and it invokes histories of silencing. The title of Weems's photograph *Sorrow's Bed* (Figure 7.7), which is part of *The Louisiana Project*, refers to *plaçage*. From

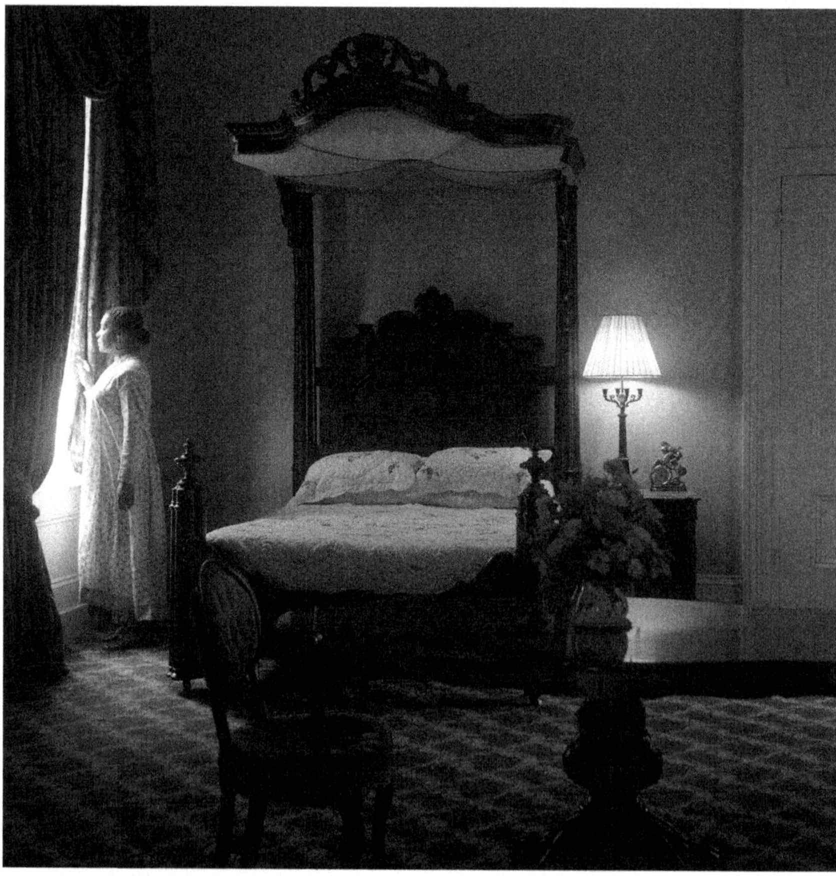

FIGURE 7.7 Carrie Mae Weems, *Sorrow's Bed*, 2003, iris print, 20 × 20 in. © Carrie Mae Weems. Courtesy of the artist and Jack Shainman Gallery, New York.

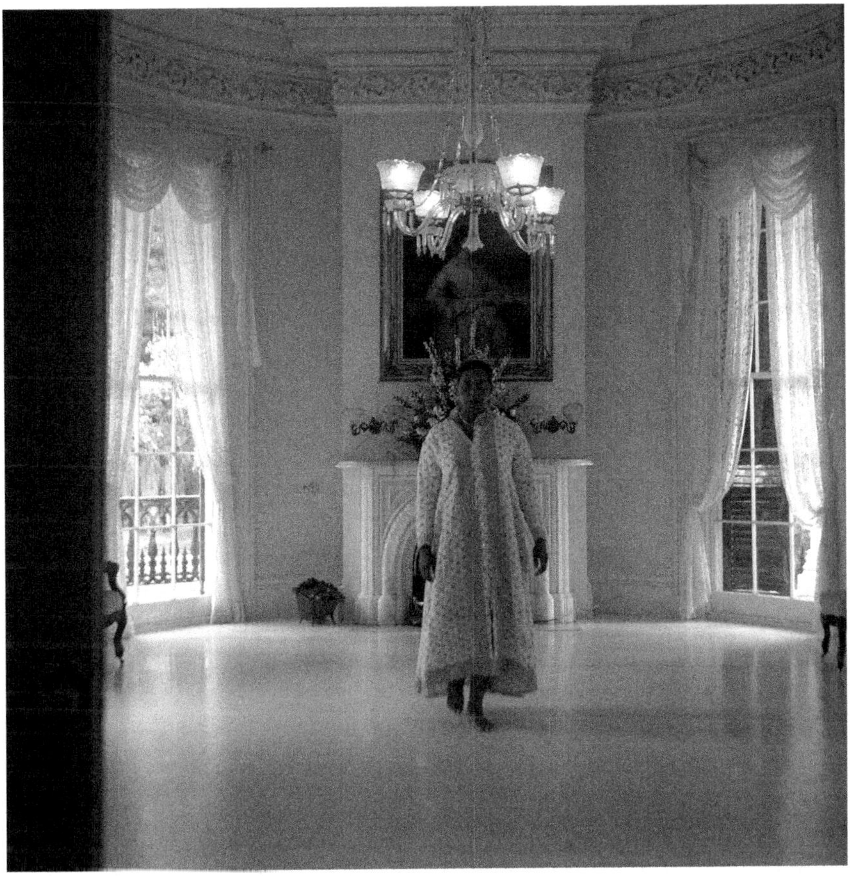

FIGURE 7.8 Carrie Mae Weems, *A Single's Waltz in Time*, 2003, gelatin silver print, triptych, 20 × 20 in. each. © Carrie Mae Weems. Courtesy of the artist and Jack Shainman Gallery, New York.

a French word that means "placing," plaçage, as practiced in New Orleans, was the system wherein men of European descent kept women of mixed African American and European descent as mistresses.[32] *The Louisiana Project* thematizes the double silencing of women enslaved or kept in plaçage; the witness figure that visually pulls together the series declaims herself, in an image central to the series: "I was the chambermaid, the whore."[33] Taking up the subjectivity of the dispossessed, Weems's photographs witness social structures of oppression. In this sense, her photographs often achieve the original aim of photography – to be a magic mirror, to show more than the eye.[34]

The other south: Sally's Mann's immediate family

Carrie Mae Weems's *Louisiana Project* and Sally Mann's *Deep South* and *Mother Land* series are roughly contemporary, works from the turn of the twenty-first century that can be read side by side, as each contains disturbing echoes of the Greek Revival architecture of the traditional South. Because Weems frames her images with staged witnessing and haunting, the architectures in her work speak of oppression and domination. Mann's work does not suggest a mode of witnessing trauma but instead repeats a nineteenth-century photographic technology, glass plate, and so her images tell of ruin with a rough and harsh nostalgia. While Weems uses twenty-first-century photographic and printing techniques and evokes haunting, Mann uses wet plate collodion emulsion to present a visceral and ominously unpeopled landscape. Mann's series title *Mother Land* unmistakably engages nostalgia – however melancholic and ambivalent – for the bucolic and ruined rural South, tying her work to that of the Southern Agrarians, intellectuals such as John Crowe Ransom, of the earlier twentieth century. In both *Mother Land* and *Deep South*, Mann comes to terms with her own inheritance of Southern culture as a wealthy, white woman whose family has a long history in the South (Figure 7.9). Yet her use of nineteenth-century landscape photographic technique means the images are so deeply backward-looking that they appear as if outside time. That is, they do not appear to be twentieth-century or early twenty-first-century scenes, and one is forced to ask exactly how, by precisely what visual marks, Mann's photographs of the southeastern United States critique the region's history of slavery and Jim Crow.

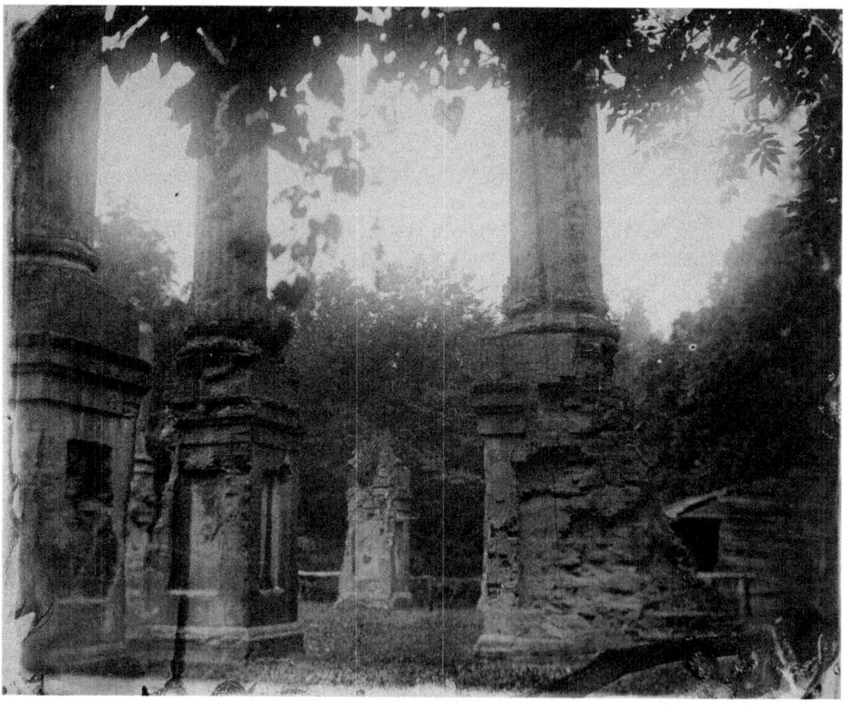

FIGURE 7.9 Sally Mann, *Deep South, Untitled (Valentine Windsor)*, 1998, gelatin silver print, 40 × 50 in. © Sally Mann. Courtesy Gagosian Gallery.

Do these works reach toward scenes of ruin that might not necessarily agitate for cultural change now? Weems's work clearly presses her viewers to think both about the South's painful history and its aftermath. Yet the lack of people in Mann's series at once makes the landscapes timeless and haunting and also, troublingly, turns away from direct engagement with the real human suffering that is part of the South's history. Nothing in Mann's images anchors in the viewer a knowledge of the South's resistance to ending the enslavement of African Americans, and so the sense of fragility and harm that the images convey could indicate any grief, a general meditation on mortality, and not a specific response to racism. Indeed, Mann's lush southern landscapes could almost cohere with the Lost Cause ideology that was still dominant in the South of Mann's 1950s childhood. To be clear, I am certainly not arguing that Mann espouses racist ideology (she has written eloquently against such). Rather, I am writing in this chapter about the ways that her photographs have been received, discussed, circulated, and acclaimed. The architectural and vista photographs of the deep South that Weems creates in *The Louisiana Project* and that Mann creates in *Deep South*, then, contrast with each other strikingly in mood, aspect, apparent meaning, and conveyance, even as they show similar architectures and represent a process of the artists steeping in the history of the American southeast.

Mann is best known, however, not for her accomplished landscape images but for her controversial 1992 book, *Immediate Family*,[35] which contains photographs undergirded by an implicit discourse of race. Working mainly in black and white, Mann created these photographs of her three children during the family's long summers at a retreat in rural Virginia. (She still lives on a farm outside of Lexington, Virginia.) Unlike her later work in landscape photography, *Immediate Family* focuses absolutely on the human figure and the human face; the series nearly exclusively showcase the faces and (sometimes naked) bodies of Mann's children, all under age 12 when she took the photographs. Anne Higonnet has argued that, in this series, Mann ingeniously solves the mother–artist conflict that has dogged women artists for generations.[36] Higonnet apparently refers to the (now defunct, we hope) belief that women who have young children have a difficult time creating serious art.[37] The argument has two forms: (a) women who have young children may not be taken seriously as artists but will instead be seen as amateurs; and (b) having young children in one's care is a structural impediment to focusing on one's art because nurturing the next generation will leach power from one's work as an artist. Needless to say, such a paradigm reflects sexist cultural patterns that require women to take primary responsibility for children.[38] Sally Mann found the time and space and the open place for creation. She found the focus without turning away from the task of creating art utterly with and among her children – because she made her three young children the focus of her art.

Critics have praised *Immediate Family* as one of the most influential photography books of the twentieth century, and, as I have mentioned, they have called Mann America's best photographer.[39] And yet some have also maligned the work as child pornography, in that it shows Mann's prepubescent children unclothed and displayed in positions of insouciance and damage, if not actual eroticism.[40] Mann's response to this charge has been to claim that a child's pleasure inhabiting his or her own naked body is natural and that only adults bring to their viewing of the images the notion of eroticism.[41] Regardless of one's views on the salutary, negligible, or damaging effects on children who are repeatedly photographed in the nude, it is clear that the controversy surrounding *Immediate Family* shaped Mann's career. The controversy also very meaningfully shows how vexed the cultural contradictions of motherhood remain.[42] By photographing her children, Mann in her best-known work becomes a public mother-photographer, and as such her career reveals much about the ideologies of motherhood and what we consider to be art.

The public furor *Immediate Family* stirred up did not question Mann's gifts as a photographer but her competence as a mother. Some claimed that photographing her children in the nude when they were much younger than the age of consent made Mann a child abuser, whereas others argued that Mann was not so much abusive as just misguided.[43] This emphasis on Mann the mother tended to set to one side the question of whether the photographs in *Immediate Family* were great photographs. It implied that Mann's supposed crimes as a mother were more important than her possible claim to artistic greatness.[44] At the time the book first circulated, even positive reviews focused on Mann's work as photography and maternity:

> In these intimate black-and-white portraits, exhibited piecemeal over the last several years, [Sally Mann] struck a vein. The fears and sheltering tenderness that any parent has felt for his or her child were realized with an eidetic clarity. A half-naked androgyne, smeared with dirt and grass stains, looks up from a leaf-strewn yard. Lithe, pale shapes move with prideful ease among thick-torsoed elders. The images seemed to speak of a familiar past that was now distant and irretrievable.[45]

Whereas I do not personally advocate circulating photographs of underage children in the nude because these images can indeed be fodder for pedophiles, the tremendously strong ties in public reception between Mann's art and her maternity make her a case study in the gendering of art.[46] And also, importantly, the photographs reflect codes of race in America. For Mann's very ability to widely circulate her photographs of her naked children depends on her privileged status as a well-to-do, well-educated, straight, married, and – above all – white woman.

The photographs in *Immediate Family* show a mother's gaze at her children.[47] They assert the mother's right to her children's bodies, to see them unclothed, to touch them, to control them. In this way, the images work against many cultural tropes of the feminine – the feminine woman is supposed to be someone who renounces her right to touch, control, and watch the bodies of others.[48] So Mann's maternal gaze pitches against cultural tropes of femininity the power of the mother to see, touch, and possibly harm the bodies of her children.[49] To see this gaze expressed through the camera is to be aware that being female does not necessarily mean being only the object of the male gaze. Being a mother, in Mann's handling of the camera, means claiming one's children as human beings nearly completely within one's power. But what does Mann's visual claim on her children's bodies say about race, class, and cultural interpretations of race and class? What does it tell us that Mann has been interpreted as a mother, and nothing else, rather than as a wealthy white mother (that is, a woman whose place in Southern culture is secured and protected by class and race)?

Notably, the trope of the powerful mother is some part of the fabric of the traditional South and arguably has its roots in the power structures of enslavement.[50] The white mother in the antebellum South often had the capacity to physically punish African Americans, male and female, enslaved by her family.[51] Some white women were known to have treated their family's enslaved African Americans violently.[52] This pattern of controlling the bodies of oppressed or disenfranchised others, then, is part of the traditional paradigm of white Southern femininity and a very troubling one.[53] Whereas I would not make the case that Mann's photographs degrade her children, the photographs clearly do depend on the children's acquiescence to pose for their mother. This vulnerability stems from their extreme youth and concomitant dependency on their mother for care (or whatever adult might have stood in her stead); indeed, their survival depends on this care.

I suggest that Mann's work in *Immediate Family* reveals not childish capers, however rough the children sometimes appear. Instead, the photographs trace the very intense and serious struggle *between* the mother and the children. It shows the power of the bond, the ferocity and even desperation of the love and need that run between the mother and her children: the mother, the photographer, fights mightily to wrest herself as an artist and to wrest her art from the powerful needs of her young children, whom she fiercely loves. It is not that Mann's photography captures her children in some feral, untouched state – not at all. What she captures in *Immediate Family* is the force of her relationship to her children, the powerful struggle to emerge as an artist while still playing the role of the devoted, white, Southern mother, a role that had already built into it a measure of violence and bodily control of those in her power.

A little-discussed but very telling aspect of *Immediate Family* is the extent to which reception of the work is immersed in the ideology of race. Precisely because Mann is white and her children are white, and precisely because they are protected in their well-to-do whiteness, their naked forms are interpreted as symbols of childhood. But by claiming that reception of Mann's work often adopts uncritically, and apparently unknowingly, the ideology of the dominant race, I do not mean to dismiss her work. It magisterially shows the raw and powerful struggle of the woman artist to emerge from the constrictive space of maternity, whatever the cost.[54] This power, the longing and the will to create art no matter what the circumstances – and no matter what inherited terms of domination are deployed in the execution of the work – is the force of Mann's *Immediate Family*.

Mother love

Weems and Mann have complicated and elliptical relationships to the tradition of documentary photography. Weems's work, from the early 1990s to the present, questions the givens of the documentary conceit – questions the idea that photographs can show the real – so that her work becomes increasingly conceptual even as it retains a clear aesthetic relationship to a certain kind of representational verisimilitude. Mann does not so much conceptually critique documentary tradition as turn it radically inward, documenting her children's infant play and nakedness, her husband's tragic illness and nakedness, and her own injury and recovery after falling from a horse. She alters documentary tradition much in the way that feminist anthropologists alter the field of ethnography, by making the case that in the domestic is not ignorance but another kind of knowledge, a painful one; beneath the surface this subtext of brooding on mortality drives Mann's lushly gothic work.

Despite its problematic racial positioning, Mann's work yet drives a feminist aesthetic because the photographs do unearth, however, the grit of the violence of motherhood, the way that mortality is its essential condition. Although decrying the violence of the racist South is not an explicit part of Mann's *Immediate Family* images, they allude to that violence – albeit in ways that most interpreters ignore and also in ways that Mann possibly did not intend. The photographs immerse themselves in the violence of being human and in the mother's violent struggle to wrest herself from eidetically merging with the children whom she passionately loves, holding them still in her gaze. The grit of the images has little to do with the children as such, but instead they are portraits of the mother's struggle with mortality, violence, and the fight for a self, all as portrayed by her astonishingly generous models, her children.

And yet Carrie Mae Weems's witnessing of the traumatic subterranean reality of American history and Sally Mann's private vision of her children are also in conversation about privacy, as privacy is a major aspect of wealthy, white privilege.[55] Mann's work does show the force and the will to create art in that space of cultural silence that is maternity. This sense of being impelled makes the work strong and feminist, overturning as it does sugary expectations of the realm of mother and child. But Weems's work speaks against a different kind of cultural silencing. The surface calm – and beauty – of her work is the result of her steely divinations, going down into the places that Americans try to forget or gloss over. The beauty of her images makes her visual protest the photographic equivalent of a long stare, the gaze of someone who does not look away. As such, Weems is quintessentially a photographer in that photography is the medium of the stare. It is the medium of gazing in stillness longer than we ever look at life. And if we look long enough and if the photograph is right, it sinks in.

In Weems's and Mann's work, the space of death is a palpable backstory, and the force of their images is elegiac, possessing a quality of history not to be undone, only to be redone. In Mann's photograph *Last Light*, as in Weems's triptych *A*

Single's Waltz in Time (here is shown the central panel of that triptych, Figure 7.8), the force of what is lost takes over the visible field. In Mann's photograph, *Last Light*, the youngest daughter, Virginia, is held by her father, whose hands – enormous compared to the child's small body – seem to take the child's pulse as the last light ebbs from the day. The little girl with her head tilted back, baring her throat to the camera, becomes a metaphor for the ebbing of light and the mortal condition in which her small body (and all human bodies) is contained. In Weems's waltz, the African American woman in nineteenth-century garb haunts a lavishly preserved plantation in the twenty-first century. Here the body's freedom to dance is implicitly and painfully contrasted with antebellum architecture as an expression of domination. The plaintive, crepuscular tones of the images make the three photographs (a triptych) of Weems's waltz in time look valedictory. And yet the dance is a new beginning in time, as Weems performs in the twenty-first century what would have been impossible in the nineteenth – an African American woman dancing freely in the formal space of an antebellum parlor. This reiterative return to origins – and releasing of images from their painful sources – is the force of this photographic work.

The original experience, as Blanchot conceives the term, not only spurs the creation of art but is, as he argues, the goal of the true artist. Weems epitomizes this force: she immerses herself in originary spaces, not just those already mentioned but also the graves and slave quarters on Sea Island, Georgia (*Sea Islands Series*, 1991–1992), the sites from which kidnapped Africans were taken into slave ships (the series *Africa* and *Slave Coast*, 1993), and more recently Abraham Lincoln's emancipation proclamation (the video *Lincoln, Lonnie and Me – A Story in 5 Parts*, 2012). The return to the origin, then, is the impetus of the works, and the origin is also the work. That is, form and content cannot be separated in Weems's sounding of key turns, and returns, in American history. "A just answer is rooted in the question," argues Blanchot, for the work itself "does not begin but is prior to any beginning."[56] Weems has spent her working life immersed in asking the questions from which emerge these just and justified images.

Mann and Weems are not photographers usually mentioned in the same breath, and yet these almost exactly contemporaneous American photographers have repeatedly sounded out questions of origin in their work. As the twenty-first century has progressed, Mann has photographed a series of self-portraits taken as she recovered after a fall from a horse and images of her husband's decline from an incurable degenerative disease, photographs of painful introspection. In the same time period, Weems's expansive progress has reached toward encompassing notions of an American family, a history in which not only the photographer but also many of her viewers are immersed, tapping film and other media in her quest to explore the original experience. Questions of privilege and privacy, of self and other, and of the interior and the expansive gaze play through these quintessential American photographers' oeuvres. Their work performs a descent into American history, an encounter with the original national experience.

Notes

1 Maurice Blanchot, "The Original Experience," in *The Continental Aesthetics Reader*, ed. Clive Cazeaux (London: Routledge, 2000): 327–329. Elsewhere, Blanchot writes, "The work is always lacking with respect to itself. For the implication is that, without the collection of all the works which incarnate it in time, art does not exist, yet that art is 'true' only in the work always still to come." *The Space of Literature* (Lincoln: University of Nebraska Press, 1982), 158.

2 Argues Blanchot, "The work is deeply concerned for art. This is to say that for the work, art is never a given, and that the work can find art only by continuing toward its own completion in radical uncertainty, for it cannot know in advance whether art is what it is." *Space of Literature*, 234.

3 Ibid., 242.

4 I discuss the controversy over Sally Mann's *Immediate Family* later in the chapter; my discussion of the controversy surrounding the work of Carrie Mae Weems can be found in *Witnessing Sadism in Texts of the American South* (London: Routledge, 2014) and in "The Crucible of Witnessing," *Meridians: Women, Race, and Transnationalism* 13, no. 1 (Fall 2015): 26–52. In short, Mann's controversial work has been discussed in the media and in criticism as bearing on the supposedly universal aspect of her motherhood, without attention being paid to how her whiteness protects her as she produces naked photographs of her children. By contrast, the controversy surrounding Carrie Mae Weems's work is enclosed in the discourse of African American art historians.

5 Brendan Lindsay, *Murder State* (Lincoln: University of Nebraska Press, 2015); Sharon P. Holland, *Raising the Dead* (Durham, NC: Duke University Press, 2000); Deborah Walker King, *African Americans and the Culture of Pain* (Charlottesville, VA: University of Virginia Press, 2008).

6 This is not to discount the photographers' inheritance from other influences, which is very rich. Please see Shannah Ehrhart, "Sally Mann's Looking-Glass House," in *Tracing Cultures: Art History, Criticism, Critical Fiction*, ed. Miwon Kwon (New York: Whitney Museum of Art, 1994), 52–69; see also, Dawoud Bey, "An Interview with Carrie Mae Weems," *BOMB Magazine* 108 (Summer 2009): 60–7.

7 Blanchot, *Space of Literature*, 235.

8 Amelia Jones, *Seeing Differently: A History and Theory of Identification in the Visual Arts* (London: Routledge, 2012).

9 Interpreting Mann's work through the rubric of her visual immersion in white Southern identity is my explicit strategy in this chapter. I choose this approach because as much as Mann's Southernness is described in media responding to her work, it needs to be critically analyzed. For example, an article discussing the terrible and grievous tragedy of her adult son's suicide frames Mann's life and work with phrases like "the depictions of the children's bodies . . . could not be completely understood outside the context of this farm. The farm is remote and sylvan, with horses grazing alongside the winding drive," evoking Southern plantations without using that word. In other words: Sally Mann's photography of her naked children has to be placed in the context of her white, Southern, and wealthy social situation, a social placement that implicitly protects her (though possibly not her children). See Hilarie M. Sheets, "After Her Son's Death, Sally Mann Stages a Haunting Show," *New York Times*, September 6, 2016.

10 This way of discussing Weems and Mann in conversation and in contrast arose during a discussion on June 18, 2016, at the African American Studies Seminar in Washington, D.C., where I have been privileged to present work. I am very grateful to the seminar group for their reading and interpretation of an earlier draft of this chapter. In particular, Wilma King and Jay Driskell offered thorough-going suggestions, and I am so thankful for their support.

11 Carrie Mae Weems and Deborah Willis, *Carrie Mae Weems: Three Decades of Photography and Video* (New Haven, CT: Yale University Press, 2012).

12 As Blanchot puts it, "What man risks when he belongs to the work and when the work is the search for art is, then, the most extreme thing he could risk: not just his life, not only the world where he dwells, but his essence, his right to truth, and, even more, his right to death." *Space of Literature*, 237.

13 Carrie Mae Weems, "INsight Conversation: Carrie Mae Weems with Deborah Willis," LOOK3 Festival of the Photograph, Charlottesville, VA, June 2013.

14 In discussing her work on "The Hampton Project," Weems lays claim to Native American as well as African American heritage. See Carrie Mae Weems, *The Hampton Project*, ed. Vivian Patterson, Frederick Rudolph, Constance Glenn, Deborah Willis, and Jeanne Zeidler (New York: Aperture, 2000).

15 Daniel Patrick Moynihan, *The Negro Family: The Case for National Action* (Washington, DC: Office of Policy Planning and Research, U.S. Department of Labor, 1965).

16 In 2016 – 26 years after its creation – *The Kitchen Table Series* was finally published as a stand-alone book by Damiani/Matsumoto Editions/D.A.P. See Hilary Moss, "Revisiting Carrie Mae Weems's Indelible Series – Almost Three Decades Later," *New York Times*, April 5, 2016. *Immediate Family*, by contrast, was published by Aperture in 1992, immediately after Mann completed the images, which she began photographing in the mid-1980s.

17 Laura Mulvey's theory of how traditional cinema structures watching, looking, from the male perspective is often extrapolated to discuss photography. However, she very specifically focuses on the narrative structures of traditional cinema, which she argues center on the male gaze. That is, the male protagonist is active in the film, and the camera's and hence viewer's gaze is sutured to the point of view of the male protagonist. By contrast, in traditional cinema the female "love interest" remains passive, still, and the camera takes the visual pleasure of showing her face and body. Laura Mulvey, "Visual Pleasure and Narrative Cinema," *Screen* (October 1975) 16(3): 6–18.

18 bell hooks theorizes the "oppositional gaze" possessed by African American women. She writes, "Reading Laura Mulvey's provocative essay, 'Visual Pleasure and Narrative Cinema,' from a standpoint that acknowledges race, one sees clearly why black women spectators not duped by mainstream cinema would develop an oppositional gaze. Placing ourselves outside that pleasure in looking, Mulvey argues, was determined by a 'split between active/male and passive/female.' Black female spectators actively chose not to identify with the film's imaginary subject because such identification was disenabling." *Black Looks: Race and Representation* (Boston, MA: South End Press, 1992), 122.

19 Ibid., 115–31.

20 Ibid., 118.

21 *Hidden Witness: African-Americans in Early Photography*, exhibition, February 28–June 18, 1995, J. Paul Getty Museum, Malibu, CA.

22 Weems, "INsight Conversation." *From Here I Saw What Happened and I Cried* has been the subject of vigorous debate in the African American art history community. I trace this debate in one section of my book *Witnessing Sadism*, 31–73.

23 Ibid.

24 Social theorist Ron Eyerman argues that African American culture experiences a deep cultural trauma resulting from the aftermath of enslavement as well as the continued corrosive effects of racism. *Cultural Trauma: Slavery and the Formation of African American Identity* (Cambridge, UK: Cambridge University Press, 2002).

25 Helaine Posner and Nancy Princethal, *The Deconstructive Impulse: Women Artists Reconfigure Signs of Power, 1973–1991*, exhibition, January 15–April 3, 2011, Neuberger Museume of Art, Purchase, NY; see also, Carrie Moyer, "The Deconstructive Impulse," *Art in America* (May, 2011), www.artinamericamagazine.com/reviews/the-deconstructive-impulse/.

26 Brendan Lindsay, *Murder State: California's Native American Genocide* (Lincoln: University of Nebraska Press, 2015).

27 On this controversy, please see Sarah Bassnett, "From Public Relations to Art: Exhibiting Frances Benjamin Johnston's Hampton Institute Photographs," *History of Photography* 32,

no. 2 (Summer 2008): 152–68. See also Holland Cotter, "Art in Review – Carrie Mae Weems's 'The Hampton Project,'" *The New York Times*, March 23, 2001.

28 Before Katrina, New Orleans was a predominantly African American city, with 67 percent of its African American citizens living below the poverty line. See Rebecca Solnit, *A Paradise Built in Hell* (New York: Penguin, 2010).

29 As Barthes eloquently states, "Many photographs are, alas, inert under my gaze. But even among those which have some existence in my eyes, most provoke only a general and, so to speak, polite interest: they have no *punctum* in them: they please or displease me without pricking me: they are invested with no more than *stadium*." *Camera Lucida: Reflections on Photography* (New York: Macmillan, 1981), 27.

30 For an introduction to Louisiana's environmental woes, and the way that environmental racism shapes the state's residential and neighborhood patterns, see Julie Cart, "A Strong Voice in Louisiana's Cancer Alley," *Los Angeles Times*, August 27, 2013.

31 Kimberle Crenshaw argues that intersections between racist and sexist oppression have a kind of teratogenic force (that is, an impact in which each toxin worsens the effect of the other toxin). "Mapping the Margins: Intersectionality, Identity Politics, and Violence against Women of Color," *Stanford Law Review* 43, no. 6 (July 1991): 1241–99.

32 For an in-depth history of one instance of plaçage and its outcome, see Gary B. Mills and Elizabeth Shown Mills, *The Forgotten People: Cane River's Creoles of Color*, rev. ed. (Baton Rouge: Louisiana State University Press, 2013). Elizabeth Shown Mills also argues that women of African descent under plaçage were not always victims. "Demythicizing History: Marie Thérèse Coincoin, Tourism, and the National Historical Landmarks Program," *Louisiana History* 53 (Fall 2012): 402–37.

33 Carrie Mae Weems, *The Louisiana Project* (New Orleans: Newcomb Art Gallery, Tulane University, 2005).

34 Geoffrey Batchen, *Burning with Desire: The Conception of Photography* (Cambridge, MA: MIT Press, 1999).

35 Sally Mann, *Immediate Family* (New York: Aperture, 1992).

36 Argues Anne Higonnet, "Along the way, Mann's work has challenged the histories of artistic, commercial, and amateur photography, as well as the reality effect that impinges on all three of those histories." "Sally Mann: The High Price of Success," in *The Woman Artist at the Millennium*, ed. Carol Armstrong and Catherine de Zegher (Cambridge, MA: MIT Press, 2006), 403.

37 Linda Nochlin takes apart many such truisms regarding women and art in her important essay "Why Have There Been No Great Women Artists?" in *Women, Art, and Power, and Other Essays* (New York: Harper Collins, 1988): 146–157.

38 And yet even without such sexist paradigms the mere facts of repeated childbirth (or even giving birth to and raising one child) could affect a woman's energy and thus her ability to create art.

39 Reynolds Price, "Time Magazine Named Sally Mann 'America's Best Photographer,'" *Time Magazine*, July 9, 2001.

40 Richard B. Woodward, "The Disturbing Photography of Sally Mann," *New York Times*, September 27, 1992.

41 Sally Mann, *Hold Still* (New York: Little, Brown and Company, 2015).

42 See Sharon Hays, *The Cultural Contradictions of Motherhood* (Cambridge, MA: Harvard University Press, 1998).

43 In her memoir, Sally Mann discusses criticism of her decision to photograph the children. See, Sally Mann, *Hold Still: A Memoir with Photographs* (Boston, MA: Little, Brown, and Company, 2015), 161.

44 "It May Be Art but What about the Kids?" *San Diego Tribune*, 1992.

45 Woodward, "Disturbing Photography."

46 James Steward, "The Camera of Sally Mann and the Spaces of Childhood," Ed. Elizabeth Goodenough, *Secret Spaces of Childhood* (Ann Arbor, MI: University of Michigan Press, 2003): 204–214.

47 Carol Mavor has argued that Mann's work compares to that of Clementina Hawarden, who also photographed her children. *Becoming: The Photographs of Clementina Hawarden* (Durham, NC: Duke University Press, 1999), 101–35. And yet, Hawarden's children were in their later teens when she photographed them and they wore clothes, which provides a psychological sense of protection. As Phillippe Sollers writes of Francesca Woodman, she is "more naked" than anyone, by which he means that Woodman risks herself more than anyone. See Hervé Chandès, ed., and Francesca Woodman, *Francesca Woodman* (Zurich: Scalo, 1998).

48 John Berger, *Ways of Seeing* (New York: Penguin, 2009).

49 Notably, while men and not women commit the overwhelming majority of cases of violence (that is, rape, battery, and child sexual abuse), women commit nearly as many cases of child abuse – physically harming a child in one's care – as men. Richard B. Felson and Paul-Philippe Paré, "The Reporting of Domestic Violence and Sexual Assault by Nonstrangers to the Police," *Journal of Marriage and Family* 67, no. 3 (August 2005): 597–610. On the mother and her connection to art, see Judith Mastai, "Anxious Dust: History and Repression in the Archives of Mary Kelly," in *Museums After Modernism: Strategies of Engagement*, Eds. Griselda Pollock and Joyce Zemans (London: Blackwell, 2007): 178–190.

50 Wilbur J. Cash, *The Mind of the South* (New York: Knopf, 1941); see also Paul D. Escott, ed., *W.J. Cash and the Minds of the South* (Baton Rouge: Louisiana State University Press, 1992) and Charles W. Eagles, ed., *The Mind of the South Fifty Years Later* (Oxford: University Press of Mississippi, 1992).

51 I do realize that this claim is controversial, with some historians arguing that white women rarely physically touched, much less harmed African American slaves, whereas others argue that there are numerous examples of white mistresses behaving physically aggressively against the enslaved people who belonged to their husbands. For measured explorations of this aspect of Southern history, see Fred W. Morrison, ed., *Mothers of Invention: Women of the Slaveholding South in the American Civil War* (Chapel Hill, NC: University of North Carolina Press, 2004). Please see also Wilma King, ed., *A Northern Woman in the Plantation South: Letters of Tryphena Blanche Holder Fox 1856–1876* (Columbia, SC: University of South Carolina Press, 1993). King points to the example of a white mistress choosing to whip an enslaved woman purportedly so that she could spare the slave the worse whipping she would receive at her husband's hands. See also, Patricia Yaeger, *Dirt and Desire: Reconstructing Southern Women's Writing, 1930–1990* (Chicago, IL: University of Chicago Press, 2000). Yaeger makes the argument that patterns of skewed parentage – with wealthy white women assuming parental power over African Americans and also over their own children as if they were possessions, a way that the culture of racism shaped white Southern femininity.

52 Henry Wiencek, *Master of the Mountain: Thomas Jefferson and His Slaves* (New York: Farrar, Straus, & Giroux, 2013)

53 I have written about this paradigm in *Witnessing Sadism*.

54 As Julia Kristeva has written, motherhood as it is scripted in the West is the space of silence and nonthought. See *Stabat Mater: The Kristeva Reader*, ed. Toril Moi (London: Wiley-Blackwell, 1991).

55 Child protection services disproportionately affect African American and Native American families. See Child Welfare Information Gateway, "Addressing Racial Disparity in Child Welfare" (Issue Brief, U.S. Department of Health and Human Services, Children's Bureau, Washington, DC, 2011); see also, Andrea J. Sedlak and Dana Schultz, "Racial Differences in Child Protective Services Investigation of Abused and Neglected Children," in *Race Matters in Child Welfare: The Overrepresentation of African American Children in the System*, ed. Denette M. Derezotes, John Poertner, and Mark F. Testa (Washington, DC: Child Welfare League of America Press, 2005): 97–117.

56 Maurice Blanchot, *The Infinite Conversation*, trans. Susan Hanson (Minneapolis, MN: Minnesota University Press, 1992), 211–39.

8

ETHNOGRAPHIES AND PORTRAITS

Mary Ellen Mark, Rineke Dijkstra, and Zoe Strauss

Photographers Mary Ellen Mark (1940–2015), Rineke Dijkstra (born 1959), and Zoe Strauss (born 1970) do not belong to one school of or one movement in photography. Working in the late twentieth and early twenty-first centuries, the photographers have created images that – by dint of differing approaches to their subject matter and by using different cameras and printing techniques, could never be mistaken for each other. I am grouping them here because each has created a photographic oeuvre that deploys the camera as a kind of ethnographic tool. The camera unearths a visual space that is both portraiture and empathetic ethnography and uses the visual to search out the self, as identity is shaped in the late twentieth century and early twenty-first century in the West.

Mark, Dijkstra, and Strauss share a largeness and specificity of vision, encompassing interior infinities in their photographies.[1] This visual claim of seeing very specifically and in great detail what is there, while also placing the specific in the context of broader cultural and global realities, allows all three to create work that is politically subtle but that always carries a political force – a force of what it means to be poor, a female, a displaced person, a soldier, a prostitute, an adolescent, or a child. Mary Ellen Mark's fidelity to analog photography makes her a fascinating study, as well. Mark, who was active as a photographer up until her death in 2015, favored the verisimilitude of analog. Her argument in favor of using film and developing film images to print (that is, not having recourse to digital technology to create her photographs) bears on the question "What is photography?"[2]

The word means *light-writing*, or light-mark (phos, φως, meaning *light* in Greek, and graph, γραφική, meaning *written mark*). As the technology was developed in the nineteenth century and used throughout most of the twentieth century, this term *light-writing* is literal. An analog photograph is an image that is produced when the light rays that bounce off a physical object are contracted through a lens onto a capture medium that is photosensitized (silver is almost always the capture medium).

An image is created on that medium that is, in a real sense, the skin of light cast by an object. Analog – or film – photography, then, uses the laws of physics to create images. The technology might have seemed miraculous when Louis Daguerre and Henry Fox Talbot successively brought it forward in 1839, but analog photography simply harnesses the laws of physics. In that sense, it works by physical laws the same way the eye does.[3]

Digital photography, by contrast, translates light's waves (via impulses caught by a light-sensitive device in a digital camera) into algorithms, mathematical functions that through yes-and-no delineations (yes meaning "here is a mark," no meaning "here is open space") create images that are pixilated. (If you sufficiently enlarge a digital image, you can see the squares.) In this sense, digital photography can be extremely accurate and refined, but it will not give you the image down to the skin in the way that a daguerreotype or a silver colloid photograph does. A digital photograph is a mathematical code; an analog photograph is a physical trace. Mark's favoring of film photography, then, reveals something about her ethos of photography: the photographer should be there, skin to skin with the world; she should be part of the physical world and the reality that her photograph captures as a physical trace.

Mary Ellen Mark

Mark shaped a career from photographing subjects who were at risk, at the fringes of society, dispossessed: she photographed women in mental institutions (*Ward 81*) and brothels (*Falkland Road*), as well as homeless children and youths who lived on the street and in abandoned buildings in Seattle (*Streetwise*, which originated in photographs she took for an article in the now-defunct *Life* magazine).[4] Her emphasis, when she chose work that expressed her personal interest (as opposed to taking assignments to keep afloat financially) often was on photographing women. Mark states:

> I photograph women a lot. I don't want to be classified, but I am a woman and a photographer. I feel that great photography is great photography whether it's male, female, or whatever. But I think because I am a woman I understand women more. And I guess I like to photograph what I understand, so I have photographed women a lot. I also believe that women are more vulnerable. It's harder being a woman, and I guess that's part of what I want to show. I relate well to men, but I feel a real link with women because I understand their plight.[5]

In making the photographs that constitute *Streetwise*, Mark's connection with one child prostitute in particular, a young adolescent girl called Tiny (Erin Blackwell), became so close that Mark continued to stay in her life. Mark's connection with her may well have been part of the reason that Tiny eventually got clean from drugs, stopped working as a prostitute, and established a life off the streets.[6] Mark took her black-and-white photographs for *Streetwise* in the early 1980s, working in conjunction with reporter Cheryl McCall. In addition, she worked on a film, also called *Streetwise*, with her husband, Marvin Bell.

Given the rough terrain of the street kids' lives, Mark would have needed courage and support (from McCall and from her spouse) to complete the *Streetwise* project. Taking photographs of homeless youths meant that Mark spent her days in the neighborhoods where child prostitutes, child drug addicts, and drug dealers lived. Getting down to the gritty truth is key for Mark's photography; she chose Seattle for her photographs of homeless youths because at the time, the early 1980s, Seattle was being hailed as America's most livable city, a kind of urban paradise. Mark wanted to show the whole truth of the city. To photoshop or manipulate images when she had gone to personal risk to get the actual image (that is, to photograph the street kids on the street and in flophouses, not in her studio and not posed) would have been against Mark's ethos as a photographer. The ethical dimension to Mark's photography, then, is paramount and yet also complex.

Streetwise

In creating *Streetwise* (as also when photographing *Ward 81* and *Falkland Road*), Mark took photographs of a vulnerable population.[7] Homeless youths are vulnerable in several ways: (a) many are underage, as most of the kids photographed in *Streetwise* were under age 18 when Mark photographed them; (b) all are by definition functionally impoverished – whether or not homeless youths come from families living under the poverty line, they lack the money to obtain a stable domicile, and that almost always means they lack the money for regular access to healthy food, or any food, and to medical and dental care; (c) homeless youths are disproportionally likely to participate in an economy of survival sex, that is, having sex with strangers as a way to get enough money for food to survive; and (d) homeless youths are frequently addicted to drugs or alcohol or both. In other words, several overlapping vulnerabilities construct the identities of homeless youths. Whether a homeless youth could meaningfully give consent to being photographed for *Life* magazine – that is, could understand what it might mean to have her or his image circulated nationally as a child prostitute, a child drug dealer, or a street kid – is questionable.

But do the ethics of photography simply turn on whether a photographic subject gives, or can give, full consent to having her image "taken"? As Susan Sontag long ago pointed out, many verbs that surround the act of photography are violent: one "shoots" a photograph, one "snaps" a photographic "shot," one "takes" a person's photograph.[8] These verbs reveal photography's inherent capacity to violate, and at least for Susan Sontag they reveal the inalienable violence of photography.

Mark photographs the children not in the nude, not having sex, but just talking and hanging out, fully clothed. These children's families have already abandoned them – or the children had to flee abusive families. Unscrupulous adults are using these children for sex and as facilitators in selling drugs, and our culture does not care about these children sufficiently to help them find meaningful ways off the street. That being the case, can we really say that Mary Ellen Mark's photographs make these children any more vulnerable than they already were? Initiating the work that would become *Streetwise*, Mark noticed the children's unwillingness to trust her.[9] Such children instinctively mistrust adults – and rightly so, given the abuse they have experienced at home and on the street. But Mark used her work as a photographer not to steal or to take something away from her photographic subjects but to form an empathetic gaze. This gaze granted these risked people a way of being seen that might render them less invisible and more dignified than the way that our culture usually views child prostitutes and drug dealers. This empathetic gaze differentiates Mark's work from photographs who might seek to sensationalize or exploit homeless youths.

Tiny

Mark's bond with Tiny (Erin Blackwell) is particularly telling in this regard. I suggest that the iconic photograph that Mark created, "*Tiny*" *in Her Halloween Costume, Seattle, Washington, 1983* (Figure 8.1), is a portrait not just of a young girl living in a terrible situation but also of a relationship between the street kid and the photographer. After Mark's death in 2015, the *Seattle Times* interviewed Blackwell, and whereas her description of the pain that watching the film *Streetwise* brings her is haunting, she closes the interview by stating clearly that she "loved being around" Mary Ellen Mark.[10] Thirty years after she was a child prostitute, Blackwell recognizes that the existence of Mark's photographs (and also of the movie that Mark made with her husband) means that she, Blackwell, is permanently caught in the public's eye as a figure of drug abuse, prostitution, and street life.[11] Even though pained by the memories these images bring to her, as well as very reasonably fearful of her children seeing the film, Tiny speaks in loving terms of Mary Ellen Mark.[12]

Photography always risks exploiting its subjects: the photograph circulates an image far outside our boundaries and control; a photograph can be shown years after it was taken; it can be shown to a nearly endless number of people; and it skews and repeats time and space in a way that can be very violative. Regardless of the photographer's intent, a photograph always invades the privacy of the person photographed to some degree, and by definition what a photograph does is circulate an image. Erin Blackwell distinguishes these risks from her relationship with Mary Ellen Mark. Her pleasure in being around Mark, an adult who tried to take care of her by buying her food and offering a place to live, an adult who did not get drunk or ask Blackwell for sexual favors, may have been the closest Blackwell came to finding a real parent. Mary Ellen Mark did not have the authority to save Blackwell from life on the streets. After shooting *Streetwise*, Mark and her spouse, Bell, invited Blackwell to live with them, stipulating that she would have to attend school if she did so; because of that stipulation, Blackwell declined the offer.[13] But Mark did have the authority to photograph Tiny in images that reveal the possibility of the young prostitute transcending her situation.

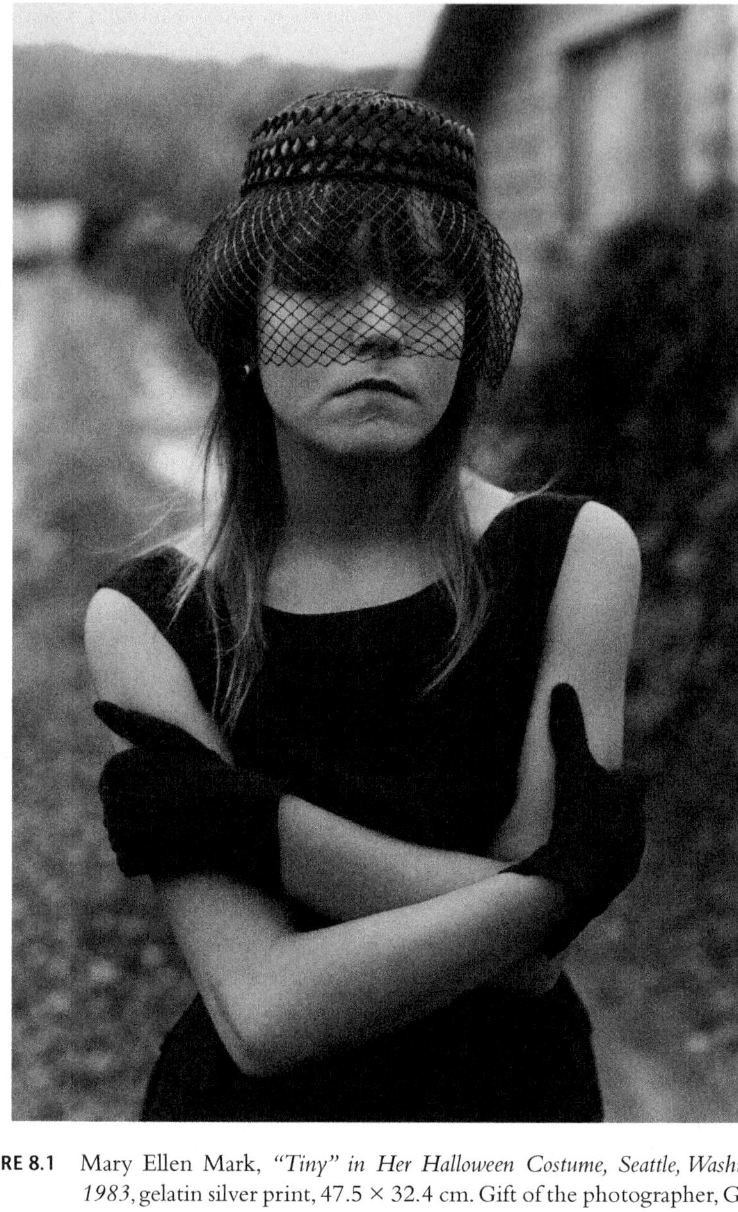

FIGURE 8.1 Mary Ellen Mark, *"Tiny" in Her Halloween Costume, Seattle, Washington, 1983*, gelatin silver print, 47.5 × 32.4 cm. Gift of the photographer, George Eastman Museum, Rochester, NY. © Mary Ellen Mark.

In "*Tiny*" *in Her Halloween Costume, Seattle, Washington, 1983*, Mark conveys the liminal social place of her subject (Figure 8.1). The crepuscular, autumnal equinox lighting that surrounds the girl governs the mood of the image – evening in late autumn – and a feeling of colder air coming in, grass and trees becoming dormant, attends the photograph. The child is scantily dressed, and she holds her own upper arms against the cold. She is mimicking the appearance of a woman, playing dress-up, and yet, despite her small stature and underdeveloped body, she has a facial expression that suggests she knows more about the toughness of life than do most adults. She is slightly older than most kids who trick-or-treat (usually by age 12 the years of roaming the neighborhood on Halloween are over), and so the photograph suggests also a sense of nostalgia for childhood, as well as the impossibility of returning to its innocence. The dead grass and withered low bush or tree behind Tiny suggest things have come to some sort of end, as autumn is always a symbol for things ending. The road behind her also dead-ends at a structure that looks like a shack. The girl is not in cheery suburban surroundings that we might associate with childhood Halloween trick-or-treating. She is alone. Her chin is scarred and stoically held as if against tears. She is strangely elegant. Her near emaciation shows off the fitted black sheath dress, the black gloves, and – paramount – the veil. She seems a very young widow, an exile, and an orphan (as indeed she was an orphan in some sense, although her alcoholic mother was still alive throughout her childhood and adolescence). The girl is someone through whom pain has passed, transfiguring her. She has no innocence (in the sense of ignorance or unknowingness) and also no guile. Her eyes are watchful, mistrusting, but not hateful. The gaze is toward someone whom she thinks would like to make things better for her but whose efforts to help she will resist.

This space of resistance is the triumph of the photograph: Tiny does not deign to seek our pity. She understands her situation, that she has gone beyond the pale of childhood and is no longer protected by anyone but herself. And yet in the carnival atmosphere of Halloween, the Lord of Misrule, as Mikhail Bakhtin (not writing about Mark's photography) might suggest, there emerges this image as a way to overturn the bad fate in which Tiny finds herself. In the subversion of identity offered by carnivalesque holidays like Halloween, Tiny, the child prostitute, might suddenly be the elegant creature Mark's photograph suggests.[14] The sense of possibility on the edge or eve of its own loss makes the photograph a deeply empathic portrait, as if you held the photograph too closely you could break the girl pictured in it. Mark imbues the image with a sense of distance and fragility; we see Tiny's wound, but Mark never allows us to touch that wound.

Rag Doll

In a different photograph from the *Streetwise* series, the word "dope" anchors the image, *Lillie, Seattle*, of a young child holding a rag doll and smoking (Figure 8.2). Mark took the photograph at an angle to the graffiti-covered wall, accentuating the vanishing point. The viewer physically feels a sense of space narrowing in the photograph; the only other person in the photograph is an adult walking away, at the edge of the image. The center of the photograph shows a young child of indeterminate gender holding a child's toy, a rag doll, and smoking intently. The child's small size, baby face, and the fact that she is holding a toy contrast sharply with the intensity and knowingness with which she smokes (marijuana or possibly

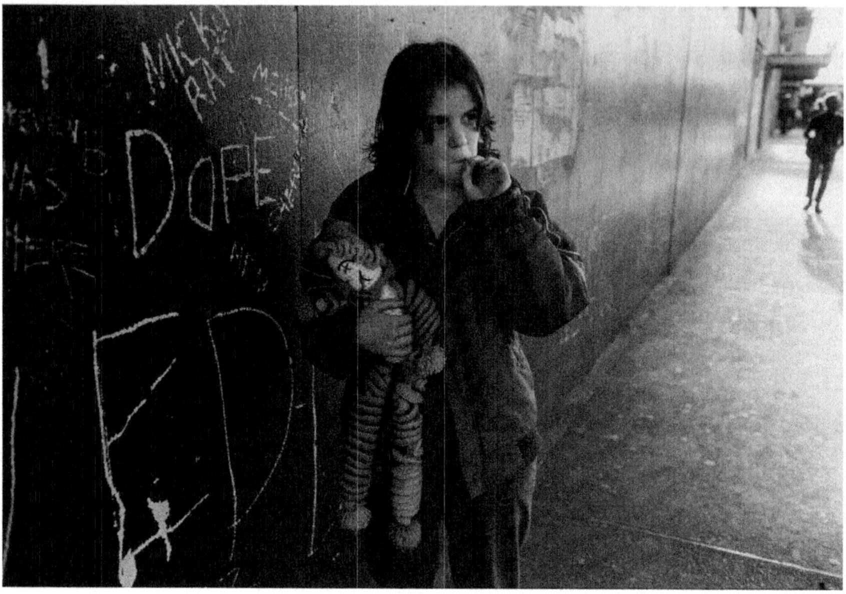

FIGURE 8.2 Mary Ellen Mark, *Lillie, Seattle*, 1983, gelatin silver print, printed 1988, 27.7 × 34.1 cm. Purchased with funds from the Charina Foundation. George Eastman Museum, Rochester, NY. © Mary Ellen Mark.

a hand-rolled tobacco cigarette) and the dirty, graffiti-covered wall before which she stands. The child's expression is almost feral, but she holds the toy so tenderly and tightly, protective of this talisman, and in so doing makes Mark's point in taking the photograph clear: for all that the child might seem to participate in illegal or unethical behavior, she is a deeply vulnerable and very young person who needs to be protected, just as she is offering protection to her doll. Mark's vision in this photograph is that the child is immersed in a world that is unjustifiably rough.

This photograph too raises the vexed question of exploitation. The numbers of young adolescents in America (or even in Seattle) who are homeless have not decreased because of Mark's photography. Hence, in this narrow sense, Mark uses the images of homeless youths to entertain and educate the middle- and upper-middle-class consumers of *Life* magazine rather than to permanently alleviate the suffering of the homeless children. But in a more expansive sense, one that Mark's visionary art calls for, her photographs honor the souls of these children. Her work opens the possibility that its viewers will see in the faces of homeless street kids their own faces, had their fate been just slightly different. This recognition will open a space for ethical response to homelessness and to the children who suffer it. One would not say that Mary Ellen Mark gives dignity to the homeless youths she photographs. Instead, her photographs *show* the dignity that is always rightfully theirs – for surviving, for making a way in their own lives no matter how unjust the terms they face.

Zoe Strauss's neighborhood

Zoe Strauss, like Mary Ellen Mark, takes photographs that participate in photojournalism and documentary photography in that Strauss's work shows painfully raw images of poverty. However, Strauss is not researching the lives of others but plumbing the depths of some aspects of her own history.[15] She documents poverty and is best understood as a war photographer whose battlefield of choice is the harsh, aching poverty that Americans tend to prefer not to recognize as their own. From a working-class background, Strauss photographs not as a stranger visiting the terrain of poverty but as an activist using her camera to give visibility to those Americans afflicted by poverty and the social dispossession that so often attends inner-city poverty. She hails from Philadelphia, and her most ground-breaking work is made up of photographs taken in Philly's rougher neighborhoods. Importantly, Strauss has made a point of showing her work not only in galleries and museums but also in the neighborhoods where she created it.

She came to the attention of the art world by placing her photographic portraits of inner-city residents along bridge underpasses in Philadelphia. By placing the photographs back in the spaces where they were taken, taping the images to pillars under the I-95 highway in south Philly, Strauss pushed against the commodification of art rampant in the twenty-first century. She refused to allow her works to wholly play the role of gentrified versions of rough life.[16] Aptly, Scott Gratson notes of Strauss's photographs that there is a "double movement of identification and alienation."[17] The rich visiting the poor for photographic consumption is an old game. Sociologist-photographer Lewis Hine photographed the poor as a form of activism. Before him, Oscar Rejlander photographed whimsical scenes of urban homeless children for his own financial gain. Rejlander played on the idea that the children were naughty and fun to look at and went so far as to use a street child, Charlotte Baker, in photographs of soft kiddie porn.[18]

The risks of photographing vulnerable subjects cannot ever be set aside, and Zoe Strauss photographs vulnerable subjects, the urban poor. By placing her photographs in an annual exhibit set in the Philadelphia neighborhood from which she culled most of the images, Strauss makes her ethics clear. She gives her photographic subjects a chance to see what her pictures show of them and a chance to be not just an image but also to respond to that image. Her photographs can be hard to look at. In them, we face people whose faces and bodies poverty has heavily worked and scarred. And yet, Strauss records not blunt suffering but human persistence, perseverance, and even humor through suffering.

Mattress flip

Her photograph *South Philly (Mattress Flip Front)* shows two young boys playing in a landscape of discarded objects, several of which are mattresses that the boys have stacked up to make a trampoline. This photograph was taken in 2001 and printed in 2003. The grace of the boy wearing the "88" T-shirt, caught in midair juxtaposed against the trash pile above which he sails, creates a vertiginous sense of possibility – as if one could float above poverty, float above the discarded trash of capitalism, and not be treated like the discarded trash of capitalism. Behind the flying boy, another slightly older boy appears ready to spring up for his turn on the ersatz trampoline. The boys' innocence and their joy in play are palpable in the photograph. This intensity of embodied joy translates the image out of the realm of pity and into one of self-recognition – that is, recognition of childhood and its pleasures – and makes the photograph such a strong critique of capitalist economic violence, especially as that violence affects children. Seeing the photograph, I am reminded of the game my childhood best friend and I used to play of counting how many backflips we could do on her trampoline. It ran up close to 100 as we would turn flips over and over, just touching down our feet before the next turn, experiencing a lightness of body, and indeed of soul, that almost no adult has. That the older boy in the photograph died, a murder victim, a few years after Strauss snapped the image speaks to the precariousness of the boys' situation, and also to the precariousness of childhood as such.[19] Strauss says of the photograph and of the boy's fate: "I'm hoping that it will be seen in many ways as honoring [Boo's] life. He lived . . . he was here, and he was loved."[20]

That Strauss had access to photograph these children speaks to their vulnerability; middle-class children playing in enclosed backyards would not be accessible to a roving photographer. And yet, given this power imbalance that is almost impossible to avoid in documentary photography of humans (one person wields the camera, the others do not, and economics are often the reason for the difference), Strauss brings forward an image of the mattress-jumping children that contains a critique of their accessibility and their vulnerability. It is not Strauss who has made the children vulnerable. Instead, she visually locates the effects of poverty and racism, as well as the force of the children's resilience. She shows the boys literally bouncing back, aloft above their circumstances.

Daddy tattoo

One of Strauss's most painful photographs, *Monique Showing Black Eye* (2006, printed 2010), is of a young woman showing to the camera her hideously beaten face. It is a terrifying image. The young woman is wounded in a way that goes far beyond bruising. The phrase "black eye" does not begin to describe what has been done to her face, the very structure of which has been taken apart by violence. Strauss had previously photographed this young woman in *Daddy Tattoo* (2004, printed 2013), and I want to focus on this earlier photograph, which foreshadows the alarming later image. Strauss's camera catches the young woman in a pose that mimics the quarter-turn of starlets, her shoulders facing away from the camera, with her face turned toward Strauss, her opposite hand delicately raised in a starlet-like gesture. With another nod toward movie stars, the girl is very heavily, almost comically made up, but the expression in her eyes snuffs any humor. She looks haunted, even hunted. Although having a photographer she does not know snap her image could partially explain that expression, the young woman does not look startled but instead looks accustomed to invasion, which lends a sense of the tragic to the image.

The tattoo that is the focus of Strauss's interest is telling in its relationship to feminism. "Daddy," of course, is diminutive for father, but in the vernacular, daddy has further meanings. Daddy can mean an older man sexually involved with a younger man. Daddy, in the phrase *sugar daddy*, means an older or more powerful man who pays for a sexual relationship with a younger and less-wealthy woman. Daddy can also be slang for a man who has power over women. And the slang phrase, "Who's your daddy?", means who has power over you. Daddy can also be slang for a pimp. In this sense, "daddy" in the young woman's tattoo signifies multiple codes of gender domination, codes that are further reified in the young woman's makeup, her posture, and her expression of hunted resignation. The idea that everything a woman creates and can make of herself she must ultimately set at the feet of a daddy is one of the hardest aspects of male domination to expose and topple.

Frequently, gifted women who want to express their gifts find the way to cultural status by pleasing men – not necessarily by sexually pleasing men but simply by pleasing them. Writing the kinds of books men decide are worthy, for example, is just as much a way of bringing it home to daddy as is trying to achieve a certain sexually alluring look with one's body. In this sense, the tragedy of male domination is condensed into this word, *daddy*, just as it is concentrated and driven into the expression in the eyes of Strauss's subject in the image *Daddy Tattoo*. The photograph is not just about poverty; it is also about gender domination. There is a chilling convergence of knowledge in this photograph: knowledge of the way that gender domination does not just mark women, it is not just a performance (even though this young woman is clearly deeply engaged in performing tropes of the traditional feminine, with her makeup, bustier, and bouffant hairdo) but also a form of annihilation. Strauss takes us to that place where we can see the logical conclusion of gender domination. If we choose to believe that only impoverished inner-city girls are harmed by it, then we have lost much of what Strauss's photograph tells us.

Portraits: Rineke Dijkstra

Dutch photographer Rineke Dijkstra differs dramatically from Zoe Strauss and Mary Ellen Mark in her subject matter. She does not photograph people living in poverty, prostitutes, or the homeless. And yet, like Mark and Strauss, Dijkstra creates a kind of extreme portraiture. Whereas the other two follow in a documentary and photojournalist tradition, Dijkstra develops her extraordinary oeuvre of formal portraits in the tradition of European painting.[21] Her work is visually distinguished by its almost hyperreal clarity, its large size when printed and framed, its lush colors, and its frequent use of sweeping natural vistas in the background.[22] The work is similar to traditional painted portraits in its aesthetic; yet, as photography, it carries a mark of pain and eeriness in its connections to the real bodies of the photographic subjects.[23] Dijkstra's early self-portrait, taken when she was recovering from injuries from a bicycle accident, gives a hint of some of her predilections in choosing photographic subjects.

Among her series of portraits are a series of young women who have just given birth and are photographed naked, holding their newborns (1994). She titles the images in photo documentary and portraiture style, that is, with very specific names, dates, and scene descriptions. The babies are frighteningly tiny and vulnerable, the mothers' bodies distended from the pregnancy and childbirth that has just occurred. One mother poses wearing sheer underwear and a pad to catch the blood that flows heavily just after childbirth. In another series of images, Dijkstra photographs bullfighters after their battles. The images show the young men's faces and clothes smeared with blood, their faces hopped-up with fear and victory, and the images are all recorded with Dijkstra's clean, dispassionate technique. But the blood shown in Dijkstra's photography is different from the blood we might expect in photojournalism. This is not the blood of catastrophe and death but of passage. The women who bleed after giving birth are not dying but moving into another phase of life, and the bullfighters she photographs are not the ones grievously wounded or killed. They are young men who emerge after facing some symbolic death. The symbolic wounds she captures with crystalline clarity in large-format portraits – an aesthetic that gives a glossy, bright sense of control, beauty, and even cheer to Dijkstra's images – are responsible for her work's paradoxical force. She seems to be showing us only the beautiful surface, but something more lies beneath that gleaming beauty.

Dijkstra is especially drawn to photographing liminal states, spaces in which the photographic subject is undergoing or has just undergone some personal transition: a young boy becoming a soldier, women who have just become mothers, a child of refugees, and, paradigmatically, her series of beach portraits of adolescents. The woman photographer as portraitist is in a tricky position: traditional femininity requires that a woman pays attention to others, not herself. To be traditionally feminine, then, her portraits would efface the photographer's presence and give the viewer sympathetic access to the sitter. Dijkstra's portraits veer subtly and meaningfully from this feminine ideal of self-suppression, and they bring forward a feminist statement in their subtle divergence from traditional feminine decorousness. In this regard, I want to focus on her photographs of adolescents on the beach, taken at the end of the twentieth century in Europe and in America. Although I will mainly discuss her photographs of adolescent girls, the very fact that Dijkstra includes adolescent boys in the series is of import. The gender equity of her vision – that if she takes photographs of semiclothed girls, she also takes photographs of seminude boys – goes against traditional gendering of bathing suit photography. (Think of *Sports Illustrated*'s iconic, and truly depressing, annual swimsuit issue, in which pretty young women bare it.) Instead, Dijkstra's beach portraits play out themes of liminality in several regards: the liminal space of the shore, the littoral zone where land becomes ocean; the boundary between being clothed and being nude; the liminality of the horizon between earth and sky; and the situation of the subjects of these portraits, adolescents on the cusp of adulthood or between childhood and adulthood. The beach photographs, then, show liminality and the possibility of transformation.

Her photographs of teenage girls are especially telling, as in them Dijkstra revises tropes of showing the female body in art. A young girl, about age 13 and wearing a peach-colored bikini, stands on the shore of an upscale resort area in the photograph *Hilton Head Island, SC, USA, June 24, 1992.* Befitting the exclusive beach area where her family is vacationing, the girl is done up sumptuously with all the markings of a certain kind of American wealth: she looks well fed and curvaceous for her young age; her bathing suit is exquisite and surely expensive; and her hair is glorious, carefully cared for. Her round baby face contrasts with her curvy body as she poses clutching her hair in a mimicry of a swimsuit model. The parallels of this photograph to Botticelli's *The Birth of Venus* (1483–1485) are obvious. In Dijkstra's photograph, the girl's lush and long blond hair, her contrapposto pose, her semi-clothed state, and her positioning at the water's edge all evoke *The Birth of Venus.* But Dijkstra gently and subtly critiques the version of femininity the goddess of love epitomizes. In the girl's face, Dijkstra captures a sense of division or separation from the role of swimsuit siren that the girl is trying to teach herself to play. She catches the girl's pride in her beauty and also her dismay in the nascent separation of self and social role that goes along with fulfilling the terms of traditional feminine beauty. The expression in the child's face, then, as well as the tender baby fat on her round cheeks, sets Dijkstra's photograph apart from pinup images of girls in bikinis. Likewise, the girl, though self-consciously posed, does not primp for Dijkstra. She may feel she is being photographed because she is pretty, but what Dijkstra shows is a child who epitomizes adolescent ambivalence and ambiguity.

Dijkstra's 1992 image of a child of similar age, a young teen, on the shore of the Baltic Sea, *Kolobrzeg, Poland, July 26, 1992* (Figure 8.3), also a large-format color print, can similarly be compared to Botticelli's *Venus* in that it features a young girl in contrapposto pose standing at the edge of water. However, unlike the South Carolina photograph, the photograph on the Baltic shore is decidedly less lush; its aesthetic is more stringent, reflecting the city's at-times embattled history, in particular during World War II when the city was devastated. (To be sure, Hilton Head Island has its own painful history of the enslavement of African Americans, but this history is deeply submerged under the tourist resorts.)

In the photograph from Kolobrzeg, above the young woman a V-shaped bank of clouds suggests the possibility of rain, and the littoral zone is broken into three pieces – water, wet sand, and dry sand – with the girl's feet crusted in sand, indicating she has just moved from water onto dry land. The bottom half of her bathing suit is wet, which further suggests recent emergence from the water and also accentuates her nether parts. The adolescent girl at Kolobrzeg is angular, womanly, shy, and severe all at once. Her sharply narrow waist and wide hips lead to very slender legs; her shoulders are narrow, and she is thin enough that you clearly see the outline of her clavicle. This slenderness makes her appear vulnerable; and, of course, adolescents are a vulnerable group to photograph, which is both the draw and the risk of Dijkstra's series. The girl's expression is not in the least come-hither.

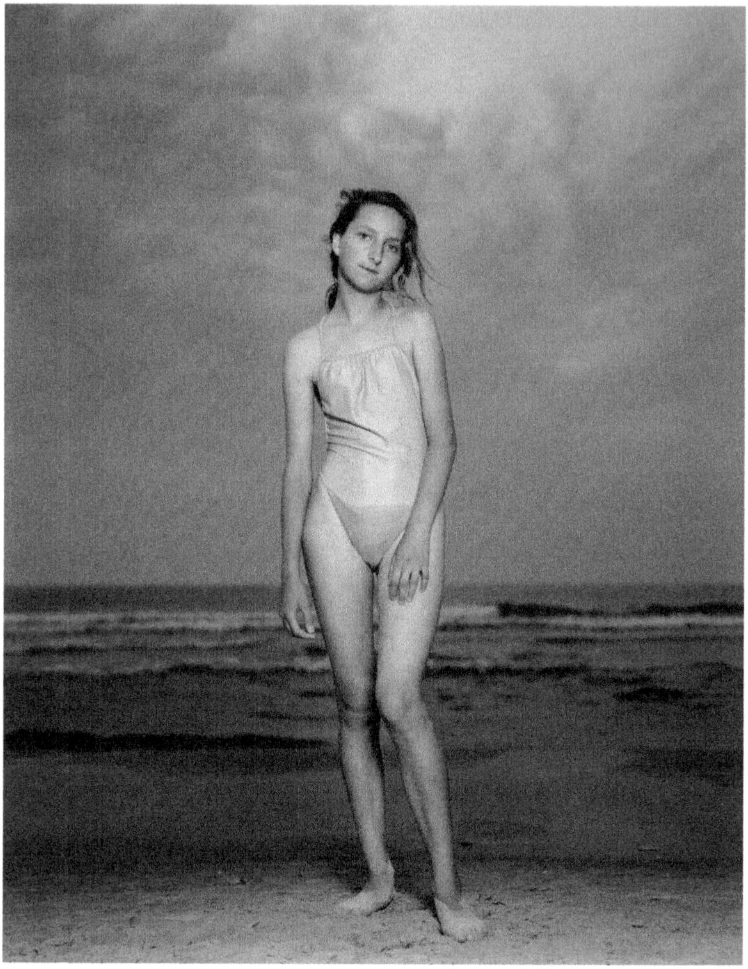

FIGURE 8.3 Rineke Dijkstra, *Kolobrzeg, Poland, July 26, 1992*, chromogenic print 117 × 94 cm. Courtesy the artist and Marian Goodman Gallery, New York and Paris. © Rineke Dijkstra.

She embodies an adolescent awkwardness and wariness, as if she were made of glass against the jeweled and somber tones of Dijkstra's seascape.

In photographing this pivot in the constraint and production of gender – adolescence, the time during which society much more strictly enforces gendered identities and young people much more emphatically express them – Dijkstra seeks and shows the variegation of the landscape. In keeping her project international, photographing adolescents on beaches in different countries, Dijkstra shows there is not one seascape, not one shore, but of course many different shores, many different boundaries. By extension, there is not one way of becoming feminine or masculine, male or female, or between. In photographing different genders and significantly different body types, cultural milieus, and different personalities, Dijkstra's photographs resist and work against containing identity in traditionally gendered typologies.

Notes

1 The phrase "interior infinite" is from Mikhail Bakhtin, signifying modes of identity after the Romantic era, that is, in modernity. *Rabelais and His World*, trans. Hélène Iswolsky (Bloomington, IN: Indiana University Press, 1984), 24.
2 Greer McNally, "Mary Ellen Mark: The Acclaimed Photographer Talks about Her Nights in the Asylum and the Death of Documentary with Greer McNally," *Digital Photographer*, www.maryellenmark.com/text/magazines/digital_photographer/933J-000-001.html. States Mary Ellen Mark: "I'm not a digital photographer. . . . I have a really good printer, Chuck Kelton, here with a lab and I work with him. . . . I use all different kinds of cameras – Canons, Leicas, and 645 cameras. I have both the Mamiya and Hasselblad and I love the Hasselblad Square. I also have a Mamiya 7, which is like a big Leica. It's a wonderful camera, really wonderful. . . . For portraiture, I prefer to use medium to large format, but 35 mm for the street and documentary work. I've also used the Mamiya 7, the Hasselblad, and the 645 for the street work."
3 See Geoffrey Batchen, *Burning with Desire: The Conception of Photography* (Cambridge, MA: MIT Press, 1999), 17–54.
4 See Carolina A. Miranda, "Street Kids, Poverty and Fortitude: Photographer Mary Ellen Mark's Stirring Last Project," *Los Angeles Times*, September 28, 2015. See also Mark, *Ward 81* (New York: Fireside Books, 1979) and *Falkland Road* (Göttengen, Germany: Steidl, 2005); see also Mark and John Irving, *Streetwise* (New York: Aperture, 1992).
5 Grace Schaub and George Schaub, *20th Century Photographers: Interviews on the Craft, Purpose, and the Passion of Photography* (Waltham, MA: Focal, 2014).
6 Efrem Zelony-Mindell, "Looking Back at Mary Ellen Mark's Iconic Photos of a Prostitute Named Tiny," *Vice Media*, January 23, 2016.
7 I use the phrase "vulnerable population" in the specific sense of social science: live subject research, when conducted with vulnerable populations, such as prisoners, has multiple safeguards to protect the subjects from exploitation. But in the context of working with vulnerable populations, Mark's empathy of vision is startlingly clear. Indeed, Mark's ability to visually query identity, to show our relationships to each other, to the other, has taken the form of two projects – the *Twins* and *Prom* photographs – that play on the trope of the double. I suggest that Tiny, in some sense, becomes Mark's double, and Mark's photographs of her evince a deep and poignant bond. See Bridget Bennett, "Double Acts: Mary Ellen Mark's 'Twins,'" *Women: A Cultural Review* 20, no. 2 (August 2009): 172–85.
8 Susan Sontag, *On Photography* (New York: Picador 1977), 15–16.
9 Mary Ellen Mark, Isabelle Allende, John Irving, and Martin Bell, *Tiny: Streetwise Revisited* (New York: Aperture, 2015).
10 Nicole Brodeur, "Three Decades After *Streetwise* Documentary, Tiny Struggles and Dreams On," *Seattle Times*, May 19, 2016, www.seattletimes.com/entertainment/movies/three-decades-after-streetwise-documentary-tiny-struggles-and-dreams-on/.
11 Ibid.
12 Ibid.
13 Ibid.
14 Bakhtin, *Rabelais and His World*, 27, 370.
15 Barry Schwabsky, "The Complete History of Everyone: On Zoe Strauss," *The Nation*, February 7, 2012.
16 Discussing Strauss's efforts to shake up the relationship between photography and museum representation, Scott Gratson considers Strauss's use of billboards and other

dialogic gestures that attempt to open the museum space, making it accessible both financially and socially to impoverished and working-class people. Gratson states, "In essence, her work focuses on counter-publics, those whose voices may be maligned or simply forgotten." "An Open Door to a Closed Society: The Incorporation of Dialogue into Museum Viewing Spaces," *International Journal of the Inclusive Museum* 5, no. 1 (2011): 29.

17 Ibid., 33–4.

18 Mark Murrman, "The Photos That Helped End Child Labor in the United States," *Mother Jones*, October 3, 2015, www.motherjones.com/environment/2015/10/kids-coal-mines-lewis-hines-photos.

19 Tara Murtha, "Photographer Zoe Strauss Took This Photo Ten Years Ago: Here Is the Story of 'Mattress Flip,'" *Philadelphia Weekly*, January 10, 2012.

20 Ibid.

21 Michael Fried, *Why Photography Matters as Art as Never Before* (New Haven, CT: Yale University Press, 2008), 191–233.

22 Anne-Celine Jaeger, "A Conversation with Rineke Dijkstra," in *Image Makers, Image Takers* (New York: Thames and Hudson, 2007), 136–45.

23 Jan Avgikos, "Rineke Dijkstra: Marian Goodman Gallery," *Artforum International* 42, no. 3 (November 2003): 188.

9

A HISTORY OF PHOTOGRAPHY

Aida Muluneh and Lalla Essaydi

> The inferno is not down below, it is here in our memories and in our minds . . . [in] the blood of false victory stitched by the threads of nostalgia . . . longing to see paradise in the dark abyss of eternity.
>
> – Aida Muluneh, artist statement for *99 Series*[1]

Photographers Aida Muluneh (born 1974) and Lalla Essaydi (born 1956) share the identity of having been educated in the West, while hailing from families that have deep ties to Africa – Ethiopia and Morocco, respectively. Muluneh and Essaydi deploy a strategy of reclaiming visual territory and of wresting from stereotype and cliché the photographic terrains of Africa and the Middle East, particularly where violent Western stereotypes have been enforced on African or Middle Eastern women. Despite marked differences in their approach to photographic work, the two artists bear comparison: their work responds to a history of photography as a form of discursive colonization. Their work speaks to and refutes images circulated in Western countries that obsessively depict women of African and Middle Eastern descent as eroticized, exoticized, and dehumanized. Muluneh's and Essaydi's work can be interpreted as intertextual in that it creates a visual response to earlier dominant and violative photographic images of women who are from Africa and the Middle East. In grouping their work in this chapter, I do not suggest that it responds in the same way to photographic history. Rather, I argue that it shares a fierce resistance to photographic images and tropes that have enacted discursive violence. Both artists resist the practice in which Western photographers and audiences dominate by looking at and circulating images that debase non-Western women. Muluneh and Essaydi create deeply symbolic and multilayered photographic works deploying cloth, paint, mask, bullet casings, and linguistic text to subvert the dominant patriarchal Western photographic gaze. Their work asserts enigmatically symbolic and historically reflective photographic images of women of African and Middle Eastern descent, reclaiming the visual text of the African and Middle Eastern woman as a space to be determined *by* African and Middle Eastern women.

Another history: Aida Muluneh's new icons

The idea of iconicity has been appropriated in the age of technological reproduction, with the putatively iconic image circulated as marketing tool. But the idea of the icon is rooted in an Eastern Orthodox faith that is mostly ignored by the West.[2] In this faith, the icon is a window to the divinity: it is a representation of a saint, an apostle, or an angel; it is an image that is not used as an idol but as a conduit or window to worship. The icon's role for the faithful is representation par excellence, representation with the ability to transform the one who sees; indeed, it is representation as transformation. Orthodoxy includes Syrian, Coptic, Greek, and Ethiopian traditions. I am approaching the photographic and multimedia works of artist Aida Muluneh (born 1974) through this lens because I see in her photographs invocation of the ancient tradition of the Ethiopian Orthodox icon.[3] That said, I certainly do not ascribe to Muluneh's photographs a straightforward reflection of or adherence to Orthodoxy. Instead, she draws from traditions of image-making that run very deep in her native Ethiopia to create a body of photographic work that refuses Western appropriation and misreading of African identity and African image-making, even as her work also radically reenvisions the patriarchal terms of traditional Eastern Orthodoxy. Muluneh's photography also invokes other aspects of African culture, as I will discuss.

Muluneh's work is deeply and searchingly concerned with questions of ethics and history, in particular Ethiopia's history and the nation's photographic visibility in the twentieth and twenty-first centuries.[4] Born in Ethiopia of Ethiopian parents, Muluneh moved with her family through several countries, including Yemen, England, Cyprus, Canada, and the United States, ultimately completing her university degree at Howard University in Washington, D.C.[5] After working for the *Washington Post* as a photojournalist, Muluneh returned to Ethiopia to focus on photography as art. By returning, she aimed to clear herself of her own (Western-influenced) misreadings of the country and transform her relationship to her homeland from one of painful nostalgia to a clear-sighted vision of a very ancient culture in a process of flux and change. Muluneh jokes that nostalgia is part of the culture of Ethiopia: "It's our national sport, in a sense, to be nostalgic."[6] Since she returned to Ethiopia and settled in Addis Ababa, her work has increasingly moved away from photojournalism and moved toward creating a symbolic and iconic vocabulary of images. The images explore past and present through Ethiopian traditions of image-making, including but not limited to that of the Orthodox icon.[7]

Muluneh's work in *99 Series*, showcased in the United States at the Smithsonian's National Museum of African Art,[8] draws from the theme of Dante Alighieri's *Inferno* and the Roman Catholic faith Dante is based in, but Muluneh pulls from those sources in a way that reverses the oppressive discursive direction that imposes Western culture on African culture. Muluneh's work deploys imagery and concepts from the earliest origins of Christianity, an image vocabulary that is Ethiopian. The

Ethiopian Orthodox faith retains the Byzantine iconography of the Eastern Church; Western Catholicism branched off from the Eastern Orthodox Church more than a millennium ago. Hence, in drawing from Ethiopian Orthodox iconography to inhabit and give visual voice to the violence and dispossession Ethiopia experienced in the famine and wars that ended the twentieth century, Muluneh radically relocates colonialist notions of center and margin. In her work, she makes the visual argument that she is not responding to the concept of heaven, hell, ethics, or eternity as taken from Western Christianity. Instead, she visually argues that Western Christianity developed its imagery and symbols from Eastern, including Ethiopian, Orthodoxy. Her work, then, visually insists both on its own originality and the aesthetic originality of African culture – a deep history reflected in her work. Muluneh taps and also complicates the history of Ethiopian image-making and the patriarchy of its traditions. To be precise, her work troubles Western appropriations of Ethiopian imagery and traditions, even as her avant-garde photographs also critique Eastern Orthodoxy's avowedly patriarchal structure. But as I note elsewhere in this book, feminist resistance is not fundamentally about gender but about domination. For Muluneh, a major force of domination is Western appropriation, misinterpretation, and erasure of African imagery. Her photographic work embodies resistance to these visual elisions of African culture that have accompanied Western political acts.[9]

Several of Muluneh's *99 Series* photographs are carefully staged portraits of a young woman who appears to be African. Her race, however, is entirely denaturalized by the application of heavy paint and makeup: her skin is deathly white, while hands painted dark red touch her face (Figures 9.1, 9.2, and 9.3). Immediately, the images convey the idea of trauma as a kind of skin enclosing the subject, and they raise the question of how skin color can matter when it is only paint, even as this paint so heavily applied conveys pain and suffocation. The white paint that covers the young woman's face also gives her a look of being a ghost or of being between life and death. Here, the woman's face is shown and not her body, emphasizing her personhood and not her reproductive capacity. The eyes of the young woman who is painted look alert and alive, yet the image also suggests she is dead or in another state. Besides suggesting distance and untouchability, the paint evokes haunting. Muluneh photographs the same model wearing heavy white paint for other images in *99 Series*. In these photographs, hands that are heavily painted and that are not shown as attached to bodies touch the model. They seem at once to be pulling at her and also protecting her. M. Neelika Jayawardane sees, in this white paint, a reference to Xhosa face painting, rightly noting that this white paint "recalls the white clay that young Xhosa men apply on their faces and bodies soon after the circumcision ceremony," correctly asserting that Muluneh's photographs are also about "transition and transformation."[10] Here, Muluneh's use of photographic symbolism is a striking departure from the conceit of naturalism in photography. Instead of creating images that appear natural, she uses the camera to record painting, that is, paint applied to the human body. In this sense, even though Muluneh is using a camera for *99 Series*, it is a multimedia work: paint, theater, and photography. The background of the photographs is empty, and so the young woman's face and the hands that touch her command the visual field. The work is emphatically centered

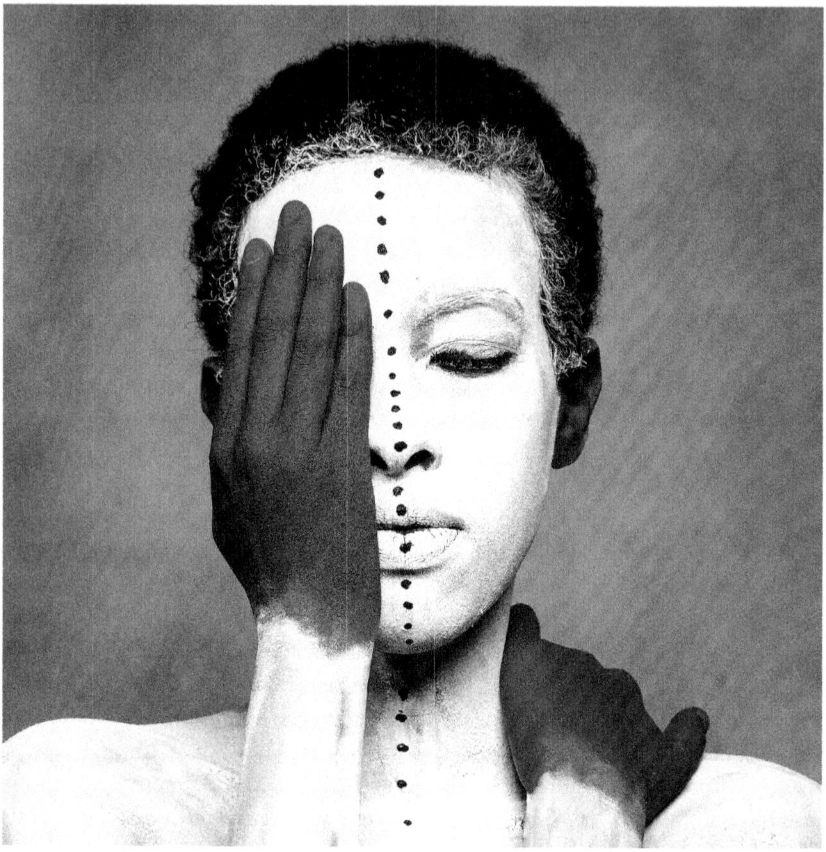

FIGURE 9.1 Aida Muluneh, *99 Series, (Part One)*, 2014, archival digital print, 80 × 80 cm. David Krut Projects, Johannesburg, Cape Town, and New York.

on a proscenium effect, giving center stage to the figure. The figure is at once isolated and encroached on; the paint that covers her stands as a second frame so that the images are produced not only in the photographic frame but also in the paint that encloses the photographic subject.

Responding to the relationship between photojournalism and the history of Ethiopia in the late twentieth century, Muluneh's photographs in *99 Series* make a sharp and absolute step away from literal representation of cultural (and embodied) pain. Muluneh comments that, as a young woman, "the stigma of the starving Ethiopian made it impossible for me to have any kind of pride in being Ethiopian."[11] When Ethiopia suffered famine in the mid-1980s, Western photojournalists circulated images of Ethiopians (and other Africans) on the brink of death by starvation. The images contributed to an international stereotype of the country as incapable of surviving and of the people as always deathly in their extremity.[12] As Jayawardane comments, the "global image of black people," reduces the image of people of African descent to "people who exist in an evolutionary past ... helpless victims without

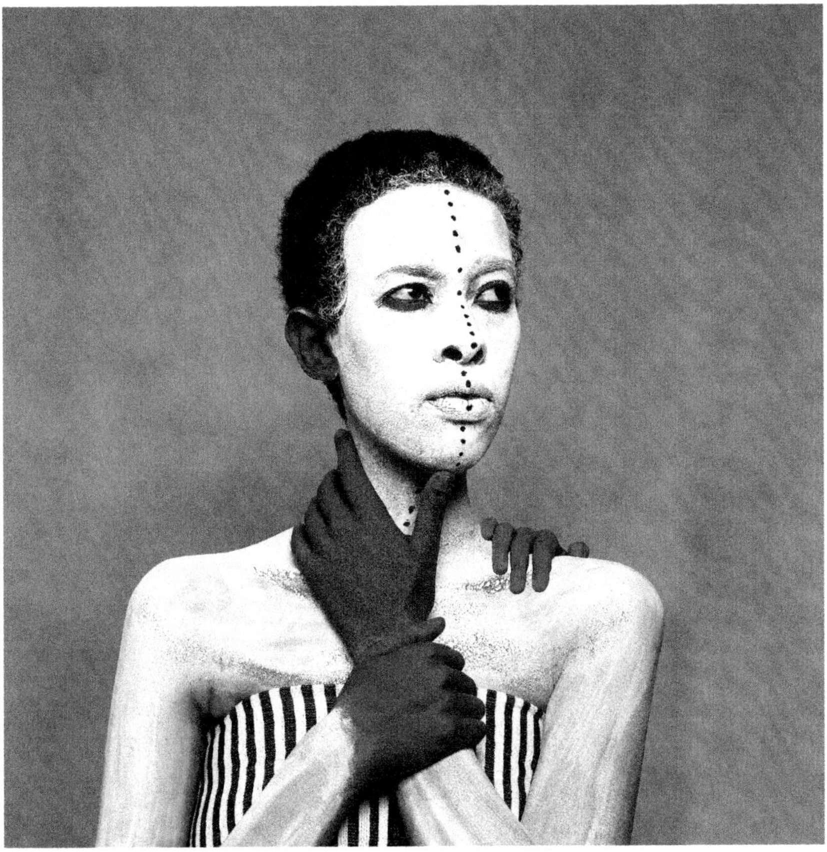

FIGURE 9.2 Aida Muluneh, *99 Series, (Part Two)*, 2014, archival digital print, 80 × 80 cm. David Krut Projects, Johannesburg, Cape Town, and New York.

agency of their own."[13] Even now, the idea that Ethiopian existence is precarious is deeply embedded in Western ideology and the Western imaginary.[14] Muluneh's *99 Series* invokes the history of suffering and dispossession that Ethiopia has experienced in the twentieth century but rebukes and turns from Western images that fuse the image of the African body with tropes of brute suffering and deathliness.[15]

Muluneh's photography works to break this fusion that Western photographers imposed on being African as if it meant being fated to suffering intense bodily harm and death. Muluneh does not turn away from the history of war and famine that her country has undergone, but she transmogrifies history into a symbolic landscape of symbol and soul. Consider Muluneh's highly symbolic and carefully posed surrealist photographs in contrast to the work of photojournalists Anthony Suau, Sebastião Salgado, and James Nachtwey, all of whom photographed African famines of the late twentieth century.[16] Among Suau's devastating and disturbing photographs from the 1980s are a series of images taken in Ethiopia that show a starving mother's shriveled, empty breast (the images do not show her face) and a

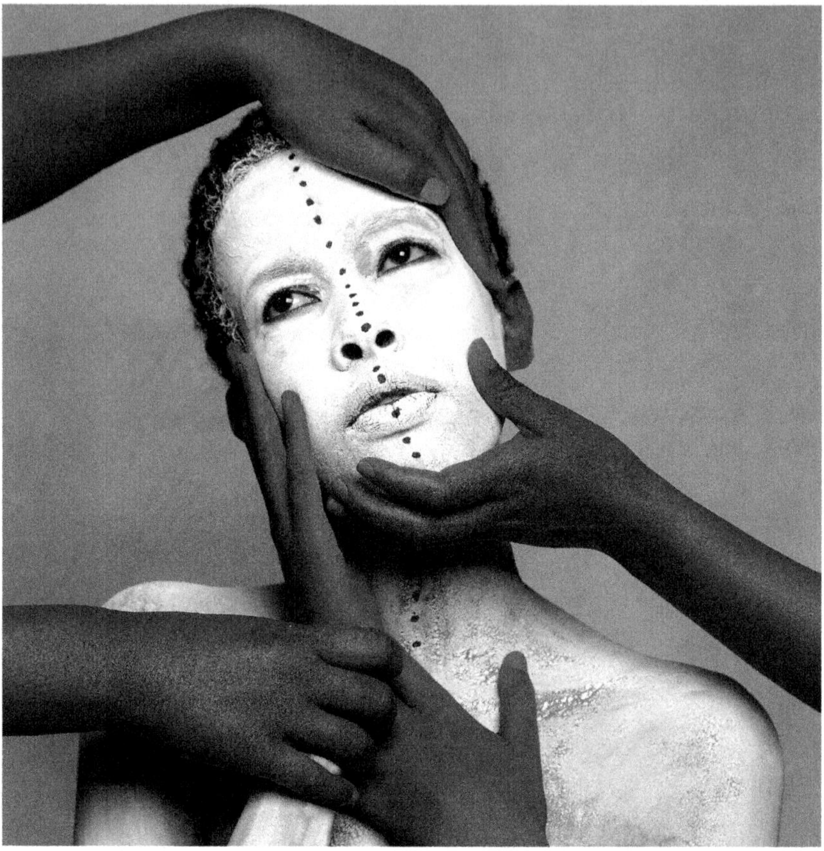

FIGURE 9.3 Aida Muluneh, *99 Series, (Part Seven)*, 2014, archival digital print, 80 × 80 cm. David Krut Projects, Johannesburg, Cape Town, and New York.

skeletal toddler tugging hungrily at it. The horror of the photographs inheres not only the pain of starvation that they show (the baby is starving, and the mother who is also starving cannot save her child) but also the invasiveness of the camera. Suau's camera treats the mother's breast as if it did not belong to a human being with a mind and a soul.

By contrast, the model Muluneh uses for *99 Series* is clearly healthy, and the images focus intently on her enigmatically pensive face. The series conveys suffering by painting the model white: white signifies mourning in many non-Western countries. Whiteness as a signifier for both mourning and transition between states also subverts Western and racist imaginaries in which white stands for purity. By painting the model for *99 Series* in stark white paint (Figures 9.1, 9.2, and 9.3), Muluneh indicates the young woman's risked position, simultaneously isolated and encroached on, alive and also symbolically cast with the dead, vivid but bearing the scars of suffering. The *99 Series* symbolically confronts and rebukes this edge of visibility insisting on the terms and frame of African visibility. In this series, paint, the photographs' frame, and the model's costumes all protect the African woman photographed. She stands in marked contrast to representations of African women in photographs by Western (and almost always male) photographers that have circulated for decades as stereotyped signs of embodied mute suffering. Muluneh's *99 Series* show only the face of the woman photographed. Here, Muluneh removes the figure from purloined visibility and transforms it into a kind of protean metaphoric enigma: we do not know why the woman is painted white, or why the hands encroach, but we see her liminal state and isolation, and her meditation on these. The meditatively symbolic photographs do not tell the specific embodied history of the woman's inferno, the hell she stands before, reckoning. Instead, the viewer of the images is pulled to contemplation without easy resolution.

These images refuse to allow the viewer to hold on to clichéd ideas of African identity and art. As cultural theorist Mel Y. Chen argues, the quality of "animacy" – that is, liveliness or being alive or, indeed, having a right to be alive – is a cultural concept that is used to signify putative and oppressive differences between West and East, male and female, and living and dead. Chen argues that the discourse of racist, colonialist, and sexist oppression takes the form of ascribing the symbolic space of life – that is, liveliness and the right to be fully alive – to people who are white, Western, and male. Meanwhile, people who have darker skin, are not of European descent, and are not male, implicitly are cast in the realm of the culturally dead, social ghosts, in particular with regard to public response to violence and environmental violence.[17] Muluneh's symbolically layered photographs confront and overturn this racist landscape of life and death, revivifying the visual elocution and articulation of African imagery and the imagery of African women. In her photographs, Muluneh claims animacy – liveliness, and full subjecthood – for African women. She is not simply rebutting white male ways of seeing African women but also creating her own symbolically layered imagery of the vivid history and liveliness of the mind and soul of her nation.

Icons of their own lives

Muluneh's work faces grief and references Ethiopian history – which in the twentieth century certainly had its share of grief – in part by taking in radical directions the tradition of the Orthodox icon. In this discussion, note that her work references an historic culture, and vibrant present, not necessarily her personal beliefs. Eastern Orthodox icons typically focus on the face of the saint or holy one portrayed, and they use inverse perspective so that the icon's face appears to be looking directly into the viewer's eyes. Icons are venerated by a traditional kiss, and so they are made to be seen very close up. Muluneh's *99 Series* uses a close-range format and dispenses with any surroundings so that we at once become intimately close with and also are narratively distanced from the model, as the blank backgrounds do not suggest a narrative. The images in *99 Series* (Figures 9.1, 9.2, and 9.3) present the woman as a figure in pain and a figure in isolation who does not seek or ask for communion with the audience. She appears holy and marked apart by white paint that covers her; she is powerful and impossible to broach. In this sense she is iconic; that is, she leads the viewer to contemplate the real, which is the role of icons in the Orthodox Church (albeit, the faithful believe the real to be the deity, and by contrast Muluneh's work engages contemporary politics and history). In *99 Series*, then, Muluneh faces not only Ethiopia's history of famine and the political instability and war that play into and cause famine, not only the flotilla of Western-produced photographs of starving Ethiopians but also the need to move forward, the insistance on life and liveliness. As the Western images denude Ethiopians of what we might call humanity in image, Muluneh's work puts on the clothes of symbolic form and history, drawing from an Ethiopian tradition of image-making that is older than any formal system of Western Christian imagery.

Emphatically, I do not mean to suggest that we should understand Muluneh's work as traditional Orthodox iconography. Her work is avant-garde and highly original. And yet she draws from the sacred Ethiopian tradition of icon painting to reinvest images of Africans with something that goes beyond dignity, moving to elegance and self-sovereignty. Her *99 Series* is enigmatic and confrontational, confessional and obscure. Orchestrating the colors of blood and death – red and white – she dresses the photographic image in paint that invokes a tradition of iconicity older than Western colonization. For instance, an Ethiopian icon of warrior saints from the fifteenth century shows the male saints dressed in colors of blood. Muluneh's haunting images in *99 Series* draw from the colors of the Ethiopian warrior saints' icons, invoking not passivity in suffering but ferocity in resistance. And she anchors this resistance in images of a woman's face.

The World is 9

The title for Aida Muluneh's exhibit *The World is 9* is a quote from the photographer's grandmother that means the world is never perfect and never complete – that is, it is never 10.[18] While certainly one could reach for a theological interpretation of the grandmother's claim (the Orthodox belief that only with the second coming of the savior will the world be redeemed), Muluneh's work in this exhibit gestures toward a far more cosmopolitan and expansive frame of interpretation. Her photograph *Sai Mado/The Distant Gaze* (Figure 9.4) brings questions of photographicity and perspectival geometry to bear on the notion of identity. In the photograph, Muluneh uses decidedly painterly techniques: the floor is checkerboarded so that, in a nod to Malick Sidibe, linear perspective establishes the space of distance in the image; the wall is decorated with a painting of the sky, suggesting that it may be not be a wall but only the back limit of the image frame. On the checkerboard floor and before the wall that is a sky, a woman sits in a dark wooden chair. She wears a vibrant red suit with bell-bottom pants, a white shirt, and a matching red tie (Figure 9.4). The woman's hands and the lower part of her face are painted blue, her eyes and forehead are painted yellow, and her hair is done up in an elaborate bun that hangs forward almost over her face. She faces an image in a picture frame

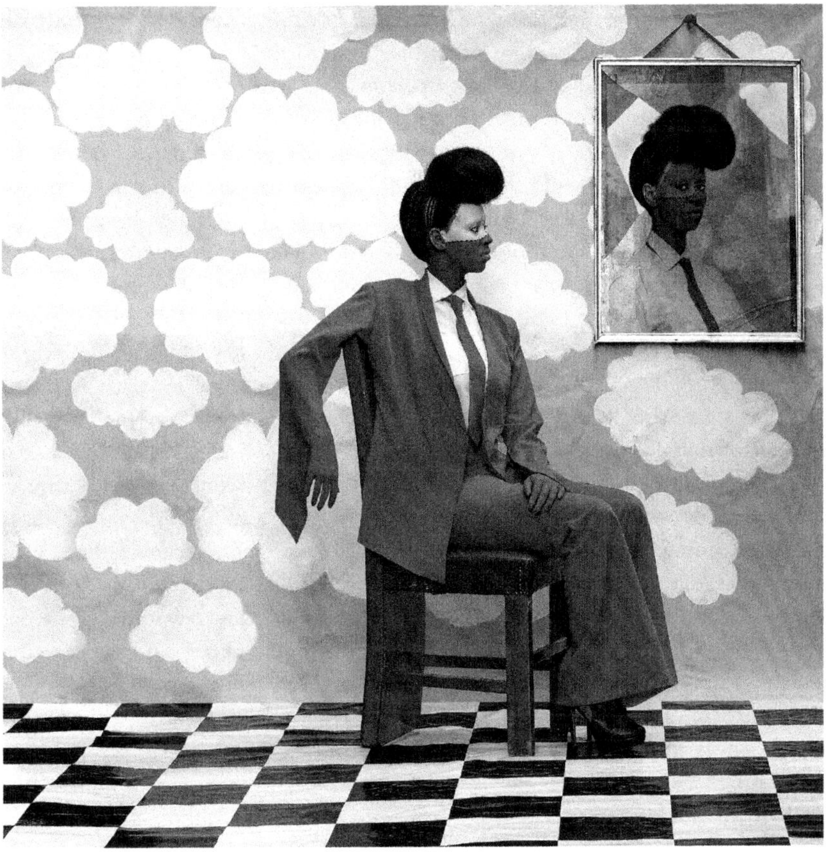

FIGURE 9.4 Aida Muluneh, *Sai Mado/The Distant Gaze*, 2016, archival digital print, 80 × 80 cm. David Krut Projects, Johannesburg, Cape Town, and New York.

that could be her mirror image or could be a photograph in black and white. The colors of the woman's painted skin and her bright garments are not reflected in the mirror-photographic image that faces her. And yet, while the viewer of the whole image sees only the woman's profile, the woman's reflection as photograph addresses the viewer. But even this address is indirect, in that the mirror-photograph image of the woman is first looking at herself, the figure in bright colors seated in the chair.

Sai Mado/The Distant Gaze troubles the idea of the photographic image as naturalistic and as showing the viewer some immediate, that is, unmediated, reality. Seeing what might be a photograph or a kind of mirror image of the model in *Sai Mado/The Distant Gaze*, we are by no means shown her direct image. Instead, the photograph works through the complexity of seeing photographically: always a reflection and never a reflection that shows what was really there, but rather how history interprets what was there. The distant gaze of the title is the gaze of the photograph certainly: the photograph presents a sense of immediacy but actually depends on several interlocking forms of vision, formal (linear perspectival), historical (art historical and cultural), and personal. *Sai Mado/The Distant Gaze* could show a young woman looking at herself (although the mirror-photograph image that gazes back at her does not show her wearing a jacket whereas the figure is wearing a jacket), or it could show a young woman looking at an ancestor's portrait. Muluneh bases the piece on an Ethiopian saying, "Temetaleh beye, sai mado, sai mado, ye lijenete eyene mouma ende beredo," which is loosely translated, "As I waited for you in a distant gaze, my eyes melted like ice awaiting your return." Of the photograph she states, "The checkered floor is my dedication to Malick Sidibe."[19] The homage to the Malian portrait photographer indicates Muluneh's taking up and redirecting the challenge of photography as chronicler of popular culture and daily life, a path that she followed in her earlier work *Past/Forward*, which in a photojournalistic style chronicled contemporary Ethiopia.[20] For *Sai Mado/The Distant Gaze* is not journalistic but surreal, symbolic, painterly, and allusive. The photograph explodes conventions of feminine desire in romantic love and presents instead a self-determining photographic protagonist. In it, Muluneh recreates Sidibe's characteristic studio portrait (the checkerboard floor and decorative wall background) as painting engulfed by photograph. In this image, the distant gaze surpasses tropes of romantic love and comes to stand for the distance (cultural and structural) in which photographs are seen, the way that photographs act as and instantiate memory as a form of distance, and the way that stereotyped Western tropes of African and feminine identity have little or nothing to do with the social, psychological, and interior world of a woman who is African. The photograph (Figure 9.4) is totally denaturalized: the model's skin is painted, the background is art deco paint, the checkerboard floor and fabricated pattern pay beautiful homage to Sidibe, and – paramount – the photograph does not reflect what was there but instead the distance that shapes the act of seeing. *Sai Mado/The Distant Gaze* meditates on the uncanniness of photography as art and as cultural memory.

The conceptual frame that Muluneh deploys for photography in *99 Series* and *The World is 9* forces a shift in the way that viewers perceive images of Africa and Africanness. And yet even as she moves away from the black-and-white photographic cultural mnemonic of her earlier works, like the well-received *Past/Forward*, the choreography of the new symbolic work is ever invested in asking ethical questions through photography. In particular, her use of the female body as the formal frame through which she visually explores the landscapes of memory, history, suffering, cultural silencing, and resistance to silencing, resistance to suffering, and hence preservation of personal and cultural memory, centers her work. Her awareness of the culturally coded body – that is, the way that the African woman's body reductively stands for Africa –presses Muluneh to deconstruct this dehumanizing way of seeing (and of being seen).[21] The photographs of *99 Series* and of *The World is 9* use the formal frame of the African woman – her face, her body – as the mode through which to interrogate and overturn Western appropriations of African imagery and culture. These womanly figures, with thickly painted skin, with clothes that act as dramatic costume, and in constructed settings that rigorously denaturalize the photographic gaze, pose feminist resistance to multiple forms of oppression. In Muluneh's *99 Series* and *The World is 9*, it is always the female gaze, embodied in this enigmatic and fierce form of the woman symbolically painted and costumed, interrogating and refusing racist domination and the patriarchal codes and discourse that support it.

Bullets and jewels: Lalla Essaydi

Born in 1956 in Marrakech, Morocco, multimedia artist Lalla Essaydi has increasingly turned to photography to create work in the twenty-first century. Educated in the United States and based in New York City, Essaydi uses the photograph as a way to economically (in terms of space and time and the image in space-time) respond to the history of representations of women in the Middle East and to the situation facing Middle Eastern women today. Essaydi's work frequently visually quotes – so as to dismantle – Western stereotypes of women from the Middle East. From the figure of the odalisque to the trope of the harem, Western colonization has oppressively configured Middle Eastern women as exotic, sexual, and categorically different from Western women.[22] This intense eroticization is formally delineated in the imagined figure of the odalisque, given form and epitomized by Ingres's *La Grande Odalisque* (1814) depicting a voluptuous, nude, and small-headed woman who is presented to the viewer as a sexual commodity that can be safely consumed because she is not a Western woman.[23] The racist and colonialist idea that women of Middle Eastern or African descent are especially sexual, and especially sexually available, reaches a kind of apotheosis in Delacroix's *Les Femmes d'Alger dans leur appartement*. (I will focus my comments on the 1834 painting.) As critic Assia Djebar has elegantly shown, the formal tropes of invasion become scopic in Delacroix's painting, presenting the fantasized view of the European male gaze. In *Les Femmes d'Alger dans leur appartement*, Delacroix visually imagines the space of the harem, or cloistered place, as accessible to a European male audience. This access doubles as conquest, and the conquest is held aloft on the racist cultural assumption that women of the Middle East and Africa are always sexually available and that therefore the processes of conquest and colonization render them always available to Western men. *La Grande Odalisque* likewise imagines the Middle Eastern woman as a concubine with a child's rounded face and a woman's voluptuously curved body.

Notable in both the Ingres and the Delacroix paintings is the elaborate depiction of cloth: wall hangings, floor coverings, clothes, and scarves are all depicted as extravagantly lush and ornate. These cloths, along with the vacant expressions given the women depicted in the paintings, cohere with Edward Said's influential concept of Orientalism: a form of discursive colonization, and domination, in which Western beliefs, theories, and practice construct a false, oppressive, and materially violent notion that (a) people not of European descent are fundamentally and categorically "other" to those of European descent and that (b) this "otherness" inheres particularly in a hypersexuality of non-European woman, of which the colonizing

Western man is free to avail himself.[24] One notes that the very fabric depicted in Ingres's and Delacroix's paintings suggests an overdetermined sensuous and sumptuous physicality. Essaydi subverts this use of cloth and returns to full subjectivity in her recent photographic works. Whereas some of these works are direct rebuttals and visual refutations of the paintings I have just mentioned, in my comments here I will be discussing a photograph in a series that responds visually not just to the Western colonizing male gaze but also to the codes of violent patriarchy that encroach on women's rights in some parts of the Middle East in the twenty-first century.[25] In *Bullets Revisited #3* (2012), Essaydi revisits the terrain of the odalisque, posing her model in the gesture of the reclining odalisque (Figure 9.5). The work is a large triptych and competes visually with the space and surface brilliance that characterize the earlier French paintings of people from territory that France was colonizing. (Algerian independence was not regained until 1962.) Algeria neighbors Essaydi's homeland of Morocco; the French colonized both countries.

But in Essaydi's photograph *Bullets Revisited #3*, she creates the lush fabric-like surfaces with patterns of bullet casings. Hence, the title of the piece (which is one of a series) shifts the sumptuousness of the scene so that rather than having a sense of easy access to the model's body, and in that access imagining a pleasantly sensuous tactility, one is made abruptly aware of the violence and risked position of the woman of Middle Eastern descent, and imaginatively confronted with the hard stop of bullet casings. Essaydi is concerned not just with the eroticized representation of Middle Eastern women as objects of Western colonialist conquest. She is also concerned with the ways in which conservative factions in the Middle East and in some parts of Africa strip away women's autonomy and bodily integrity. Her photographic triptych presents an image of gorgeous terror: the young woman is divided and flattened, as if pressed against the bier or bed on which she is reclining, and the jewels that surround her and cover her are bullet casings.

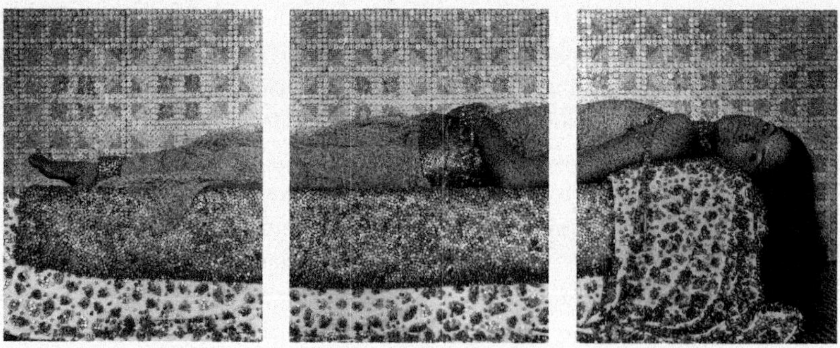

FIGURE 9.5 Lalla Essaydi, *Bullets Revisited #3*, 2012, chromogenic print mounted on aluminum, in three parts, each: 60 × 48 in.; overall: 60 × 144 in. Miller Yezerski Gallery, Boston. © Lalla Essaydi.

Photographs, unlike paintings, do not have brushstroke textures, and unless a photograph is incorporated into multimedia, to give it actual physical texture, it is a flat image, however much it relies on perspective to create the illusion of depth. The cast of this image works toward photographic flatness, and Essaydi uses this material flatness and hard glossiness to convey a visceral sense of the subject's risk and the limits of risk's representation.

Essaydi's *Bullets Revisited #3* works directly against the illusion of depth and interiority, on which both Ingres's and Delacroix's paintings depend. The French paintings invite the viewer into a space of depth, allowing the viewer to visually experience, by metonymic displacement, penetration into the presented African and Middle Eastern women's private places. The apartment room inhabited by the women in Delacroix's painting, like the alcove in which Ingres's odalisque is placed, act as doubles for the women's bodies, and the viewer's masculinized gaze becomes proxy for the viewer's capacity to enter the women's space as conquest. By contrast, Essaydi's photograph flattens and breaks visual space – it is a triptych that also flattens, by foreshortening, the plane in which the model is presented. The glittering background matches the model's shining garments – which further flatten the plane, reflecting light up to the surface of the image – and is visually echoed by the opulent surface of the bed or bier on which the model reclines. All of these elements cohere visually to revoke depth and, hence, access to the interior. The bullet casings seem to be jewels but are actually signifiers of violence, and the young woman is draped with them.

Essaydi's photograph, *Bullets Revisited #3*, brings together in a visual cataclysm the contrast between (a) the Orientalist Western gaze and fantasy of women of Middle Eastern descent as exotics always sexually available and (b) the risks of violence (from extremist groups at home) and subjugation (from Western fantasies of conquest) that broach the person of Middle Eastern and African descent who appears to be a woman. Essaydi turns the trope of cloth, lush surface, and faux interiority (the perspectival geometry endemic to photography) into a photograph that is terrifying in its gleam because its glittering beauty derives from bullet casings. Breaking the frame, she shapes a triptych that fractures the viewing experience. Foreshortening the photographic gaze, she brings the young woman in the photograph into a place of confrontation with the viewer. Essaydi's words, in Arabic writing, cover the photograph's skin. In so gleaming a rebuttal to multiple forms of patriarchal domination, Essaydi makes photography her field of protest.

Notes

1 Aida Muluneh, *The 99 Series.* Muluneh's work was part of the exhibition, *The Divine Comedy: Heaven, Purgatory, and Hell Revisited by Contemporary African Artists*, National Museum of African Art, Smithsonian Institution, Washington, DC, April 8–August 2, 2015.

2 Martin Kemp, *Christ to Coke: How Image Becomes Icon* (Oxford, UK: Oxford University Press, 2011).

3 I make no claims about Muluneh's personal religious beliefs. Instead, I am discussing Orthodox icons as art and as a form of image-making that stems from Ethiopia.
4 Karen E. Milbourne, "African Photographers and the Look of (Un)Sustainability in the African Landscape," *Africa Today* 61, no. 1 (2014): 114–40.
5 Please see M. Neelika Jayawardane, "Between Nostalgia and Future Dreaming: Aida Muluneh's Ethiopia," *Transition* 120 (2016): 118.
6 Ibid., 128.
7 Sionne Neely, "'Preserving Memory as Future': An Interview with Aida Muluneh," *ACCRA [dot] ALT Radio* (blog), May 22, 2013, https://accradotalttours.wordpress.com/2013/05/22/preserving-memory-as-future-an-interview-with-aida-muluneh/.
8 Muluneh, *The 99 Series*.
9 Jennifer Bajorek and Erin Haney, "Eye on Bamako: Conversations on the African Photography Biennial," *Theory, Culture and Society* 27, no. 7/8 (2010): 263–84.
10 Jayawardane, "Between Nostalgia and Future Dreaming," 127.
11 Jayawardane, "Between Nostalgia and Future Dreaming," 126.
12 American photojournalist Anthony Suau won the 1984 Pulitzer Prize for Feature Photography for his work documenting the famine in Ethiopia in the mid-1980s. James Nachtwey, who also published photographs of the drought and famine in Africa at the end of the twentieth century, later brought out a book largely composed of photographs taken in Africa titled *Inferno* (New York: Phaidon Press, 1999). Sebastião Salgado also photographed African famine in the late twentieth century, creating images that, like Nachtwey's work, are of considerable formal beauty. Although I admire Nachtwey, Salgado, and Suau for their determination, skill, and virtuosity of photographic form, and I respect the personal risks they have often undergone to get these images, it cannot be denied that as successful, male Western photojournalists, they have shaped the visual discursive image of Africa in the later twentieth century.
13 Jayawardane, "Between Nostalgia and Future Dreaming," 125.
14 "Ethiopia's Drought: On the Edge of Disaster: The Government's Achievements Appear Increasingly Precarious," *Economist*, February 27, 2016.
15 Jimmy Ogonga, "The Scars of Dissipation: Memory, Catharsis and the Search for the Aesthetic," *African Identities* 9, no. 2 (2011): 233–7.
16 To be sure, the photographers listed here saw themselves as showing the world the suffering of Africans and hence giving Africans a voice. I do not impugn their motives, merely point out the effect, on Ethiopians, of the mass circulation of the suffering of Ethiopians.
17 It is hard to do justice in this short space to Mel Y. Chen's fascinating and complex book, *Animacies: Biopolitics, Racial Mattering, and Queer Affect* (Durham, NC: Duke University Press, 2012). In it, she maps out persuasively how discourses of life and death – and about who has the right to be alive and to be considered fully alive – implicitly charge through the political landscape of power and domination.
18 Jayawardane, "Between Nostalgia and Future Dreaming," 128
19 Aida Muluneh, wall label, "Local Understanding," Jenkins Johnson Gallery, 464 Sutter Street, San Francisco.
20 Aida Muluneh, "Past/Forward: Photography in Ethiopia," Art Department lecture, Colby College, Waterville, ME, April 23, 2015.
21 Jayawardane, "Between Nostalgia and Future Dreaming," 122.
22 Assia Djebar, *Women of Algiers in Their Apartment*, trans. Marjolijn de Jager and Clarisse Zimra (Charlottesville: University of Virginia Press, 1999). See also Edward W. Said, *Orientalism* (New York: Pantheon Books, 1978); Roger Benjamin, ed., *Orientalist Aesthetics: Art, Colonialism, and French Africa, 1880–1930* (Berkeley: University of California Press, 2003).
23 Tamara Hunt and Micheline Lessard, *Women and the Colonial Gaze* (New York: New York University Press, 2000).
24 For further discussion of Said's groundbreaking concept applied to art, see Todd Porterfield, *The Allure of Empire: Art in the Service of French Imperialism* 1798–1836 (Princeton,

NJ: Princeton University Press, 1998); see also Ruth Bernard Yeazell, *Harems of the Mind: Passages of Western Art and Literature* (New Haven, CT: Yale University Press, 2000).

25 For example, Essaydi's photograph *La Grande Odalisque*, which takes its title directly from Ingres's work, responds very obviously to Ingres's imagery. In Essaydi's photograph (which is housed in the Toledo Museum of Art, Toledo, Ohio), the model's face does not look passive and inviting but confrontational, and she is not nude but draped in mourning clothes with Arabic lettering covering her skin and garment.

10

COUNTERDISCOURSE, SEEING ANEW

Rebecca Belmore and Matika Wilbur

The political position of indigenous people in the United States and in Canada has deep and disturbing ties to nineteenth-century photographic practice.[1] In the nineteenth century, photographs of Native Americans were circulated as trophies and proof of conquest; they were cataloged and stored in natural history archives as part of early anthropology's racist discourse; they were sentimentalized in a push to "ghost" or make socially invisible the actual lives of living North American Indians.[2] In the attempted genocide of indigenous North Americans, the photograph was not just a coincidental bystander or a by-product of domination and oppression, but it also played a key role in circulating and upholding the ideology of conquest and domination of North America's people.[3] Photographs of indigenous North Americans taken by photographers of European descent were used as scientific proof of racial inferiority and were used as evidence of the "disappearance" of native peoples. Examples of the latter include Edward Curtis's well-known photograph, *The Vanishing Race* (1904), and Gertrude Käsebier's less-well-known but equally troubling photograph, *The Red Man* (1900).

Both Curtis and Käsebier considered themselves friendly to and supportive of North American Indians, photographers seeking to save and preserve a people whom they romanticized and believed were on the cusp of extinction.[4] Their photographs *The Vanishing Race* and *The Red Man* not only shape indelible stereotypes of Native American life and lives but also visually put forward the notion of Native Americans as disappearing. These early twentieth-century photographs are posed and show Native American subjects who agreed to be photographed almost certainly without full knowledge of the photographers' intent; the subjects in these photographs are discursively silenced even as they are displayed as photographic emblems, a kind of nostalgia after conquest. Curtis and Käsebier were not photographing Native Americans as they in fact lived at the turn of the twentieth century but rather as Curtis and Käsebier imagined they lived. Curtis's photograph *The*

Vanishing Race shows a group of people on horseback retreating into the distance. The conceit of the photograph is that it somehow shows the viewer what Native Americans looked like before Europeans invaded the continent; the image is literally a backward glance – a posed, choreographed, and imagined one. The faces of the people riding horses cannot be seen because they are riding away, facing away from the camera. All that can be seen is the photograph's merging of human and animal form, its intimation that Native Americans are entirely different from Europeans and, therefore, incapable of sustaining existence of any kind. Toward the end of the nineteenth century, Native Americans were relegated to a place of dispossession in the United States, the so-called Indian Wars having come to a close. The title of Curtis's photograph leaves little to the imagination: just in case the viewer did not see the disappearance of Native Americans in the photograph itself, his title tells the viewer that Native Americans are effectively dead people, ghosts.

This "discursive colonization" places Native Americans in a cultural space in which a romanticized veil obscures the reason native populations were dwindling at the end of the nineteenth century: aggressive governmental policy toward displacing and killing indigenous North Americans and toward terminating American Indian identity.[5] Likewise, the photograph pretends that Native Americans' disappearance is a done deal, when in fact native populations have rebounded from a nadir in the early twentieth century. Such visual evocations of implicit cultural mythologies radically undercut the agency and voice of the very subjects, North American Indians, whom Curtis went to great lengths to record.[6] I do not mean to state here that Curtis or Käsebier had vicious motives. On the contrary, these photographers are emblematic of the problem of cultural ideology and its enfolding and intermingling with photographic imagery. They thought they were creating the last images on earth of Native Americans and "saving" the last record of this population.

Even beyond its offensive title, Käsebier's photograph, *The Red Man*, obviously constructs a stereotype: having photographed one person, one man, Käsebier gave the image a title that suggests that he stand for all North American Indians. This is an extraordinary fallacy given that the North American continent was fully populated at the time of European invasion. Hence, having one Native American man stand for all Native Americans would be like claiming that a photograph of a Lithuanian accurately represents all Spaniards, Greeks, French, Germans, and so on. To support this visual idea that *The Red Man* stands for all indigenous North American people, Käsebier's photograph obscures all aspects of personal history other than the man's face and expression. The image is shot so close to his face that we do not see what he is wearing, except that he is shrouded in a kind of cloak; we do not know where his home is, what his livelihood is, or who his family is. He is shown to us stripped of almost all the signifiers that we use to decode identity in modernity – except we do see his expression, wry and fully aware. Many of Käsebier's photographic subjects were Native Americans who performed in Buffalo Bill's Wild West show, forced by impossible economic circumstances to earn their livings by playing out – for white audiences – the very wars and battles in which European Americans attacked Native Americans. In Käsebier's photograph, the subject's expression seems to indicate he was fully aware of the impossible position in which he has found himself. He agrees to the photograph not with pleasure, but with despair tempered by a desire to survive.

In addition to Curtis and Käsebier's fine art versions of romanticized Native Americans as specters, the U.S. government also archived numerous photographs of Native Americans.[7] These images served the purpose of asserting governmental control over indigenous people. In particular, during the late nineteenth century, when delegations came to Washington, D.C., to represent their tribes in treaty negotiations, the government would request that the delegates sit to have their portraits taken. The government then retained these portraits, categorizing each person by tribe. The photographs served as precursors to broken treaties; that is, the photographs were an ideological embodiment of the government's taking possession of Native Americans as emblems of conquest, rather than bourgeois photographic subjects.[8] Portrait photographs of nineteenth-century and early twentieth-century Americans of European descent slanted toward memorializing the personality and personhood of the photographed subject. In contrast, turn-of-the-century photographs of Native Americans – taken by photographers of European descent – tended to present their subjects as either a taxonomy of race or a romanticized elision of history. Notably, these photographs were created to be circulated almost exclusively among white viewers: for the most part, such photographs were not created for or given to the indigenous North Americans pictured in them.

Matika Wilbur

Twenty-first-century photographer Matika Wilbur (who is Native American, of the Swinomish and Tulalip tribes) has created a visual response to the history of European American photographers recording Native American subjects.[9] She has created *Project 562*, in which she is taking and archiving photographs of American Indians, categorizing her photographs in part according to the tribal membership of her photographed subjects.[10] An extraordinary example of photography as activism and resistance embodied in image, *Project 562* is an archive that faces the earlier photographic archives of Native Americans and radically turns the field of portraiture. Instead of showing human beings reduced to specimens, Matika Wilbur (born 1984) deploys photography to show personalities, personages, and individuals who also identify collectively through tribal cultures. Wilbur's overarching idea for *Project 562* is the creation of photographs of all the federally recognized tribes – 562 is the number of all the tribes that were federally recognized when Wilbur began the project. Hence, Wilbur categorizes her photographs according to the tribal identity of the sitter.[11] This project eerily echoes the organization of Native Americans photographed by and for the U.S. government in the nineteenth century. The U.S. government's photographs were also archived according to tribe, usually with the name of the photographic subject's tribe written onto the photograph as if in taxonomy. In this sense, Wilbur's project directly responds to the degrading history of photography as a tool to categorize and objectify Native Americans as possessions of the United States.[12] Her photographs, portraits set in landscape vistas, reclaim indigenous identity; the images are black and white, shot variously in digital or film, and then tinted – usually around the outline of the human subject – in adroitly applied color. The *Project 562* photographic portraits are subtle, equanimous, and unique – Wilbur never repeats a pose or a setting – each image reflects a conversation between the photographer and the sitter about how that sitter wants to be presented.

Wilbur's work blurs the boundary between fine art photography and social activism, but it is precisely in this duality that the work is most successful: its aesthetic fineness is achieved because the photographer has a goal other than getting her work in the hippest gallery. The images are often set on landscapes that suggest a boundary, the subjects often in natural surroundings (near lakes, trees, fields, rocks). The combination of black-and-white photography with tint applied delicately and sparingly by hand creates a look as if the photographs were taken in the late afternoon or early evening – a boundary time, a time of transition. The expressions of her photographic subjects seem more wary, more careful, and further from the audience than what one might find in the work of comparably accomplished portrait photographers. (For example, see Scottish American Graham MacIndoe's very fine group of portraits taken of a handful of successful artists and writers in the urban Northeast.) Wilbur's portraits for *Project 562* show her subjects always slightly wary, notwithstanding the humor apparent in images such as adult twin brothers skinny-dipping in a lake. Wilbur's subjects approach the camera, and Wilbur's camera approaches them; both carry a knowledge of the history of the photograph and its capacity for violence, but also its capacity for transformation.

Wilbur directly avows the purpose of her project as a desire to create counterimages – images that will work against older, destructively stereotypical visions of Native Americans that persist in North America and the world. In this sense, her photographs can be understood in the way that Michel Foucault describes counterdiscourse, that is, the turning of terms in the very place of their use that radically alters their meaning.[13] Wilbur takes up the tool – the camera – that historically has been used to dehumanize American Indians and creates images that perform as counterdiscourse, at once refusing and reenvisioning images of indigenous Americans. Her photographs counter not simply negative stereotypes but also, more expansively, entrenched ways of seeing Native Americans as the original "other" to the idea of American-ness. For Wilbur's portraits, sensitive, searching, and always on the boundary between melancholy and pleasure show indigenous North Americans who are not "other" to a "real" America, but who *are* the *real* America. *Real* America is a concept impossible to define decisively; the concept is always shifting and changing and, unmistakably in Wilbur's work, includes indigenous North Americans.

Wilbur's photograph of Anna Cook, a teenager also of the Swinomish and Tulalip tribes, epitomizes this sense of claiming place and is tinged with some grief at having to make that claim (Figure 10.1). In the blog that accompanies Wilbur's photographic journey, she suggests that the young Anna Cook has been a victim

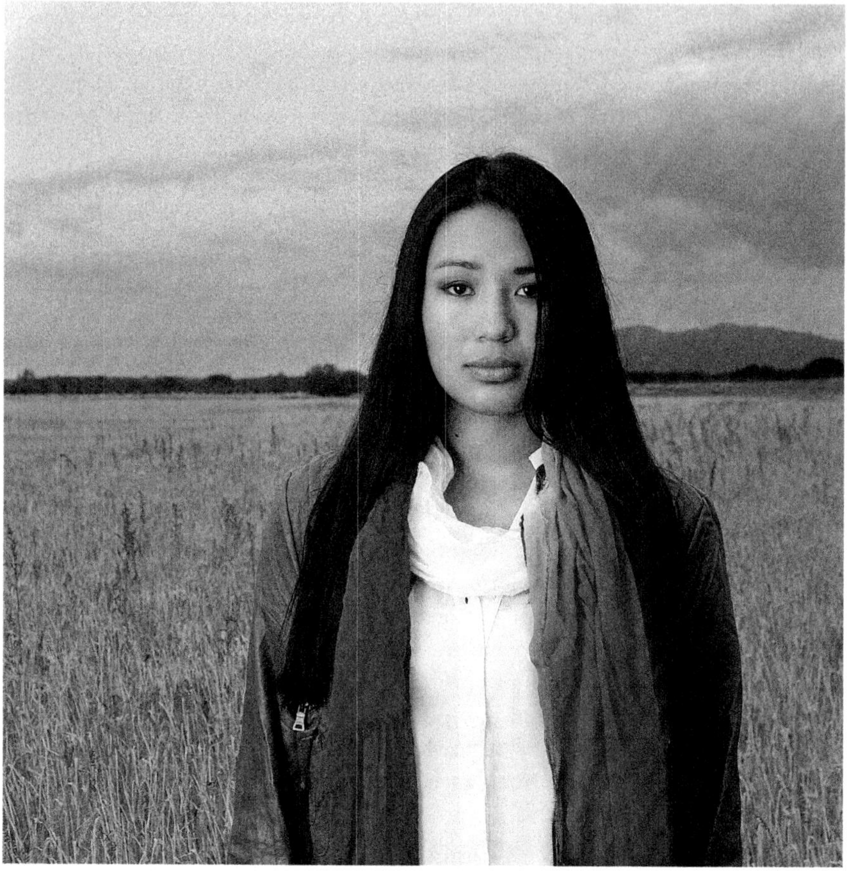

FIGURE 10.1 Matika Wilbur, *Project 562, Anna Cook*. © Project 562.

of racist teasing in her school from girls of European descent. In Wilbur's portrait, we see in Cook's eyes the effects of this teasing. She looks somewhat defensive, but Wilbur's portrait shows us unequivocally how beautiful Cook is and how this beauty redefines sexist and racist ways of seeing.

As Wilbur sets her subject, Cook seems to own the field and the sky before which she stands. The grays of the photograph match Cook's jacket with the tones of the low mountain behind her. The tall grass echoes the girl's very still, graceful, and face-center stance. The romanticization of Western conquest ends in this image, taken in the American Northwest: here is the end, geographically, of conquest, and also the end – as in the rebuttal – of conquest. The photograph positions the young girl staring back at conquest. The land before her is incontestably hers by rights of the photograph's aesthetic. Thus the image achieves much more than just showing that Native American girls should not be judged by European standards of beauty. It shows the girl's transformation into womanhood and, in particular, into a womanhood that claims its place and space (geographical place and social space) in America on the land that is hers.

Wilbur's photograph emphasizes Cook's serious gaze and strong upright stance. It emphatically is not an eroticized depiction of the young girl. In this, the photograph performs as resistance and rebuttal not only to our culture's obsessive eroticization of the bodies of young women generally, but also to the specific history of indigenous North American women as victims of gender-based violence.[14] The sexual victimization rates of indigenous North American women reflect a blend of misogyny and racism in the deep history of the formation of North American nation-states. In this history, the conquest of land and the conquest of indigenous women were ideologically fused.[15] Matika Wilbur's photograph of Anna Cook responds to, resists, and refuses the terms of such conquest, seeing anew a field and boundless sky of potential for the young woman. She is photographed as the possessor of the land, the portrait reaching beyond the terms of resistance and toward a manifold sovereignty.

Wilbur's portrait of Robert and Fannie Mitchell, an elderly Diné couple, depicts a subject that race theory and feminist theory are sometimes at odds with: heterosexual love (Figure 10.2). I want to briefly tease apart this conflict and connect it with Wilbur's moving photograph of the couple. African American theorist bell hooks makes a Marxist argument that upper- and middle-class white women experience lesbian identity still in the context of their economic support from white men: fathers, brothers, uncles, and even the more general ease with which white women can act as economic agents in capitalism. hooks then makes the case that other African American feminist theorists have echoed: African American women

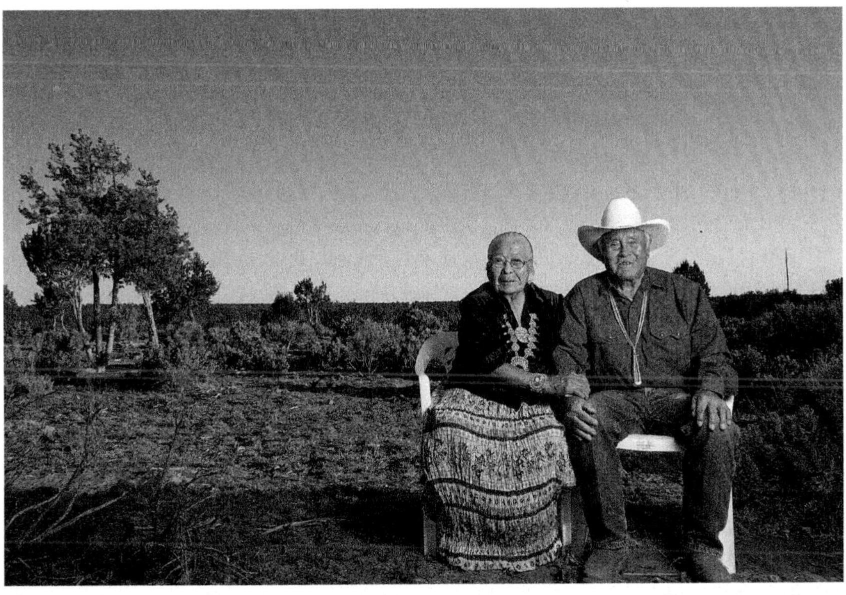

FIGURE 10.2 Matika Wilbur, *Project 562, Fannie and Robert Mitchell.* © Project 562.

are more tightly connected economically and culturally to African American men than they are to white women.[16] Native American feminists have also made the case that Native American women share bonds with Native American men that supersede and are more meaningful than any gendered connection with white women.[17] Wilbur's photography evinces such solidarity, as she honors, in *Project 562*, a large number of Native American men with sensitive and moving photographic portraits. I want to raise the issue, then, of who thinks they own feminism? If feminism has any power at all, it has to have the power to undo multiple systems of oppression. Therefore, feminist theory cannot be a doctrinaire script written by a small number of privileged white academics.

Emphasizing the beauty of the elderly couple, Wilbur's tender photograph of the Mitchells shows the pair nicely dressed in what looks to be their best or favorite clothes. Fannie wears a bead necklace, and Robert wears a bead necktie. They are sitting on land that appears to be in the American southwest (in U.S. government parlance, Diné are called the Navajo). The land on which the Mitchells sit appears to be their own: their body language lays claim to it. The setting in which they are photographed is spare and the land dominates the scene, with the couple set to the far side of the photograph. They are sitting on outdoor chairs, smiling ever so slightly, enjoying the process of being photographed. They are holding onto each other, with Fannie reaching her hand around Robert. They look solid, hewn rightfully on their land. The land and sky reach behind them, without houses, buildings, shopping malls, or cars. None of the trappings of capitalism and nation-state appear in the photograph, except the plastic chairs and the couple's garments, which are standard clothes almost certainly purchased in stores. The power of the photograph is the sense of immensity that unfolds behind and around the old couple, the land, and the sky: it is their place. Their eyes and facial expressions also express a sense of immensity: their love for each other, their happiness in survival, and, I believe, also their joy in participating in Wilbur's *Project 562*. It is a chance to be part of resistance to racism and part of a movement for social change. This joy contrasts markedly to the situation of indigenous North Americans photographed in the early twentieth century by Curtis and Käsebier. Wilbur takes the tool of the camera and turns to face down the colonizer's gaze, thus creating an archive of images for the people.

To return to a point made earlier in this chapter, although Wilbur did not create the images of *Project 562* for the Internet – that is, the photographs exist as objects not merely as scanned images – she uses her personal website as an archive for the images. On this website, she accompanies the images with a running blog that describes the photographic subjects and her interaction with them, with the photographic locales, and with the tribe or tribes in which the sitters are enrolled members. In this presentation, the work is a twenty-first-century multimedia effort, for the website presentation merges the blog and the images. (Also on this website, one can view images not embedded in a blog). This merging of language and image, then, is arguably the work of art – the blog does not just enhance the images, it is fundamentally part of *Project 562*.

Similarly, Wilbur's nomadic existence as she takes the photographs for *Project 562* – traveling in a van up and down and across the continent for years as she takes the photographs for this project – bears comparison to philosophers Gilles Deleuze and Felix Guattari's theory of political resistance exemplified by nomadism: "A path is always between two points, but the in-between . . . enjoys both an autonomy and a direction of its own."[18] Deleuze and Guattari's theory of nomadism is not only about people actually moving around, but rather it is about thoughts and ideas moving across nation-state borders. In this sense, Matika Wilbur's *Project 562* very forcefully resists the containment of that identity in the state apparatus even while tracing the federal definition of indigenous North American identity. In this spirit of resistance to domination inheres the feminist torque of her work.

Rebecca Belmore's vivid revenants

Anishinaabe Canadian artist Rebecca Belmore (born 1960) has focused her career on performance art, and she also has created film and multimedia exhibits and photographs that intersect with her performance pieces. Her photographs go far beyond simply cataloguing her performances, and they stand as works in their own right.[19] The artist's political commitment to reassembling the threads of damaged First Nations culture and history, to profoundly resisting the ideology of white domination, is clear and lifelong.[20] To encompass Belmore's career in performance art, photography, film, and multimedia would require more space than I have in this book. Her photography is just one of many arts that she deploys to create images, performances, and events that convey a counterhistory of First Nations identity. The heart of Belmore's work, discussed in this chapter, can be thought of as a formal representation of haunting. That implies haunting in the sense of invoking the dead and haunting as revisiting history. But most of all, it implies haunting as the potent and very powerful sense of threatening the status quo with the truth that dominant ideology tries to suppress and elide.[21]

Prime examples of the power of haunting in Belmore's work include the performance piece, *Vigil*, and the film and multimedia exhibit, *The Named and the Unnamed*. The works are dedicated to protesting and reenvisioning the meaning of the abduction and murder of First Nations and Métis women from the late 1970s into the twenty-first century.[22] During these decades, local, white police in Vancouver, British Columbia, did not consider the disappearances of these women important, and so the women continued to disappear; that is, they were made to disappear by violence inflicted on them.[23] In the early twenty-first century, a white farmer living outside of Vancouver was found guilty of multiple counts of murder.[24] For decades, he had systematically abducted and killed women of several races, and a disproportionate percentage of his victims were indigenous and Métis (that is, of mixed indigenous North American and Euro-American heritage). The problem of violence against indigenous North American women continues.[25]

Belmore's performance commemorating the disappeared indigenous women of Vancouver takes place on a street corner in a neighborhood in that city called "the low track," a place where many of the women were abducted, almost all of whom were involved in sex work. Belmore goes to this already haunted neighborhood and subverts, turns around, the terms of its haunting in her performance.[26] She begins on her hands and knees scrubbing clean the corner of sidewalk where she will perform. Then she reads aloud the names of the dead. Some of the murderer's victims remain unnamed – known only as DNA samples found in his domicile and its surroundings – and as she yells each name, Belmore draws through her mouth a rose. Each of the named dead, then, receives a rose and the forceful and somber invocation of her name. Belmore then dons a red dress and uses a hammer to nail its long skirt and bodice to a telephone pole. Thus caught, she tears herself free by tearing the red dress to shreds, stepping free dressed only in a camisole and underwear. The performance ends when a man, her partner, arrives in a white truck. (The victims, the disappeared, were abducted by getting into the murderer's vehicle.) Belmore gets into the truck, and as the two ride away, the song "It's a Man's World" blares through the truck's windows.[27]

This performance of haunting is at once direct and visceral and also abstract. Belmore voices the names of the dead by yelling them out to the neighborhood from which the women were abducted. She performs a symbolic expiation of their suffering by tethering herself – via a red dress – to the telephone pole with hammer and nails. Then she symbolically performs their death by tearing the red dress to shreds as she removes herself from the pole to which she is nailed. Both this performance and Belmore's film and multimedia exhibit, *The Named and the Unnamed*, work back and forth between symbolic registers; red for blood, rose for woman, names to remember the dead, and images to commemorate the unnamed dead.[28] Belmore's performance leverages grief and rage in a way that confronts the racism that engineered the women's deaths: the racism of the perpetrator who focused especially on indigenous women in his decades-long killing spree and also the racism of the police who ignored the situation for decades, thus treating the indigenous women as expendable and invisible.

Belmore brings to her photography a similarly complex layered vision.[29] Her still photographs are haunted by what it means to appear in a gallery or a museum, where art is a commodity and a tool of class-based oppression. Her performances, films, and photographs are haunted by what it means to perform as art for a largely white audience in a capitalist system in which art is bought and sold. They create troubling and revolutionary images of First Nations women, presenting anew indigenous Canadian women in ways that subvert and resist white expectations while honoring, commemorating, and signifying these women's vivid presence. Belmore's photographs are often elegiac, invoking a suggestion of the afterlife, that is, the persistence of the dead, their continuing and forceful presence among the living. The trope of the revenant, or the person who appears to be both living and dead, suggests a political force of the dispossessed, of those who have had power taken away from them but who also resist disempowerment. The more disempowered the revenant, the greater her force in refusal and subversion of the terms that disempower her. In this visual resistance, Belmore is extraordinarily eloquent.

Her photograph *Fringe* was originally shown much larger than life, as a billboard, inhabiting the urban landscape as a statement. In it, a woman who might be indigenous North American (she has slightly dark skin and straight dark hair) is shown reclining on a white surface that looks less like a bed and more like a slab. Already the positioning of this woman puts in play the question of whether the woman is alive or dead or somehow between these states. She is slender and appears to be young; a white sheet covers part of her body, but a slanting wound slashes through the exposed back, and a raised keloid scar emerges from that wound. Instead of blood, strings laden with deep burgundy-colored beads fall from the wound. The photograph plays through several levels of signification. Hollywood representations in the Western movies so popular throughout the twentieth century generated the idea of "fringe" or beaded garments as stereotypically Native American.[30] These films are partly responsible for the racist image of indigenous North Americans that many white people have even now, as traditional Westerns typically depict Native Americans as violent, monosyllabic, and dressed in garments that Hollywood costume designers created, pastiche that included the use of decorative fringe. Needless to say, Hollywood fabricated its representation of indigenous North Americans, and this depiction did not reflect actual indigenous lives and choices, sartorial and otherwise.

Belmore, then, takes up this cliché of fringe, and gives it a twist, depicting the racist stereotype as an actual wound down the back of the model. The cut is long and crosses the woman's entire back. It is not a real cut but an image of a cut with red beads standing for blood. Were a woman to actually suffer a deep wound of this massive size, she would most likely not survive. Hence, in its stillness and in its representation of the cut as not a recent event but one that the woman lives with, the photograph also raises the idea that the woman so wounded by racism is both alive and dead, killed by stereotype even while surviving. The word "fringe" also indicates a position of liminality and of being cast out, as in the fringe of society, a place of dispossession. Confronting dispossession, the liminal space of the photograph is echoed on several levels: the photograph inhabits the city skyline because it is a billboard, and thus it places the image of the young woman's body in urban space that is otherwise occupied by tall buildings, telephone lines, and electrical wires. The woman so pictured is also possibly dead or possibly alive – the photograph does not tell us which. What is clear, though, is that she bears a wound. This wound is the harm of being mis-seen and of being racially stereotyped – racist actions that result not in some trivial transient embarrassment for its victims but in a kind of annihilation, a death in life. By choosing the venue of the billboard, Belmore rejects the gallery space as a bourgeois field of consumption and takes her message to the public.

Belmore's photograph *State of Grace* also complicates its own position in the art world of the gallery and museum. In it, a young woman who appears to be indigenous North American sleeps in a deeply soft and white bed, and the photograph is cut through with regular careful cuts so that it is actually in strips. Hung on a gallery wall, the photograph then moves when wind currents in the room cause it to move. This gives the photograph a life of its own; it moves and breathes and is not passive and inert on the gallery wall. It haunts viewers, suggesting that the young woman in a state of grace may be dead, but if so she can still act and enter the social space of the gallery. She is not the visual possession of the gallery visitor but instead moves out toward the viewer as breath and wind currents move through the room.

The spectral aspect of this photograph brings up the question of discursive "ghosting" that I mentioned at the beginning of this chapter. If North Americans of European descent have created the stereotype of indigenous North Americans as "ghosts" (that is, as a vanished people), then how does Rebecca Belmore return to this trope to subvert it, to turn it over, and to turn it around? She does so first by invoking history: in *State of Grace*, Belmore reckons with disappeared murdered indigenous and Métis women whom she commemorates in *The Named and the Unnamed*.[31] *State of Grace* presents a resolution of some kind to these and other indigenous women's disappearances. It shows a woman who appears to be First Nations Canadian, or possibly Métis, and who may be dead. But in death, she hovers at the edge of the living, she has been given a place of honor, in this image, signifying that she is among the innocent. She inhabits a state of grace, this being a condition of being free from sin – either because she has never sinned or because she has been entirely absolved. The peacefulness and sorrow of the photograph do not cover up the violence of the abduction and murder of indigenous North American women, but instead the image faces that fact with a concern for the remembrance of the dead. It commemorates the women who are blameless for the violence that was done to them. In Belmore's *State of Grace*, the model performs symbolically as the holy dead; she gives the dead voice, body, and space, much as Belmore herself performs this role in *Vigil*.

White thread

I close my discussion of Rebecca Belmore's photography with a look at Belmore's early twenty-first-century photograph *White Thread*. This image, like *Fringe* and *State of Grace*, is eloquent of the contestation of power that takes place in vying for and performing in gallery and museum spaces. The photograph, like many of Belmore's early twentieth-century images, is lit with proscenium lighting, an effect that consciously presents the central figure – a woman bound in red cloth – as a performed image. The photograph apparently is Belmore's response to the United States' invasion of Afghanistan in 2001, and it connects this war, which Belmore interprets as colonialist aggression, with the multiple wars European Americans waged against indigenous North Americans. *White Thread* presents a young person with straight black hair and somewhat tan skin who is bent, doubled over, and held in this uncomfortable position by strips of red cloth that are threaded around her body. We cannot see the subject's face, and the red cloth significantly obscures the gender of the person. But the bound person is feminine with slender ankles, narrow shoulders, and a slightly curved figure.

No other person and no other object are shown in *White Thread*: only the person photographed and the red cloth threaded through with white that binds this person are visible. The fact that the figure is shown as on a stage, and framed by proscenium lighting, emphasizes the dramatic and self-aware positioning of the photograph as it assumes its position as fine art in a capitalist system.[32] Although the figure is not clearly presented as belonging to any race or gender, with relatively dark skin and straight black hair the figure may be said to represent people who are not pale skinned and blond. *White Thread* presents the person as bound, constrained, and silenced. The photograph's feminist aesthetic works to subvert and overturn the suppression of the oppressed and the violated. The figure in *White Thread* appears almost genderless and yet suggestively feminine; not decidedly racially identified and yet with visibly dark skin and black hair. In its position, the figure represents all those oppressed and constrained and violated. It also suggests the racist and sexist direction that political domination often takes. And yet from this position of being doubled over and bound in thread – Belmore's symbol for violence, war, conquest, and murder – the model in *White Thread* is also poised, tensile, strong, and graceful, ready to spring into an upright stance, transformed and transformative. In this figuring forth of resistance, this articulation of the oppressed person's capacity for power and transformation – if the thread that binds her can be raveled – Belmore's photograph *White Thread* is most deeply feminist.

Notes

1 See Mick Gidley, "Visible and Invisible Scars of Wounded Knee," in *Picturing Atrocity: Photography in Crisis*, ed. Geoffrey Batchen, Mick Gidley, Nancy Miller, and Jay Prosser (Chicago, IL: University of Chicago Press, 2012): 25–38; Paula Richardson Fleming and Judith Luskey, *The North American Indians in Early Photographs* (New York: Dorset Press, 1986); Lucy Lippard, ed., *Partial Recall: Essays on Photographs of Native North Americans* (New York: The New Press, 1992).

2 See Samuel J. Redman, *Bone Rooms: from Scientific Racism to Human Pre-History in Museums* (Cambridge, MA: Harvard University Press, 2016); Melissa Banta and Curtis M. Hinsley, *From Site to Sight: Anthropology, Photography, and the Power of Imagery* (Cambridge, MA: Peabody Museum Press 1986).

3 Benjamin Madley, *An American Genocide: The United States and the California Indian Catastrophe* (New Haven, CT: Yale University Press, 2016).

4 Christopher Lyman, *The Vanishing Race and Other Illusions: Photographs of Indians by Edward S. Curtis* (Washington, DC: Smithsonian Institutions Press, 1982).

5 Renee Bergland, *The National Uncanny: Indian Ghosts and American Subjects* (Lebanon, NH: University of New England Press, 2000).

6 Timothy Egan, *Short Nights of the Shadow Catcher* (New York: Mariner Books, 2013).

7 Paula Richardson Fleming, *Native American Photography at the Smithsonian* (Washington, DC: Smithsonian Books, 2003).

8 For a discussion of how photographs that categorize human subjects as "specimens" differ aesthetically from those that are created as portraits, please see Allan Sekula, "The Body and the Archive," in *The Contest of Meaning: Critical Histories of Photography*, ed. Richard Bolton (Cambridge, MA: MIT Press, 1992), 343–89.

9 Susan Bernardin, "Indigenous Wests: Literary and Visual Aesthetics," *Western American Literature* 49, no. 1 (2014): 1–8.
10 Wilbur is archiving her images on her personal website, www.matikawilbur.com, and in gallery shows. See also Natanya Ann Pulley, "Indigetechs: The Original Time-Space Traveling Native Americans and Our Modern World Hyper-Pow-Wow," *Western Humanities Review* 68, no. 2 (2014): 95–101.
11 Kristen Williams, "Reimagining Native America: Matika Wilbur's Project 562," *Cultural Survival Quarterly* 38, no. 2 (2014): 6–7.
12 Laura Levis, "Planting Seeds of Culture," *Harvard Magazine*, May 5, 2016, http://harvard magazine.com/2016/05/seeds-of-culture.
13 Michel Foucault, *Language, Counter-Memory, Practice: Selected Essays and Interviews*, ed. with a preface by Donald F. Bouchard and trans. Bouchard and Sherry Simon (Oxford, UK: Blackwell, 1977), 151.
14 Sarah Deer, *The Beginning and End of Rape: Confronting Sexual Violence in Native America* (Minneapolis, MN: University of Minnesota Press, 2015).
15 Annette Kolodny, *The Lay of the Land: Metaphor as Experience and History in American Life and Letters* (Chapel Hill, NC: University of North Carolina Press, 1975).
16 bell hooks, *Feminist Theory: From Margin to Center* (New York: Routledge, 2015).
17 Lee Maracle, *I Am Woman: A Native Perspective on Sociology and Feminism* (Richmond, BC: Raincoast Books, 2002); see also Renya K. Ramirez, "Race, Tribal Nation, and Gender: A Native Feminist Approach to Belonging," *Meridians* 7, no. 2 (2007): 22–40.
18 Gille Deleuze and Felix Guattari, *Anti-Oedipus: Capitalism and Schizophrenia* (New York: Penguin Classics 1972/2009), 380.
19 Jolene Rickard, "Rebecca Belmore: Performing Power," in *Rebecca Belmore: Fountain*, Eds. Jessica Bradley, Jann Bailey, and Scott Watson (Vancouver, BC: Morris and Helen Belkin Art Gallery, University of British Columbia, 2005), 68–76.
20 Elizabeth Kalbfleisch, "Women, House, and Home in Contemporary Canadian Aboriginal Art: Hannah Claus, Rebecca Belmore, and Rosalie Favell," *Frontiers: A Journal of Women Studies* 33, no. 3 (2012): 1–30.
21 Laura Beard, "Playing Indian in the Works of Rebecca Belmore, Marilyn Dumont, and Ray Young Bear," *The American Indian Quarterly* 38, no. 4 (2014): 492–511.
22 Native Women's Association of Canada/L'Association des Femmes Autochtones du Canada, "Fact Sheet: Missing and Murdered Aboriginal Women and Girls," Akwesasne, Ontario, 2010, https://nwac.ca/wp-content/uploads/2015/05/Fact_Sheet_Missing_and_Murdered_Aboriginal_Women_and_Girls.
23 Despite heroic activism on the part of First Nations women, the problem of "disappeared" indigenous American women and girls continues to be a major issue in Canada and, indeed, in the United States. Please see, *Forever Loved: Exposing the Hidden Crisis of Missing and Murdered Indigenous Women and Girls in Canada*, eds. D. Meemee Lavell-Harvard and Jennifer Brant (Bradford, Ontario: Demeter Press, 2016).
24 Mali Ilse Paquin, "Unsolved Murders of Indigenous Women Reflects Canada's History of Silence," *The Guardian*, June 25, 2015, www.theguardian.com/global-development/2015/jun/25/Indigenous-women-murders-violence-canada.
25 Jaskiron Dhillon and Siku Alooloo, "Violence Against Indigenous Women Is Woven into Canada's History," *The Guardian*, December 14, 2014, www.theguardian.com/commentis free/2015/dec/14/violence-indigenous-woman-canada-history-inquiry-racism.
26 Laura Levin, *Performing Ground: Space, Camouflage and the Art of Blending in* (London: Palgrave Macmillan, 2014).
27 Julia V. Emberley, *Testimonial Uncanny* (Albany, NY: SUNY Press, 2014), 151–5.
28 Claudette Lauzon, "What the Body Remembers: Rebecca Belmore's Memorial to Missing Women," in *Precarious Visualities: New Perspectives on Contemporary Art and Visual Culture*, ed. Olivier Asselin, Johanne Lamoureux, and Christine Ross (Montreal: McGill–Queens University Press), 155–80.
29 Of Belmore's quiet and quite radical resistance, Charlotte Townsend-Gault writes: "Belmore has always been clear that she is not 'a traditionalist'. . . . She maintains a keen eye

for the traditions of contact, including language loss, racial stereotyping and the commodification of sewing. She shows zero tolerance for the ludicrous or lethal compromises made between authority and those whom a paternalistic colonialism entrusted to its 'care'" (727). See Townsend-Gault, "Rebecca Belmore and James Luna on Location at Venice: The Allegorical Indian Redux," *Art History* 29 (January 2006): 721–55.

30 See M. Elise Marubbio, *Killing the Indian Maiden: Images of Native American Women in Film* (Lexington, KY: University of Kentucky Press, 2009). Here, Marubbio explores the use of the image of the Native American woman (often performed by a non-Native woman) as a figure for conquest, whose subsummation into white ideology of domination takes the form of a metaphorical death (metaphorical, that is, in the sense that film and multimedia exhibits always present metaphor).

31 See Amber Dean, "Space, Temporality, History: Encountering Hauntings in Vancouver's Downtown Eastside," in *The West and Beyond: New Perspectives on an Imagined Region*, ed. Alvin Finkel, Sarah Carter, and Peter Fortna (Athabasca, Alberta: Athabasca University Press, 2010), 113–31.

32 See India Young, "Culture v. Capital: The Rebecca Belmore Case," *Contemporaneity* 3 (2014): 77–95. States Young: "The strategic employment of several socio-cultural systems allows Belmore's work to be categorized both as art object and cultural property. Her works are sites of activism embedded within dominant cultural structures of the commercial and capitalist oriented art world . . . these works epitomize the interconnectedness of Indigenous knowledge systems" (86).

POSTSCRIPT

Exergue, on Dayanita Singh

For Dayanita Singh, photography no longer exists. For her, "there is only the frame."[1] Singh uses her extant photographs to create combinatory sculptures that she calls museums – displays of multiple photographs in frames that are part bookcase and part shadow box. Her point in creating these portable museums for her work is to disrupt the gallery or museum experience so that the viewer and the image are never in a one-to-one correspondence; that is, the viewer never gazes at a single image without awareness of its relationship to many other images.[2] Her work, then, is sculptural, processual, and conceptual, as Singh sometimes creates her museums by removing photographs, leaving only the structures of bookcases, shadow boxes, and frames, such as in her exhibit *Museum of Shedding*. In part, Singh's recent work responds to the advent of digital photography, which permits instant creation of what we might call photographic (created by light) images that can be shared through the Internet and then vanish. (The mobile app Snapchat is the extreme version of this quickness, casting up an image for a limited time while being capable of showing an unlimited stream of images across time.) Singh interprets the photograph not as a finished object to be set on a wall but as a building block in an ongoing compilation of fragmented pieces of vision.[3]

Singh's work in the twenty-first century uses images as building blocks of signification to create and to endlessly shift an array of photographic narratives. She uses her photographs to create books and, as discussed above, museums. In her museums, Singh draws on photographs she has taken long ago and more recent images, shifting the connections between the photographs. She sees the photographic images she creates as "raw," not art in themselves, and uses these raw images to create what she sees as her real work: the shifting combinations of images that function as a museum or as a library, a book, or both.[4] It is this combination of her photographic images – their fluidity as combinatory functions – that Singh considers art.[5] Hence, she is not a photographer but a writer who writes with images. One might also suggest that in her museums and books she moves the photo-collage and photo-essay in radical new directions. As I will be drawing on Roland Barthes' book *S/Z* throughout this postscript, it seems appropriate to reflect that Singh's photography is "writerly," as Barthes here defines the term:

> The writerly text is ourselves writing, before the infinite play of the world is traversed, intersected, stopped, plasticized by some singular system, which reduces the plurality of entrances, the infinity of languages. The writerly is the novelistic without the novel, poetry without the poem, the essay without the dissertation, production without product.[6]

In keeping with this notion of the fluidity of image and concept, the photographic as raw material rather than certain sign, Singh interprets all human beings as both male and female.[7] Even so, in her museums, Singh's images and image groupings comment strikingly on gender: *The Museum of Little Ladies* displays photographs taken by Singh's mother of Singh and her sisters as children, interspersed with photographs taken by Singh of young girls, and photographs of Mona Ahmed, regarding which I will say more shortly.[8]

Born in 1961 in New Delhi and educated at the National Institute of Design, Singh got her start as a photojournalist, but she very soon came to disagree with the clichéd and voyeuristic way that photographs presented India – her natal country and the country in which she now lives – to the West as always exotic and impoverished.[9] Drawing from the work of theorist Edward Said, one would say that Singh objected to the Orientalist gaze that photography created for the West casts at India; she objects vigorously to the visual creation of a narrative of India as poor and extraordinarily strange compared with a putatively normative West.[10] As Chandra Talpade Mohanty explains in her article "Under Western Eyes," some aspects of Western feminist theory have an Orientalist bent, in that Western feminists have a drive to appropriate, take, misinterpret, and otherwise assert discursive dominion over non-Western women and feminisms.[11] In particular, Western feminists have tended to use the non-Western woman as the discursive site of an imagined injured and vulnerable body. Western feminists have tended to linguistically force Asian, South Asian, and African women to perform as the wounded and vulnerable feminine site of Western feminists' recuperative drive. As Mohanty makes clear, such use of feminist theory is discursively violent and serves to rhetorically protect Western feminists from having to consider their own embodied vulnerability. Singh's photography vehemently refuses to perform the vulnerable body for the Western gaze.

Visual libraries

In the last decade of the twentieth century, Singh began moving photography in radical directions. She did so in response to profound concerns about the risks of being interpreted in a limiting way as a woman photographer from India – that is, being interpreted as an artist who is female and foreign in relation to the largely

Western, white, and male social power structure that receives photography and gives it its status as art. Singh has now gone as far away from photojournalism as a photographer can, although at the time of my writing, she still uses a camera.[12] She has focused on creating books of photographs rather than photographic works that might mimic paintings, and she has consequently become obsessed with the concept of visual libraries, a sort of garden of forking paths for the prosthetic (that is, photographic) gaze.[13] Her second book brought forward a haunting relationship between the photographer and her friend Mona Ahmed.[14] *Myself Mona Ahmed* pushes to its edge the concept of the photographic essay, dissolving the boundary between the photographic subject and the photographer who watches and records, making the book about the relationship between photographer and subject, Mona Ahmed.[15] It is an insider's view of Ahmed's difficult existence. Hence, the text of *Myself Mona Ahmed* can stand at once as a statement declaring the identity of Singh's photographic subject and also as a statement of the photographer's fusion with her subject. The problem of feminist theory and what it might offer or say to Ahmed is raised by Singh's project of photographing Ahmed.[16] Ahmed is a *hijra* who visually appears to be between genders and whose personal story is bound up in her experience of motherhood and the loss of her child (who was taken away because Ahmed, a loving and gentle mother, was considered an inappropriate parent).

Il n'y a pas de hors-texte, argues Jacques Derrida; that is, the text encompasses its readings and the readings of the text are part of the text.[17] I offer, then, a reading of Singh's work that stands at the periphery of the texts she produces but not outside them. I offer this reading not to contest Singh's clearly stated disagreement with categories like "woman" and "photographer," but to trace how these overlapping categories "woman" and "photographer" might intersect with and diverge from the singular corpus of work that Singh has created. In this necessarily brief postscript, I cannot possibly cover all the questions that one might raise about her works' relationship to the politics of viewing gender, nationality, and photography, but I think it is paramount to be aware that her work does radicalize these terms.

As I have argued in the introduction, gender is not an internal condition of self but instead is a way of being seen. Often one is seen as a woman because one has been born female and become an adult who has not (by dint of surgery, hormones, clothing, or other actions and substances) transitioned into being a man. In the proto-space – always hallucinatory, autoscopic, and embodied – of a photograph, the diacritical mark of the creator's body is never entirely absent.[18] Nor is that mark ever entirely present. I have been clear that one cannot read the gender of a photographer conclusively just by looking at a photograph, but at the same time I have suggested that some women photographers do practice "seeing differently," as Amelia Jones argues.[19] Living in a male-dominated culture means that people who appear to others to be women experience many aspects of domination – some painful and others just odd or slanted. Likewise, such an embodied and disembodied (that is, autoscopic) experience of self is heavily racialized in our world: orientalism is one expression of such racism. We may understand Singh's very presence in Mona Ahmed's life through Singh's difference from men (who may have paid Ahmed for sex) and Singh's cultural familiarity (as a person born and raised in India of Indian parentage) with Mona Ahmed's situation.[20] Gender and nationality, here, lay a foundation for trust, even sisterly love between Singh and Ahmed, because Singh is in the cultural position to understand the social contours and meanings of Ahmed's life as a hjira, even as Singh is herself not at all part of the hijra community. Gender in particular becomes a form of trust because Ahmed comes to lean on Singh as a source of sisterly nurture, and Singh is moved by and drawn to the maternal warmth of Ahmed. Here, I do not suggest that sororal and maternal nurture and warmth are qualities "natural" to people born female. Instead, they are qualities socially associated with femininity, and they are expressed by Mona Ahmed, a person born male who lives between genders. In the relationship to Ahmed, through this photographic mirror, Singh becomes feminine; that is, she moves into a sororal social regard.

The development of the years-long photographic project that becomes the book *Myself Mona Ahmed* is decidedly outside the boundaries of what we might think of as masculinist paradigms of career success. Singh photographs Ahmed for years because she is her friend. As she creates this body of work, Singh makes no effort to publicly circulate the photographs. Only when an elderly Ahmed asked that her story be told did Singh decide to make the images public. One could argue that using photography as a means of visual communication and friendship between the photographer and her beloved subject shapes a difference. That difference is marked by the gendered qualities of warmth, care, and devotion to others – qualities that we often associate with femininity – instead of personal ambition. Here, I do not mean that biological women actually are typically warm and caring. Indeed, my point is that Mona Ahmed – born male, a person of a third sex who performs the feminine – is warm and caring, and Singh's handling of this photographic subject mirrors Ahmed's gentleness.

Affected by her relationship with Ahmed, Singh develops a difference of vision that is a hallmark of her work: her photographic images are oneiric and often hover on the boundary of the surreal, always between the actual and the lost, always liminal. The photographs in the book *Dream Villa* are paradigmatic in creating this sense of presence and disappearance at once: of really being there and never having been there, of emanating from the photographer's memory rather than reflecting what is just there.[21] The photographs have a liminal quality, as if all were taken near the ocean – the littoral zone. The photographs of *Dream Villa* read like a dream that is not necessarily a nightmare – they have the quality of condensed symbolic work that can never be entirely forced to make sense in the waking world of daylight. The sense that home is a place that is always just lost and that one is just on the tip of arrival but that the place is always restless and beyond stasis, characterizes Singh's *Dream Villa* sequence of images.

Even though the goal of her work is for images to coexist and not to be seen locked in isolation on a gallery or museum wall, I only have the space to discuss two single images from *Dream Villa*. One shows a woman in a creamy sari standing beneath a slanting electrical pole, one hand on her hip. The night sky is cobalt blue, royal blue, and the lush landscape looks as if it has just received heavy rain. What appears to be water along the road, at the edge of which the woman stands, reflects a shockingly bright electric light. The pale sari and the bright electric light reflecting in the water visually echo each other four times in the image. The dark street and dark water likewise echo each other. The plants growing on both sides of the street parallel each other. The shape of the trees is echoed by faint clouds. Even the woman's stance, slightly slanted, seems to avow the slant of the utility pole. With these recurrent doubling motifs, the photograph creates the sense that one cannot entirely tell where the photograph ends and the landscape begins. The frame shimmers with intuited possibility. A suggestion of farther, deeper water (maybe an ocean) pulls to the left of the road; the woman stands on this side of the road before an immensity that the image suggests but does not show. In this photograph we see only the edge and not the center, but by this luminous edge we see a way into the center. The woman stands as a kind of sentinel or provocateur: a double for Singh, who displaces notions of interiority even as her photographs suggest the symbolically laden spaces of interiors.

When one views a Dayanita Singh photograph, a sense of being both inside and outside the frame occurs. This visual liminality is appropriately answered by her use of photographs as raw signifiers to build visual lexicons and narratives – her photographic hypertext. In this constant shifting of representation, Singh intimates a space of emptiness that can always admit the viewer: the work is not a closed field, shutting out the viewer, but a shifting phantasm, beckoning. This intense visual awareness of the periphery, of the strangeness of all things, functions as a metaphysics in which Singh states her philosophy of randomness and of chance, but always randomness and chance seen by a careful observer with an acute eye. Singh embraces the muteness of photography, its secrecy, aiming to photograph the unsayable, and to combine these images into visual narratives that speak.[22]

One might combine the *Dream Villa* photograph I have just described with another *Dream Villa* image, one that shows a slightly battered car parked before a wall. Has the woman just gotten out of the car? What has placed her on this road at night? To say that Singh creates visual narratives is not to suggest she creates tidy stories. Her photographic words shift and recombine, never forming a singular or clear story line. In this sense, they also resist the enframing devices – or boxes – into which we are forced by codes of gender domination. The self, in Singh's photographic world, is elusive, mutable, and not to be settled.

S/Z – myself

Singh began her work photographing Mona Ahmed relatively early in her career, and their relationship remained close until Ahmed's death; hence, the photographic work chronicling Ahmed cannot be settled easily into one phase of Singh's oeuvre. Still, this work is pivotal to understanding both how she presents gender in her photographs and how she interprets the question of gender *tout court*. In an email conversation with me regarding this book, Singh argued that we are all both male and female. While perhaps reflecting the argument, popularized in *Sexing the Body*, that there is significant variation within and between the categories that our culture strives to define as male and female, this belief in gender's double aspect may also stem in part from her long and devoted friendship with Mona Ahmed, a member of the third sex.[23] This friendship opened the boundaries of photography for Singh.

It began for Singh as an assignment for the *London Times* to photograph Indian hijra.[24] But when Mona Ahmed learned that the photographs Singh had taken of her would be seen in London where Ahmed had family, she asked Singh to throw away the film. Singh, feeling emotionally drawn to the warm and maternal Ahmed, agreed. Thus began the friendship during which Singh photographed Ahmed and, in particularly moving and poignant images, Ahmed's adopted daughter, Ayesha.[25] What comes through so powerfully from these images is Ahmed's motherliness: she is tender and devoted to her daughter, far more so than many biologically female mothers.[26] When Ayesha is cruelly taken away from her adoptive mother Ahmed, the hijra's heart is broken. She yearns to adopt "a hundred" daughters to give them all the love that is so bountiful in her heart.[27] Hence, one may say that Singh's work, *Myself Mona Ahmed*, shows us that not only is gender fluid, but it is also a source of pain.[28] In other words, the fluidity of gender is something of a missed metaphor, in that gender tends to be experienced more as boundary than boundlessness. As chronicled by Singh's emotive photographs, Ahmed's life takes a path that is harsh: she ends up living in the graveyard among her family's tombs, longing for the daughter who was taken away from her and developing maternal attachments to animals that Singh's photographs document with a painful elegance.

The 2014 photograph *Dear Mr. Walter – Mona and Myself* (Figure 11.1) shows Ahmed reclining in a pose like an odalisque on a sofa.[29] Above her is a cluster of

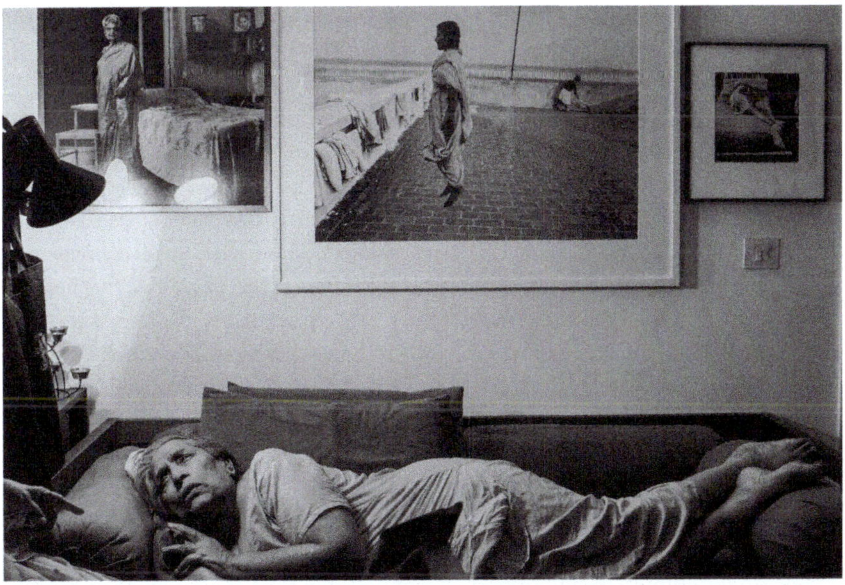

FIGURE 11.1 Dayanita Singh, *Dear Mr. Walter – Mona and Myself*, 2001. From *Mona Ahmed and Sing, Myself Mona Ahmed* (Zurich: Scalo Publishers, 2001).

Dayanita Singh photographs, including one of a woman who seems to be levitating on a jetty and an image of a young girl's legs as she lies on a bed. Toward Mona, a delicate, feminine (though not necessarily female) hand is reaching, to offer comfort. The pain on Mona's face is answered by this reaching hand.[30] If the hand reaching toward Mona Ahmed is Singh's hand, one may say that the photograph is also reaching toward its subject as a loving gesture. This photograph is, in its way, already a museum; this one Singh photograph contains multiple other Singh photographs. And thus, in its multiplicity, the image resists deciphering: the figure on the couch, between genders, the photograph a photograph of photographs. Likewise, whether the figure will be helped through her pain and whether her pain is physical or emotional is undecided in the image. The jetty reaching into water in the photograph directly above the couch imparts an uncanny vista to the domestic scene. Looking at a photograph that contains other photographs, we are caught in a kind of *mis en abyme* of looking: we see the frames of the other images and know that the image in which we are immersed is also only a framed piece of time and space. The body is paper – frame and form – as it is caught here, both in pain and in receiving comfort, both elegant and disheveled, both male and female, both remote and intimate.

Poesis

As I mentioned at the beginning of this postscript, Singh's goal is developing a poetry of images with her photographs. In the book *Camera Lucida*, Roland Barthes argues that photography aspires to be a language but cannot be language. The photographic image as a signifier always laminated to its referent cannot achieve the independence of meaning that a language needs to function.[31] And yet, in Singh's museums of photographs, the fact that a constantly shifted series of photographs cannot tell a story with the clarity of words is not a hindrance but a goal: it is the dreamlike indeterminate nature of photographic sequences that lures Singh. The image without a code does precisely what she wants her art to do, be evocative and ambiguous, even undecidable.[32]

The theory Barthes develops in *Camera Lucida* about the pensive image, the photograph that makes us think, resonates with his earlier work *S/Z*.[33] There he develops an argument for the power of the pensive text; that is, the verbal text that resists being completely comprehensible through narrative and symbolic codes.[34] It is precisely such a resistant text – one that cannot be entirely decoded – that causes one to think and that becomes memory. In *S/Z*, the question of undecidable gender is at the heart of the undecidable text, that which resists completely being read. Indeed, the title and signifier that Barthes deploys, *S/Z*, indicates precisely this between-gender inscription. *S/Z* signifies the way that gender moves between characters and, in its shifts, marks the figure between genders as of great and terrifying import in whose body is symbolically held the violence of the system of domination that we call gender. The forms of gender domination become most clearly legible in these interstices: at these boundaries where the necessity of feminist vision is most clear. In her photography, Singh gives the figure of the third gender, Ahmed, as a figure who is treasured and who grants treasure, but she also recognizes in Ahmed dispossession and outcast status, and she shows in Ahmed's face and gestures the rough and unjust social configuration of gender.

Singh's photography of Ahmed, then, carries the feminist aesthetic of resistance to domination because it obsessively returns to these boundaries and, ultimately, becomes a photography of limits. For the gendered terms of Ahmed's suffering cannot be disavowed: in Singh's photographs of Ahmed, gender as ideology is adumbrated and mourned. And so Mona Ahmed teaches Dayanita Singh to shift the frame. Through her friendship with Ahmed – a bond that Singh likens to that of two long-time girlfriends from school days – Dayanita Singh has been well nurtured, becoming a photographer whose work always pushes to the edge of the visible.

The idea of a feminist aesthetic I have developed in this book is a radical reenvisioning of the political through the reinvention of the photographic image. In this specific sense of opening new ways to interpret the visual and to use the visual, my definition of *feminist* is in some ways atypical. It blends structural and poststructural perspectives to analyze the political and social force of images. In photography, aesthetic means that which is visible and engages the viewer in the difficulty of thinking: an image functions as a visible object, icon, or sign, and it has an aesthetic force if it can be thought with difficulty. Photography that singularly fuses fine art with the vernacular, the cultural with the ineffable, the machine with the human, presents a limit case for changing how we, as a society, see. A feminist aesthetic, then, charges photography with the potential to alter the political landscape. My goal in this book is not to smooth the disparate photographers represented herein into one unified field, but on the contrary to show that the force of feminist vision is its capacity for newness and difference, across time, place, and culture. If photography was once called a magic mirror, one may also see that gender itself is a mirror, although not magical but chimerical. As one can use mirrors to focus light and create a spark, the feminist revisions of the photographic that I have discussed in this book are expressed not only in the photographs, which are captured light, but also in the light they cast, the sparks they ignite.

Notes

1 Dayanita Singh, personal communication with the author, July 26, 2016.
2 Singh's reworking of the concept of museum reminds me of some lines from Lawrence Weschler's *Mr. Wilson's Cabinet of Wonder* (New York: Vintage, 1996): "The museum affords this marvelous field for projection and transference. It's like a museum, a critique of museums, and a celebration of museums all rolled into one" (40).
3 Stephanie Rosenthal, ed., *Dayanita Singh: Go Away Closer* (London: Hayward, 2012), 33–61.
4 Dayanita Singh, personal communication with the author, July 26, 2016.
5 Jyoti Dhar, "The Architecture of a Conversation: Dayanita Singh," *Art Asia Pacific* 87 (March/April 2014): 68–77.
6 Roland Barthes, *S/Z*, trans. Richard Miller (New York: Hill and Wang, 1974), 5.
7 Dayanita Singh, personal communication with the author, July 26, 2016.

8 It is important to note that Singh's "museums" are not museums in the architectural sense of the word: they do not have a fixed geographic locale. Instead, the very point of her assemblages is to disrupt the hubris and power of the architectural museum space and in its place insert, or assert, a fluid set of constantly shifting photographic images.

9 Even so, she is often interpreted as a visual chronicler of India. See Jane Rankin-Reid, "Dayanita Singh," *ArtUS* 17 (March/April 2007): 5.

10 Edward W. Said, *Orientalism* (1978; repr., New York: Vintage Books, 1994).

11 Chandra Talpade Mohanty, "Under Western Eyes: Feminist Scholarship and Colonial Discourses," *Boundary 2* 12, no. 3 (Spring/Autumn, 1984): 333–58.

12 Antawan I. Byrd, *Art Cities of the Future: 21st Century Avant-gardes* (London: Phaidon, 2013).

13 An Ho Rui, "Dayanita Singh," *Art Asia Pacific* 82 (2013): 126; see also Dayanita Singh, "Artist Intervention: File Room," *Future Anterior* 11, no. 1 (2014): 107–10; Milena Tomic, "Dayanita Singh," *Art in America* 101, no. 4 (2013): 122.

14 "In Conversation: Dayanita Singh and Jyotindra Jain," *Marg, a Magazine of the Arts* 61, no. 2 (December 2009): 70–9.

15 Mona Ahmed and Dayanita Singh, *Myself Mona Ahmed* (Zurich: Scalo Publishers, 2001).

16 Maura Reilly, "Curating Transnational Feminisms," *Feminist Studies* 36, no. 1 (2010): 156–9.

17 Jacques Derrida, *De la grammatologie* (Paris: Éditions de Minuit, 1967).

18 See John Tagg, *The Disciplinary Frame: Photographic Truths and the Capture of Meaning* (Minneapolis, MN: University of Minnesota Press, 2009).

19 Amelia Jones, *Seeing Differently: A History and Theory of Identification in the Visual Arts* (London: Routledge, 2012).

20 Dayanita Singh and staff, "It's Her Story," *The Hindu*, February 3, 2002, www.thehindu.com/thehindu/mag/2002/02/03/stories/2002020300230400.htm.

21 Singh now considers herself primarily a bookmaker. See Dayanita Singh, *Dayanita Singh: Dream Villa* (Gottingen: Steidl, 2010).

22 "Rearranging the Furniture: Dayanita Singh at the Gardner," *Art New England* 26, no. 4 (June/July 2005): 14–15. On the concept of the unsayable, see also Daniel Martin Varisco, *Reading Orientalism: Said and the Unsaid* (Seattle, WA: University of Washington Press, 2007).

23 Anne Fausto-Sterling, *Sexing the Body: Gender Politics and the Construction of Sexuality* (New York: Basic Books, 2000). It is also significant that *hijra* are a very ancient and traditional part of South Asian culture. This fact, then, suggests that the notion of what Fausto-Sterling calls significant variation within biological sex categories, as well as the recognition that intersex people are not a rarity but part of humanity, is not new with Fausto-Sterling's book but has long been recognized in South Asian culture.

24 Hijra, a third sex, are a traditional part of South Asian culture. They often earn their livings as prostitutes, in which they play the feminine sexual role; yet, they are also seen as sacred or instrumental to rituals surrounding the celebration of the birth of a child, for example. Singh's photographic subject, the hijra Mona Ahmed, is a Moslem. This fact is important because Ahmed ultimately comes to live in her family's burial plot (Hindu do not bury their dead), and some of Singh's most extraordinary images are photographs of Ahmed in this context. Even so, Ahmed follows Hindu customs in much of her life as a hijra. Despite the hijras' sacred role in some aspects of South Asian culture, they live apart from society in ways that might make close and dear friendships with outsiders, such as that between Singh and Ahmed, rare and unusual. Daniel Ehnbom, personal conversation with the author, August 26, 2012.

25 Ruth Rosengarten, "How Close Is Closer? Dayanita Singh: Go Away Closer," *londongrip.co.uk*, December 2013, http://londongrip.co.uk/2013/11/ruth-rosengarten-how-close-is-closer-the-work-of-dayanita-singh/.

26 Dayanita Singh, *Dayanita Singh: Myself Mona Ahmed* (London: Scalo, 2001).

27 Dayanita Singh and staff, "It's Her Story," *The Hindu*, Sunday, February 3, 2002, www.thehindu.com/thehindu/mag/2002/02/03/stories/2002020300230400.htm.
28 Ibid.
29 See http://moma.org/collection/works/192759?locale=en.
30 It is interesting to compare this image, in its reflection of Ahmed's self-presentation, to nineteenth-century Indian photographs of courtesans. The commonplaces of self-presentation between courtesan and hijra are resonant. See Darogah Abbas Ali, "The Beauties of Lucknow," *Tasveer Journal*, April 22, 2014, http://tasveerjournal.com/2014/04/22/the-beauties-of-lucknow-2/.
31 Roland Barthes, *Camera Lucida*, trans. Richard Howard (New York: Hill and Wang, 2010), 6. Writes Barthes, "[the photograph] aspires perhaps to become as crude, as certain, as noble, as a sign, which would afford it access to the dignity of a language; but for there to be a sign there must be a mark." For Barthes, the photograph is not a mark because it disappears into what it presents – its referent.
32 Ibid., 88.
33 Barthes, *Camera Lucida*, 38; see also Barthes, *S/Z*, 226–7. Honoré de Balzac's novella *Sarrasine*, the text on which Barthes builds *S/Z*, is cast in the Orientalizing mold of locating the complexity of gender in an eroticized other. (In *Sarrasine*, an Italian castrato is both the utterly beautiful romantic hero and also the grotesque monster of the story, which is set in France. Balzac's story contrasts the idea of a "civilized" France to the idea of a "barbaric" Italy.) This problem, of empire and its gaze, is not worked through in Barthes's analysis. And yet, in Barthes's analysis it is clear that gender is the name for the endless *othering* of ourselves and our fellow human beings, and so how could all of its ramifications and manifestations be worked through in the scope of one analysis?
34 Barthes, *S/Z*, 226–7.

SUGGESTIONS FOR FURTHER READING

Feminist Aesthetics

Armstrong, Carol and Catherine de Zegher, eds. *Women Artists at the Millennium*. Cambridge, MA: MIT Press, 2006.

Armstrong, Meg. "'The Effects of Blackness': Gender, Race, and the Sublime in Aesthetic Theories of Burke and Kant." *Journal of Aesthetics and Art Criticism*. 54 (1996): 213–236.

Battersby, Christine. *Gender and Genius: Towards a Feminist Aesthetics*. Bloomington, IN: Indiana University Press, 1989.

———. *The Sublime, Terror and Human Difference*. London: Routledge, 2007.

Braidotti, Rosi. "Feminism by Any Other Name." *Differences: A Journal of Feminist Cultural Studies*. 6.2 (1994): 47.

Brand, Peg and Mary Devereaux, eds. "Women, Art, and Aesthetics." Special issue of *Hypatia*. 18.4 (2003).

Brand, Peggy Zeglin and Carolyn Korsmeyer, eds. *Feminism and Tradition in Aesthetics*. University Park, PA: Pennsylvania State University Press, 1995.

Butler, Judith. *Bodies That Matter: On the Discursive Limits of "Sex."* New York: Routledge, 1993.

———. *Gender Trouble: Feminism and the Subversion of Identity*. New York: Routledge, 1990.

Chadwick, Whitney. *Women, Art, and Society*. London: Thames and Hudson, 1990.

Cixous, Hélène. "The Laugh of the Medusa." (1975). Trans. Keith Cohen and Paula Cohen. *Signs* Vol. 1, No. 4 (Summer 1976): 875–893.

Copjec, Joan. *Imagine There's No Woman: Ethics and Sublimation*. Cambridge, MA: MIT Press, 2002.

Creed, Barbara. *The Monstrous Feminine: Film, Feminism, Psychoanalysis*. London: Routledge, 1993.

de Lauretis, Teresa. *The Practice of Love*. Bloomington, IN: Indiana University Press, 1994.

Devereaux, Mary. "Feminist Aesthetics." *The Oxford Handbook of Aesthetics*. Jerrold Levinson, ed. New York: Oxford University Press, 2003. 647–666.

Eaton, Anne. "Feminist Philosophy of Art." *Philosophy Compass*, 3/5 (2008): 873–893.

———. "Feminist Standpoint Aesthetics." *A Companion to Aesthetics*. Stephen Davies and Kathleen Marie Higgins, eds. Malden, MA: Wiley-Blackwell, 2009: 272–275.

Florence, Penny and Nicola Foster, eds. *Differential Aesthetics: Art Practices, Philosophy, and Feminist Understandings.* Aldershot, UK: Ashgate, 2000.
Hein, Hilde. "Looking at Museums from a Feminist Perspective." *Gender, Sexuality, and Museums.* Amy K. Levin, ed. London: Routledge, 2010: 53–64.
hooks, bell. *Feminist Theory: From Margin to Center.* New York: Routledge, 2015: 115–133.
hooks, bell. "The Oppositional Gaze." *Black Looks.* Boston: South End Press, 1992.
Jones, Amelia. *Seeing Differently: A History and Theory of Identification and the Visual Arts.* London: Routledge, 2012.
Klinger, Cornelia. "Aesthetics." *A Companion to Feminist Philosophy.* Alison M. Jaggar and Iris Marion Young, eds. Malden, MA: Blackwell, 1998. 343–352.
Kokoli, Alexandra. *Feminism Reframed: Reflections on Art and Difference.* Newcastle-upon-Tyne: Cambridge Scholars Publishing, 2008.
Kristeva, Julia. *The Powers of Horror: An Essay on Abjection.* Trans Leon S. Roudiez. New York: Columbia University Press, 1982.
Meyers, Diana Tietjens. *Gender in the Mirror: Cultural Imagery and Women's Agency.* New York: Oxford University Press, 2002.
Mulvey, Laura. *Visual and Other Pleasures.* London: Macmillan, 1989.
Musgrave, Ryan, ed. *Feminist Aesthetics and Philosophy of Art: The Power of Critical Visions and Creative Engagement.* Dordrecht: Kluwer/Springer, 2013.
Nead, Lynda. *The Female Nude: Art, Obscenity and Sexuality.* London: Routledge, 1992.
Neumaier, Diane, ed. *Reframings: New American Feminist Photographies.* Philadelphia, PA: Temple University Press, 1995.
Nochlin, Linda. *Women, Art, and Power and Other Essays.* New York: Harper and Row, 1988.
Parker, Rozsika and Griselda Pollock. *Old Mistresses: Women, Art and Ideology.* New York: Pantheon Books, 1981.
Pollock, Griselda. *Differencing the Canon: Feminism and the Writing of Art's Histories.* London: Routledge, 1999.
———. *Vision and Difference: Femininity, Feminism and the Histories of Art.* London: Routledge, 1988.
Reckitt, Helena, ed. *Art and Feminism.* London: Phaidon, 2001.
Robinson, Hilary, ed. *Feminism – Art – Theory: An Anthology, 1968–2000.* Oxford: Blackwell, 2001.
Silverman, Kaja. *Male Subjectivity at the Margins.* New York: Routledge, 1992.
Ziarek, Ewa Plonowska. *On Feminist Aesthetics and the Politics of Modernism.* New York: Columbia University Press, 2012.

Artists

Julia Margaret Cameron

Olsen, Victoria C. *From Life: Julia Margaret Cameron and Victorian Photography.* New York: Palgrave Macmillan, 2003.
Wolf, Sylvia, Stephanie Lipscomb, Debra N. Mancoff, and Phyllis Rose. *Julia Margaret Cameron's Women.* New Haven, CT: Yale University Press, 1998.

Clementina Hawarden

Dodier, Virginia. *Lady Hawarden: Studies from Life, 1857–1864.* New York: Aperture, 1999.
Mavor, Carol. *Becoming: The Photographs of Clementina, Viscountess Hawarden.* Durham, NC: Duke University Press, 1999.

Claude Cahun

Cahun, Claude and Marcel Moore. *Don't Kiss Me: The Art of Claude Cahun & Marcel Moore*. New York: Aperture, 2006.

Doy, Gen. *Claude Cahun: A Sensual Politics of Photography*. London: I.B. Tauris, 2008.

Lee Miller

Burke, Carolyn. *Lee Miller: A Life*. Chicago, IL: University Of Chicago Press, 2007.

Penrose, Antony. *The Lives of Lee Miller*. London: Thames & Hudson, 1995.

Dorothea Lange

Gordon, Linda. *Dorothea Lange: A Life Beyond Limits*. New York: W.W. Norton, 2010.

Spirn, Anne Whiston. *Daring to Look: Dorothea Lange's Photographs and Reports from the Field*. Chicago, IL: University Of Chicago Press, 2009.

Imogen Cunningham

Lorenz, Richard. *Imogen Cunningham: On the Body*. New York: Bulfinch, 2001.

Alinder, Mary Street. *Group f.64: Edward Weston, Ansel Adams, Imogen Cunningham, and the Community of Artists Who Revolutionized American Photography*. New York: Bloomsbury, 2014.

Diane Arbus

Arbus, Diane. *Diane Arbus: Revelations*. New York: Random House, 2003.

Gibson, Gregory. *Hubert's Freaks: The Rare-Book Dealer, the Times Square Talker, and the Lost Photos of Diane Arbus*. New York: Harcourt, 2008.

Vivian Maier

Cahan, Richard and Michael Williams. *Vivian Maier: Out of the Shadows*. Chicago, IL: City-Files Press, 2012.

Maloof, John. *Vivian Maier: A Photographer Found*. New York: Harper, 2014.

Ana Mendieta

Viso, Olga. *Ana Mendieta: Earth Body*. Berlin: Hatje Cantz Publishers, 2004.

———. *Unseen Mendieta: The Unpublished Works of Ana Mendieta*. New York: Prestel USA, 2008.

Francesca Woodman

Berne, Betsy, Johanne Binotto, Elisabeth Bronfen, and Gabriele Schor. *Francesca Woodman: Works from the Sammlung Verbund*. New York: Distributed Art Publishers, 2014.

Raymond, Claire. *Francesca Woodman's Dark Gaze: The Diazotypes and Other Late Works. New* London: Routledge, 2016.

Nan Goldin

Goldin, Nan. *The Ballad of Sexual Dependency*. 1986. New Edition. New York: Aperture, 2014.

Nikki Lee

Lee, Nikki S. *Parts*. Berlin: Hatje Cantz Publishers, 2006.

Catherine Opie

Halberstam, Judith. "An Introduction to Female Masculinity: Masculinity without Men." *Female Masculinity*. Durham, NC: Duke University Press Books, 1998: 1–45.

Zackary Drucker

Drucker, Zackary and Rhys Ernst. *Relationship*. New York: Prestel USA, 2016.

Carrie Mae Weems

Delmez, Kathryn E., ed. *Carrie Mae Weems: Three Decades of Photography and Video*. New Haven: Yale University Press, 2012.

Willis, Deborah. *Reflections in Black: A History of Black Photographers, 1840 to the Present*. New York: W.W. Norton, 2000.

Sally Mann

Mann, Sally. *Hold Still: A Memoir with Photographs*. New York: Back Bay Books, 2016.

———. *Immediate Family*. 1992. New Edition. New York: Aperture, 2015.

Mary Ellen Mark

Mark, Mary Ellen. *Tiny, Streetwise Revisited*. New York: Aperture, 2015.

Rineke Dijkstra

Blessing, Jennifer, Sandra S. Phillips, and Jan van Adrichem. *Rineke Dijkstra: A Retrospective*. New York: Guggenheim Museum Publications, 2012.

Zoe Strauss

Barberie, Peter, ed. *Zoe Strauss: 10 Years*. Philadelphia, PA: Philadelphia Museum, 2012.

Aida Muluneh

"Aida Muluneh." *Ethiopian Passages: Dialogues in the Diapsora*. Exhibit Webpage. Washington, DC: Smithsonian National Museum of African Art, 2003. https://africa.si.edu/exhibits/passages/muluneh.html.

Lalla Essaydi

Essaydi, Lalla. *Crossing Boundaries, Bridging Cultures*. Paris: ACR Edition, 2015.

Rebecca Belmore

Belmore, Rebecca. *The Named and the Unnamed*. Vancouver, BC: University of British Columbia Press, 2003.

Bradley, Rickard. *Rebecca Belmore: Fountain*. Vancouver, BC: University of British Columbia Press, 2005.

Matika Wilbur

Wilbur, Matika. *Matika Wilbur Photography*. Website. www.matikawilbur.com.

Dayanita Singh

Singh, Dayanita. *Go Away Closer*. London: Hayward Publishing, 2014.

Singh, Dayanita. *Myself Mona Ahmed*. Zurich: Scalo, 2001.

INDEX

Figures are indicated by page numbers in italic type.

For Product Safety Concerns and Information please contact our EU representative GPSR@taylorandfrancis.com Taylor & Francis Verlag GmbH, Kaufingerstraße 24, 80331 München, Germany

Printed and bound by CPI Group (UK) Ltd, Croydon, CR0 4YY
29/04/2026
02099862-0003